for professor william twinning,
   In deep admiration
      and
   many thanks for your
   Support,
      warmest,
         pratiksha
         delhi, 2015

PUBLIC SECRETS
OF LAW

PUBLIC SECRETS
OF LAW

RAPE TRIALS IN INDIA

pratiksha baxi

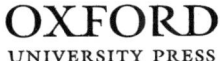
OXFORD
UNIVERSITY PRESS

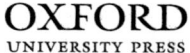

OXFORD
UNIVERSITY PRESS

Oxford University Press is a department of the University of Oxford.
It furthers the University's objective of excellence in research, scholarship,
and education by publishing worldwide. Oxford is a registered trademark of
Oxford University Press in the UK and in certain other countries

Published in India by
Oxford University Press
YMCA Library Building, 1 Jai Singh Road, New Delhi 110 001, India

ISBN-13: 978-0-19-808956-8
ISBN-10: 0-19-808956-2

Typeset in Adobe Garamond Pro 11/13
by The Graphics Solution, New Delhi 110 092
Printed in India by Sapra Brothers, New Delhi 110 092

For
Upen and Prema

Contents

≈∾

Acknowledgements

I owe the first enunciations of my desire to explore the world of law to my inspiring father, Upendra Baxi, whose life and work has been constitutive of my academic journey. Together, my parents, Upen and Prema, created a home always open to friends and colleagues who brought work and politics to our living room more oft than not cluttered with piles of cyclostyled petitions, books, and reports. I remember snippets of conversations amongst an entire generation of spirited and dedicated legal academics committed to inventing new meanings of what it meant to research, teach, and practice law. I especially wish to pay tribute to Professors Lotika Sarkar, B.B. Sivaramayya, S.P. Sathe, Gyan Sharma, Chhatrapati Singh, Damodar Wadegaonkar, Rani Jethmalani, and Justice D. A. Desai—all sadly no more—who were extraordinary people, whose life and work remains inimitable. My earliest memories hark back to the now iconic Mathura Open Letter when Upen and Lotika Sarkar worked furiously on the reform of the rape law in the 1980s. Inheriting the legacy of the Open Letter has not been easy, yet I must acknowledge the debt I owe to my father in choosing to research the rape law. The decision to locate my research project in a trial court was entirely inspired by my mother, Prema, whose struggle to train as a lawyer and ability to negotiate the male dominated courts in Delhi was truly salutary.

At the Delhi School of Economics (D-School), Veena Das supported and defended my decision to research rape trials, which was a project not without its sceptics at the time. She helped me think through terribly difficult ethical questions during my fieldwork. After she joined Johns Hopkins University, where she invited me for a year, she continued to engage with my writing, and has remained since one of the most important presences in my life and my work.

Deepak Mehta has witnessed this work grow from its inception, read countless drafts, and shared exciting readings. He has an incredible nurturing engagement with a student's writing and profound sensitivity towards what it takes to research violence. His friendship remains an invaluable gift of a past life at D-School.

Although it was unusual for a sociologist to seek permission to research criminal trials, Hon'ble Justice R.A. Mehta, Gujarat High Court, graciously granted me permission to access court records. I especially wish to thank Hon'ble Justice Chetan Bhuch, presiding Judge of the District and Sessions Court (Rural) Ahmedabad, for permitting me to sit at *in camera* trials. He provided me immense support and encouragement. Late Justice N.J. Pandya's help was immeasurable in accessing the field. I remain in the debt of the Additional Session Judges, who made me feel very welcome in their courtrooms facilitating the research infinitely. Several sitting judges spoke to me at length and generously gave me their invaluable time, for which I remain extremely grateful. I am equally indebted to the Additional Public Prosecutor, and his colleagues for believing that this research was legitimate and for helping me in every possible way. I thank all the lawyers, police officers, medico-legal experts, and witnesses who shared their views with me. The names of these judges, prosecutors, experts, and lawyers cannot be mentioned owing to restraints of confidentiality.

I especially wish to thank R.M. Bihola and Bhavnaben Jadeja for walking me through every step of my research and helping me finish this project. Conversations with Girishbhai Patel, Achyut Yagnik, Kajalben Patua, Amiben Yagnik, Gagan Sethi, and Swaroopben were infinitely helpful. Razia Khan helped me transcribe court proceedings during fieldwork. Without Anand Yagnik's help, I would not have been able to find my way around the city and its courts. I appreciate the help and support I received from Hinaben, Nupur, Joy, Tanushree, Wilfred, Megha, Bhakti, and Viraj. Sophia and Razia Khan made my last memories of Ahmedabad very special. I remain extremely grateful for these memories—the city remains tragically transfigured after 2002. Lajja Gandhi who helped me translate police documents passed away so young leaving her friends bereft. So did my friend Bina Srinivasan who I know would have been happy to read this book had she lived.

Above all, I am deeply indebted to all those who shared with me their experiences lived in the aftermath of sexual violence. I had scarcely hoped to receive such trust, rapport, and generosity. I hope I have been able to translate their trust into responsible writing.

Alongside this research, I found my voice working with friends in the *Gender Study Group* and later the *Forum against Sexual Harassment* in the University of Delhi. I am grateful to friends who forged our campaigns against sexual violence in the university and elsewhere in the 1990s and for etching their presence into the deepening conversations about the politics of protesting sexual violence during the recent protests in Delhi. I also wish to acknowledge the learning I gained from my association with activists and academics at the Alternative Law Forum, Centre for Enquiry into Health and Allied Themes (CEHAT), Centre for Women's Development Studies (CWDS), Forum against Oppression of Women, Jagori, Lawyers Collective, *Majlis*, *Nyayagrah*, *Sahiyar*, and *Saheli*.

Many friendships flourished at the University of Delhi making way into life that found me after I left the neighbourhoods of Chhatra Marg. Janaki Abraham, Jinee Lokaneeta, Jyotsna Sivaramayya, Renu Addlakha, and Yasmeen Arif gifted me a wholly undeserved lifetime of intellectual, political, and emotional companionship. Jinee and Sangay Mishra left me with no option but to feel totally showered with care. Lester Coutinho, Ishita Ghosh, and young Ishan have inspired like none other. At different points of time, Ashley Tellis, Bharati Mohan, Mahuya Bandyopadhyay, Navin Vasudev, Shoma Choudhury, Savithri Subramanium, and Vasudeva Rao sought me out to reminiscence, encourage, and share. At D-School, late Sujata Ghosh taught some of us how our institutions need to learn how to care.

Mani Shekhar Singh, Suman Bisht, and Sushma Gupta enlivened my life with so much laughter, meaning, care, and affection, marking extraordinary friendships for which I feel blessed. I am grateful to Mira and Varun for simply enchanting me. The two years spent in Surat introduced me to the generosity of late Professors S.P. Punalekar and Devyani Punalekar—whose stories of fieldwork captivated me. Their daughter Mitali Joshi has maintained the bonds of friendship since.

Never allowing scepticism to find me, Uma Chakravarti read and commented upon everything I wrote, contributing to the

making of this book foundationally. Niraja Gopal Jayal and Shirin
Rai have engaged with my work and life with stunning generosity
and honesty. In England, I found camaraderie in Brenna Bhandar,
Dwijen Rangenkar, Gauri Raje, Shraddha Chitageri, Stewart Motha,
and Sukhwant Dhaliwal. Srila Roy, whom I first met at Warwick,
has enriched this work infinitely by sharing her work, engaging with
everything I wrote and sustaining a deep friendship. I must also thank
Abdul Paliwala, Anupama Roy, Ann Stewart, G. Arunima, Farah
Naqvi, Flavia Agnes, Indira Jaising, Justice Dr S. Muralidhar, Madhu
Mehra, Nivedita Menon, Patricia Uberoi, Pradeep Jeganathan,
Radhika Chopra, Rajni Palriwala, Roma Chatterji, Srimati Basu,
Ujjwal Kumar Singh, Usha Ramananthan, Ved Kumari, and Vrinda
Grover for being such important interlocutors. Professors Kamala
Sankaran, Kalpana Kannabiran, Mary E. John, Pradeep Jeganathan,
Peter Fitzpatrick, Sally E. Merry, Shaheen Sardar Ali, and Shalini
Randeria gave their feedback on various chapters, hugely enriching
this book.

I am deeply grateful to a number of friends, some of whom
also helped forge the Law and Social Sciences Research Network
(LASS*net*), for leading me to texts, ideas, and conversations, which
otherwise would not have been mine to contemplate. Conversations
with Aaron Goodfellow, Anitha Abraham, Anuj Bhuwania, Arudra
Burra, Arvind Narrain, Bikram Jeet Batra, Chandan Gowda, Jawahar
Raja, Lawrence Liang, Mayur Suresh, Mathew John, Prita Jha,
Priya Thangaraj, Rinku Lamba, Roger Begrich, Shylashri Shankar,
Siddharth Narrain, and Shrimoyee Nandini Ghosh have been
formative to the making of this book. I remain extremely grateful to
Shrimoyee and Mayur for their insightful reading of the manuscript;
Dwij for scanning chapters of Modi 1922 from the British library;
Anusha and Moi for helping compile case law for Chapter 6; Anuj
and Lawrence for finding exciting readings and arguments for me;
Priya, Anita, and Prita for looking after me most emphatically.

In Jawaharlal Nehru University (JNU), Jaivir Singh, Amit Prakash,
Navroz Dubash, Jayati Srivastava, and Parnal Chirmuley have been
most wonderful colleagues and friends. I truly do not know what
I would have done without the warm support extended by my
generous and lovely colleagues and students at the Centre for the
Study of Law and Governance (CSLG) in JNU. They also allowed

me to travel to Kate Hamburger Kolleg, *Recht als Kultur* in Bonn for five months in 2011 and 2012 and to Paris on the Hermes fellowship at the Centre of Himalayan Studies in 2010 for three months. I am hugely indebted to friends from time spent in conversation in Paris on the Just-India project especially Daniela Berti, Devika Bordia, Gilles Tarabout, Joëlle Smadja, Jeff Redding, France Bhattacharya, and Nicolas Jaoul. I am truly grateful to Professor Werner Gephart and Dr Raja Sakrani who invited me to Bonn finding me invaluable time and space to finish my manuscript. I have yet to meet others like Werner and Raja who extend and sustain such amazing hospitality and friendship to colleagues from abroad. This book owes a huge debt of gratitude to Kate Hamburger Kolleg, *Recht als Kultur*.

Profound thanks to the anonymous reviewers, whose sensitive and detailed comments helped enormously. I am indebted to the editorial team at Oxford University Press for seeing the manuscript through the review process and working on it beyond the call of duty. I am most indebted to Hon'ble Justice Gautam Patel, Bombay High Court, for allowing me to use, as a cover page, his photograph of the carving of the image of justice etched in the pillars of the Bombay High Court at a time when it was inaugurated amidst much publicity.

Every research is also made possible due to the incredibly important work of librarians, archivists, and photocopyists. I wish to acknowledge the Ratan Tata Library at D-School and the libraries at the Faculty of Law, Delhi University, CWDS, Indian Law Institute, CSLG, JNU Library, and the Gujarat High Court. For photocopying research materials, I am heavily indebted to the support extended by Shyam Singhji in D-School, and by Ashish Das in SSS-1, JNU. Dada's café and J.P. Tea Stall in D-School; and Shambhu's canteen alias the faculty club in JNU were places of many welcome infractions. I have been lucky that my itinerant household has been looked after by very caring people. I must thank Bhairav Dutt, Hira Devi, and Savitri for helping me organize my everyday life with so much affection.

Since home has been mostly in Delhi, I did not meet my maternal grandmother Bhogi Jiandani much. She was a stunning woman who survived the trauma of Partition with incredible grace and sense of humour. My truly inspiring paternal grandparents Muktaben and Vishnuprasad were my first windows into Gujarat. I truly miss them. In Ahmedabad, my uncle Madhusudhan Baxi and my aunt,

Bharti Kharod—and their families were extremely supportive during fieldwork. My cousin Dr Hemang Baxi was very generous in helping me find my way around hospitals and labs in Ahmedabad. In Delhi, my brother Viplav, my sister-in-law Shalini and their beautiful children, Paripoorna and Sambhav have been sources of unmitigated joy and support. I adored Shalini's mother, late Kamalni Sane, who was simply a wonderful teacher. And Professor Krishna Sane, her father, whom we lost as this book went to press, continues to inspire. This book belongs to my parents, Prema and Upen, who have heard every story from the field, read every draft, and supported every decision I have made in my life. They have been true friends, critics and mentors. I dedicate this book to them for it is their love, which allowed me to find myself. The limitations of this book however must be mine to answer.

An earlier version of Chapter 2 was published in Kalpana Kannabiran (ed.), *The Violence of Normal Times: Essays on Women's Lived Realities* (New Delhi: Women Unlimited/Kali for Women, 2005, pp. 266–311).

Chapter 4, now revised, was originally published as 'Justice Is a Secret: Compromise in Rape Trials' in *Contributions to Indian Sociology*, Vol. 44, No. 3: 207–33 (2010).[1] It has been republished in Flavia Agnes and Shoba Venkatesh Ghosh (eds), *Negotiating Spaces: Legal Domains, Gender Concern and Community Constructs* (New Delhi: Oxford University Press, 2012), in association with Majlis Legal Centre.

Chapters 4, 5, and 6 draw upon 'Habeas Corpus in the Realm of Love: Litigating Marriages of Choice in India', *Australian Feminist Law Journal*, Vol. 25: 59–78 (2006) and a working paper 'Habeas Corpus: Juridical Narratives of Sexual Governance', published by the Centre for the Study of Law and Governance, Jawaharlal Nehru University (CSLG/WP/09).

NOTE

1. Copyright © 2010 Institue of Economic Growth, Delhi. All rights reserved. Reproduced with the permission of the copyright holders and the publishers, Sage Publications India Private Limited, New Delhi.

Table of Cases

Introduction

A woman clerk in the Gujarat High Court admonished me for researching rape trials:

> Women should not do work like this. It is only when you have misconceived ideas of bringing change that you do work like this. It simply means inviting trouble. It is partly women's fault that they are raped. I have learnt a lot from practical life. Women are helpless. We have no power. I can tell you all of this.

Vehement that research could not change the rape cultures that colonize our courts, she believed that it was dangerous for women to reveal such public secrets. For her, researching rape meant refusing to know 'what not to know' (Taussig 1999: 3). Based on an ethnographic project in the rural district and sessions court in Ahmedabad over eighteen months from 1996 to 1998, as well as readings of the juridical archive, this book describes the multiple ways in which public secrecy is subjected to specific revelations in rape trials in India.[1]

While the theme of secrecy has been dwelt on at length in anthropological writing, my focus in this book is on the relationship between law and public secrecy. We know that anthropologist Michael Taussig has famously argued that a public secret is 'that which is generally known, but cannot be articulated ... knowing is essential to its power, equal to the denial. Not being able to say anything is like testimony to its power' (1999: 6). Further, citing Walter Benjamin, Taussig emphasizes that '... it is the task and the life force of the public secret to maintain that verge where the secret is not destroyed through exposure, but subject to a quite a different sort of revelation that does justice to it' (1999: 3). In this book, I have argued that public secrecy finds specific revelation in rape trials in India, which does not bring justice to a rape survivor but addresses and reinforces deeply entrenched phallocentric notions of 'justice'.

At the outset, I must underline that this work does not aim to stage an exposé or uncover a core secret. Rape trials far from destroying secrets, are privileged sites of the production, negotiation, and management of public secrets. I therefore move away from the commonplace view that courts as public spaces destroy secrets. Nor do I catalogue the public secrets of law, for secrecy 'is not laid down as a set of culturally observed rules, as if written in stone. Secrecy is instead a cultural performance, the eventualities of which cannot be predicted in some kind of ethnographic inventory' (Jong 2004: 268). Secrecy is something that is achieved, important not on account of its content 'but the way it was performed' (Jong 2004: 273). The ethnography of rape trials that follows describes how a series of illegitimate legalities (or legitimate illegalities) fold into the law, structuring specific forms of public secrecy that constitute actively that which we must know not to know.[2] In some cases, secrecy 'may be performed to create an impermeable boundary *vis-à-vis* the State and the Court' (Jong 2004: 261). In other cases, secrecy may be performed to create a boundary *vis-à-vis* the affinal family of the victim or the larger extended family (see Chapters 3 and 4).

If rape is a public secret in the sense that we all know about it but find it difficult to articulate, how do ethnographers talk about rape in the field? Talking about rape, whether in academic or everyday contexts, is a 'cultural and political process' (Nordstrom 1996: 156). Herman argues that the study of sexualized violence against women becomes possible in the context of the attempts to counteract 'ordinary social processes of silencing and denial' (1992: 9). The increasing attention to sexual violence as a legitimate field of research and subject of pedagogy must also be insistently located in relation to the discursive contexts created by feminist protests against sexual violence in India (see Kumari 1994). In 1980, the Open Letter written by four law professors to protest against the acquittal of policemen who raped a tribal girl created space for critical engagement with the way judicial writing inscribes violence on women's bodies (see Chapter 1). The protest that ensued resulted in an amendment to the rape law defined in Sections (ss.) 375 and 376 of the Indian Penal Code (Act no. 45 of 1860) [hereafter IPC].[3] This was first time that the rape law was amended in independent India since its enactment by the British in 1860. Having inherited this history, I decided to study how the 1983 amendment was implemented in trial courts. Equally, the work of scholars such as Veena Das (1995, 2006), Urvashi Butalia (1998), Ritu Menon and Kamla Bhasin (1998) on sexual violence during the Partition marked a critical shift in social science research on rape in India. Situating its making in these contexts, *Public Secrets of Law* describes the everyday socio-legal processes that underlie the making of rape trials. Ethnographic writing about rape trials, however, demands practices of transformative reading that displaces horror, shame, or titillation. Such academic writing fails to transform the things we do with feminism, if it excites, horrifies or paralyses (also see Jeganathan 1998).

The very project of researching rape trials typically produces social anxiety or even excitability. Such forms of anxiety surfaced repeatedly when I mentioned my research topic, whether the response was hostile or laudatory.[4] Typically, I would be asked, 'But why did you take up this topic? Why could you not research 306[5] or something else? It is difficult to talk about it.' When I asked why talking about rape was so problematic, I was repeatedly told that it was difficult, especially for male lawyers, to talk to me since I was an 'unmarried' woman—'I can't be free with you'. Not surprisingly, I was expected to script shame and embarrassment in my interviews. This motif of shame was accompanied by the idea that the act of witnessing rape trials wounds women. One lawyer advised me not to document the circulation, witnessing, and recitation of narratives of sexual violence. He said, 'You see, your work will affect you. You see varieties of men in the court. You have already seen a lot. It will have a psychological effect on you.' For him, talking about rape did not offer the possibilities of transformation, or that 'meanings, in as much as it is established in a chain of signifiers, can always slide, producing new meanings' (Aretxaga 1997: 20).

I do not wish to suggest that lawyers do not know that the testimony of rape survivors who are silenced, or on whose behalf men speak, is more than a confession or merely coming out. They know that testimony 'works as an act, a reclaiming of history, and does so in a particular manner which asserts the fragility of the silence which counters it. In this way, testimony is a coming to voice, an insistence on speaking and not being silenced or spoken for' (H. Feldman 1993: 17). Every lawyer knows that women's testimonies are distorted, disciplined, and misrepresented in rape trials. Defence lawyers talk, sometimes boastfully, about how courtroom speech routinely converts the testimony of rape into a confession of consensual sex. Judges know that courtroom talk in rape trials typically titillates, excites, and provokes. We know that legal records freeze this drama of sexualizing the raped body in stylized ways (see Chapter 1). Even when a trial results in a conviction, the law addresses a phallocentric notion of society, or deploys male standards of injury, thereby causing trauma to survivors testifying against rape.

Researching rape offers many provocations to the social and legal mechanisms of silencing women from speaking out against rape. Talking to male lawyers as an expert (and even as an equal) meant transgressing social boundaries, wherein transgression itself is an experience of alterity. Transgression is not alterity in the sense of being a subversion of that which it violates (Jervis 1999). Instead, transgression implies the interrogation of the mechanisms of power and authority that articulate the limit, while at the same time engages complicitously with that which it prohibits. This means that the very process of conducting ethnographies of rape trials, to an extent, is complicit in the making of the public secret.[6] Such ethnography of rape trials offers pictures of the social and political process that script research as shameful, shape out-of-court negotiations, traffic in inducements, bargain with terror, and purchase dignity. The process of research also brings an uncanny awareness of the elsewhereness of the women's movement's critique of dominant and dominating ways of thinking about rape by foregrounding the very premises of researching rape.

ON CONSTITUTING THE SITES OF RESEARCH

While doctrinal pictures of law that treat of cases as texts have been critical to furthering our understanding of how judicial reasoning extinguishes voices of suffering, such readings of the rape trial are at times inflected by categories constituted by appellate judgments, equating legal discourse with 'written law'. I contend that law reform has not paid attention to the way power is deployed through language when survivors of rape testify to rape in courtrooms (O'Barr 1982; Mateosian 1993; Philips 1998; Taslitz 1999). I believe that the emphasis on everyday processes of the law providing accounts of subjection and resistance is important as it allows us to re-think the categories that are normalized by the doctrinal picture of law. Perhaps we need to review how legal categories inflect feminist discourses, marking the power of law to authorize meaning and elide the socio-legal processes that underlie the making of testimony to rape.[7]

I situated the ethnographic project in a trial court to interrogate the doctrinal picture of law, provided by what Galanter (1966) calls 'lawyer's law', or law in books. This expression, invented by Dean Roscoe Pound (1910), suggests an authoritative hierarchy of legal norms within which the practices of lawyering make internal sense (see also Pound 1943; Cohn 1965). Doctrinal legal materials such as appellate judgments, law commentaries, medico-legal textbooks, and case documentation present an ethnographer with some formidable complexity, if only because these stand constituted diversely. The confounding traffic in categories, techniques, and certification across different temporalities remain constitutive of the ethnographies of the rape trial in India. Providing an ethnographic understanding of authoritative legal materials entails unpacking their density as these craft the destiny of violated subjects of law. The ethnographic accounts of the rape trial do not aim to supplement 'detailed accounts of local conditions' (Galanter 1989: 10). Nor do I re-enact the well-worn contrast between law in books and law in action (see Pound 1910; Stone 1999).[8] Rather, I suggest that state law is transformed in its localization, often to the point of bearing little resemblance to written law.

Legal anthropologists have argued that the study of conflict mirrors social structure, social solidarity, or the norm (Durkheim 1933; Gluckman 1955; Llewellyn & Hoebel 1941; Turner 1957). Merry (1990) suggests that the everyday lives of litigants in courts cannot be meaningfully understood by only thinking of the court hearing as a dramatic revelation of the norm. She points out that in 'lower' courts, law acts on the consciousness of litigants, inflects their everyday life, and changes their perception about the case as it unfolds over time. Moreover, when feminist scholars contend that the rape trial is constituted as a sexualized spectacle, they do not only mean that the trial dramatically mirrors phallocentric norms of sexuality. Rather, as Carol Smart argues, the rape trial does not merely reflect patriarchal norms, but it also imparts a 'specific disqualification of women and women's sexuality' (1989: 26).

Although the trial is a privileged site where we may trace how the law constitutes its truth, legal anthropologists have favoured the extended case method within legal anthropology not merely as providing 'opportunities for the elaboration of doctrine' but as 'imperatives that stem from community life' (Nader 2002: 97, see also Epstein 1978; Nader & Todd 1978). Nader says:

> An extended case may comprise a series of related cases through time, involving some or all of the same actors; or it may comprise one detailed case unsettled over a period of months and years ... the dispute in question is viewed within the social context in which it develops and is played out, allowing the analyst to trace developments and shifts in the balance of power between the individuals involved. (1965: 14)

While Llewellyn and Hoebel (1941) argued that 'trouble cases' describe the norm or are 'the safest main road into the discovery of law', other scholars argue that 'the case method with its focus on institutionalized dispute settlement or conflict resolution, is unduly restrictive if one is interested in getting a full range of socio-legal occurrences or in grasping differential knowledge of the law' (Nader 2002: 97). Nader suggests that since Llewellyn and Hoebel were not 'interested in what genocide does to law-ways', while describing the 'juristic beauty' of the *Cheyenne*, they constituted the case method as 'safe' (2002: 95–9). The 'extended case method' allows one to trace the shifting legal norm while defying the imagination of the ethnographic project as a 'safe' highway for the discovery of law-ways.

Rather than follow a case from the court to the community, a method which could generate a different set of narratives, I followed routine cases that evaded the glare of publicity directed at landmark trials in the trial court. I do not examine the case to illuminate the legal norm, rather I am interested in looking at how the picture of the norm shifts as the case unfolds, and moves from one site to another. In this book, I suggest that there is no singular or linear framework that reflects the 'truth' of a case. Rather, each ethnographic account of the rape trial reflects multiple perspectives, each existing in tension with the experiential or the everyday. More importantly, how does the legal norm, as a shifting norm, constitute the legal subject? The over-determination of analysis by appellate law has shifted attention from the way in which written records efface those operations of power that make it difficult to read the agency of women other than as victims or manipulators of the law.[9]

Such operations of power are far more complex than the usual framing of a legal subject as victim, prosecutrix, witness, or complainant suggests, since a single legal subject may occupy different juridical identities simultaneously. Nor is the category of victim or complainant a stable category in the life of a trial. By focusing on the making of the rape trial, I wish to suggest how the culture of a courtroom alters the very meaning of rape from the point of view of the woman or child. Further, I do not claim that the ethnographic accounts of rape trials that follow in this book are exhaustive or even representative. The hesitation to label these cases as typical trials or as exceptions stems from my understanding of the ways in which the socio-legal processes underlying the rape trial insert contingency at the heart of state law.

The juridical field does not appear in one institutional site (Foucault 1975).[10] Rather than limit the analysis of the trial to one segment of the legal proceedings, I analyse the production of expert knowledge in relation to different institutional sites. Different effects of power and knowledge congeal to disqualify the testimony of rape at the various sites of the law including the police station, forensic science laboratory, the hospital, and the court. The legal manual, the clinician's table, the laboratory, the chamber, and the witness stand materialize courtroom talk. Courts rise and sit to hear cases. The police file complaints, carry out investigations, and bring the cases to the court. Medical practitioners and forensic experts diagnose, analyse, and testify in courts. Under-trials are locked away in prisons. Numerous kinds of expert knowledge and different institutional sites constitute the object within their particular expertise. Law, however, retains its power over other expert knowledge by annexing these to authorize its truth claims (see Smart 1989). For the law to inscribe its violence on legal subjects, these institutional sites separate and mediate as 'offensive frontiers' (de Certeau 1986) between law and bodies. Equally, legal ethnographies are imbued with an uncanny awareness of law's relationship to interpretation and violence.[11]

THE *NYAYA MANDIR*

Although hostility towards women as lawyers, judges, witnesses, or petitioners is built into the architecture of law, projects of law reform have paid insufficient attention to how courts are constructed. Typically court buildings are permeated by a bewildering array of intimidating sights, smells, and sounds, such that 'the outsider is subjected, through admiration and astonishment, to monumental law' (Haldar 1994: 199). While comparison of the architecture of different courts may yield stories of how such forms of scripting admiration and astonishment to monumental law varies according to judicial hierarchy between courts, court buildings typically separate the quotidian from the sacral. Haldar argues that 'it is through architecture that law paradoxically enforces itself as select, secluded, and sacral in nature and yet at the same time celebrates its regulation over an outside community of subjects by drawing them within the singular and absolute extent of this jurisdictional space' (1994: 187).

The Mirzapur court in Ahmedabad, still under construction, was set apart from a street that led into a bustling market in the walled city by a large court compound and an imposing flight of stairs. The Indian flag and a signboard marked out the court building as the Nyaya Mandir, which literally means temple of justice in Gujarati and Hindi. The noisy court compound comprised a parking lot where police vans of prisoners were a common sight, and was usually crowded with typists, touts, and litigants. The building had eight floors, with the ground floor comprising spaces for lawyers to work. Scores of lawyers worked on chairs and tables that were placed close to each other and secured with iron chains. The court canteen was located at the other end. The first floor opened into the District and Sessions Judge's courtroom at one end, and the Additional District and Sessions Judge's courtroom on the other. The second floor housed the assistant District and Sessions Judges' courtrooms. The public prosecutors' office was located here. The upper floors were allocated to magistrates of various ranks, the rank decreasing in the hierarchy from the lower floors to the upper floors.

This spatialization of hierarchy pointed towards the way in which the different powers allocated to the various judges and magistrates were mapped by the court architecture.[12] Spatial arrangements both divide up space opening it up for the enactment of visibility of legal hierarchies, and enclosing it to make invisible legal persona from public gaze. While fewer experts occupy larger and more private workspaces, hierarchy is maintained between legal experts and litigants by assigning scarce spaces and resources to a large mass of non-experts, mainly litigants. The visibility of hierarchy is accentuated by the creation of a mass presence of litigant bodies in small, concentrated spaces. It is this space that the rape survivor as a prosecution witness occupies.

The principles of judicial hierarchy that rest on isolation, privilege, and exclusivity, embodied in the judicial persona, stand dramatized to their fullest realization in a courtroom. Goodrich (1990) points out that the ritual character of legal proceedings is marked by the ceremonial dress donned by the legal actors or the features of address and procedure, which are highly systemized. The courtroom falls silent and rises each time the judge enters or leaves the courtroom. The judge has to be addressed with a bow whilst entering or exiting the room. The judge is never addressed by his or her name but in metonymic form as the court or bench. In fact the judge embodies the court, for a court sits where the judge sits. Hence, we find the words 'judge' and 'court', usually prefixed with 'the Hon'ble', are used interchangeably in legal discourse. The sitting and rising of the court accompanied by its codified forms of address, behaviour, and speech or silences, is performed in these other spaces from metonymic association.[13]

On my first day in the courtroom, I remembered Peter Goodrich's words:

> The day in court is likely to be experienced in terms of confusion, ambiguity, incomprehension, panic and frustration, and if justice is seen to be done it is so seen by outsiders to the process. Nor is justice likely to be heard to be done by the participants in the trial. The visual metaphor of justice as something that must be visible and seen enacted has a striking poignance in that it captures the paramount symbolic presence of law as a façade, a drama played out before the eyes of those subject to it (1990: 191).

The noisy, busy, and sweaty courtroom with simultaneous hearings was a bewildering scene. Over time I learnt that during a trial, the defence and the prosecutor stand in the well facing the judge. The witnesses take the witness box on the right side of the judge and the accused on bail stands on the left (diametrically opposite the witness box). The accused in custody occupies the dock situated at the end of the courtroom facing the judge and the constables accompanying him sit on a bench next to the dock.[14] Behind the witness box is a row of chairs reserved for lawyers. Right behind these a few rows of chairs for the litigants, public, journalists, or other witnesses are placed. On that unforgettable first day in a courtroom, I made many mistakes. The court was yet to begin its session. I looked around and sat down on a comfortable chair reserved for lawyers, and was at once chastized. Abashed, I walked to a bench, which was reserved for the accused. Again I was severely chided. Then I walked to the first row of chairs, to be told yet again that this row was reserved for witnesses. As days passed by, I managed to mark a chair with a broken armrest nearest to the witness box as my place in the court. Sometimes when I was lucky I could secure permission from the court to sit at the lawyer's table, from where I could hear the proceedings better.

Even from the first chair (towards the witness box) reserved for the public, it was difficult for me to hear what was being said. The accused separated spatially cannot hear most of what is said, but views the proceedings from the distance. I agree with Goodrich that the court is an auditory space organized on the principle of 'visibility of justice rather than its audibility' (1990: 191). I noted that the greater the audibility the closer an individual is to privilege. More often than not, depending on the viewing and listening positions of the actors in a courtroom, the courtroom is experienced as 'theatrical autism with all actors speaking past each other' (Carlen 1976 cited in Goodrich 1990: 193). The ethnography that follows conveys this sense of speaking past each other.

After the first few days of sitting in the court, a middle-aged male lawyer who knew about my work gestured to me to follow him. Hesitantly I followed him to his chamber, not knowing who he was. Hirabhai, one of the five additional public prosecutors (hereafter, APP) then began to interview me. Soon I was incorporated as a researcher amongst his juniors, mostly women. One of his junior lawyers, Beenaben, became a confidante and defended the validity of my research, which was keenly contested by lawyers in the court. In the chamber, my research was supported and defended. Hirabhai's journalist friend wanted to do a story on my 'courage'. When a woman clerk gossiped that I was shameless to do research like this, Beenaben stoutly defended me and refused to talk to her. Later she added, 'Do not be discouraged. These people are very narrow-minded. They do not know how courageous you are. Women like you and me are very few. We are different.' Hirabhai was appointed as my 'guide' by one of the judges whose courts I used to observe. Over time, I was situated like one of the juniors, as if I too must be trained in the art of prosecution, yet learn to observe judicial hierarchy.

Twenty cases of rape, abduction, or kidnapping were assigned to Hirabhai.[15] Not all of them were heard during this period. I could not choose which rape trials to follow. I followed six over a period of one and a half years, over a hundred hearings. I followed five cases prosecuted by Hirabhai (see Chapters 2, 3, 4, and 5).[16] I followed one case with the assistance of another APP, Mr Rajput (see Chapter 6). These cases concern complaints of statutory rape (of children below sixteen years); and rape, abduction, and kidnapping of minors (applicable to girls below eighteen years). None of the cases I have documented were routed through any non-governmental organization or women's group.[17] In this book, I have chosen to write about four cases studies of the six trials. Two of these trials went on appeal to the Gujarat High Court (see Chapters 3 and 6). Sufficient time has now elapsed between the trials and the appeals for these cases to be written about.

Although the district and sessions judge had granted me permission to document *in camera* trials, I also secured consent from the complainant in each case to follow the case. Consent for me did not mean the routine ways of securing informed consent but was based on full disclosure of my location and my work. The interviews were difficult in the absence of support services for victims or their families. In the case of statutory rape, the anxiety generated by the legal proceedings, my inability to develop a relationship with young children in the space of the court, and above all the fear of harm to the children precluded the possibility of ethnographic interviews (see Chapter 6). I also found that the parents perceived that talking to a stranger was therapeutic, while revealing what happened to the extended family was perceived as a source of stigma with long-term, deleterious consequences for the child's future (see Chapters 3 and 4). Rapport, then, was not a measure of the amount of time spent with the person interviewed, nor did it remain a given as the case unfolded over time (see Chapters 3, 4, 5, and 6). I was present in the courtroom during their testimonies, yet we would never meet again or keep in touch.

Most interviews with the complainants and their families happened in court corridors. The lack of privacy posed a problem as time went by. I was nicknamed 376 by some male lawyers, after the section on rape, posing an indexical relationship between my presence and the topic of my research. Once when I was interviewing Dhirubhai—whose ten-year-old daughter had been raped—four male lawyers who were passing by stopped (see Chapter 6), pointed to his daughter, and said, 'This is the one, look at her, so small and she has been raped.' I asked the men to leave and stopped the interview. The fact that I was seen in their presence directed a gendered gaze on the child—an identification I struggled with. Where I felt that it was unethical to interview rape survivors, I refused the help of lawyers or the police to set up such interviews. I have included in the analyses of these cases fragmentary conversations in between the court proceedings with child survivors of rape.

In all these cases, I have fictionalized the identities of the survivors and their families, witnesses, accused, prosecutors, lawyers, policemen, and medical experts in order to protect the identity of the rape survivor and the complainant. Likewise, I have altered or omitted references to dates and places. Anonymity has also been maintained where I have cited court documentation or appellate judgments. In cases where courts have cited the victim's name in published judgments, now available online, the name has been bracketed (indicated by the victim's initials in brackets). I have only retained the names of those survivors who have protested publically against law's injustice to them, or those women who acquired iconic status in the women's movement. These women's and children's contribution to feminist legal critique is immeasurable and deserving of acknowledgement. They have taught us how to do things with feminism—lessons further explored in the first chapter.

LEARNING THE VOCABULARY OF RESEARCHING RAPE

Courts have typically been described as intimidating, chaotic, and confusing spaces for a non-expert. Not unlike criminal trial courts,

Srimati Basu describes family courts as suffused with an 'atmosphere of tension and terror of public spectacle', although family courts are 'visualized as a utopian site of new meanings of marriage and empowerment' (2012: 484). In contrast to other field sites, one cannot 'hang out' in a court. A lawyer hurrying to court once paused to say to me, 'Miss Baxi, if you want to learn law, you must walk faster.' If the fast pace or stride (which often breaks off into a run) marks the lawyer's sense of time, a completely different sense of time marks litigants. Unlike the animated gait of the lawyers, a marked boredom and exhaustion characterized the litigants, for whom time dragged for endless hours and often after waiting nothing seemed to happen. Marked as a researcher desirous of learning the ways of law, my pace had attracted comment. I had to walk purposively as if I were headed towards the lawyers' library, the prosecutor's office, the record room, or the courtroom.

The ethnography unfolded alongside conversations with defence lawyers who boasted about their prowess at securing acquittals in rape trials, mocked women defence lawyers who defended men accused of rape, and gossiped endlessly about women lawyers. Conversations about sexual affairs among lawyers were common during lunches in chambers, and stories about sexual harassment abounded. I recorded several stories of women lawyers resisting sexist comments, even in open court—in one instance, a woman lawyer slapped a male lawyer during court proceedings. Researching rape itself was unsafe, attracting the charge of indecency, sexist comments, and even sexual harassment. In this predominantly male space, lawyers often swapped stories about rape cases in other courts in Gujarat. One such conversation took place in Mr Rajput's chamber when a defence lawyer, whom I call Mr Patel, walked in. After eager enquiries about how my research was progressing, he proceeded to tell me that he won an acquittal in a case in Himatnagar. He laughed, 'I cited one case, amongst three, on the character of the woman. And got an acquittal'. Continuing to flaunt his prowess as a good defence lawyer, he said:

P: In one case, in Gandhinagar, the woman who was from Delhi did not come back to complete the cross [*laughs*]. The case is pending.

PB: She was so scared of your cross?

P: Yes [*laughs*].

The boast of successfully terrorizing a rape victim during a cross-examination and the slandering of a woman's character typify defence lawyering. Mastery over questions designed to intimidate and finding pleasure in crafting a humiliating cross-examination embody the practice of defence lawyering in rape cases.

Initially, no one was willing to speak to me about ongoing rape trials. I had yet to learn the vocabulary of how to speak about rape in the court. Just as I had begun to despair, Hirabhai introduced me to a young woman in a statutory rape and kidnapping case he was to prosecute. He then took me to the courtroom, where he asked the bench clerk for the case papers. We sat at the far end of the lawyers' table, and he turned to the medico-legal aspects of the case. Turning to the accused's medical certificate, in his usual booming voice which echoed in the half-empty courtroom, Hirabhai said, 'You know what a man's primary sexual organs are, don't you?' A little taken aback, I nodded. Then he turned to the victim's medical certificate. After going over the other details about bodily development and superficial injuries, he asked me, 'Do you know what a hymen is?' I responded in the affirmative. Rather theatrically, he drew a vagina on small piece of paper to explain the technical terms for injury on the *labia minora* or *labia majora*. The discussion continued on in the chamber where he instructed Beenaben to explain 'it' to me. After he had left she said, 'Pratiksha, do you know that a man cannot rape a woman by simply touching her, or kissing her.' I nodded, even more puzzled and curious now. She carried on, 'Well, how do I explain how a man rapes?' I replied, 'Beenaben, do you mean partial or complete penetration?' She nodded in relief.

In performing a specific revelation of the public secrets of rape, Hirabhai directed my attention to the vocabulary by which I could research rape. Insisting that medical jurisprudence separates the social from the clinical, Hirabhai maintained that a 'decent' legal practice could coexist with frank discussions on the topic of rape.[18] The route to generating this 'frank' space initiating the research, as he put it, enabled him to teach his woman juniors how the prosecution could successfully fight rape cases more freely. This linguistic route became his way of teaching me facts of anatomy, sexuality, and the rape law.

Hirabhai and his junior Beenaben made it possible for me to undertake this research in many ways. Hirabhai—whom I called 'sir', unlike other women juniors, who addressed him by fictive kin terms—was like a teacher instructing me in the ways of the court. He did not hesitate to reprimand me on many occasions. I was instructed on whom to speak to and whom to avoid. I stopped wearing bright colours to the court. I was taught what constituted decent modes of dress, appearance, gait, posture, and speech. While I was schooled to 'fit into' the scenes of the court, I remained an outsider. It was this status as an outsider that allowed me access, although on the verge of experiencing alterity. As if aware of this, Hirabhai would reassure me without any obvious cause for it: 'Baxi, you are safe here.' When I was leaving the field, almost reflexively, Hirabhai said to me, 'I don't know why, Baxi, but I never looked at you with that kind of gaze [*nazaar*]. I liked you because you work so hard. Do invite me to your marriage.'

The complicity with adopting medico-legal vocabulary as the modality of talking about rape was deeply problematic. I was tutored not to ask direct questions about rape. For instance, I could not ask direct questions about what lawyers and prosecutors meant when they said that women are habituated to sex. I knew that the determination of whether or not a woman is a *habitué* is on the basis of a clinical test, which doctors conduct routinely. This test, popularly known as the two-finger test, is used to determine the absence or presence of the hymen, and whether it is distensible or not. If the doctor finds that the hymen is broken and there are old hymeneal tears, they may write that the rape survivor was habituated or used to sexual intercourse in the medico-legal certificate. When a prosecutor or defence lawyers reads a medico-legal certificate that declares a woman to be a *habitué*, more often than not, they conclude that she has lied about being raped. A defence lawyer routinely uses such medical findings to establish past sexual history (see Chapter 2). I wanted to know why prosecutors who purportedly represent the victim exploit the category of the *habitué*.

Towards the last phase of the research (fifteen months after the preceding conversation), I decided to ask direct questions which may have been thought of as talking about secrets men do not share with women as equals in a professional setting. These secrets 'appear in ethnographic texts as signs of alterity' (Jong 2004: 257). I cite here a discussion with Mr Rajput, who argued that women could not be raped unless there is grievous violence, and women who were habituated to sex without marks of injury frequently lied about rape. This was not an uncommon view in the court. He pursued this question in the privacy of his chamber to explain to me why he thought that 'habituated' women were liars. He asked me to sit in a chair beside him and lowered his voice so that his colleagues could not overhear him through the wooden partitions that separated the chambers of the public prosecutors. He spoke in English.

> R: That day you were saying about habituated. I did not say anything because other people were around. A woman cannot really be raped.
>
> PB: Why?
>
> R: It becomes quite large. The opening in a habituated woman therefore becomes quite large therefore habituated.
>
> PB: You mean the vaginal canal?
>
> R: Yes, that's why two fingers go in quite easily.
>
> PB: But that's what I was discussing with Dr B [a forensic expert]— that is, the finger test is quite unreliable. What about masturbation?
>
> R: That is there. But see if two fingers go in easily (mimicking such penetration with his fingers) it means that she is habituated, the entire hole, that's why I say a woman cannot really be raped.
>
> PB: But that was not my point of view. I was trying to say that why must her past sexual history be linked to her credibility?
>
> R: But it must.
>
> PB: Why? Why should it be considered against morality?
>
> R: Because it is. Because with married women rape is not possible, and in our society sex before marriage is not allowed.
>
> PB: Why do women have to experience rape as worse than death or shameful that they will kill themselves? I am arguing for another point of view.
>
> R: But a woman cannot be raped unless … how do I explain? Do you know what secondary sexual organs are? Do you know why doctors write secondary sex organs are well developed?
>
> PB: You mean…?
>
> R: The organ develops after a woman has an erection, that's why they are well developed, that's how they find out she is habituated. How do I explain this to you?

R: The woman becomes wet. The penis cannot go in unless the woman is not willing. She cannot be willing unless she is wet—like a machine—a rod cannot go in without lubrication. (gestures)

PB: But what about cases in which there is partial penetration?

R: I have not found such cases, they all claim complete penetration; that is why I am saying that a woman cannot be raped.[19]

Mr Rajput stopped speaking when a colleague walked in and I was hugely relieved to put an end to this conversation. He added, 'You see I am an MSc in Biochemistry. We were taught all of this. I have worked in a hospital for one year. Come again we will discuss this.'

This lesson in 'biochemistry' was a lesson in alterity—of how men experience pleasure while talking about rape and women's bodies. The prosecutorial body itself becomes a desiring body inserting in talk about rape male passions to possess and objectify. During a trial, a survivor knows that her testimony gives men pleasure and experiences the questions put to her as unbearable humiliation, yet since such talk is staged in a court of law, the process is imbued with the values of objectivity and such talk is classified as evidence.

SIGNPOSTS

Chapter 1, 'Doctrinal Pictures of Rape Trials: How to Do Things with Feminism' explicates the doctrinal pictures of the rape law. I narrate stories of landmark trials in relation to the women's movements' critique of the rape law. Taking a cue from Shoshana Felman, we may think of landmark trials as sites where key elements of previous trials are repeated (Felman 2002; Sarat & Kearns 2002). It is this intertextuality that leads us to critically trace the operation of the precedent like a ritual 'gaining in force with each repetition' (Dayan 2002: 184). Yet the force of precedent cannot be fully understood by limiting our analysis to written law.[20] For instance, feminists archive numerous precedents of injustice against rape survivors which are not written into the law as 'formally recorded precedents evoked under the doctrine of *stare decisis*' (Darian–Smith 2007: 64). Darian–Smith has argued that precedents of injustice are not merely 'silenced and written out of the text of law, but yet periodically resurface over time at particular moments of perceived crisis and threat' (2007: 64).

Hence, spoken law, which does not form the official record, becomes critical to ethnographically informed critique of the rape law. By indicating how courtroom speech is paraphrased, translated, and discarded in the making of the record, I suggest that we cannot understand the precedents of injustice without understanding the power of spoken law. Indeed, spoken law all too often re-writes the written law (*lex scripta*). The customariness of spoken law is scarcely recognized in doctrinal pictures of law. Rather than think of doctrinal law as parallel to spoken law, I believe that we must juxtapose these to trace circularity in the way in which law materializes the memory of precedents of injustice.[21] If written law discards those precedents of injustice which are inscribed on the bodies of witnesses, the speech of witnesses is equally inflected by categories stabilized by written law. I believe that the circulation, standardization, and stylization of categories; modalities of courtroom talk; tonalities of speech; forms of gestures; stylization of courtroom performances; and production of affect are constitutive of courtroom cultures. This emphasis on oral scripts of law formative to the making of rape trials is based on readings that shift registers between the juridical archive and the lived experience of law. Chapter 2 is crafted to direct the reader's gaze to this method of reading rape trials.

Chapter 2, 'Medicalization of Consent and Falsity: The Figure of the *Habitué* in Indian Rape Law', traces the emergence of medico-legal categories that medicalize consent and falsity. The colonial institution of the technique of the two-finger test to determine signs of habituation to sex rests on the idea that the surface of the female body can be read to provide 'scientific' evidence of consensual heterosexual experience. This is one of the most primitive forms of truth technology deployed on women's bodies. I argue that the medicalization of consent and falsity is the defining feature of rape trials in India. By juxtaposing excerpts from medico-legal manuals side-by-side with a segment of a rape trial of a twelve-year-old child, I demonstrate how medico-legal manuals provide a script to the defence lawyer structuring his cross-examination frame by frame. I contend that defence lawyers feign ignorance by treating diagnostic categories as if these are experiential categories. Even in the instance of statutory rape, medico-legal textbooks provide defence lawyers with the resources to suggest that the child is actually a child-adult, a seductive child who really could not have been raped in nature. The medicalization of consent in a statutory rape trial where consent is not relevant may be thought of as a paradigmatic case of public secrecy.

In Chapter 2, I introduce ethnographic transcripts of court proceedings. The court records were written in Gujarati. Most witnesses were examined in Gujarati. At times, Hindi and English were spoken in court during the proceedings. I have indicated the language spoken where it is germane to the testimony. The court record was not a verbatim record of everything that was spoken in court; rather a specific process of translation was followed whereby the judge dictated the testimony to the typist in Gujarati. I wrote down the question–answer sequence, not always audible to me, in the language spoken.[22] The ethnographic excerpt of courtroom talk includes my observations and transcription of the proceedings, as well as the dictation in Gujarati by the judge, which forms the official record as indicated in the text as J(d). The ethnographic record thus combines my record of courtroom speech, which may be regarded as the 'oral script' and the dictation by the judge to the court typist, the 'written transcript'. It is the juxtaposition of the oral script and written transcript that finds further elaboration in the next chapter.

In Chapter 3, 'The Child Witness on Trial', I draw attention to courtroom talk that imagines rape as belonging to the realm of adult normativity.[23] I demonstrate what it means to argue that the rape trial is a pornographic spectacle. The structure of the cross-examination bears strong resemblances to the structure of pornography. In a statutory rape trial spoken law inserts questions which feign ignorance that the victim is really a child, and in the ultimate analysis it is her childhood that is on trial. Here, we encounter the power of spoken law not translated verbatim in the official script; the violence of the oral script is paraphrased, sanitized, or elided.

These oral scripts, where we actually find children embodying the wounding effects of precedents of injustice, which are repeated in case after case, defeat the guidelines issued by appellate courts. It is therefore insufficient to think of the precedent merely in doctrinal ways. Instead, courtroom talk, which evades projects of judicial reform, wounds the raped survivor mimetically to produce evidence of the injury caused to society. It is not surprising then that despite repeated guidelines issued by the Supreme Court, rape trials continue to display a child's body to a sexualized gaze, forcing her to recount the trauma repeatedly in adult ways, challenging her everyday knowledge about the world and inscribing blame on her for being raped.

In Chapter 4, 'Justice Is a Secret: Compromise in Rape Trials', I point to the culture of compromise that is constitutive of our courts.[24] I follow the story of a minor whose story is mediated through a bewildering set of records and events that never quite allow us to determine how she may have narrated her own story. I illustrate how the out-of-court settlement, which revolves around an upper-caste father's sense of dishonour performs public secrecy to do 'justice' to the compromise between men of unequal status. Although it is illegal to settle, compound, or compromise a rape case, it is a public secret that rape cases are routinely compromised (also see Berti 2010, 2011). In such cases, the trial is abridged, witnesses turn hostile, and the official script is emptied of the danger of revealing what really happened. The case law reveals terrifying consequences for women who are assaulted, murdered, or forced to commit suicide by the men who raped them when they refuse to compromise. Judicial delay, lack of witness protection, and social stigma that accrues to a rape complainant create the material conditions for cultures of compromise to flourish.

In such cases, far from being a dramatic revelation of the norm, the trial conceals it. It institutes illegality at the heart of state law. More importantly, the shadowy figure of the woman on whose behalf a compromise is enacted, now hostile to the prosecution, remains vulnerable to charges of perjury. The criminal trial becomes a site of contestation over the monopoly for fashioning an out-of-court settlement between the accused, the complaint, the family, the defence, and the prosecution. The term 'culture of compromise' indicates a field of power and violence where the monopoly over compromise often means terror for the subject on whose behalf compromise is brokered. In everyday legal discourse, compromise cases are dubbed as 'false' cases. The equivalence between compromise and falsity is a semantic obfuscation that negates coercion, terror, and censorship as the material condition of testimony. To characterize compromise cases as 'false' is to ignore the lack of control a woman has over her story in the contestation over the monopoly to settle a case. Every other rape trial is marred by the contestation over the monopoly to compromise, a practical modality of power which the cunning of judicial reform refuses to address. My imagery of the narrative monopolies over compromise in rape trials is thus directed at a different understanding. I hope to show in some bloodied detail that, far from signifying any visions and versions of the 'rule of law', rape trials all too often signify a 'reign of terror' for the subject on whose behalf compromise is brokered (see U. Baxi 1994).

In Chapter 5, 'Love Affairs and Rape Trials in India', I reflect on the criminalization of love as rape. I narrate the Kafkaesque experiences of a young woman who was jailed for abetting her own rape, kidnapping, and abduction for refusing to heed her family's demand that she bring a rape prosecution against the man she was in love with. This case study forcefully explicates the simultaneity of juridical identities ascribed to the legal subject as victim, abettor, accused, and scene of crime—identities totally incommensurable with lived experience. The incommensurability between the experiential and the legal record finds specific rendition when love is classified as rape.

Chapter 6, 'On Interpreting Rape as/and Atrocity' draws attention to those forms of targeted sexual violence aimed to debase and humiliate specific communities. I turn to the Scheduled Castes and Scheduled Tribes (Prevention of Atrocities) Act, 1989, Act 33 of 1989 (henceforth, PoA Act), which names the rape of Dalit and tribal women as an atrocity. I indicate the complexity of the jurisprudence that has emerged in naming rape as atrocity or reading rape with atrocity.[25] Atrocities are legally defined as those crimes listed under the PoA Act against a Scheduled Caste or Scheduled Tribe, committed by a person who does not belong to these communities.[26] This special law justifies the need for protective legislation to redress and prevent specific forms of degrading violence against these 'enumerative communities' (Das 2003: 10).[27] I contend that the judicial interpretation of the PoA Act is concerned with how dominance is enacted, communicated, and displayed between men of unequal status rather than addressing the trauma of Dalit and tribal women on its own terms. I highlight the judicial narratives of Dalit women whose testimony we encounter in judicial records to pose specific questions to the sanitized sociological pictures of caste. In other words, I argue that rape trials furnish scripts of the social via the juridicalized bodies of violated women.

These rape trials are not about the memorialization of what Lucie White calls epic styles of memory, 'a legacy of wrong doing' that courts are 'constitutionally committed ... to transcend' (White 1995, cited in Sarat & Kearns 2002: 18). In contrast to such epic styles of narrating stories about race, 'claims about sex discrimination ... focus on how men and women differ and whether that difference makes a difference. When a historical story is told, it is a history of social attitudes rather than a history of national or constitutional dimensions' (Sarat & Kearns 2002: 18). By inscribing rape as an act of lust, the outcome of natural sexual differences, rape is neither inscribed as an act of political violence nor set as the scene of historical discrimination. These trials are split from histories of violent sexual humiliation as if women's biographies are emptied of all historical content. Such a 'tragic style of remembering' is particularly poignant since judges fail to memorialize sexual violence as a historic wrong even when called to interpret a special law aiming to historicize the wrongdoing to Dalits and tribals (White 1995 cited in Sarat & Kearns 2002: 14).

Yet again, I make the point that statutory rape trials allow us to explicate that this opposition between caste and gender, or the epic and tragic styles of remembering, are adult contestations over what to remember and memorialize. When a statutory rape trial is staged as special atrocity trial, the Dalit child must not only gaze at her body through adult categories, but she also learns to inherit the humiliations of caste. In this case, techniques of policing embedded in the politics of caste divest the child of the means to prove injury. I contend that when a law does not differentiate between atrocities committed on adult women and children, it assumes an adult understanding of what it means to be named as Scheduled Caste or Scheduled Tribe for a child. This notion haunts the jurisprudence on rape as atrocity.

Although I researched a trial court in Ahmedabad, I suggest that the ethnography speaks to routine trial practices in other trial courts in India, and in this sense, this book is not only about rape trials in Gujarat. Yet I was intrigued by specific claims about rape in Gujarat as compared to other regions in country. I encountered the commonplace view that sexual violence did not 'really' exist in Gujarat other than a few aberrant cases of child sexual abuse fairly routinely during my fieldwork.[28] As a high court judge told me, most cases posted for bail hearings were 'errors' committed under 'excitement or anxiety', which the woman now interprets as 'rape' and later as 'sex'.[29] Rather than expose such men whose experimentations with sex purportedly went awry to the dangers of prison, judges deployed the category of 'heinous' crime to distinguish rape from sex. I found that most lawyers I interviewed believed that the real and heinous rape cases are the ones committed on children between seven and twelve years of age. I was struck by how the public discourses picturing Gujarat as safer for women as compared to other regions, especially North India, underplayed the nature and extent of sexual violence in Gujarat. Commenting specifically on the official statistics of rape, a police officer (Crime Branch, Ahmedabad) said to me that the occurrence of rape is low in Gujarat since most registered complaints arose out of parents filing criminal cases when an underage daughter eloped. He maintained that 'real' rape cases were truly few (see Appendix 2).

A male government pleader in the Gujarat High Court said to me:

> The overall situation in Gujarat is such that except in Porbandar, girls can travel independently from here [Ahmedabad] to Rajkot or Jamnagar. Gujarati girls like to wear ornaments and walk on roads without fear. Only in riotous situation, it is difficult. But that is not a permanent situation. It is a phase for ten or fifteen days or one month. Once life becomes normal ... this is not possible in Delhi or Patna.

In this view, the riot is constituted as temporary and everyday life as the return to *normality* unmarked by the *temporary* sexual terror of the riot. Such aberrations do not threaten everyday discourses of public morality. This is an imagination framed by a picture of dangerous temporality representing Gujarat as non-violent towards women during phases of normality as compared to contexts of riots. Such pictures of violence that portray the riot as a temporal aberration enact powerful erasures of the accounts of rape in situations not defined as a riot, while rationalizing rapes that do occur during riots.

It remains a painful fact that the nature of sexual violence documented during the communal violence in Gujarat in 1992 and 2002 presented one of the most horrific faces of rape culture in India. A comment on mass sexual violence follows in the conclusion. Rather than catalogue the exceptional forms of violence that unfolded in Gujarat 2002, I reflect on exceptional forms of testimony that unfolded in the trials where the very material conditions of testimony had to be first created. If jurispathic governance marked the judicial and political response to the chilling events of Gujarat 2002, survivors, lawyers, and activists struggled to 'record and write history by creating narratives of present injustices', and insisted 'on memory in the face of denial' (Sarat & Kearns 2002: 13). These are voices, to quote Sarat and Kearns, which 'choose Justice over the jurispathic tendencies of the moment', exemplified poignantly the Bilkis Bano case (2002: 13). I provide an account of the Bilkis Bano case, the first to result in a conviction of rape during a communal riot in independent India. As the jurisgenerative potential of this trial unfolds, it also exposes the venal forms of jurispathic governance in Gujarat, offering us yet another Kafkaesque picture of the rape law in India.

NOTES

1. There are two trial courts in Ahmedabad city as the district is divided into the city and the rural districts. The district and session court (rural) where this fieldwork was conducted, located in the old city, was known as the 'Mirzapur' court after the name of the location. The city court is known as the 'Bhadra' court in local parlance. The proceedings of the court were conducted and recorded in Gujarati. In some instances, the proceedings were conducted in Hindi. Legal experts also spoke in English in court.

2. Conceiving of rape as a public secret, Nordstrom has argued that such 'Public secrets tend to coalesce around matters of power and abuse. They are thus generally imbued with relations of domination, contestation and resistance. The fact that public secrets are maintained as generalised secrets means ... that which is formally illegitimate is sufficiently legitimated in practice' (1996: 147).

3. The rape law has been defined in ss. 375 and 376 of the IPC . Related procedural law is defined in Section (s.) 114 of the Indian Evidence Act, 1872, (Act no. 2 of 1872) [hereafter IEA]. S. 155(4) IEA that permitted the defence to prove immoral character of the rape survivor was finally deleted on 31 December 2002 [see The Indian Evidence Act, 2002, Act No. 4 of 2003 (An Act further to amend the Indian Evidence Act, 1872)]. *Public Secrets of Law* went into press at a time when the legal landscape on sexual violence irrevocably changed. The efforts of women's groups and child rights groups resulted in the enactment of the Protection of Children from Sexual

Offences Act, 2012 (No 32 of 2012) [hereafter POCSO], which came into force on 14 November 2012. For the first time, the law distinguished between adult and child survivors of sexual violence. Until November 2012, rape was seen as an adult crime, denying children's voices a rightful place in judicial discourse. It is this judicial place inhabited by children in our courts of law, when child sexual abuse was not named as a specific offence, which finds ethnographic description in this book. The POCSO Act envisages a newer way of architecting children's testimony in special courts for children, adjudicated by special prosecutors, by adopting distinct courtroom procedures. Yet how the potential of this Act will be actualized remains to be seen. This book perhaps allows insights into the difficulties of displacing the rape culture that inhabits our courtrooms, wherein the disqualification of children's voices in courts of law remains routine.

In 2013, ss. 375 and 376 of the IPC were amended twice by virtue of the Criminal Law (Amendment) Ordinance, 2013 (No. 3 of 2013) and the Criminal Law (Amendment) Act, 2013 (No. 13 of 2013), marking a historic moment in the contemporary law reform debate on rape in India. The Criminal Law (Amendment) Act, 2013 passed by the Lok Sabha on 19 March 2013, and by the Rajya Sabha on 21 March 2013, received Presidential assent on 2 April 2013, and came into force retrospectively from 3 February 2013. It replaced the Criminal Law (Amendment) Ordinance, 2013 promulgated by the President on 3 February 2013 as emergency legislation to address the crisis following the gangrape in Delhi in 2012.

This legislative change followed unprecedented and sustained protests in the aftermath of the brutal gangrape and subsequent death of a 23 year old woman in a bus in Delhi on 16 December 2012. As the details of the brutality on the young woman and her male friend who boarded a private bus after watching a film at a mall hit the media, it seemed as if the threshold of toleration of sexual violence had broken down. No longer confined to the women's and queer movements, rape was talked about by everyone publically and privately across generations. Brutal gangrape, mutilation of body parts, and intolerable sexual humiliation in a public space could not be confined to zones of emergency inscribed on bodies of dalit, tribal, religious or sexual minorities, some place out there which did not really hurt us. Perhaps there was recognition that we are all living in states of sexual emergency, producing an unparalleled circulation and outpouring of affect.

Following the protests, the government appointed a three-member committee chaired by Justice JS Verma along with Justice Leila Seth and Gopal Subramanium. The Verma Committee, which received more than 80,000 submissions, and organized a two-day hearing with women's groups, activists and experts who had worked on the issue of sexual violence, submitted their report in 29 days. After the release of the report, the government enacted the Criminal Law (Amendment) Ordinance, 2013 on 3 February 2013. The government did not accept many important recommendations of the Verma Committee. There was strong opposition to the Ordinance on many grounds including for naming sexual assault as gender neutral without any exceptions, which also meant women could be accused by men of sexual assault. The opposition was not about recognizing sexual violence is an emergency that women experience everyday, rather the question was what is recognized as an emergency, and when. By retaining the marital rape exemption, it was clear that the government did not think that marital rape is a permanent sexual emergency for married women. Further, the rape of women by security agencies such as the army, a state of permanent sexual emergency in the northeast, continues to need sanction for prosecution from the government. Those in positions of power and authority to stop unimaginable and targetted sexual and reproductive violence were not seen as criminally authoring and authorizing states of sexual emergencies. The Ordinance did not recognize the states of emergencies declared against young people who choose to marry against social norms of caste, community, and religion by raising the age of consent to eighteen. The Ordinance did not recognize that each medical examination of a rape survivor is experienced as a re-rape by virtue of the two-finger test; and that this is an emergency. Nor did it name the routinized violence on dalit women, such as stripping and parading especially of those who are punished for transgressing caste hierarchies as a state of emergency.

Protests, lobbying, and networking followed to craft a law, which resulted in the Criminal Law (Amendment) Act, 2013. Several far-reaching amendments were brought about in the rape law and new offences were introduced such as acid attacks, trafficking of persons for physical or sexual exploitation, sexual harassment, assault with intent to disrobe, stalking, and voyeurism. It is beyond the scope of this work to analyse the new legislation comprehensively, however, the 2013 amendments have been footnoted where relevant.

It must be noted that until now, despite many protests, the rape law had been amended only once in 1983 since its enactment in 1860. It is the story of the 1983 amendment that this book narrates. In doing so, I hope that this ethnography of rape trials offers to the readers not only a perspective on the history of the rape law as it unfolds in practice but also proffers insights into the challenges that continue to haunt us despite the legislative changes that made history in 2013. The violence of spoken law, yet again, escaped the agenda of judicial reform. In this sense, *Public Secrets of Law* speaks insistently to the necessity of detailing the practice of law and challenging official models of law reform, which domesticate critique.

4. If the field I had chosen to research was impractical for many in the court, institutionally the practicality of researching rape was also an issue. Women researchers working in patriarchal contexts, living or travelling alone, interacting with male informants, and researching in areas conventionally inaccessible to women have often confronted the question of securing their safety (see Bell et al. 1993; Gupta & Ferguson 1997; Huff 1997; Mattley 1997; Moreno 1995; Panini 1991; Thapan 1998; Winkler & Hanke 1995). Women have often been urged to research in 'practical' field sites (see Dua 1979; Sivakumar 1979). At the same time, the gender-neutral image of the 'heroic' fieldworker has unquestioningly valourized sexualized violence or its threat (see Gupta & Ferguson 1997). The implicit assumptions that a competent fieldworker would not 'get herself in such a situation' accrue notions of blame and incompetence to women field workers (Moreno 1995). Moreno suggests that the denial of gender at the academic workplace normalizes the division between the professional persona of the anthropologist and relegates the experience of violence to the personal, as if gender were the site of the personal alone. In her words, it is as if 'anthropologists do not get harassed and raped. Women do' (Moreno 1995: 246). The idea that vulnerability equals weakness consigns such experiences to the realm of the personal and unmentionable.

5. This refers to the IPC provision on abetting suicide.

6. George E. Marcus suggests that we must move away from thinking of complicity as a 'partnership in evil', but links complicity to the sense of being 'complex, or involved' (1997: 100).

7. The concerns of feminist jurisprudence also address anthropology, when ethnographic texts move into courts of law as evidence in cases of rape. Shalini Randeria's (1992) doctoral research on caste *panchayats* was cited in the Gujarat High Court to persuade the court that caste *panchayats* exist in the region. This evidence was furbished in a case of rape where the woman concerned had claimed that she had been divorced by a decision of a caste *panchayat*. The court initially refused to believe that she was divorced on the grounds that caste *panchayats* did not function any more in the region (personal conversation with Achyut Yagnik 1996; also see Takhtani 1997).

8. In his famous essay 'Law in Books and Law in Action', Pound argued that 'it is the work of lawyers to make the law in action conform to the law in the books, not by futile thunderings against popular lawlessness, nor eloquent exhortations to obedience of the written law, but by making the law in the books such that the law in action can conform to it, and providing a speedy, cheap and efficient mode of applying it. On no other terms can the two be reconciled ... Let us not become legal monks. Let us not allow our

legal texts to acquire sanctity and go the way of all sacred writings. For the written word remains, but man changes' (1910: 36).

9. Mardorossian (2002) argues that 'it was precisely at the historical moment when women became active in fighting to dismantle the oppressive structures that subordinated them that the category of "victim" was reinflected and ideologically redefined to support the depoliticization of gendered class relations. ... being [a] victim did not mean being incapacitated and powerless. It meant being determined and angry (although not a pathologically resentful) agent of change' (2002: 767). In this book, the use of the word victim or survivor similarly emphasizes being angry, bearing the capacity to protest, and articulating determined demands for justice. I believe that the debate that the opposition between women as victims and women as agents is not creative or even productive for the simultaneity of juridical identities is far too complex.

10. Here I am thinking of Foucault who looks at a 'case' of parricide as the 'intersection of discourses that differed in origin, form, organization, and function'; in their 'tonality and their variety they form neither a composite work nor an exemplary text, but rather a strange contest, a confrontation, a power relation, a battle among discourses and through discourses' (1975: x). He argues that a case offered an opportunity to examine 'the way in which a particular kind of knowledge (e.g., medicine, psychiatry, psychology) is formed and acts in relation to institutions and the roles prescribed in them (e.g., the law with respect to the expert, the accused, the criminally insane and so on)', hence providing a 'key to the relations of power, domination and conflict within which discourses emerge and function' (1975: xi).

11. Any ethnographer in a court has to remain mindful of the fact that her location in a court implies the pain of law's violence in the face of the violation of its authority. For instance, the threat of being charged with contempt of court even when a fieldworker does not intend to offend the court. An uneasy awareness of the potential of harassment, ridicule, or violence in everyday interactions in the court was a constant condition of fieldwork.

12. The spatialization of hierarchy between courtrooms is also marked out in the differences in the quality of the furniture between different courtrooms. The District and Sessions Judge's courtroom, for example, was furnished with the finest chairs in the court, uniformly for all litigants and lawyers. The Additional Sessions Judge's courtroom reserved more comfortable chairs only for lawyers. With the decline in hierarchy between judges and corresponding increase in the floors, the chairs and benches became more uncomfortable, inexpensive, and scarce.

13. When a judge walks down a corridor, passageway, or flight of stairs through the court, lawyers fall silent, make way, and even bow or nod.

These norms of the court seem to tighten as the hierarchy between courts increases. In the Gujarat High Court, a judge is led out by a court attendant who emits a low hissing sound and waves a baton in the air. Thus, physical contact between a judge and other people is spatially ordered to maintain the exclusivity of law. Other spaces in the court are also exclusively marked out for judges. For instance, judges and lawyers have separate law libraries, separate entrances, bathrooms, and social spaces.

14. The criminal manual issued by the Gujarat High Court outlining the procedures to be followed in the court specifies that 'the accused person should be informed by the court at the beginning of every trial that he may sit, if he desires to do so, and chairs or benches should, whenever available, be provided for this purpose. ... The accused must, however stand up, whenever he is addressed by the court. At the time of hearing of the criminal case against the accused who are on bail the accused, instead of being made to sit in the dock, be allowed to sit at a convenient place set apart in the Court room, a distance from the dias where the judge or magistrate sits' (Gujarat High Court 1977: 59).

15. I could not generate a list of the number of ongoing rape trials. The cases were not classified according to the nature of the offence but were organized according to the quantum of punishment and sessions number. Following Garfinkel (1967) we can argue that this is not an instance of 'bad record' keeping; rather it reflects the classificatory practices organized on the principle according to which courts are hierarchized, that is, the quantum of punishment definitive of the jurisdiction of each court. I subsequently relied on listing the number of ongoing cases in the additional public prosecutor's office.

16. The other three additional public prosecutors, including a woman prosecutor, did not allow me to follow cases assigned to them.

17. Of the two groups I approached, one had worked with rape survivors by providing counselling and legal support. However, I did not get permission to document their records or work out of their office.

18. Yet another viewpoint insists that the disciplinary location configures desire and gaze in specific ways that de-sexualizes male gaze. As Hirabhai said to me, 'Baxi, if I were to look at a naked dead woman in a morgue I would be dispassionate. Even though I am a man. I would not see her with the same kind of gaze. Same is with doctors. One does not gaze at a nude dead woman as if she were a woman.'

19. Note here that the use of the category of 'lubrication' conflates biological changes with pleasurable sex. Lees has rightly argued that 'sexual arousal may cause the vagina to lubricate but this does not mean that a moist vagina necessarily implies sexual arousal' (1997: 97–8).

20. Hence, I do not follow the method of engaging in statistical or quantitative analysis of appellate judgments (see Shankar 2009). Nor do I list numerous precedents on various aspects of the doctrinal law of rape. My attempt is to trace how oral scripts index the circulation of standardized categories when translated into written transcripts.

21. Chatterji and Mehta alert us to 'how the unfolding of history influences the memory of survivors of violence', such that apart from other conditions of testimony, 'the speech of the testifier is informed by the archive of the communal riot' (2007: 29–30).

22. I did not follow the route set out by Mateosian (1993) who combines structuration theory with conversational analysis to study courtroom talk in rape trials, specifically the cross-examination of the survivor of rape. Mateosian is right when he says that 'the "mere" recitation, and incantation of "boring" details in courtroom talk, which Holmstorm and Burgess, and Largen lament, might well organise the sonorous rhythmic design found in charismatic discourse' (1993: 21). It was impossible for me to replicate the techniques of recording and transcription that may generate 'such a density of conversational detail that literally thousands of utterances and conversational properties become available and analytically relevant' (Mateosian 1993: 65). The method itself presupposes the possibility of recording trial proceedings on tape or video (see Epstein 1978).

23. Although I use the category of raped 'women' where relevant, I argue that the testimony to rape is constituted through categories of an adult legal discourse. Hence, female children testifying to rape have to grapple with medico-legal procedures, procedures for court appearances and questions during the trial as if they were adults, and yet have to retain childlike qualities to be believed (see Chapter 3). The contradictions in the rape law in relation to children remains a public secret whereby the injuries caused by the law remain unacknowledged in public discourse and accepted as an inevitable necessity. I read the records of rape on adult women and children simultaneously in order to point out the distressing incapacity of the judiciary to relate to children's words and their worlds in the aftermath of sexual violence.

24. Cultures of compromise are not unique to rape trials. We find that the culture of compromise manifests in other non-compoundable crimes, such as murder and riots. Nor is compromise unique to the trial courts even though it unfolds most dramatically in trial courts.

25. The PoA Act was implemented on 30 January 1990. The characterization of cases under the PoA Act in judgments and public discourse varies. In Gujarat courts, the PoA Act is abbreviated as the 'Atrocities Act' and the judges designated as 'special atrocity judges'. In other

courts, the PoA Act is referred to as the SC/ST Act. The manner in which I have abbreviated the Act retains the emphasis on the aim of the legislation to prevent and redress atrocities rather than maintain the connotation that the legislation itself produces atrocity as indicated by the abbreviation, 'Atrocities Act'.

26. The Constitution of India has specifically abolished untouchability. It lists the castes and tribes for which the state provides certain provisions, such as reservation of seats in the Parliament and state legislatures, and posts in government institutions. Thus, Scheduled Caste and Scheduled Tribe are juridical categories. The Constitution also mentions Other Backward Classes (OBCs), who are also entitled to certain provisions in individual states. The Scheduled Caste communities are also referred to as Harijan, which literally means 'people of God', a contested category (Mendelsohn & Vicziany 1998). I have preferred to use the word Dalit to refer to communities named as untouchables formerly. Dalit, a word used in Marathi language, is defined as 'ground' or 'broken or reduced to pieces generally'. It has been associated with the radical politics of self-assertion and dignity. Dalit has encompassed the juridical categories scheduled caste and other backward classes (that are coterminous with so-called lower castes).

27. The category of Scheduled Castes replaced an earlier category, 'depressed classes', under the Government of India Act of 1935 (Das 2003; Galanter 1972, 1984). As Das reminds us, 'initially untouchability was to be the criterion for the inclusions of castes into the list of Scheduled Castes. Galanter has described the difficulties of arriving at a list, given the differences in the south and the north of India' (2003: 10). The 'names of castes that were finally included in the state lists formed a kind of unity only through a "common relationship their members have with government"' (Duskin 1972 cited in Das 2003: 19). This marked the generation of what Veena Das calls 'the conception of community as an enumerative community, which has a strong influence on processes of political representation' (2003: 10).

28. In the opinion of a Gujarat High Court Judge, there are four kinds of rape cases, 'cases of rape which are not rape. These are false cases. Then there are cases where there is implied consent but not full consent. These semi-consent or consent cases are reported only if someone has come to know; otherwise, the crime would not have been reported. When the girl is between twelve and sixteen, due to lack of sex education and anxiety on the part of the girl, she is vulnerable to exploitation. Up to the age of ten, children are victimized by aged men. These are heinous crimes where bail is not granted.'

29. In the words of the high court judge, 'bail is not normally granted when the victim is very young, a child has been raped or he poses a threat

to the victim. Otherwise, bail should be granted. Most cases are of consent and semi-consent. Though these are serious offences, it is heinous unless it is 100 per cent against the wish or the will of the girl. Given the conditions of Indian jails, and on top of that rape cases! He may have committed an error under excitement or anxiety. If you send them to jail, it may permanently teach these men other crimes. Until it is not heinous, for example, a three-year-old or a father–daughter rape, the impact of the decision of the court would affect him adversely. You would be punishing him before the trial, for the victim may become hostile and say it had happened with her consent'.

CHAPTER ONE

Doctrinal Pictures of Rape Trials
How to Do Things with Feminism

Judicial words bear illocutionary force as acts or mandates for deeds (Austin 1975). In a basic sense, 'a legal world is built only to the extent that there are commitments that place the body in line … the interpretive commitments of officials, are realized, indeed, in the flesh' (Cover 1995: 208). In this chapter, I elaborate such judicial interpretations executed in the flesh of the women testifying to rape. Further, I wish to present a reading of appellate law on rape to trace how judicial precedent represses the violence that underlies its development. By juxtaposing landmark cases from different Indian courts to read the rape law, I hope to describe the written and unwritten precedents of injustice that haunt projects of law reform. In doing so, I focus on the effects of the 1983 amendment in relation to the Indian women's movement's critique of the rape law.

Although landmark trials repeat elements of earlier precedents of injustice, such trials also act as laboratories for judicial reform. The cunning of judicial reform lies in folding the measure of reform into the structure of the trial without displacing the character of the rape trial as a sexualized spectacle. I suggest that even where newness seems to be introduced in trials we find the repetition of elements of other trials. Hence, trials that act as laboratories for judicial reform and yet repeat earlier precedents of injustice have been characterized as landmark trials. I do not aim to provide a prescriptive model of how the rape law ought to be reformed. Instead, I call attention to how we may think of projects of reform as embodied and lived experiences that inscribe violence on the very legal subjects on whose behalf judicial reform speaks.

SITUATING THE RAPE LAW IN INDIA: THE 1983 AMENDMENT

In India, each contemporary account of the rape law has referred to the extraordinary political mobilization that took place against the Supreme Court judgment[1] acquitting two policemen of charges of rape and assault in 1979. The national campaign against rape (1980–3) that followed this judgment introduced a public discourse that critiqued existent social discourses of shame and honour regulating speech against rape in public spheres (see Gandhi & Shah 1992). It challenged practices of power that constructed public testimony to rape as indecent or pornographic (Agnes 1983). In its construction as a legitimate social problem, testimony of rape entered the realm of politics. The movement challenged the popular 'psychopathological' model of rape that constructed rape as the act of a few perverted men or an isolated act of uncontrolled male sexuality (Albin 1977).

The distinction between sex and violence was questioned (Menon 2004). Catherine Mackinnon (1989) famously argues that the distinction between violence and sex is problematic since rape is as sexual, for the man, as it is violent. The threat of rape coerces women into compliance and mystifies the control by calling this process seduction to which consent is central. Mackinnon (1989) contends that the very category of consent is problematic, since it is not apparent what it is that women consent to. She suggests that violence itself has become sexualized or sexy, such that the only criterion that separates battery from rape is that the latter is defined genitally. Other feminist scholars such as Carol Smart depart from this position by arguing that 'there is a difference between saying that we should not call rape violence because this means we fail to face the larger and more difficult problem of phallocentric sex, and saying that we should not call rape violence because all (hetero) sex is violence' (1989: 44). Similarly, Nivedita Menon critiques Mackinnon since 'such an understanding that all (hetero)sex is violence reduces one to paralysis. It denies one the possibility that women can redefine and affirm themselves outside the rigid codes of a male-defined sexuality. If violence is sexuality and sexuality is male, there is a daunting seamlessness to male dominance' (Menon 2004: 115). Such an affirmation can only come about if the women's movement 'shifts its focus from the law…to work towards transforming commonsense understandings of rape and sexual violence in general' (Menon 2004: 156).

Feminists have challenged phallocentric commonsense that assigns blame to women for 'provoking' rape.[2] Feminists have also critiqued victim-blaming assertions which assert that women who wear provocative clothes, smoke, go out after dark, or travel alone 'invite' rape; or that most rape survivors are lying and vengeful women. The commonplace assumption that rape is an isolated crime committed by strangers has also been challenged, as most often the rapist is a relative or an acquaintance. Thus, sociological studies that relate the high incidence of rape to social structures suggest that rates of rape do not merely signal a statistical normality but also indicate that rape is an extension of normative sexual behaviour (Walby 1994).

The shift in thinking of rape from 'pathology' to 'normality' was forwarded by feminists who questioned the assumptions that underpin normal heterosexuality, making explicit the links between male violence and male sexuality (see Griffin 1971). Brownmiller (1975) argued that rape is a normal mode of exerting patriarchal power. Rather than endorsing the view that rape is the outcome of overpowering male sexual urge, rape was defined as intentional, premeditated, and political violence against women. In other words, men do not rape because they are sexually frustrated; they rape because they experience the desire in rape.

Rape then may be understood as a form of preferred political violence (Brownmiller 1975). The 1980s campaign put together statistics to show the 'normality' of rape both in terms of their incidence and frequency. The statistical frequency of rape indicates that rape is a preferred form of violence against women. Simultaneously, the campaign identified the law courts (which acted as a unified signifier of the state) as *the* institutional site that normalizes violence against women by converting the testimony to rape into evidence of consensual sex.

The national campaign resulted in the first amendment of the colonial rape law since it was enacted in 1860. One of the most significant changes in 1983 was the re-naming of the section on rape as 'sexual offence', emphasizing the construction of rape as sexual violation.[3] Siddique's definition of rape as a traumatic instance of 'illegal sex and violence' aptly sums up this legal understanding of rape (1993: 452). Section 375 IPC defined rape as follows:

A man is said to commit rape who, except in the case hereinafter excepted, has sexual intercourse with a woman under circumstances falling under any of the six following descriptions:

First: Against her will.

Secondly: Without her consent.

Thirdly: With her consent, when her consent has been obtained by putting her or any person in whom she is interested in fear of death or of hurt.

Fourthly: With her consent, when the man knows that he is not her husband, and that her consent is given because she believes that he is another man to whom she is or believes herself to be lawfully married.

Fifthly: With her consent, when, at the time of giving such consent, by reason of unsoundness of mind or intoxication or the administration by him personally or through another of any stupefying or unwholesome substance, she is unable to understand the nature and consequences of that to which she gives consent.

Sixthly: With or without her consent, when she is under sixteen years of age.

Explanation: Penetration is sufficient to constitute the sexual intercourse necessary to the offence of rape.

Exception: Sexual intercourse by a man with his own wife, the wife not being under fifteen years of age, is not rape.

The explanation to s. 375 has been held to mean that penile penetration is necessary to constitute the offence of rape.[4] Courts have held that evidence of partial penile penetration is sufficient to constitute the offence of rape. Until 2013 rape by the metonymic substitutes of the penis like sticks, fingers, and other objects did not constitute the legal meaning of rape. This hetero-normative emphasis on rape based on penile penetration may be related to the way in which patrilineal descent is traced in society, to which control over female sexuality is central.

It has been further argued that rape is 'a crime against female monogamy (exclusive access by one man) than against women's sexual dignity or intimate integrity' (Mackinnon 1989: 172). This argument is illustrated by the state's consistent refusal to criminalize adult marital rape. In other words, all forms of heterosexual rape are not criminalized. An underage girl could not consent to sex until she was sixteen years of age, but she cannot withhold consent from her husband after she turns fifteen.[5] We can then argue with Mackinnon that 'the law of rape divides women into spheres of consent according to indices to men. Which category of presumed consent a woman is in depends upon who she is relative to a man who wants her, not what she says or does' (1989: 175).

The 1983 amendment reflected such dividing practices clearly when it reduced the punishment for men who rape child wives between the age of twelve to fifteen by making the offence bailable, non-cognizable, and punishable by a maximum imprisonment of two years (see Appendix 1).[6] The 1983 amendment also named rape on a judicially separated wife as 'illicit sexual intercourse not amounting to rape'.[7] This bailable and non-cognizable offence was punishable by a maximum imprisonment of two years. Commenting on this provision, the Joint Parliamentary Committee opined that 'in a case where the husband and wife are living separately under the decree of judicial separation, there is a possibility of reconciliation between them until a decree of divorce is granted. Hence, the intercourse by the husband with his wife without her consent during such period should not be treated as, or equated with rape' (JPC Report 1982: 8). The distinction between rape and consensual sex from the point of view of the separated wife was blurred for the law, which not only described rape as illicit sex but also normalized it for the sake of 'reconciliation' (P. Baxi 2000).[8]

The 1983 amendment deployed adult standards to define rape (see Chapter 3).[9] Until the enactment of the POCSO Act in 2012, female children were constituted as victims of rape only if there was evidence of partial or complete vagino–penile penetration. The 1983 campaign did not offer a critique of the naming of rape of children as 'unnatural' sexual offences under s. 377 IPC. Unnatural sexual offences are defined as follows:

> Whoever voluntarily has carnal intercourse against the order of nature with any man, woman or animal, shall be punished with imprisonment of life, or with imprisonment of either description for a term which may extend to 10 years and shall also be liable to fine.

The explanation holds that 'penetration is sufficient to constitute the carnal intercourse necessary to the offence described in this section'. Not only did this colonial law name rape of children—male or female—as 'unnatural' sex, 'the lack of a consent-based distinction in the offence has made homosexual sex synonymous to rape and equated homosexuality with sexual perversity' (Gupta 2006: 4815).[10]

In other words, this law posits penile penetration of the vagina as normal and natural while pathologizing sodomy as an offence against nature. While such a law in its emphasis on penile penetration does not consider sexual relationships between women a possibility, it criminalizes sodomy with or without consent in homosexual or heterosexual relations. However, Gupta's analysis of the judicial meaning of unnatural sexual offences makes it clear that 'there has been a tendency in Indian courts to create an association between the sexual acts and certain kinds of persons, who are more likely to commit the act—thereby giving a character and face to sodomy in the form of a homosexual' (2006: 4816).

This law has not been repealed despite demands from several queer, feminist, and human rights groups. The petition challenging the constitutionality of s. 377 succeeded in the Delhi High Court in 2009, when the court read down s. 377 IPC excluding from its purview consensual adult same-sex relationships (see Narrain and Gupta 2011). This case, popularly known as the Naz Foundation case, is now pending on appeal in the Supreme Court.[11] The Delhi High Court made it manifest that a consenting partner can no longer be construed as an abettor. With the enactment of the Protection of Children from Sexual Offences Act, 2012, the argument that s. 377 is essential to prosecute child sexual abuse ought to have been made redundant, paving the way for repealing this discriminatory law, yet ironically, the POCSO Act continues to be read along with s. 377 IPC. The debates on how to name rape, child sexual abuse, and queer rights in the last twenty years are integrally linked, although the journey of such devastating critiques of the rape law has taken different and somewhat divergent routes. I cannot do justice to the complexity and nuance of these debates in this book, but I will flag some of the issues that prefigure them.

The debates in the 1980s not only focused on critiquing the pernicious effects of the rape law on women, but also introduced new legal categories of rape.[12] Custodial rape was denounced as an extreme form of state violence against women—the direct means of violence through which state power is inscribed on women's bodies. Such cases are rarely prosecuted; when heard, it is usually the rape survivor who is maligned and portrayed as a lying *habitué* (PUDR Report 2004). Arguably the conceptualization of custodial rape is one of the most important contributions of Indian feminists in drawing the attention of political theorists to the sexual politics of the state. Making such assertions, Gangoli argues that Indian feminists diverged from mainstream Western feminist analyses of rape in 'primarily interpersonal terms of expression of male power against women' (2007: 84). The anti-rape campaign focussed on 'sexual violence by the police on the most marginalised', by mobilizing protests against the state's sexual repression of 'poor, lower caste and minority women' (Gangoli 2007: 21), thereby challenging everyday legal discourses that make invisible the sexual politics of class, caste, or community.

The 1983 amendment recognized four sites of custodial rape. Following the 1983 amendment, ss. 376(2) (a)–(d) criminalized custodial rape by a policeman, a public servant, the management or staff of a jail, remand home or any other place of custody, or the management or staff of a hospital. Further, it included as an aggravated offence, rape of a pregnant woman (s. 376[2][e]), a child when she is under twelve years of age (s. 376[2][f]), and gangrape (s. 376[2][g]). These offences carried a minimum sentence of ten years. Thereby introducing enhanced punishment for 'aggravated' forms of rape.[13]

The courts were however empowered by this law to provide 'adequate and special reasons', as long as these were recorded, for a term lesser than the mandatory minimum sentence.[14] Agnes (1998) argues that rapists were routinely given less than the mandatory minimum requirement of punishment in the aftermath of the 1983 amendment.

Agnes' (1998) review of appellate judgments following the 1983 amendment is dismaying. It was clear that these amendments failed to deliver the outcomes hoped even though the 1983 amendment shifted the burden of proof under s. 114(A) of the Indian Evidence Act (IEA) in the above-mentioned aggravated rape cases under ss. 376(2)(a)–(e) and (g). Reversal of burden of proof meant that if the prosecution were able to prove sex it would now be presumed that the woman did not consent. Although there has been criticism of this provision for expanding the use of exceptional procedures into criminal law, in effect the provision has been defeated since it has increased a reliance on medical certification of the woman's past sexual history to establish consent (see Chapter 2).[15] Further, new provisions such as s. 327 CrPC which mandated that rape trials would be held *in camera*[16] and s. 228 A IPC a provision prohibiting disclosing or publicizing the identity of the rape survivor did not displace the rape trial as a pornographic spectacle (see Appendix 1).[17]

The admissibility of the past sexual history of the rape survivor has historically been one of the most degrading and discriminatory evidentiary provisions in legal history. In India, the past sexual history clause is enshrined in s. 155 (4) IEA, which held that 'when a man is prosecuted for rape or an attempt to ravish, it may be shown that the prosecutrix was of generally immoral character'. This was not repealed in 1983 despite the insistent demand by women's groups. After twenty years of protest, the Indian Evidence (Amendment) Act, 2002 (Act 4 of 2003) omitted this clause with effect from 31 December 2002. Even after the deletion of the past sexual history clause, from 2003 onwards, we find that the past sexual history of the victim has continued to inform the jurisprudence on rape (see Chapter 2). Following the many disappointments generated by the implementation of the 1983 amendment, we see the emergence of intense lobbying for further amendments of the rape law, the use of public interest litigation and scores of protests. In the ultimate analysis, this disappointment stemmed from the judicial inability to do things with feminism.

For Agnes (1992) the law then is what the judges say it is and judicial will could be pressed into service by systemically monitoring the impact of the new rape law (also see Agnes 1998). Hence, legal history is also shaped through forces outside it (Sarat & Kearns 2002). It is fair to argue that the 1983 amendment did not result in a jurisprudence which reflected the idea that rape is an act of sexualized power, and thus a conscious mechanism through which patriarchy maintains its domination. Indian judges by and large do not share the feminist viewpoint that rape is the form of political domination of women and instead of symbolizing its breakdown rape maintains phallocentric social orders (Mackinnon 1989). Or that rape itself must be conceptualized as social structure as it is both systemic and persistent across time and space, with sufficiently consistent and patterned outcomes in the legal system (Walby 1994).

Das (1996) argues that judicial interpretation of rape lies at the intersection of regulatory discourses of sexuality and alliance. The judicial discourse on rape classifies women into those who can potentially be integrated into structures of alliance as distinct from those women who are found to be 'habituated', 'loose' or exhibiting 'easy virtue'.[18] Das argues that rules of alliance

> ...[i]mplicitly state that men may only treat those women as sexually available who are not integrated into the structure of alliance. Thus, those men who recognise each other in the 'matrimonial dialogue of men' to use the evocative phrase of Levi Strauss, are normatively required to constitute the women as signs, as women carrying significance in this dialogue. If, on the other hand, a woman is not chaste and is therefore without significance, in the exchange between men, then she may be seen as available for sexual experimentation. (1996: 2416)

A specific form of sexual objectification of women's bodies ensues in a typical rape trial that sorts bodies into those which can be exchanged in matrimony and those which cannot. Das notes,

> [T]he first question in a rape trial that the judges seek to determine is whether sexual intercourse has occurred. A whole way of talking about the sexualised body comes into play here; is the hymen intact; how much of a finger could be inserted into the vagina under medical examination; is penetration to be understood as vulval or vaginal; etc. Thus, a whole topology of signs is created that move on the surface of the body, territorialise it, and constitute it as a sexual body, fit or unfit for exchange. The body is objectified in ways that become a kind of judicial pornography. (1996: 2415)

The woman is expected to name her body parts, what the accused did to them, with which parts of his body. Such extreme form of sexual objectification is on display in the trial. Smart points out that 'the naming of parts becomes almost as a sexual act, in that it draws attention to the sexualised body. But her account, distorted by the cross-questioning techniques of the defence does not only sexualise her, it becomes a pornographic vignette' (1989: 39).

Further, the characterization of a rape survivor as a prosecutrix captures the experience of being positioned outside the trial. In the rape trial, a contestation between the state (represented by a public prosecutor) and the accused (represented by a defence lawyer), the victim is positioned as a witness.[19] Even though the word prosecutrix literally means a female prosecutor, she is perceived as a malevolent persecutor.[20] As Smart says, 'the trial is truly Kafkaesque for the woman who has experienced terror and/or humiliation but who is treated like a bystander to the events she apparently willed upon herself and for which she is seen as seeking an unjustified and malevolent revenge' (1989: 34).

The critique of the discourse of shame and honour thus has particular salience in the organization of the rape trial in India. Women perceive their own bodies as shameful, such that the act of naming one's sexual parts itself is shameful. On the one hand, it is considered shameful for women to talk of their own bodies and sexuality, let alone trying to verbalize the trauma of rape, and on the other hand, the victim has to graphically describe her body and the act of rape to prove that she is not lying. The Supreme Court, recognizing such social frameworks of rape, has observed:

> ...rape is the 'ultimate violation of the self'. It is a humiliating event in a woman's life, which leads to fear for existence and a sense of powerlessness. The victim needs empathy and safety and a sense of re-assurance. In the absence of public sensitivity to these needs, the experience of figuring in a report of the offence may itself become another assault.[21]

The popular belief that rape is worse than death and the ultimate violation of the self, premises repeated rigorously in Indian courts,[22] leads judges to look for marks of resistance, failing which women have been routinely disbelieved. The dictum that rape is worse than death constructs the female body as a wound, a violable inner space such that 'feminine fear seems to entail a complete identification of a vulnerable sexualized body with the self' (S. Marcus 1992: 394). Sharon Marcus suggests that a re-definition of female sexuality as an inviolable inner space may help women combat rape, since fear concentrates 'the self on the anticipation of pain' and on 'the conviction that the self will be destroyed on violence' (1992: 394–5).[23]

The feminist critique of the discourse on rape as worse than death or as shameful does not direct itself to some agency external to the individual from which repressive power flows. Rather, the discourse itself is internalized and becomes constitutive of the female self. As Vishwanath says, 'what feminism has tried to show is that there is a link between shame and sexual violence. If women feel shame at their body as sexual, then the experience of rape gets linked with the experience shame as a permanent state of body' (1994: 12). Hence, power is not conceptualized as something feminists can give to or withhold from women. The mode of empowerment here is not prescriptive, handing down a list of dos and don'ts. Women's groups act as 'brokers' in a dialogical engagement with individual women's needs and desires. Political agency for feminists, then, is not 'given but achieved' and is 'the effect of situated practices' (A. Feldman 1991: 1). In naming sexual violence, the women's movement collates women's experiences as the ground of their praxis to critique the law.[24] The legal method, however, distorts the experience of sexual violence, as will be manifest by the Kafkaesque stories of landmark trials, which follow.

TUKARAM AND ANR V. STATE OF MAHARASHTRA

Several precedents of injustice informed the conceptualization that underlay the first national campaign against rape.[25] I wish to flag one landmark case, which is pertinent to our reading of the national campaign since elements of this case find repetition in later cases of custodial rape. In March 1978, protests by civil liberty groups were sparked in Andhra Pradesh when four policemen gangraped an eighteen-year-old Muslim woman, Rameeza Bee, and beat her husband to death. The Justice Muktadar Commission set up subsequent to the protests, recommending that the prosecution 'found the policemen guilty of the offences of rape, assault, and murder with a common intention to do all this' (Kannabiran 2008: 83–4). The case was transferred to a district court in Raichur, Karnataka, on the grounds that the Enquiry Commission, headed by a sitting judge of the Andhra Pradesh High Court, would vitiate the trial. Finally, the policemen were acquitted.

Kannabiran argues that the proceedings during the enquiry that ensued 'aggravated the trauma of [the victim's] rape and loss' (2008: 84). The defence portrayed Rameeza as a prostitute, challenged the legality of her marriage to her slain husband, and positioned her as a lying *habitué*. Naming her as a prostitute also meant that she was divested symbolically of the right to mourn legitimately for her slain husband. Kannabiran remarks, 'what was one of the most horrifying events of the Enquiry itself was the sight of *burqa*-clad Rameeza standing quietly as one man after another entered the witness box to swear that he had had sex with Rameeza on a certain day at a certain place after paying Rs 10 or 15. Rameeza would then be asked to lift her *burqa*, revealing her face for the man (and the packed, tense courtroom) to stare at before he affirmed that she was indeed the same woman' (2008: 86). Indeed, 'this repeated public unveiling enabled a moral displacement of Rameeza and her reconfiguration as a prostitute: Prostitutes should not veil themselves and must be open at all times to public gaze' (Kannabiran 2008: 86). Further, 'for the State, Rameeza encapsulated within her body the "immorality" and "blasphemous character" of the Muslim community, a "fact" corroborated by other similar members of her community, while for "her" people she encapsulated the trials and tribulations of a community fighting to survive with dignity and integrity' (Kannabiran 2008: 89).

Such bias found the Supreme Court, which characterized the lived experience of Mathura, a sixteen-year-old tribal victim, as a lie. *Tukaram and Anr* v. *State of Maharashtra* (1979), popularly known as the Mathura case[26] dramatized s. 155(4) IEA, which allowed the 'immoral character' of the woman testifying to rape to be considered as relevant evidence. The facts of the case as provided in the judgment are as follows.

In 1972, in the Desai Ganj police station (Chandrapur District, Maharashtra) Mathura's brother had filed a criminal complaint against Mathura's lover on the charge of abduction. On 26 March 1972, she was brought to the police station with her brother and lover to record her statement at nine o'clock in the night. She was subsequently detained and raped twice (once in the toilet) by Ganpat, one of the two policemen charged with rape. The other accused,

Tukaram, sexually assaulted her and attempted to rape her.[27] When Mathura did not emerge from the police station a crowd gathered outside. Upon hearing that Mathura had been raped, they insisted that Mathura's complaint be registered. Mathura and the accused were sent for medical examination nearly twenty hours after the incident. According to the medical report, there were no marks of injury on Mathura's body. The medico-legal certificate noted that the vagina 'admitted two fingers easily', which the court later cited to infer that Mathura was 'habituated to sexual intercourse'.[28]

On 1 June 1974, the Sessions Judge (Chandrapur) acquitted the policemen on the grounds that there was no evidence to prove that Mathura was below the age of consent, and therefore her consent was legally relevant. The judgment held that Mathura was a 'shocking liar' whose testimony was 'riddled with falsehood and improbabilities'.[29] The court further held that although it could be established that Mathura had sexual intercourse with Ganpat, it was not rape. The court remarked that there was a 'world of difference between sexual intercourse and rape.'[30] He reasoned that 'she (Mathura) could not have admitted that of her free will, she had surrendered her body to a police constable. The crowd included her lover Ashok, and she had to sound virtuous before him'.[31]

The Nagpur Bench of the Bombay High Court reversed the order of acquittal and considering the same facts convicted Ganpat under s. 376 IPC (rape) to rigorous punishment of five years, and Tukaram was sentenced under s. 354 IPC (use of force with the intent to outrage modesty) to rigorous imprisonment for one year. The high court maintained that though there was a world of a difference between sexual intercourse and rape, the sessions court had not appreciated the difference between consent and passive submission. Lack of injury did not mean consent to sexual intercourse. The high court remarked that 'mere passive or helpless surrender of the body and its resignation to the other's lust induced by threats of fear cannot be equated with the desire or will, nor can it furnish an answer by the mere fact that the sexual act was not in opposition to such desire or volition'.[32] After the high court decision, Tukaram and Ganpat were dismissed from police service. They filed an appeal against the conviction in the Supreme Court, which was heard on 15 September 1978. The high court judgment was reversed and the Supreme Court acquitted the two policemen. The court held that Mathura did not raise any alarm and 'meekly followed Ganpat', so her consent could not be understood as 'passive submission'.[33] Why was *Rao Harnarain* v. *the State* (1958), cited by the Bombay High Court, which distinguished between passive submission and consent, not seen as relevant to Mathura. In the recounting of this landmark trial, the question 'who was Rao Harnarain Singh?' is of critical importance.

WHO WAS RAO HARNARAIN SINGH?

Rao Harnarain Singh was an advocate and an additional public prosecutor in Gurgaon. On the evening of 18 April 1957, he threw a party for his friend Mauji Ram, who was the deputy superintendent of the jail in Gurgaon on the eve of his transfer. One of the men accused in this case was Kalu Ram, who lived with his nineteen-year-old wife, S, in a room in Rao Harnarain Singh's house. In the words of the court:

> Mst. [S] is said to be an attractive girl of 19 years. ... Rao Harnarain Singh is said to have required Kalu Ram to send Mst. [S] for the carnal pleasures of himself and his guests. Kalu Ram, who had a very humble station in life, after initial protests was induced to provide his wife to satisfy the carnal lust of Rao Harnarain Singh and his guests. It is said that the girl protested vehemently against the outrageous demand, but under the pressure of her husband, she was induced to surrender her chastity. It is alleged that three accused persons Rao Harnarain Singh, Ch. Mauji Ram and Balbir Singh ravished her during the night & she died almost immediately. It is also alleged that her shrieks were heard by some Advocates living in the neighbourhood.[34]

The distinction between passive submission and consent is founded on the abject fact of being raped to death. What is even more elusive is that we know nothing about S from the judgment except that she was attractive, young, married, dependent, and poor. The judgment recounts the grounds on which the defence lawyer Mr Bhagat Singh Chawla pressed for bail:

> According to him, the girl was produced for the satisfaction of the carnal pleasures of Rao Harnarain Singh and his guests with the consent of the girl's husband Kalu Ram. He further urged that the

girl was also a consenting party and she surrendered her body to three persons willingly and with the approval and the bidding of her husband. Mr Bhagat Singh also suggested that she was a grown up girl of 19 years, and a married woman and death could not result as a result of sexual intercourse with her by three persons. *Her death, he thought, was fortuitous and probably due to sudden failure of the heart.* In his words, Rao Harnarain Singh and his guests were having 'a good time' and gathered there for a bit of 'gaiety and enjoyment'. He also said that his two clients were 'respectable persons', one being an Advocate and the other a Deputy Superintendent of Jail, and for this reason deserved to be set at large. He lastly urged that the gathering of three accused in the evening and their act in ravishing Mst. [S], young wife of Kalu Ram, might be morally reprehensible but it was not such an act which should stand in the way of the accused, from being released on bail.[35]

Observing that it was under the husband's pressure that [s],

'after vehement protestations resigned herself to the disgrace that awaited her. There is also material with the prosecution that her shrieks pierced through the walls of the room and were heard by some Advocates living in the neighbourhood just before her voice was fatally silenced. Such a submission on her part cannot be called by any stretch of language, "consent".'[36]

Defining consent as an act of reason that is free and voluntary and not induced by terror, the court held:

A mere act of helpless resignation in the face of inevitable compulsion, quiescence, non-resistance, or passive giving in, when volitional faculty is either clouded by fear and vitiated by duress, cannot be deemed to be 'consent' as understood in law. ... There is a difference between consent and submission. Every consent involves a submission but the converse does not involve consent. ... Consent implies the exercise of a free and untrammelled right to forbid or withhold what is being consented to; it always is a voluntary and conscious acceptance of what is proposed to be done by another and concurred in by the former.[37]

The court denied bail to the accused since they were in a position to hamper the investigation. We find, however, that the court was unimpressed with the defence's equation between the status of the accused and respectability. While I do not know the outcome of the trial, we do know that there was a great deal of publicity to this case.

A Hindi and Urdu newspaper, *Mewat* covered the trial hearing after hearing, extremely critical of these '*sufaid-posh*' (white collar or well-to-do) men who used their position to rape and murder a young girl. The high court found the editor of the newspaper in contempt and fined him Rs 200, warning him not to publicize the case in ways that would attract contempt again.[38]

The publicity of the trial, circumscribed by the law on contempt, is marked by the outrage against the impunity vested in state officials to rape and kill. The judicial distinction between passive submission and consent is founded on extremely brutal sexual violence, indicating the kind of violence it takes for judicial toleration of sexual violence to break down and for the court to speak on behalf of a dead raped woman. The notion of a 'good' or 'innocent' victim who is chaste and bears undisputable marks of violence—in this case, death—underpins this historic judgment. Rameeza Bee or Mathura, by contrast, who lived to testify, were not constructed as *good* victims and positioned as *habitué*s or prostitutes who could never *really* be raped. Judicial interpretation of who is a *good* victim continues to underlie the outcome of the cases even today.

THE OPEN LETTER

Four law professors—Upendra Baxi, Lotika Sarkar, Vasudha Dhagamwar, and Raghunath Kelkar—wrote a public letter to the Supreme Court, popularly known as 'Mathura Open Letter' (hereafter, referred to as 'The Open Letter') critiquing the Supreme Court for acquitting the policemen who raped and molested Mathura. The Open Letter questioned the judicial interpretation of consent,[39] and I quote:

> ...does the Court believe that Mathura was so flirtatious that even when her brother, her employer and her lover were waiting outside the police station, she could not let go the opportunity of having fun with two policemen and that too in the area adjoining a police station latrine? Does it believe with the Sessions judge that Mathura was 'habituated to sexual intercourse' to such an extent? And therefore further think that the semen marks on Mathura's clothing could have come from further sexual activities between the police incident and the next morning when she was medically examined ... from the facts of the case all that is established is submission, and not consent.

Could not their Lordships have extended their analysis of 'consent' in a manner truly protective of the dignity and of Mathura (U. Baxi et al. 1979: 5–7)?

The Open Letter critiqued the Supreme Court for offering legal redress only to affluent, urban, and educated women, while it condemned 'illiterate, labouring, politically mute Mathuras of India … to their pre-constitutional Indian fate' (U. Baxi et al. 1979: 7)?[40]

The Open Letter was circulated to all progressive individuals, civil liberty groups, and women's organizations.[41] The response to the letter was overwhelming. On 17 March 1980, women's groups in Delhi demonstrated outside the Supreme Court and demanded the re-opening of the case.[42] The Chief Justice of India at the time, Justice Chandrachud, advised the women's organizations to file a review petition.[43] The Bharatiya Mahila Federation and the Women Lawyers' Council filed the petition, which came up for hearing on a bench headed by the Chief Justice on 28 March 1980. The Chief Justice directed the case to be heard by the same bench that had delivered the judgment originally. On 2 April 1980, laying down the conditions under which such review would be heard, the court held that:

> the decision would be decided only by circulation among themselves and not by a hearing in the open court. Further, the judges will decide whether the women's organisations have any legal right at all to appear in the case. Even if they conclude that any such right exists, their lordships declared that none of them would be allowed to file written arguments.[44]

These are the now forgotten scenes of judicial activism that pre-date the emergence of public interest litigation.

At the commencement of proceedings, the three judges who had heard the original appeal held that the various women's associations and organizations had no *locus standi* in the whole matter, and they would hear the arguments made by the lawyer appearing on behalf of the Maharashtra government. The scene in the court describes women lawyers such as Hingorani and Kapoor arguing for permission to file written arguments,

> …after Mrs K. Hingorani … refused to sit down the judges sternly told her that systematic and consistent attempt had been made to pressurise

the court and they would decide the matter only by circulation instead of an open hearing. … When Mrs Hingorani still persisted and Mrs Urmilla Kapoor, appearing for another women's organisation, also intervened, Mr Justice Untawalia told them that they did not like this at all. … Mr Justice Untawalia added: 'As officers of the court we must protect the prestige of this court. It is our duty.' … Mrs Hingorani was still arguing on being allowed to file written arguments when the judges arose and walked back to their chambers.[45]

On 3 April 1980, Justice N.W. Untawalia upheld the Supreme Court decision. It was held that women's organizations had no *locus standi* to file a review petition.[46] Finally, Tukaram and Ganpat were acquitted. The drama in the courtroom indicated that the case was constructed as a scandal producing deep anxiety about the sanctity of the Supreme Court (see Pillai 1980).

YAD RAM V. STATE OF RAJASTHAN

The *Mathura* case brought to public attention how past sexual history was used to discredit the rape victim. Far from fading into insignificance, s. 155(4), the past sexual history clause continues to inform the structure of rape trials today (see Chapter 2). In 2001, the Andhra Pradesh High Court heard a public interest litigation challenging the constitutionality of the past sexual history clause, which the petitioner claimed violated the equality provisions defined under Article 14 of the Constitution of India.[47] In *Gopalakrishna Kalanidhi v. Union of India*, the petitioner challenged the law on the grounds that 'the character of an accused becomes irrelevant in terms of Section 54 of the Evidence Act whereas the same is used against a prosecutrix in terms of sub-section (4) of s. 155 thereof'.[48] The Andhra Pradesh High Court maintained that 'it is now well settled that rape is not only an offence, it has been held to be an infringement of fundamental right of a person guaranteed under Article 21 of the Constitution of India'.[49] Further, the court noted that 'the apex court has also categorically held that even if it be found that the prosecutrix was woman of a bad character and even a prostitute her right of privacy cannot be violated by any person and the accused must be punished for commission of rape irrespective of her general character'.[50]

Further, citing *Chairman, Railway Board & Ors* v. *Mrs Chandrima Das & Ors,*[51] the Andhra Pradesh High Court noted that not only has rape been seen as 'violative of human dignity', but the Supreme Court has also inaugurated 'constitutional tort' as a 'public law remedy', which is also applicable to foreigners.[52] The high court held:

> [T]he interpretation of Section 155(4) of the Evidence Act would thus be totally dependant upon a sea change made in the outlook of the court as regards the offence of rape or otherwise atrocities committed on women.[53]

A brief digression is necessary to point to the judicial interpretation of rape as a violation of right to life as elaborated in *Chairman, Railway Board & Ors* v. *Mrs Chandrima Das & Ors.*

Chandrima Das, an advocate in the Calcutta High Court, filed a petition under Article 226 of the Constitution against the Indian railways claiming that the victim, a Bangladeshi woman, must be given compensation, as she was brutally gangraped by railway employees in a room at Yatri Niwas at Howrah Station of the Eastern Railway. Holding that rape violates the right to life of all women whether or not they are citizens or foreigners, the Supreme Court pointed out the judicial meanings accorded to 'life'. Life means 'something more than mere animal existence'.[54] It is the 'right to live with dignity, free from exploitation' and extends 'even to those faculties by which life is enjoyed'.[55] It was held that the employer is vicariously liable if its employees rape a woman, irrespective of her citizenship. This judgment opened a new chapter in the jurisprudence of rape by bringing sexual violence in the purview of constitutional tort law.

Citing this judgment, the Andhra Pradesh High Court noted this 'sea change' in judicial attitudes towards rape. Dismissing the petition, the court held:

> Having regard to the aforementioned decisions of the apex court, Section 155(4) of the Evidence Act for all intent and purport has fell [*sic*] into insignificance and thus it is not necessary to pronounce the said provision as unconstitutional. Furthermore, it is a well settled principle of law that this Court in exercise of its jurisdiction under Article 226 of the Constitution of India cannot direct the Parliament to amend the law. Separation of powers envisaged under the Constitution clearly forbids such a direction unless it may become

absolutely necessary for the apex court to do so in exercise of its constitutional power under Article 142 of the Constitution of India. Such power this Court does not have.[56]

However, it remains a grim fact that the important shifts in jurisprudential thinking of rape as violative of the right to life or as an infringement of fundamental rights do not translate into the way rape trials are conducted.

Although judgments only provide us frozen pictures of the nature of questioning directed at a rape survivor, by reporting trial proceedings, appellate judgments reveal the pornographic structure of the rape trials (Das 1996). Twenty-seven years after the Mathura hearings, the sexual objectification of the body in rape trials finds shocking elaboration in a case reported by the Rajasthan High Court in 2007. During the cross-examination in a trial court in Jaipur district, the victim 'was asked as to in what posture [sic] she was raped. She was made to lie on the bench available in the trial Court to demonstrate her posture'.[57] Here it is not sufficient that a woman 'must talk in public of her breasts, her vagina, her anus and of course what the accused did to these parts of her body and with what parts of her body' (Smart 1989: 39). Rather the posture of the body being raped must be enacted in flesh. Such a performance, classified as a feature of cross-examination, rests on techniques of defence lawyering that feign ignorance about the manner in which women are raped.

Somewhat critical of the role of the presiding judge in this trial, the Rajasthan High Court observed that 'while the victim was cross examined, the trial court was sitting as a silent spectator and did not effectively control the recording of evidence in the court'.[58] The high court remarked that the trial court ought to have ensured that 'cross examination is not made a means of harassment or causing humiliation to the victim of crime'.[59] Surely compelling a rape victim to mime how she was raped amounts to an extreme form of sexual objectification of the body, which is put on display for the voyeuristic consumption of the men including the accused present in court.

Is the court only a silent spectator when a defence lawyer asks a victim to lie down to demonstrate the posture when she was raped? Or does the enactment of the rape give 'pleasure in the way pornography gives pleasure' (Smart 1989: 39)? This re-violation is not merely metaphorical; as Smart observes, 'the judge, the lawyers, the jury and the public can gaze on her body and re-enact her violation in their imaginations' (Smart 1989: 39, also see Mackinnon 1989). Unlike a photograph, Smart points out, 'the woman is "in flesh in court" to "experience" being raped twice over' (1989: 40). The defence constructs a soft-porn scenario in which the victim is supposed to 'stoutly deny'—a phrase often used in Indian courts—her part (Smart 1989). Such prolific and excited pictures of women's sexuality betray judicial pleasure in telling stories of what men do to women's bodies. The excited declarations of extreme habitation of women to sex amount to extreme sexual objectification of women and rape trials are designed to be *recreational*, enhanced by the mimetic performances forced upon a raped victim to demonstrate how she was raped.

The testimony to rape in courts of law, like other criminal trials, depoliticizes the crime. Unlike other crimes, in a rape trial the question is whether rape was possible at all and not whether the specific offender committed the crime. As Hannah Feldman puts it,

> The nature of a rape defence rests on proving that there was no rape that, there was, instead, consensual sex. Similarly, a case for rape must prove that no consent was offered and that force was used to allow penetration despite unreciprocated desire. Even when survivors of sexual assault, men and women, are allowed to tell their stories, they are constrained by the necessity of telling about a rapist's desire, his experience—projected, of course—and still cannot tell their story (1993: 17).

In other words, the rape trial is not a vehicle for communicating the violence of rape; rather, it becomes an occasion for sexualizing the woman's body and re-enacting mimetically the desire of the rapist.

MOURNING PHULMONEE DASEE: THE DEBATE ON AGE OF CONSENT AND MARITAL RAPE

The strident opposition in the parliament debating the reform of the rape law in 1983 prevented the criminalization of marital rape (see P. Baxi 2000; Gangoli 2007). Among the many arguments, the criminalization of marital rape was seen to transgress Indian culture (*sanskriti*). The only exemption possible to such readings of Indian culture was the criminalization of rape in marriage of underage girls as a means to deter and prevent child marriages (see Gangoli 2007). The confounding link between regulating child marriages and criminalizing marital rape harks back to colonial debates on the age of consent. Tanika Sarkar (2001) powerfully narrates the predicament of colonial legislators who could not introduce new legislation to regulate early child marriage, and instead chose to amend the age of consent by increasing the age from ten to twelve after the scandal that followed the rape and murder of Phulmonee Dasee (also see Anagol 2006; Kapur 2005).

In 1890 much publicity was directed at child marriage when the thirty five year old accused Huree Mohun raped his eleven year old wife Phulmonee to death.[60] In the trial that ensued, Huree Mohun was not found guilty of rape—at the time, the age of consent was ten years for wives. Rather Huree Mohun 'was found guilty of causing death inadvertently, by a *rash and negligent act*, and was sentenced to a year's rigorous imprisonment' (Kannabiran 2008: 82, *emphasis in original*). Further:

> ...the women of Phulmonee's family testified that since caste codes do not permit pre menstrual cohabitation, the couple had been kept apart till, on the night of her death, the husband had stolen into Phulmonee's room and forced himself on her, [yet] the English Judge, Wilson accepted the husband's version that as they had cohabited several times earlier, intercourse was not the cause of death. The charge of rape did not arise because she was clearly over 10 years of age. (Kannabiran 2008: 82)

By regarding the rape and murder of a child wife as a 'rash and negligent act', the jury and the judge preserved 'custom as well as the male right to the enjoyment of the female body' (Kannabiran 2008: 82). Tanika Sarkar further notes that the judge made no adverse comments about the husband who raped and murdered a child, nor did he make 'any judgmental comparison between the ways of husbands' (2001: 212).

The 1983 parliamentary debates fully analysed by Gangoli (2007) preserve the link between child marriage and age of consent. The debates reveal that while it is imperative for the postcolonial state to regulate rape in child marriages, it is invested in maintaining its difference from the West since the 'concept of rape upon one's own wife is rather foreign to our country' (JPC Report 1982: 22). In other words, we can surmise that for the parliamentarians 'the level of acceptable force is adjudicated starting just above the level set by what is seen as normal male sexual behaviour including the normal level of force, rather than the victim's or woman's point of violation' (Mackinnon 1989: 173). Although narratives of horrifying sexual violence in marital relationships haunt every rape law reform measure, the state insistently denies the trauma of marital rape. The emphasis on preserving marriage marked the 172nd Law Commission Report,[61] which, despite recommending a new definition of sexual assault and gender neutrality, did not accept the feminist demand that the marital rape exception should be deleted. The rationale of the Law Commission was that such a law would amount to 'excessive interference with the marital relationship' (Law Commission Report 2000 at para 3.1.2.1, also see Sen 2010). Noting this, Ratna Kapur has argued:

> [T]he criminalisation of some activities—such as rape, adultery, and sodomy—and the non-criminalisation of other activities—such as the rape of a woman by her husband—are marked by the idea that there are certain forms of sexuality that are private, culturally accepted, and exercised legitimately within the family. ... Despite the intense feminist lobbying to reform laws relating to sexual violence, these laws continue to sustain the public/private distinction, and the dominant sexual ideology and cultural assumptions on which they are based. (2005: 32)

This dominant sexual ideology works to preserve the institution of marriage, producing social and legal indifference towards the conditions of sexual terror in marriage.

SUDESH JHAKU V. K.C.J. AND OTHERS

For the first time, the interpretation of penetration as defined under s. 375 was challenged in the Delhi High Court in *Sudesh Jhaku* v. *K.C.J. and Ors.*[62] The *Jhaku* judgment describes the testimony by a six year old child, B, to continuous sexual abuse by her father KCJ— an undersecretary in the Ministry of Home Affairs—and his friends, as the 'yin yang of pain and lust'.[63] The judgment describes what happened as follows:

> This little girl used to be taken by her father to his office and from there to a hotel in and around the Pavilion hotel. The others to

accompany them were the persons named above. Ensconced there, they would consume alcohol, watch what are generally known as 'blue films' and revel in sexual orgies. And, during those naked games of raw flesh, KCJ would make his daughter consume alcohol, remove her clothes, and thrust his fingers in her anus and vagina. If the girl is to be believed, she was not safe even within the four walls of the house she called home.[64]

The judicial prose is startling since the representation of sexual abuse of the six-year-old child is hermeneutically sealed from the summation of feminist definitions of rape as an act of power found later in the judgment. The interpretative strategy that describes child sexual abuse as a sexual orgy and a male pornographic fantasy frames rape as a psychopathological sexual offence, thereby negating the painful realities of child sexual abuse.

Arun Jaitley (who would later become the union minister of law) argued the case, challenging the judicial interpretation of the words 'sexual intercourse' and 'penetration'.

> The grievance of Mr Jaitley was that the learned Additional Sessions Judge had arbitrarily interpreted the word 'penetration' as appearing in S. 375 of the Code to mean penetration of the male organ into a woman's vagina and that the interpretation so put failed to acknowledge the alarming increase in the incidence of sexual abuse and completely ignored not only contemporary understanding of rape but also larger issues of humiliation, degradation and violence that occur when the penis is substituted by other body parts or foreign objects.[65]

Arguing for a 'realistic' interpretation of penetration as defined under ss. 376 (rape) and 377 IPC (unnatural sexual offence), Mr Jaitley drew the court's attention to contemporary sexual assaults laws in Western Australia, the Canadian Criminal Code, and Washington State law. The judgment addressed the following questions:

1. Is 'rape' as defined in s. 375 of the Indian Penal Code confined only to penile penetration of vagina?
2. What about penetration of a bodily orifice (vagina, anus or mouth) by a penis or other part of the body, or by an object?
3. Would it fall within the meaning of the words, 'sexual intercourse' and 'penetration' as used in the said provision?[66]

Endorsing the common-law definition of penetration and sexual intercourse, the judge held that 'the Indian Penal Code, like most penal codes worldwide, incorporates a definition of rape evolved almost entirely on the basis of common law. Penetration, it has been held under the common law, is the act of inserting the penis into the female organs of generation'.[67] The court cited a colonial judgment that was published in 1923, which held that 'to constitute the penetration it must be proved that some part of the virile member of the accused was within the labia of the pudendum of the woman, no matter how little'.[68]

The court argued that this is the plain meaning of the term, shared and understood most commonly by legal subjects, for, the court opined, 'is it not true that in India too "sexual intercourse" and "penetration" have always been taken to mean penile penetration of the vagina'?[69] The court reasoned against the construction of rape as sexual assault on the lines of the Michigan Statute, which rids 'the crime of its common law baggage' and invents unique rules of proof and evidence.[70] The court further held:

Rape is a serious matter though, unfortunately, it is not attracting serious discussions. Not even in law school (Susan Estrich, Teaching Rape Law, the Yale Law Journal [1992]). The seriousness of the offence with respect to oral intercourse or vaginal penetration otherwise than with penis is not realised though it involves an act of sadism which is likely to cause the victim far greater pain and physical damage than rape itself (Jennifer Temkin, Towards a modern law of rape, The Modern Law Review 1982). Take for example vaginal penetration by a bottle. In such a case the shock, trauma and long term psychological damage to the victim will be at least as serious as that which befalls rape victims and yet it would not be rape as defined in section 375. ... This surely fails to protect the integrity of women and shows a bias against them—a bias continuing right from the days when the law of rape was concerned with the theft of virginity and protection of property. And when we think of integrity of the person's violation of which 'society cannot and must not tolerate' (Susan Estrich, Teaching Rape Law, The Yale Law Journal) we must not think only of women clad in chiffon, draped in misty soft powder sprinkled with a swansdown puff challenging to sink ships and stop heartbeats, though they are no less important, but also those bare-faced *a la* Bankim Chandra imprisoned within the confines of female subordination and restricted life chances.[71]

The Jhaku judgment (as it has been dubbed) is important for at least two reasons. First, this judgment demonstrates how judges construct law's histories through a 'complex genealogical operation that affords them enormous discretion, and yet allows them to claim that they are fully and completely bound by the past.... History in this sense is not only a source of authority but of legitimacy' (Sarat & Kearns 2002: 5). The judgment distances itself from the colonial past, where rape was constructed as theft of virginity and an offence in order to protect property, while at the same time uses this past as an authoritative source to legitimize the construction of rape as penile penetration of female generative organs. Hence, we are told that the expansion of the definition and scope of rape law could not be achieved through the interpretative process of the court but must be subjected to the legislative process. Second, the judgment marks a different feminist contestation of the rape law. We see how feminist arguments are appropriated as rhetorical devices and the limit of judicial interpretation is staged by using the trope of the suffering of rape victims. This case marks the beginning of the use of judicial activism to challenge the settled definitions of the rape law in a bid to expand its scope through judicial interpretation rather than only push for legislative change.[72]

THE SAKSHI WRIT PETITION IN THE SUPREME COURT

Sakshi, an intervention centre in violence against women based in Delhi, filed a writ petition in the Supreme Court 'in response to the travesty of ... the Jhaku case' (Puri 2011: 210). A Delhi-based NGO, Intervention for Support Healing Awareness (IFSHA); the All India Democratic Women's Association (AIDWA); as well as the National Commission for Women (NCW) were included as co-petitioners. The writ appealed to the Supreme Court to enlarge the definition of penetration to include 'a wide range of penetrations, a directive to law enforcement agencies to regulate cases under s. 375 that were related to the broadened scope of sexual assault, and to ask for law reform' (Puri 2011: 210). On 9 August 1999, the Supreme Court directed the Law Commission to examine whether the extant definition of rape was inadequate, and if so, how it could be amended. The 172nd Law Commission Report on the Review of Rape Law was submitted to the Supreme Court on 25 March 2000. The Law Commissioners consulted three groups—Sakshi, IFSHA, and AIDWA—as well as the NCW. The Law Commission recommended:

...[a] shift from rape to a wider scope of sexual assault that includes assault against male children, raising the age of the married girl from 15 to 16; strengthening the punishment for sexual assault against adults, children and pregnant women perpetuated by people on positions of authority or by multiple perpetrators, deletion of Section 377 since it would no longer be necessary to prosecute sexual assault on children (Puri 2011: 210).

Taking note of 'the dramatic increase of violence, in particular sexual violence against women and children' Sakshi argued for the inclusion of 'offences such as sexual abuse of minor children and women by penetration other than penile/vaginal penetration, which would take any other form and could also be through use of objects whose impact on the victims is in no manner less than the trauma of penile/vaginal penetration as traditionally understood under Section 375/376'.[73] Yet these offences 'have been treated as offences failing under Section 354 of the IPC as outraging the modesty of a woman or under Section 377 IPC as unnatural offenses'.[74] They argued that:

...the narrow understanding and application of rape under Section 375/376 IPC only to the cases of penile/vaginal penetration runs contrary to the existing contemporary understanding of rape as an intent to humiliate, violate and degrade a woman or child sexually and, therefore, adversely affects the sexual integrity and autonomy of women and children in violation of Article 21 of the Constitution.[75]

Further, Sakshi argued that 'a plain reading of Section 375 would make it apparent that the term 'sexual intercourse' has not been defined and is, therefore, subject to and is capable of judicial interpretation',[76] and that 'the explanation to Section 375 IPC does not in any way limit the term penetration to mean penile/vaginal penetration'.[77]

Turning down the petition, the Supreme Court, gave the following reasons for not expanding the meaning of penetration:

The entire legal fraternity of India, lawyers or Judges, have the definition as contained in Section 375 IPC engrained in their mind and the cases are decided on the said basis. The first and foremost requirement in criminal law is that it should be absolutely certain and clear. An exercise to alter the definition of rape, as contained in Section 375 IPC, by a process of judicial interpretation, and that too when there is no ambiguity in the provisions of the enactment is bound to result in good deal of chaos and confusion, and will not be in the interest of society at large.[78]

Feminist commonsense was not in the interest of society and only when the legislature had imbibed it could feminists hope for a change in the rape law.

Susan Brownmiller's *Against Our Will* makes a guest appearance in the Sakshi writ petition, as follows:

> ... in rape ... the intent is not merely to 'take', but to humiliate and degrade ... Sexual assault in our day and age is hardly restricted to forced genital copulation, nor is it exclusively a male-on-female offence. ... And while the penis may remain the rapist's favourite weapon, his prime instrument of vengeance ... it is not in fact his only tool. Sticks, bottles and even fingers are often substituted for the 'natural' thing. And as men may invade women through other offices, so too, do they invade other men. Who is to say that the sexual humiliation suffered through forced oral or rectal penetration is a lesser violation of the personal, private inner space, a lesser injury to mind, spirit and sense of self?[79]

Brownmiller's guest appearance in the Sakshi petition was also accompanied by the court's frank acknowledgement that Brownmiller's powerful text and feminist legal jurisprudence at large had made little impact on the legal fraternity in India.

The petitioners further asked the court 'whether non-consensual penetration of a child under the age of twelve should continue to be considered as offences under section 377 ("Unnatural Offences") on par with certain forms of consensual penetration (such as consensual homosexual sex) where a consenting party can be held liable as an abettor or otherwise'.[80] Further the court observed that:

> The legislative purpose of Section 377 IPC ... clearly intended to punish certain forms of private sexual relations perceived as immoral. Despite the same, the petitioner submits, the respondent authorities have, without any justification, registered those cases of sexual violence which would otherwise fall within the scope and ambit of Section 375/376 IPC, as cases of moral turpitude under Section 377

IPC. It is submitted that the respondent authorities and their agents have wrongly strained the language of Section 377 IPC intended to punish "homosexual" behavior to punish more serious cases of sexual violence against women and children when the same ought to be dealt with as sexual offences within the meaning of Section 375/376 IPC in violation of Articles 14 and 21 of the Constitution of India.[81]

However, judicial hetero-normativity was fully re-inscribed by Mrs G. Mukerjee, Director in the Ministry of Home Affairs, who argued before the court that

> ...penetration of the vagina, anus or urethra of any person with any part of the body of another person other than penile penetration is considered to be unnatural and has to be dealt with under Section 377 IPC. ... Child sexual abuse of any nature, other than penile penetration, is obviously unnatural and are [sic] to be dealt with under Section 377 IPC.[82]

A stance that was radically challenged in the 172nd Law Commission Report (2000), which recommended that s. 377 IPC ought to be repealed. There is no doubt then that the histories of sexual offences and unnatural sexual offences cannot be read separately. Jyoti Puri has rightly argued that 'sections 375/376 are proximate to section 377 in judicial reasoning and, until recently, also in the reach for social justice' (2011: 203). This intersecting history is surprisingly apparent when we turn our gaze to the judge–made law of corroboration.

CORROBORATION: JUDGE MADE LAW

In 1952, *Rameshwar* v. *The State of Rajasthan*[83] famously pronounced on the rule of corroboration, historically rooted in jurisprudential caution against believing rape survivors. It is not so well known that this judgment arose after an eight-year-old girl was raped by Rameshwar, who was first convicted by the assistant sessions judge in Sawai Jaipur, then acquitted by the sessions judge at Jaipur and then convicted by the high court at Jaipur. In this case, the Supreme Court noted:

> As regards her credibility, the learned trial Judge, who recorded her evidence and saw her in the box, has believed her, so has the High

Court; and it is important to note that the learned Sessions Judge
who acquitted the accused has not disbelieved her. On the contrary
he says he is morally convinced. All he says is that in the absence of
corroboration it will be unsafe to convict because the Privy Council
and other cases advise corroboration as a matter of prudence.[84]

Agreeing with the high court, the Supreme Court observed that it
was safe to rely on the victim's statement to her mother as providing
corroboration. Having dealt with this case, the court considered the
question of the necessity for corroboration in rape cases. First, the
court noted that the Indian Evidence Act did not state anywhere that
there ought to be corroboration in cases of rape. However, s. 114
(b) IEA stated that the 'court may presume that an accomplice is
unworthy of credit unless he is corroborated in material particulars'.[85]
At the same time, s. 133 IEA held that 'an accomplice shall be a
competent witness against an accused person; and a conviction is not
illegal merely because it proceeds upon the uncorroborated testimony
of an accomplice.'[86]

Second, Justice Vivian Bose noted that a rape victim is not an
accomplice, since 'if she was ravished she is the victim of an outrage'.[87]
If she consented, then no offence is established except in the case of
an adulterous consensual relation, 'but adultery presumes consent
and so is not on the same footing as rape'.[88] Third, the learned judge
held that 'in the case of a girl who is below the age of consent, her
consent will not matter so far as the offence is concerned, but if
she consented her testimony will naturally be suspect as that of an
accomplice. So is the case of unnatural offences'.[89] In other words,
in the case of statutory rape, if the girl consented, she could be
considered an accomplice (see Chapter 3).

Noting that in rape cases 'a large volume of case law has grown
up which treats the evidence of the complainant somewhat along
the same lines as accomplice evidence', Justice Vivian Bose observed
that 'the position now reached is that the rule about corroboration
has hardened into one of law'.[90] To distinguish between the rule
and the rule hardened into law, the court cited Lord Reading in
King v. *Baskerville*. In this case, Baskerville had been 'convicted of
committing acts of gross indecency with two boys'[91]—positioned 'as
abettors because they were freely consenting'.[92] The question then
arose whether Baskerville could be convicted of gross indecency. Was

the uncorroborated testimony of these two boys safe? Lord Reading, we are told, opined that while 'it has long been a rule of practice at common law for the judge to warn the jury of the danger of convicting a prisoner on uncorroborated testimony of an accomplice or accomplices, and in the discretion of the judge, to advise them not to convict upon such evidence', it is necessary for the judge 'to point out to the jury that it is within their legal province to convict upon such unconfirmed evidence'.[93] The *hardening* of the rule of corroboration did not suit English judges, who wished to punish such acts of gross indecency.[94]

Drawing from this case, Justice Bose held that judges could convict without corroboration. He further clarified:

> ...in these cases it is necessary that the judge should give some indication in his judgment that he has had this rule of caution in mind and should proceed to give reasons for considering it unnecessary to require corroboration on the facts of the particular case before him and show why he considers it safe to convict without corroboration in that particular case.[95]

Such a rule of precedence, then, must animate every judicial mind; however, it must be considered in every case even though it is not applied as if a rule.

> The tender years of the child, coupled with other circumstances appearing in the case, such, for example, as its demeanour, unlikelihood of tutoring and so forth, may render corroboration unnecessary but that is a question of fact in every case. ... There is no rule of practice that there must, in every case, be corroboration before a conviction can be allowed to stand.[96]

In the 1980s, following the anti-rape campaign, the reasoning around corroboration seemed to have undergone a shift. For instance, the Supreme Court held:

> [I]t is true that old English cases, followed in British Indian courts, had led to a tendency on the part of a judge made law that the advisability of corroboration should be present to the mind except where the circumstances make it safe to dispense with it ... what girl would foist a rape charge on a stranger unless a remarkable set of facts or clearest motives were made out? The inherent bashfulness, the innocent naiveté and the feminine tendency to conceal the outrage

of masculine sexual aggression are factors which are relevant to improbalise the hypothesis of false implication.[97]

In 1983, the Supreme Court developed this viewpoint in *Bhoginbhai Hirjibhai* v. *State of Gujarat*. The court held that the 'refusal to act on the testimony of a victim of sexual assault, in the absence of corroboration as a rule is adding insult to injury'.[98] Western (or Westernized) women, the Supreme Court ruled, were more likely to levy false accusations due to economic reasons, to wreck vengeance against one man or all men, complain at the behest of another man for economic or political gain, due to jealousy, on being repulsed, to win sympathy, to gain notoriety, for publicity, or simply to feel self-important.[99]

Finding such motivations irrelevant to the Indian conditions, with the exception of urban elites, the court ruled that Indian women would not foist a false case on any man for the following reasons: the rape survivor would lose her chastity, friends and families would ostracize her, she would risk her husband's love for her, if unmarried she would never be able to find a 'respectable' husband, she would experience a great sense of shame in narrating what happened to her, her family would wish to avoid the shame and stigma, she would be afraid of being blamed, considered promiscuous or responsible for inviting the assault, she would be deterred by facing the humiliation of a rape trial and risk of disbelief.[100] Such essentialization of Indian and Western women classifies women into chaste and promiscuous, to enable sorting between those who are fit to be exchanged in the structure of alliance as distinct from those who are not (Das 1996). This judgment is a typical example of how the legal discourse absorbs and expands the discourse of normalization that Foucault (1977) alerted us to.

In 1996, the Supreme Court called the insistence on corroboration as productive of conditions of 'testimonial tyranny'.[101]

> Corroboration as a condition for judicial reliance on the testimony of the prosecutrix is not a requirement of a law but a guidance of prudence under given circumstances. It must not be overlooked that a woman or girl subjected to rape is not an accomplice to the crime but is a victim of another person's lust and it is improper and undesirable to test her evidence with a certain amount of suspicion, treating her as if she were an accomplice. Inferences have to be drawn from a

given set of facts and circumstances with realistic diversity and not dead uniformity lest that type of rigidity in the shape of rule of law is introduced through a new form of testimonial tyranny making justice a casualty (cited in Bhatt 2003: 36–7).

Even though the Supreme Court has clarified that 'evidence has to be weighed and not counted',[102] typically the rule of corroboration structures courtroom talk (cited in Bhatt 2003: 148).

Assurance Short of Corroboration

Although there was been an attempt to transform the use of the standard of corroboration in rape cases, judges have advocated that they can look for assurance falling short of corroboration in cases where they need further support to determine the outcome of the case. In order to explain what this means, I turn to Justices Vivian Bose and Faizal Ali in *Kashmira Singh* v. *State of MP*.[103] In this murder trial of a five-year-old boy, the question was whether the confession of an accomplice against a co-accused could be used to lend assurance to other evidence against him. Such evidence is weak when not taken on oath, in an accused's presence, or even tested on cross-examination. It could be used only in the instance when a judge needed to strengthen his confidence in that which he could not have accepted without the assurance provided by such a confession.

Kashmira Singh is cited in *State of Maharashtra* v. *Chandraprakash Kewalchand Jain* (1990).[104] Like the Mathura case, this case too narrates a gruesome story about a police officer's pursuit of a young Muslim couple married in the face of opposition by their family. He picked up the couple from a hotel and brought them to the police station. He made advances towards the young woman and then beat her up upon rejection. The husband was beaten up too, and a false case registered against him. The police officer then sent the woman to a hotel where he raped her twice. She told her husband what had happened after he was released on bail. While the trial court convicted the policeman for a sentence of five years, the Bombay High Court did not believe the victim, taking the view that 'except in the "rarest of the rare cases" where the testimony of the prosecutrix is found to be so trustworthy, truthful and reliable that no corroboration is necessary, the Court should ordinarily look for corroboration'.[105]

Disagreeing with the Bombay High Court, the Supreme Court confirmed that rape survivors are victims and not accomplices. Further, the court asserted that the Indian Evidence Act does not state that a rape victim's statement is unacceptable unless corroborated. Pointing out that as a competent witness, her testimony should be weighed at par with a witness who is injured in other forms of physical violence cases, the Supreme Court further noted that:

> What is necessary is that the Court must be alive to and conscious of the fact that it is dealing with the evidence of a person who is interested in the outcome of the charge levelled by her. If the Court keeps this in mind and feels satisfied that it can act on the evidence of the prosecutrix, there is no rule of law ... which requires it to look for corroboration. If for some reason the Court is hesitant to place implicit reliance on the *testimony of the prosecutrix it may look for evidence which may lend assurance to her testimony short of corroboration required in the case of an accomplice.*[106]

Unlike the *Mathura* case, the Supreme Court upheld the trial court's conviction and sentenced the policemen. The punishment pronounced, however, was less than the minimum sentence of ten years.

It may be noted that several judgments have held that judges may seek assurance short of corroboration as in the case of accomplice evidence.[107] The route of assurance allows judges to define the exception. In other words, far from being an empty signifier, assurance continues to be haunted by legal interpretation of the testimony to rape as accomplice evidence.

POWER RAPE

In 1983, the demand to include 'power rape' as a legal category was set aside on the grounds that it would be misused by women. Carrying this demand to the Parliament, Geeta Mukherjee argued for the inclusion of power rape, which was defined as:

> ...where a woman is raped under economic domination or influence or control or authority, which includes domination by landlords, officials, management personnel, contractors employers and moneylenders, either by himself or by persons hired by him, each of the person shall be deemed to have committed power rape (Lok Sabha debates 1983: 412).[108]

The movement named all forms of rape as an act of power. The suffixing of power to rape here intended to underscore economic domination, influence or authority over victims and therefore, addressed marginality of all women placed in systemic domination on the basis of class and caste. Moreover, the idea that criminal law needed to address the reality that powerful men hire other men to rape women was an important recommendation. The sexual politics of systemic forms of social, economic, and political domination which the category of 'power rape' sought to name at the time, however did not identify marginality with the juridical or governmental categories of caste and tribe.

Here, we turn to the nationwide protests that ensued in 1992 when Bhanwari Devi, a forty-year-old potter (*kumhar*), was gangraped in the village of Bhateri (Bassi *tehsil*, forty-five kilometres from Jaipur) in Rajasthan. Bhanwari worked as an agent of change—*sathin* (literally: friend)—with the Women's Development Programme (WDP), which came into existence in 1984 in six districts in Rajasthan. The *sathins* were chosen from the deprived and underprivileged sections of society, especially Dalit and tribal women. An experiment that drew on linkages between the government and some women's groups, the work of the *sathin* included intervening in cases of rape or domestic violence as well as attempting to challenge the power of all-male caste panchayats (see Chakravarti 2006; Kannabiran 2008; Mayaram 2002).

In 1992, the government of Rajasthan decided to launch a campaign against child marriage, a common practice in the state. A fortnight-long campaign was launched. The prevention of child marriage became a matter of achievement for the programme. In Bhateri, Bhanwari tried to prevent the marriage of a one-year-old daughter of a powerful man belonging to the caste group of Gurjars. The marriage was secretly solemnized in the dead of night (see Mathur 1992). On 22 September 1992, when Bhanwari and her husband were working in their field,

> While Mohan had gone to relieve himself in the neighbouring field, five men Ram Sukh Gujar, Ram Karan Gujar, Badri Gujar, Gyarsa Gujar and Shravan Sharma attacked him with *lathis* and beat him up. … Taking advantage of Mohan's temporary unconscious state, two men Shravan and Ram Karan Gujar bodily held Mohan down, while

Ram Sukh Gujar caught hold of Bhanwari, Badri and Gyarsa took turns to rape her (Mathur 1992: 2222).

Bhanwari could only reach the police the next morning. The police initially refused to file her complaint on the grounds that she was lying. After intervention from WDP activists, the complaint was lodged. After a number of protests, the accused were arrested.

In April 1994, the high court released the co-accused and the two main accused were to stay in jail for two years till the district and sessions judge finally decided the matter in November 1995 after over 180 hearings. Five judges changed and the sixth judge who gave the judgment had not heard Bhanwari's testimony. On 14 November 1995, the sessions judge acquitted the accused of rape. He held them guilty for conspiring and beating up Mohan and manhandling Bhanwari, sentencing the accused to six months rigorous imprisonment and three months simple imprisonment. They were given one month to appeal. The Rajasthan High Court refused to assign the case to a fast-track court.[109] By 2007, two accused had died. The appeal is pending as a miscellaneous case in the Rajasthan High Court since it was filed in 1996.

The trial court held that the two 'respectable' men, Gyarsa and Badri Gurjar, forty and sixty-years old respectively, could not commit gangrape, as only teenagers would be capable of gangrape. The court further held that:

> But it is beyond comprehension that those who live in a rural culture, including Gyarsa, who Bhanwari Devi says is a respectable person and who some in the village listen to, would in this manner commit a rape. Particularly in collusion with someone in who is forty years of age and that in broad daylight in the jungle in presence of other men. The court is of the opinion that Indian culture has not fallen to such low depths: that someone who is brought up in it; an innocent, rustic man; will turn into a man of evil conduct who disregards caste and age differences and becomes animal enough to assault a woman. How can persons of 40 and 60 years of age commit rape, while someone who is seventy years old watches by?[110]

It is imperative to evoke here the public speeches of Bhanwari Devi, who by speaking out against rape, provided an impetus to look at how the ideology of shame and stigma may be 'turned around' in framing public protests against rape (Menon 2004: 133).

The judgment, which provoked national outrage, rests on a specific reading of practices of untouchability (Chakravarti 2006; Gangoli 2007; Mathur 1992; Menon 2004). The court found it impossible to believe that rural, older, and upper-caste men would gangrape a 'lower-caste' woman in broad daylight. Yet, the court believed that a 'lower-caste' woman would lie about it. This is indicated by the assumption that to rape a 'lower-caste' woman is to disregard caste differences. The 'reasonable man' in this legal text is upper-caste, rural, and marked by age. The law then mimes the humiliation the rapists intended to inflict on their victim by acquiring caste through its interpretative practices. In acquiring caste, it makes rape unreal. Would judges be able to make rape real, if they thought of caste— following Ambedkar—as a system of 'graded inequality in which castes are arranged according to ascending scale of reverence and a descending scale of contempt' (cited in Chakravarti 2003: 7)? What kind of jurisprudence could emerge if judicial interpretation were framed by a critique of Brahmanical patriarchy, which regulates women's sexuality by valourizing upper-caste women's sexuality and normalizing sexual contempt for women perceived as low-caste (Chakravarti 2003)?[111]

In such cases, it seems judges find it easier to convict the accused of other penal crimes, rather than rape. The difficulty of prosecuting sexual violence as a caste crime is a public secret. This was dramatized in the Sirasgaon trial in 1963.[112] According to Rao (2009), this was one of the first cases in Maharashtra after the Untouchability (Offences) Act, 1955, was passed. The court heard testimonies of how four Dalit women were stripped naked and paraded by dominant caste men in Sirasgaon. The court found ten out of the eleven men guilty of the charges of unlawful assembly, illegally trespassing the victims' property, causing hurt, committing an obscene act in public, and outraging their modesty. The accused were sentenced to six months imprisonment and fined Rs 10,000. They were acquitted of offences on the ground of untouchability. In this case, the judicial reading of the 'public practices of untouchability' created a distortion since the accounts of the violence did not 'fit standard descriptions of caste crime—denial of access to roads or common water tap' (Rao 2009: 227). Rao argues that this kind of legal reasoning is pernicious precisely because 'ritualized humiliation and public exhibition of gendered vulnerability' is 'occluded by judicial narratives of crime and victimhood in which the constitutive fact of sexual violation remained invisible and unsayable' (2009: 229).

The politics of untouchability, far from implying absence of touch or contact, regulates sexual violence. Dalit feminists point out that untouchability as a complex practice of subjugation and stigma does not outlaw different forms of sexualized touch or sexualized violence (Chakravarti 2003; John & Nair 1998; Malik 2003; Punalekar 1995; Rao 1999; Rege 1995, 2003; also see Guru 2003). Rao argues, 'the secrecy around sexual violence is double sided. Perpetrators do not conceive it as violation except when they encounter resistance, in which case they brutally assert their rights. Its victims experience humiliation as gendered violence and as collective punishment of the family and community' (2009: 222). At the same time,

> …the brutal violence against Dalit men accused of desiring upper-caste women further illuminates the double jeopardy of sexual violence as caste violence. If Dalits' political awareness has intensified caste conflict, … a crucial but invisible consequence of Dalit politicization is that the desire for upward mobility was recast as a desire for sexual access to upper-caste women … just the hint of transgressive desire was catastrophic; it became an alibi for anti-Dalit violence. (Rao 2009: 235–6)

On the question of sexual access, André Béteille says in an influential essay:

> Although it is difficult to be categorical, it would appear that upper-caste men have less easy access to untouchable and tribal women than they did it in the past. From this I am inclined to believe that material sanctions are more decisive than ritual ones in restricting such access. When the balance of political power made the risk of material sanctions relatively small, ritual sanctions were not very effective in preventing the sexual use of untouchable or tribal women by upper caste men. The balance of power has now changed, though perhaps not very radically, and this has altered not so much the attitudes of upper caste men as their horizon of possibilities. (1990: 494)

Kannabiran and Kannabiran (2003) would perhaps not agree with this picture of caste as they have argued that the lack of control over land does not necessarily deplete the power of the dominant caste.[113] They cite the abject story of Muthamma, who was stripped and paraded in the streets of the village by Reddi men 'who neither belonged to the village nor owned much land there. And yet it was their caste privilege that protected them' (Kannabiran 2003: 258). However, the category of sexual access used by sociologists and feminists is not a useful analytical one (see John & Nair 1998; Rao 2009). The word 'access' retains the ego as masculine, and therefore the description of what upper-caste men do to women they consider inferior elides the experience of the woman (read: object) by blurring the distinction between rape and seduction. Should we then use the normalizing language of access when describing the politics of untouchability?

In recent years, several stabilized forms of sexual humiliation in public spaces have been documented such as parading, stripping, mutilation, rape, and sexual harassment. These intimate and public forms of violence have been categorized as 'traditional' in the contemporary catalogue of violence. In their book *The Untouchables*, Mendelsohn and Vicziany (1998) argue that some forms of violence against the Dalits by caste Hindus have been traditional modes of exerting power. They carefully delineate the more 'traditional' and the emergent forms of violence as backlash to the Dalit claims of self-assertion. They say, 'with the crucial exception of sexual assaults/coercion of women, ... the most contemporary acts of violence against Untouchables should not be classified as "traditional"' (Mendelsohn & Vicziany 1998: 47).

Mendelsohn and Vicziany (1998) are accurate in reading that the violence directed against Dalit women is traditional in so far as these continue to be stable targets of dominant caste violence; however, the forms of sexual violence have undergone a transformation in contemporary contexts of caste wars. This is evident from the massacre in Laxampur-Bathe in December 1997, where Ranvir Sena killed sixty-one Dalits. The Human Rights Watch Report (1999) tells us that the perpetrators attacked the villagers of Laxmanpur-Bathe because the Bhumiyars wanted to appropriate fifty acres of land earmarked for redistribution amongst the landless labourers, some of whom had the support of the Naxalites. The massacre that followed was targeted violence aimed at mutilating and killing women so that they would not give birth to 'rebels', and it would *teach them a lesson* not to resist the landlords in the future. One of the witnesses who saw the rape, mutilation, and murder of five girls reported to Human Rights Watch:

> Everyone was shot through the chest. I also saw that the panties were torn. One girl was ... was 15 years old. ... They also cut her breast and shot her in the chest. ... The girls were all naked, and their panties were ripped. They also shot them in their vagina. There were five girls in all. All five were raped. All their breasts were cut off (1999: 60–1).

This mutilating account of violence against young girls is akin to the practices of violence against women and children during war or war-like conditions. Such forms of rape are not merely the aggregate of different forms of assault or variations of traditional forms of violence. Is it then possible to think of newness as Rabinow (1996) does in the field of science and technology to displace the treatment of emergent social phenomena as variations or aggregations of the traditional? Such displacement finds articulation with the promulgation of the Scheduled Castes and Tribes (Prevention of Atrocities) Act (PoA Act) in 1989. The PoA Act names crimes against the scheduled castes and scheduled tribes as atrocity in cases where the accused is not scheduled caste or scheduled tribe. It does not address all dalit women belonging to other so-called lower castes or backward classes. While I detail the juridical discourse on rape as atrocity later, it is important to note that the discourse on the rape law reform has yet to engage with the question whether naming rape as atrocity has produced newer meanings (see Chapter 6).[114]

SUO MOTO V. STATE OF RAJASTHAN

Let us now turn to the Rajasthan High Court, where Bhanwari Devi's appeal[115] is still pending, to look at judicial notice of sexual violence on its own accord by the High Court. The innovation in this case presents a different face of judicial activism. *Suo Moto v. Rajasthan*[116] opens with the following facts. In 2005, a forty-seven-year-old Mrs [PW] a German national and an employee with Lufthansa Airlines, was abducted and gangraped by an auto-rickshaw driver on the bank of the Jojari river in Jodhpur. The villagers who heard her screams, took Mrs PW to a police station where she lodged a complaint. The two men were arrested. The Rajasthan High Court *suo moto*[117] took cognizance of the case, and issued an order directing a speedy investigation.

The court directed the government to compensate the survivor for the duration she had to stay back for the investigation and trial.[118] Such steps were essential since the court held that 'rape is serious crime whether it is of a foreign tourist or any other woman. However, it leaves a question mark on the safety of the foreign tourist in the City of Jodhpur. It is likely to create panic amongst the tourists visiting Jodhpur and the other parts of the country'.[119] Taking cognizance of the incident, the court directed the registry to register the *suo moto* petition as public interest litigation. The State of Rajasthan through its Secretary, Department of Home, the Director of Tourism and Superintendent of Police (City) Jodhpur were impleaded as respondents. The court issued further directions to ensure the investigation of the case at the earliest. The forensic science laboratory (FSL) was ordered to submit its report in three days. After the charge-sheet was filed, the sessions judge was instructed to hear the case within a month. The court directed that the police give protection to the victim; the government cover all her costs, the quantum of compensation be decided later; and a copy of the order be given to the victim.[120] The court then provided the chronology of the case to showcase the time taken to complete a rape trial when assigned to a fast-track court.

Expressing great satisfaction in the German tourist case, the court said that 'the State has every reason to feel proud'.[121] Although the Rajasthan High Court stated that its guidelines were equally directed at Indian women as they were towards foreigners, this trial became a vehicle of directing publicity to the efficacy of fast-track courts. By highlighting this landmark case, I wish to note three points. First, the survivor's caste, class, community, or nationality inflects judicial treatment of rape cases. Second, the outcomes of rape trials are equally a function of how judges constitute the bureaucratic cultures of courts. Third, while rape trials may be thought of as laboratories for judicial reform, not every trial where publicity is directed is safe enough for judicial innovation—clearly it was not safe enough to fast-track Bhanwari Devi's appeal or take *suo moto* cognizance of the protests that ensued after this terrible act of violence, thus indicating that the politics of prosecuting rape is integral to law, politics, and governance.

THE GLARE OF PUBLICITY

I now turn to the story of the implementation of s. 327 Criminal Procedure Code, 1973 (CrPC), mandating that rape trials must be conducted *in camera*, in order to examine how this amendment regulated the glare of publicity. This provision, when implemented, perhaps reduced the presence of a number of men present in the trial who could consume the rape testimony as spectators, but it did not displace the pornographic spectacle. A rape survivor testifies in a room dominated by men, with an occasional presence of a woman, in front of the accused. Often defence lawyers bring a number of male juniors to the trial, and there may be more than one police constable with the accused. Addressing trial procedures,[122] the Supreme Court held in *Sakshi* v. *Union of India* (2004)[123] that 'a screen or so such arrangements should be made where the victim or witnesses (who may be equally vulnerable like the victim) do not see the body or face of the accused.'[124] The court clarified that:

> ...section 273 CrPC merely requires the evidence to be taken in the presence of the accused. The Section however, does not say that the evidence should be recorded in such a manner that the accused should have full view of the victim or the witnesses. Recording of evidence by way of video conferencing vis-à-vis Section 273 CrPC has been held to be permissible.[125]

The use of video-conferencing in rape trials has been instituted in some courts in Delhi. Vrinda Grover, an eminent lawyer practising in Delhi, narrated to me the details of a trial titled *State* v. *Manish Kumar* as an exemplary application of the *Sakshi* guidelines. The trial in the Patiala House Court was held by Justice Sanjeev Jain on a holiday to ensure that the child was not subjected to the routine environment of the criminal court. The judge conducted the trial in his chamber with a video camera and a monitor. He allowed the child's grandmother to be present while he testified so that the six-year-old male child victim did not have to face the accused, and a monitor was placed in the courtroom. The accused, his lawyers, and the lawyers with the prosecution were seated in the courtroom and were able to watch the proceedings taking place in the chamber. The child did not need to *see* the accused except when he was asked to identify the accused through video transmission. The list of 450 questions by the prosecutor and the defence were given to the judge, who put these questions in his own words to the child.

This was in stark contrast with another case, which was dubbed as the first video trial in a rape case, reported in the *Times of India* on 3 October 2007 (Mahapatra 2007). In this case, a Delhi trial court in Rohini accepted the Delhi Commission of Women's plea to use video-conferencing facilities in the rape trial of a twelve-year-old girl who had been raped by her father. Unlike the case cited above, although the technology was used, the image of the accused's image was beamed across from Tihar Central jail's video-conferencing room. Although the child was not in the same room as the accused, she was forced to confront his image, now larger than life. Ordinarily, when on the stand, at least the child has the option of not looking at the accused, although she feels his gaze upon her (see Chapter 3). The accused was permitted to exercise his right to cross-examine the victim (also, it bears repeating, his daughter), as his lawyer was not present on the day of the hearing. The intent of the *Sakshi* guideline was defeated during this trial. The mere use of technology was publicized as successful judicial reform. The media did not direct public attention to the fact that such reform does not displace the terrifying effects of the reorganization of gaze and publicity on a victim by zooming upon her a larger than life image of the rapist. In other words, rape trials function as laboratories of judicial reform—wherein the cunning of judicial reform lies in concealing law's violence towards the victim in the witness box.

***

Far from being celebratory, feminist readings of judicial reform have produced a melancholic discourse on the place of law in feminist praxis (Agnes 1993; Kapur 2005; Menon 2004; Roy 2009). Extending Roy's (2009) argument, one may argue that melancholia is productive in so far as feminists have not abandoned the project of law reform, as is evident from the intense mobilization to change existing definitions to redress mass sexual violence, to the debate on whether rape should be gender-neutral, and to the fierce criticism of how rape survivors continue to be subjected to legal humiliation in courts of law. Feminist engagements with judicial reform, as suggested in this chapter, have taken the form of agitations, public interest litigation, formulation of draft bills, and judicial training. Rather than summarize the different models of rape law reform or the fissures in the reform debates, I am more interested in the question of how the feminist engagement with judicial reform negotiates with its awareness of the cunning of judicial reform.

A specific method of reading law underlies feminist debates on how the rape law ought to be reformed. This method of reading law critiques the way legal history is written and how judges represent their own history to themselves to authorize law from within, thereby displacing the idea of precedent, normally understood as the way in which judgments exert a binding force in similar cases. Instead, a precedent is read as a failure of justice that is repeated over and over again. Each model of rape law reform memorializes and critiques specific precedents of injustice, and yet the cunning of judicial reform lies precisely in folding in this critique into the structure of the rape trial, without de-centring the historical injustice to women.

Choosing to recount some of the landmark rape trials in India, I argue that the Rao Harnarain Singh case shows how the violence underlying the development of doctrine is repressed. Most law digests cite this precedent without reference to the terrible violence that led to such a judicial pronouncement in a bail hearing. It is not, then, merely a question of whether a case is cited, but how is it cited. No law digest records whether Rao Harnarain Singh was convicted or not. The *Rao Harnarain Singh* case repeats itself in the *Mathura* trial not as a precedent of rule but as a precedent of injustice. In the *Mathura* case, the distinction between consent and passive submission is set aside. However, the precedence of injustice is repeated, and the manifold lawlessness that allows custodial rape to operate as political violence to keep working-class, Dalit, or tribal women in states of sexual subjugation is upheld.

Similarly, the Phulmonee Dasee trial is the spectre that haunts the debate on marital rape and age of consent. That wives are assigned states of sexual subjugation by the very words of law, granting husbands impunity from rape prosecutions, remains the limit of the law reform project. Even today no legislature is willing to allow the criminalization of marital rape. The courts re-direct publicity on the injustice of legalizing sexual violence towards wives to the legislature and the legislature loops such publicity back to a society supposedly 'not yet ready' to recognize and name the injustice of marital rape. There have been instances when judges have suggested that a rape victim marry the man who raped her.[126] In such cases, the rapist is in effect given the licence to rape his victim in the future, since as his wife—the survivor—would never be able to bring a rape prosecution against him again. Such forms of judicial speech places women in the zone of legal exceptionalism, which is at the heart of the institution of heterosexist marriage.

The women's movements' repeated demand to criminalize marital rape is at the heart of their recognition of the cunning of official models of law reform.[127] Agnes (2002) points out that although the 172nd Law Commission report recommended that sexual assault ought to be legislated as a gender neutral crime, the Commission found it 'necessary to retain gender specifity' in its refusal to recognize marital rape as a crime (2002: 846). Further feminist opposition arose since 'gender-neutral language in the case of perpetrators poses a threat against women and same-sex sexualities by allowing the possibility of wrongfully prosecuting them' (Puri 2011: 218). While the women's movement achieved a consensus that sexual assault must be seen as a crime of men, there is an uneasy consensus on extending the language of gender neutrality to survivors of sexual assault.[128]

The unwritten precedents of injustice highlighted during the challenge to s. 377 IPC brought publicity to men and transgendered persons as survivors of unspeakable sexual violence. The PUCL report (2003) highlighted the targeted forms of sexual violence against *hijra*s and *kothi* sex workers in Bangalore. In particular, the sexual violence experienced by transgendered persons in prisons and by policemen had earlier not been the grounds for theorizing custodial rape. Moreover, as Puri argues that:

> …when women's and queer groups attempt to revise laws such as Sections 375/6 and 377, the very constitution of those denied into 'women' or 'gay' ends up recreating numerous exclusions—hijras, kothis, forms of violence whereby women are sexually assaulted not only *qua* women, but also as bearers of gender, religion, and ethnicity, as in the genocide against Muslims in 2002 or the 1984 pogrom against Sikhs in Delhi. (2011: 223)

Further, the debate on gender neutrality led to a nascent discussion on how to legislate male/male rape especially in the contexts of caste domination, communal violence, police torture and as a form of punishment for transgressing sexual norms. These experiences of sexual violence have yet to find serious engagement in the Indian women's movement, despite the repeated and painful illustrations of sexual humiliation of the male body as a technique of economic, political and social domination. Sivakumaran rightly points out that rape of men by men, remains a 'cause without a voice'—often misrepresented as a violent manifestation of same-sex sexuality or 'confined to a footnote' in feminist writing on rape (2005:1280–81).

Although the language of sexual assault animates appellate law and the discourse of law reform, the shift to naming rape as sexual assault in law reform discourse analysed insightfully by Sen (2010) is squarely linked to the vexed question of gender neutrality. Child sexual assault was named in the POCSO Act since it retained gender neutrality of both perpetrators and survivors. Yet even the POCSO Act did not displace the colonial meaning of rape of children by men, since the Act did not specify that s. 377 IPC will not be applied in child sexual abuse cases. In other words, the conjunction of the language of sexual assault with that of unnatural sex suggests that different temporalities of legal discourse continue to frame the naming of sexual violence of children. Thereby the cunning of judicial reform does not displace the widespread belief that rape of children, is a product of sexual perversity, while re-inscribing the validity of the intolerable criminalization of 'offences against the order of nature'.

The debate on naming rape as sexual assault, however, is also intimately related to the transformation of the procedures of recording complaints and testimonies. This book, limited in its focus on the 1983 amendments, points to the importance of thinking through the definitional imperatives in law reform in relation to other judicial sites where humiliation is produced. Indeed, can reform of the rape law succeed if the meaning of sexual violence bears little resemblance to the model of reform put forward in the first place? This question of resemblance figures even when there is innovation in court procedures through videos, screens, guidelines, or fast-track courts. In the same high court where Bhanwari Devi's appeal remains buried in a file not to be heard, fast-track courts became a site of publicity in the German tourist case. While Bhanwari Devi's struggle against rape led to guidelines on sexual harassment at the workplace, her struggle did not result in particularized justice, giving her case closure.[129] Her appeal file, an artefact of injustice, is not the site where publicity is organized. It remains a precedent of injustice that exposes in painful ways the cunning of judicial reform.

Publicity is also organized around fast-track courts with the view to calibrate judicial efficiency and reduction of delay, without regard to the principles of fair trial. In *Digambar Iranna Majkure* v. *the State of Maharashtra*,[130] the accused was found guilty of rape, sodomy, and murder in a fast-track court within six months of the offence. It was found, however, that no legal aid lawyer was appointed to defend the accused, even though he petitioned the court that he could not afford to hire a lawyer. Noting that the accused had already served five years in prison, the Bombay High Court held that:

> We are certainly of the view that though the Fast Track Courts should act fast and justice should be delivered as quickly as possible, decision of a criminal trial cannot be speedily given at the cost of justice. To deny legal aid, though statutorily required to be provided and constitutionally mandated by the Constitution, would be certainly infringe the right guaranteed to every citizen by Article 21 of the Constitution of India ... Had the learned Judge granted adequate time and legal aid to the accused, may be the trial would have been over by the end of year 2001, whatever the result. Presently the accused is languishing in jail for last five years with a blatant illegality committed in his trial. In the event of the fresh trial ending in acquittal of the accused, valuable five years of the man would have been lost due to a mistake which could well have been avoided by a Judge of the experience and knowledge of the Presiding Officer. It is rather unfortunate that such a seasoned and experienced Sessions Judge was in blissful ignorance of statutory provisions contained in Section 304 of the Code of Criminal Procedure and the provisions of Article 21 and Article 39A of the Constitution of India. The right to life given by Article 21 is now ... interpreted to mean opportunity to live which would include right to legal assistance and aid because without such a aid, a person without having means to engage a lawyer will be denied the right to live if he is denied the legal aid.[131]

Digambar Iranna Majkure illustrates that even though publicity is organized in specific ways to produce an image of a judiciary responsive to critique, fast-track trials produce unjust outcomes.[132] Publicity directed at such laboratories of law reform, does not displace the rape trial as a pornographic spectacle since it keeps in place the figure of the habitué, a product of medico-legal techniques—the subject of the next chapter.

NOTES

1. See *Tukaram & Anr.* v. *State of Maharashtra* (1979) 2 SCC 143.

2. Analysing the 'vocabulary of motives' employed by incarcerated rapists 'to diminish responsibility and negotiate a non-deviant identity by presenting themselves in culturally appropriate and acceptable ways', Scully and Marolla point out how rapists do not emphasize the violence of the act but the sexual aspect of the crime (1984: 531).

3. The re-naming also allowed legislators to create a new category of offences under ss. 376A, B, C, and D, which though not amounting to rape were criminalized as unlawful sexual intercourse, punishable by a maximum of five years. While s. 376A (intercourse by a man with his wife during separation) was non-cognizable, bailable, and triable by a sessions court, ss. 376B, C, and D (intercourse by man who is a public servant, a superintendent of a jail or remand home; or staff of a hospital of a woman in his custody) were cognizable, bailable, and triable by a sessions court with the stipulation that no arrest could be made without an order of a magistrate.

4. In 2013, the definition of rape was amended as follows:
A man is said to commit 'rape' if he—

(a) penetrates his penis, to any extent, into the vagina, mouth, urethra or anus of a woman or makes her to do so with him or any other person; or

(b) inserts, to any extent, any object or a part of the body, not being the penis, into the vagina, the urethra or anus of a woman or makes her to do so with him or any other person; or

(c) manipulates any part of the body of a woman so as to cause penetration into the vagina, urethra, anus or any part of body of such woman or makes her to do so with him or any other person; or

(d) applies his mouth to the vagina, anus, urethra of a woman or makes her to do so with him or any other person, under the circumstances falling under any of the following seven descriptions:—

Firstly—Against her will.

Secondly—Without her consent.

Thirdly—With her consent, when her consent has been obtained by putting her or any person in whom she is interested, in fear of death or of hurt.

Fourthly—With her consent, when the man knows that he is not her husband and that her consent is given because she believes that he is another man to whom she is or believes herself to be lawfully married.

Fifthly—With her consent when, at the time of giving such consent, by reason of unsoundness of mind or intoxication or the administration by him personally or through another of any stupefying or unwholesome substance, she is unable to understand the nature and consequences of that to which she gives consent.

Sixthly—With or without her consent, when she is under eighteen years of age.

Seventhly—When she is unable to communicate consent.

5. Although Criminal Law (Amendment) Act, 2013 raised the age of consent to 18 years, girls above the age of 15 years cannot withhold consent from their husbands.

6. The Criminal Law (Amendment) Act deleted this provision by virtue of s. 376 (1) IPC which prescribes minimum sentence of seven years which may extend to life imprisonment in all rape cases, which are not defined as aggravated offences under s. 376 (2) IPC. However, rape of a child-wife by her husband is not seen as an aggravated offence, even though rape of a sixteen year old girl now constitutes an aggravated offence.

7. The 2013 rape law amendment not only retained the marital rape exemption but it also included other kinds of sexual acts in its purview, no longer limited to forced penile penetration of the child wife's vagina. The law now holds that 'sexual intercourse or sexual acts by a man with his own wife, the wife not being under fifteen years of age, is not rape'. Under s. 376B IPC, the only concession made for separated wives, was that such separation is no longer limited to one granted by judicial decree. For such an offence a minimum sentence of two years and a maximum of seven years may be awarded. Further, all forms of sexual intercourse not amounting to rape by persons in authority were organized under s. 376 (C) IPC in 2013. Section 376 (3) specifies that a man in a position of authority or in a fiduciary relationship [s. 376 (C) (a)]; or a public servant [s. 376 (C)(b)]; or superintendent or manager of jail, remand home or any place of custody established by or under the law, children's or women's institution [s. 376 (C)(c)] or on the management or staff of a hospital [s. 376(C)(d)] who induces or seduces any woman either in his custody, charge or who is present on the premises to have sex with him, when such sex does not amount to rape, will be punished by imprisonment of minimum five years which may extend to ten years.

8. See Gangoli (2007) for a reading of matrimonial law in relation to the rape law. Gangoli suggests that the provision of restitution of conjugal rights

in the Hindu Marriage Act, 1955, although gender neutral, 'colludes with, if not actively validates marital rape' (2007: 58). Sexual violence now is a ground for seeking relief under the Protection of Women from Domestic Violence Act, 2005.

9. In 2012, the Protection of Children from Sexual Offences Act, 2012 was enacted.

10. Gupta argues that 'the growing linkage between sodomy, perversity and homosexuality sans a discussion on a private space for consensual sexual acts was solidified in the case of Pooran Ram vs State of Rajasthan where a homosexual was equated with a rapist. The court in Pooran Ram held that "perversity" that leads to sexual offences may result either in "homosexuality or in the commission of rape"' (2006: 4817, also see *Pooran Ram* v. *State of Rajasthan* 2001 Cri LJ 91).

11. *Naz Foundation* v. *Government of New Capital Territory of Delhi and Others* Delhi Law Times 160 (2009) 227.

12. It may be noted that the 1983 amendment enlarged the notion of consent to include two new changes. First, until 1983 the third clause of s. 375 held that consent would be vitiated only in the circumstance of putting the victim in fear of death or hurt. Now consent would be vitiated also when the victim is forced to consent when put in fear of death and hurt to 'any person she is interested in'. Second, a new section under 'fifthly' was added where consent is vitiated on the grounds of unsoundness of mind, administration of a stupefying substance or intoxication wherein the woman is unable to understand the nature and consequences of what it is that she consents to. The 1983 amendment did not accept the 84th Law Commission's recommendations to replace consent with 'free and voluntary consent' to signal active consent in contrast to consent presumed from passive submission (Law Commission 1980).

13. In 2013, newer categories of aggravated rape have been introduced. These include: rape by a relative, guardian, or teacher of, or a person in a position of trust or authority [s. 376 (2) (f)], rape of a woman during communal or sectarian violence [s. 376 (2) (g)], rape of a woman incapable of giving consent[s. 376 (2) (j)], rape of a woman when the accused is in a position of domination and control over her [s. 376 (2) (k)], when a woman suffers from a physical or mental disability [s. 376 (2) (l)], when grievous bodily harm is caused or the woman is maimed, disfigured or her life is endangered [s. 376 (2) (m)], or she is raped repeatedly [s. 376 (2) (n)]. Further, the amendment defines as an aggravated offence, rape of children until the age of 16 [s. 376 (2) (i)], as compared to the earlier 12 years. Section 376 (2) (c) makes it an aggravated offence if any member of the army forces in an area deployed by the Central or State government

commits rape on a woman in such area. Section 376 (2)(a) further holds that rape by police officers as an aggravated offence by specifying that such a rape will be considered aggravated when the crime is committed, within the limits of a police station to which the policeman has been appointed or in the premises of any station house or when the woman is in custody of such a police officer or his subordinate. The minimum punishment for these offences is ten years and the maximum extends to life imprisonment, where life means till the remainder of the convict's natural life. A new section, s. 376A was added which held that when rape causes death or the rape victim is reduced to a persistent vegetative state then a minimum of twenty years imprisonment with a maximum of life until the remainder of natural life or death may be awarded. Section 376D enhanced the punishment for gang rape to a minimum sentence of twenty years, which may be extended to life imprisonment for the remainder of the person's natural life. This section specifies that the fine imposed should be sufficient to cover the victim's medical expenses and must be paid directly to the victim. Section 376E specifies that punishment for repeat offenders will warrant the life sentence for the remainder of the person's natural life or the death penalty.

14. For two excellent studies on sentencing in rape cases see Varghese 1992 and Satish 2013.

15. In 2013, s. 53A was inserted in the Indian Evidence Act which states that the evidence of the character of the victim or of such person's previous sexual experience with any person shall not be relevant on the issue of consent or its quality. Further, s. 146 was amended to substitute the previous proviso which states that under ss. 376, 376A, 376B, 376C, 376D and 376E IPC (or attempt to commit any of these offences) it shall not be permissible to adduce evidence or to put questions in the cross-examination of the victim as to the general immoral character, previous sexual experience of the victim to prove consent or the quality of consent.

Section 273 CrPC which describes the conditions which require the presence of the accused during the trial was further amended in 2013 by way of a proviso which now held that while recording the evidence of a woman below the age of 18 who is subjected to rape or any other sexual offence, the court will see it to it that the woman is not confronted by the accused while at the same time ensuring his right to cross-examination.

16. Section 273 CrPC which describes the conditions which require the presence of the accused during the trial was further amended in 2013 by way of a proviso which now held that while recording the evidence of a woman below the age of 18 who is subjected to rape or any other sexual offence, the court will see it to it that the woman is not confronted by the accused while at the same time ensuring his right to cross-examination.

17. Until 2013, disability did not feature as a ground for amending laws of procedure and evidence. For an insightful critique of the conduct of rape trials in relation to shifting the burden of intelligibility on disabled women see Mandal 2013. The 2013 Amendment inserted s. 54A CrPC to specify that in case of a person identifying the accused is mentally or physically disabled, the process of identification will take place under the supervision of the Judicial Magistrate using methods the witness is comfortable with and such a process will be videographed, if the person arrested is mentally or physically disabled. Further, s. 154 which now holds that the first information given by a woman in rape cases should be recorded by a woman police officer or any woman officer, specifies that if the victim is temporarily or permanently mentally or physically disabled then such information shall be recorded by a police officer at the residence of the complainant or any other place convenient to the complainant in the presence of an interpreter or special educator. Section 164 CrPC was amended to state that the Magistrate shall take the assistance of an interpreter or a special educator to record the statement of the person against whom such an offence is committed is mentally or physically disabled; and this will be videographed. Such a statement will be considered a statement in lieu of examination-in-chief and such a statement could be cross-examined without the need for recording the statement at the trial stage.

18. While there are judgments proclaiming that even a prostitute has the right to protection against rape, in practice such prosecutions are rare.

19. In *Delhi Domestic Working Women's Forum* v. *Union of India* (1995), the Supreme Court held that legal representation is a right that can be exercised by the survivor of rape. Such lawyers do not displace the role and function of the prosecution, but they supplement the legal representation available to the survivor of rape, keeping her interests in mind as a victim of sexual violence. Further, the court clarified that the survivor of rape must not be constituted as a passive bystander to a legal case fought between the state and the accused. Further, the Supreme Court holds that the brief of the victim's lawyer would be to assist the victim right from the stage of filing a complaint to the time the case is heard in the court. Such lawyers would be appointed by the court and are empowered to act in police stations even before taking permission from court. Such lawyers have been entrusted with the task of explaining the legal procedure to the victim, assist the survivor in filing the case in the police station, prepare her for the testimony, and make information available to her in case she needs counselling or medical assistance. The judgment makes it binding on the police to inform the victim of her right to legal representation. The police have been instructed to maintain lists of advocates willing to represent survivors of rape [see *Delhi Domestic Working Women's Forum* v.

Union of India (1995) 1 SCC 14]. The impact of such normative departures in trial courts remains highly variable.

20. The term 'prosecutrix' does not find reference in any other law except in s. 155(4), Indian Evidence Act. Although the section has been deleted, the word 'prosecutrix' dominates appellate legal discourse.

21. *State of Madhya Pradesh* v. *Babulal* (2008) 1 SCC 234 at para 27.

22. Ibid.

23. Sharon Marcus (1992) has found critique for thinking of rape as a scripted interaction between men of unequal status. Marcus (1992) has argued that rape is a manifestation of a gendered grammar of violence. This gendered grammar of violence predicates men as subjects of violence and men are extolled to constitute their bodies as weapons or objects of violence without experiencing the same kind of fear as women (S. Marcus 1992). Challenging the idea that women can disrupt the social script that pre-exists rape in identical ways, irrespective of the states of mind, location, and cultures, Mardorossian argues that 'a model like Marcus' therefore downplays the "materiality of gender" and ignores that social inscriptions—that is, our physical situatedness in time and space, in history and culture—do not simply evaporate because we are made aware of them' (2002: 755).

24. In this sense, consciousness-raising allows women to 'understand that an experience they might previously have perceived as interpersonal in nature is in fact rooted in historical and social relations. ... As a site of collective enunciation, it politicizes rape even as it allows victims and survivors to examine the very terms they use to describe their experience' (Mardorossian 2002: 764).

25. The pre-histories of this campaign against rape were marked with protests against rape by civil liberty groups who saw rape as primarily a law and order problem at the time. Dalits groups also protested rape of Dalit women as crimes against all Dalits. In 1978, protests by Dalits ensued after a young Dalit woman was raped by a landlord's son in the Kathada village in Dasadataluka of Surendra Nagar district (Patel 2009).

26. See *Tukaram & Anr* v. *State of Maharashtra* (1979) 2 SCC 143.

27. The court described the accused's criminal behaviour as an act of fondling the victim's private parts. Such legal language normalizes the violence of a deeply humiliating form of sexual assault. To describe such forms of violent and inappropriate touch as fondling is to adopt the rapist's point of view (see ibid).

28. Ibid. at para 3.

29. Ibid. at para 3.

30. Ibid. at para 3.

31. Ibid. at para 3.

32. Ibid. at para 4.

33. Ibid. at para 5.

34. *Rao Harnarain Singh* v. *State of Punjab* (1958) Cri LJ 564.

35. (1958) Cri LJ 564 at para 4, emphasis added.

36. Ibid. at para 6.

37. Ibid. at para 7.

38. *Rao Harnarain Singh Sheoji Singh* v. *Gumani Ram Arya* (1958) Cri LJ 952.

39. The 2013 amendment now specifies that 'consent means an unequivocal voluntary agreement when the woman by words, gestures or any form of verbal or non-verbal communication, communicates willingness to participate in the specific sexual act', 'provided that a woman who does not physically resist to the act of penetration shall not by the reason only of that fact, be regarded as consenting to the sexual activity'.

40. It must be remembered that the Open Letter was written one year after Justice Krishna Iyer had passed strictures against the practice of calling women to police stations (as a violation of s. 160 [1] of the Criminal Procedure Code, 1973) in the case of Nandini Satpathy who was the Chief Minister of Orissa at that time [see *Nandini Satpathy* v. *PL Dani* (1978) 2 SCC 424].

41. The Open Letter was first published in a newspaper in Pakistan before the Indian press picked up the story (see U. Baxi 1994). The first organization to respond critically in support of the Open Letter was Jyoti Sangh in Ahmedabad. Jyoti Sangh wrote to women's groups such as the All India Women's Conference (AIWC) seeking action on the case. Soon the Forum against Rape (FAR) was formed in Bombay, marking the beginnings of the autonomous women's movement in India (see Gangoli 2007). Gujarat was the first state to issue directions to the police not to call women after dark to the police stations.

42. U. Baxi writes, 'in our Open Letter we had, however suggested that if the court wished it would review this decision because we were interested in the court itself learning from a public acknowledgment of its ways. As it happened, the State of Maharashtra itself asked for review. But the women's organizations by now wanted to associate themselves with the review … we wanted to court to decide for itself; nor did we seek a re-conviction of offenders in this case if the court thought it unjust to do so. We only aimed at the court declaring the law, by correcting its erroneous proposition that consent could be presumed in custodial rape' (1994: 73).

43. The advocates at the Supreme Court expressed their displeasure at the Chief Justice of India's public address at the Indian Law Institute (Delhi) one day before the review petition was to be heard.

44. *Hindustan Times*, 3 April 1980, p. 1 and p. 5.

45. Ibid.

46. The women's groups were constructed as militant, populist, trade unionist, and lacking legal understanding. Two women's groups were chastised in Parliament. Ram Jethmalani, an eminent jurist, said, 'we are a society governed by a rule of law and the women's movement today is beginning to manifest itself in some forms which with all respect to the intelligent females in this country, I wish to say are not consistent with the rule of law. Only the other day the High Court of Delhi allowed an appeal. The judges honestly did their duty. They thought on evidence that the man was not guilty and they passed a judgment of acquittal. And sir, there were demonstrations outside the High Court and all kinds of ugly scenes had been witnessed. Sir, these are somewhat unproductive and I think they ought to be avoided' (Lok Sabha Debates, dated 1 December 1983, Vol. 42, no. 6, p. 410).

47. *Gopalakrishna Kalanidhi* v. *Union of India* Writ Petition No. 33582 of 1998, dated 28.03.2001, High Court of Andhra Pradesh, available at http://www.indiankanoon.org/doc/1192673/ accessed on 18 September 2012.

48. Ibid. at para 1.

49. Ibid. at para 7.

50. Ibid. at para 9.

51. AIR 2000 SC 988.

52. *Gopalakrishna Kalanidhi* v. *Union of India,* Writ Petition No. 33582 of 1998, dated 28.03.2001, High Court of Andhra Pradesh, available at http://www.indiankanoon.org/doc/1192673/ accessed on 18 September 2012, at para 9.

53. Ibid. at para 7.

54. *Chairman, Railway Board & Ors* v. *Mrs Chandrima Das & Ors* AIR 2000 SC 988 at para 34.

55. Ibid. at para 34.

56. *Gopalakrishna Kalanidhi* v. *Union of India,* Writ Petition No. 33582 of 1998, dated 28.03.2001, High Court of Andhra Pradesh, available at http://www.indiankanoon.org/doc/1192673/ accessed on 18 September 2012, at para 9.

57. *Yad Ram* v. *State of Rajasthan* RLW (2008) (2) Raj 1659 at para 7.

58. Ibid. at para 8.

59. Ibid.

60. *Queen Empress* v. *Huree Mohan Mythee* XVIII ILR (Cal) 49 (1891).

61. Available at http://lawcommissionofindia.nic.in/rapelaws.htm, accessed on 18 September 2012.

62. 1998 Cri LJ 2428.

63. Ibid. at para 2.
64. Ibid.
65. Ibid. at para 6.
66. Ibid. at para 1.
67. Ibid. at para 14.
68. *Natha* v. *The Crown,* AIR 1923 Lahore 536: cited in ibid. at para 19.
69. Ibid. at para 26.
70. Ibid. at para 27.
71. Ibid. at para 28, emphasis in original.
72. In *Sakshi* v. *Union of India* [(1999) 6 SCC 591], the Supreme Court found that the 156th Law Commission Report did not deal with the issue of child sexual abuse as raised in the writ. The Law Commissioners were requested to re-examine the specific issues listed in the writ and examine the feasibility of making recommendations for the amendment of the law in order to plug the loopholes. This second wave of calls for legal reform has come on the heels of the campaign to demand for legislative change to treat child sexual abuse by way of distinct legal procedures, and this campaign has used public interest litigation as a mode of pushing for legislative change.
73. (1999) 6 SCC 591 at para 2.
74. Ibid.
75. Ibid. at para 3.
76. Ibid. at para 4.
77. Ibid.
78. Ibid. at para 22.
79. Ibid at para 6. Susan Brownmiller's *Against Our Will* makes a guest appearance in *Sakshi,* as follows:

> ...in rape ... the intent is not merely to 'take', but to humiliate and degrade ..... Sexual assault in our day and age is hardly restricted to forced genital copulation, nor is it exclusively a male–on–female offence. ... And while the penis may remain the rapist's favourite weapon, his prime instrument of vengeance... it is not in fact his only tool. Sticks, bottles and even fingers are often substituted for the 'natural' thing. And as men may invade women through other offices, so too, do they invade other men. Who is to say that the sexual humiliation suffered through forced oral or rectal penetration is a lesser violation of the personal, private inner space, a lesser injury to mind, spirit and sense of self?

80. Ibid. at para 9 f.
81. Ibid at para 7.
82. Ibid. at para 10.
83. (1952) SCR 377.

84. (1952) SCR 377 at para 16.

85. Ibid. at para 18.

86. Ibid.

87. Ibid. at para 19.

88. Ibid.

89. Ibid.

90. Ibid.

91. (1916) 2 KB 658, cited in Ibid. at para 20–1.

92. Ibid.

93. Ibid. at para 21.

94. The court tells us that 'there is a class of cases which considered that though corroboration should ordinarily be required in the case of grown-up woman it is unnecessary in the case of a child of tender years. *Bishram* v. *Emperor* (1) is typical of that point of view' (ibid. at para 23). Another set of Privy Council cases maintained that 'conviction should not ordinarily be based on uncorroborated evidence of a child witness' (ibid. at para 23; see *Bishram* v. *Emperor* AIR 1944 Nag 363.

95. Ibid. at para 21.

96. Ibid. at para 23.

97. *Krishnan Lal* v. *State of Haryana* 1980 Cri LJ 972.

98. *Bhoginbhai Hirjibhai* v. *State of Gujarat* (1983) Cri LJ 755.

99. 1983 Cri LJ 755.

100. 1983 Cri LJ 755 at 757.

101. See *State of Punjab* v. *Gurmit Singh and Ors*, 1996 2 SCC 384.

102. See *State of HP* v. *Raghubir Singh*, 1993 2 SCC 622.

103. (1952) AIR 159.

104. *State of Maharashtra* v. *Chandraprakash Kewalchand Jain* MANU/SC/0122/1990.

105. MANU/SC/0122/1990 at para 13.

106. MANU/SC/0122/1990 at para 16, emphasis added.

107. *State of Himachal Pradesh* v. *Shree Kant Shekhari* 2004 (7) SCALE 647.

108. P. Venkatasubbaiah replied, 'to criminalise "rape by economic domination" would be "counter productive"… There will be instances where some unscrupulous women may take advantage of it and try to blackmail or may do some character assassination of such people … So, one should be very careful in this matter' (Lok Sabha debates, dated 1 December 1983 at pp. 432).

109. Vij Shivam, 'A Mighty Heart', Tehelka, 13 October 2007, available at http://www.tehelka.com/story_main34.asp?filename=hub131007A_MIGHTY.asp, accessed on 9 August 2012.

110. English translation of the judgment of the District and Sessions Court, Jaipur, in *The State* v. *Ramkaran and Others*, dated 15 November 1995 at pp. 17–8, on file with the author.

111. Chakravarti argues that 'brahmanical patriarchy' describes 'a set of rules and institutions … where women are crucial in maintaining the boundaries between castes. Patriarchal codes in this structure can ensure that the caste system can be reproduced without violating the hierarchical order of closed endogamous circles' (2003: 21, also see Chakravarti 1993).

112. Although Article 17 of the Indian Constitution, abolished untouchability or its practice in any form, the Constitution presumed its existence without defining it. In 1955, the Untouchability (Offences) Act was passed. It was amended in 1976 and re-named the Protection of Civil Rights Act (Act 22 of 1955). The latter included certain offences against the STs as well. Galanter (1972) has amply demonstrated how difficult it was under this law to prove that a violation was committed on the grounds of untouchability. Upendra Baxi has also argued that since untouchability was not juridically named, what it meant was 'that it was open to the accused to demonstrate that the action against a member of scheduled caste was not done on the ground of untouchability but on other grounds. If this was accepted, then the burden of proof would shift to the prosecution to prove that the action was committed on the ground of untouchability' (1994: 127).

113. Also see John's (2003) critique of the ethnocentric romanticization of Dalit women's freedom or resourcefulness. John critiques the position that 'gender relations are more egalitarian amongst lower castes, and become increasingly unequal as one moves up the caste hierarchy, implying therefore that "the status of women falls, when their husbands' rises"' (2003: 221–2).

114. Forms of terrifying and mutilating sexual violence, which have been paradigmatic to the experiences of dalit and tribal women, seemed to have become the norm, and therefore, became one of the .grounds for such a widespread protest in 2012–13. However, the complex experiences of prosecuting rape and atrocity did not inform the debate on law reform. Sadly enough, even ritualized forms of sexualized humiliation such as stripping and parading were not recognized as specific forms of historic wrong. Rather, following the Verma Committee Report, s. 354B was inserted in the IPC which criminalized assault or use of force to compel any woman to be naked or disrobe her for a minimum sentence of three years and a maximum sentence of seven years. This new section however does not redress the specificity of the humiliation of being stripped and paraded in front of a public, which consumes such a degrading spectacle. Nor were further amendments to strengthen the prosecution of rape of dalit or tribal women under the PoA Act recommended by the Verma Committee.

115. Also see *Bhanwari Devi* v. *Ram Karan and Ors*, CRLR '54' of 1996–R, Division Bench, registered on 24/1/1996, pending for orders– Misc. Cases.

116. MANU/RH/0034/2007.

117. This means a court taking judicial notice on its own motion without a case being filed.

118. MANU/RH/0034/2007 at para 1.

119. Ibid.

120. On the same day, the Rajasthan High Court issued directions to the State of Rajasthan to pay three lakh rupees as compensation to the survivor within three months. The State Government was directed to set up a state-level special cell, to coordinate and control different agencies towards quick and scientific investigations in sexual violence cases. The court directed that the police officers must try to ensure that the investigation is completed in one week. All district superintendents were directed to submit quarterly reports to the special cell, which would be collated and submitted to the registrar (fast track) of the Rajasthan High Court. The administrative judge would peruse these reports for further directions. The first such report was to reach the direction in the first week of August 2005. The court further directed the sessions judges to ensure that the trial in cases of sexual violence is completed in four months from the date of filing the charge sheet. The sessions judges were directed to submit quarterly reports about rape trials to the administrative judge (fast track) through the registrar (fast track) starting from the first week of August 2005. The court directed the state government to prepare a scheme within to ensure necessary financial, medical, psychological, and social assistance to rape survivors. If the survivor is a tourist or under threat, her statement is to be recorded immediately before she leaves the country, and if she stays back to depose, the government must cover her costs. Further, the Rajasthan High Court directed that the victim should not be harassed by restating her trauma more than once, her statement be recorded on the date she is called to court except for special recorded reasons, and she should be provided accommodation while on the premises of the court and not be required to wait beyond two hours. Most of these guidelines were not implemented.

121. MANU/RH/0034/2007 at para 9.

122. The court maintained that 'the questions put in cross examination on behalf of the accused, insofar as they relate directly to the incident should be given in writing to the presiding officer of the court who may put them to the victim or witnesses in a language which is clear and is not embarrassing' (ibid. at para 34).

123. AIR 2004 SC 3566.

124. Ibid. at para 34.

125. Ibid. at para 31.

126. See Rakesh Bhatnagar, 'Woman Can Marry Her Rapist if She Wishes: Chief Justice of India', 8 March 2010, Daily News and Analysis, available at http://www.dnaindia.com/india/report_woman-can-marry-her-rapist-if-she-wishes-chief-justice-of-india_1356464, accessed on 8 September 2012.

127. It is not only important to argue for a deletion of the marital law exemption, but it is also important to include in the law an explanation that consent between the complainant and the accused ought not be presumed in the event of an existing marital relationship. Similarly although there is no explicit bar, which prevents a sex worker from filing a rape prosecution, there are no provisions, which explicitly state that sex work would not be prejudicial to filing a complaint.

128. This consensus reflected in the definitions of rape and sexual assault recommended by the Justice Verma Committee. However, the Criminal Law Ordinance 2013 disregarding this recommendation brought in a definition of sexual assault, which was gender neutral in relation to victims and perpetrators, while it retained the marital rape exemption in relation to wives. The effect of the Ordinance was that technically speaking husbands could bring a charge of sexual assault against their wives but women could not lodge a complaint of sexual assault against their husbands. After much opposition, the Criminal Law Amendment Act, 2013 which repealed the Ordinance not only retained the gender specificity of the offender but also of the victim—thereby denying recognition to the experiences of sexual violence faced by adult men and sexual minorities.

129. *Vishakha and Ors* v. *State of Rajasthan* AIR 1997 SC 3011.

130. Judgment of the Bombay High Court, dated 26 September 2006, available at http://indiankanoon.org/doc/671685/, accessed on 20 November 2012.

131. Ibid. at paras 5 and 6.

132. The demand for fast-track courts and reduction of delay in rape trials dominated the protests in 2012–13. The 2013 Amendment amended s. 309 CrPC by adding ss. (1) that any inquiry or trial relating to an offence under s. 376, s. 376A, s. 376B, s. 376C, s. 376D or s. 376E IPC shall be as far as possible completed within two months from the date of filing charge sheet. Such proceedings shall be held everyday until all witnesses have been examined and reasons for any adjournments have to be recorded.

CHAPTER TWO

Medicalization of Consent and Falsity
The Figure of the *Habitué* in Indian Rape Law

A defence lawyer who had practiced criminal law for twenty years in the Mirzapur and Bhadra courts in Ahmedabad drew my attention to the central place of medical jurisprudence textbooks in rape trials.[1] He said to me, 'I specialize in criminal law. I have dealt with eighty to ninety rape cases. Most of the cases are false cases. Look at Modi or Lyon. They have even cited cases. Modi, for example, talks of how because of feud, a father injured his daughter'. The frequent references to 'Modi' or 'Lyon' in Gujarat courts illustrated the critical role of medical jurisprudence textbooks, which acted as a medium of both pedagogy and prescription, and often determined the structure of questions posed in a trial. For any ethnographic understanding of rape trials in India, it is important to detail the proliferation of medico-legal categories such as 'habituated to sex', 'partial penetration', and 'technical rape'. These categories are products of medical techniques used on women's bodies that are relatively autonomous from the juridical apparatus, yet constitutive of the way in which rape trials are structured in Indian courts.

In this chapter, I do not aim to engage in an exhaustive review of the medical jurisprudence on rape. Instead, I focus on explicating my claim that Indian rape trials medicalize consent and falsity, thereby causing harm to the rape victim. Medico-legal categories, which derive from judicial interpretations of medical jurisprudence manuals, remain obscure as ethnographic categories if we do not trace how these become diagnostic in the first place. A typical medico-legal textbook is disconcerting to read since the techniques and frameworks deployed by medical jurists during the colonial period are juxtaposed with newer additions about forensic techniques and therapeutic approaches to victims of violence. Recent editions of medical jurisprudence manuals are marked by different temporalities, retaining sexist and racist colonial constructions of the lying, colonized female subject alongside more contemporary discussions on the trauma of rape (see also Agnes 2005).[2] Agnes therefore asserts that change will be possible only when 'at each juncture of writing newer editions, the experts … abandon the trend of slavishly copying from the older texts, outdated examples and the archaic sexist presumptions' (2005: 1866). The simultaneity of temporalities in rape trials poses a specific puzzle about how we may read the construction of women's biographies emptied of historical contexts.

It remains a terrifying fact that one of the most powerful ways by which sexualized violence has been made invisible is through the use of the twin categories of self-inflicted injury and false charges. I argue that the medicalization of falsity is not a neutral representation, but a specific combination of power and knowledge—following Michael Foucault (1977)—authorizing the idea that science can be used to make a female body speak despite, or even to spite, her testimony.[3] Further, the specificity of the rape trial in India derives from one of the earliest forms of truth-technologies inscribed on women's bodies, what was popularly referred to in the trial court as the 'two-finger test' (clinically known as the bimanual examination). During my fieldwork, I found that alongside the case history, age, and descriptions of injuries, it was commonplace to record 'P/V (Per Vagina): two fingers admissible' (or 'inadmissible', as the case may be), in medico-legal certificates.[4] The interpretation of the findings of the two-finger test provided in these certificates provided an insight into how these are further translated in juridical discourse as 'habituated to sexual intercourse', 'habitual', or 'used to sex'. In other words, the medico-legal certificate issued after a medical examination of the victim becomes a means for a defence lawyer to bring in past sexual history, now no longer permissible in the law, during the trial. The characterization of a woman as a *habitué* or as 'habituated', which we routinely come across in appellate judgments, is used to transform a testimony of rape into a statement of consensual sex.

I define this movement through the technique of the two-finger test—which enables the transformation of coercion into consent—as the medicalization of consent. I suggest that the use of the colonial category of 'habituated to sex' in the everyday vocabulary of legal and medical experts is mediated by the canonical space inhabited by medical jurisprudence textbooks, which bear the signature of scientific authority.

All raped victims—irrespective of age—are subjected to an invasive mimicry of the act of sexual violence via the two-finger test.[5] I argue that even though consent is not relevant in statutory rape cases, the medico-legal expert diagnoses whether the child's body has been sexualized by partial penile penetration of the vagina, or whether the hymen is ruptured. 'Partial penetration' is a medico-legal category, which means that even a minor degree of penetration is sufficient to meet the existing definition of rape—a category deployed almost entirely in child sexual abuse cases. To understand the sexualization of children's body in this manner, I draw attention to the characterization of statutory rape as 'technical rape' in legal discourse.[6] Technical rape is not merely a 'folk' category in law used by lawyers to denote statutory rape. Rather, the translation of statutory rape as technical rape signals that what is disallowed in law is possible in nature. The body of a growing female child is seen as having potential for seducing an adult man. The juridical verification of the sexualized body flows from treating medico-legal categories as if these exist in the child's experience, thereby obfuscating the meaning of rape.

THE HABITUAL LIAR

The commonplace insistence that most complaints of rape are false and that women's bodies should bear marks of stiff resistance to prove rape was foundational to the establishment of colonial medical jurisprudence in India (Kolsky 2010). Indeed, 'medical jurisprudence was a particularly significant investigative tool because it enabled the colonial state to circumvent oral testimony by locating truth in and on the body' (Kolsky 2002: 405). The corpus of works by Taylor (1845, 1856, 1866), Baynes (1854), Chevers (1856), Lyon (1918, 1921, 1953), and Modi (1922, 1940, 1969, 1972) not merely medicalized the suspicion towards raped women but also consolidated the role of medical experts in colonial India (also see Agnes 2005; Kolsky 2010). Medicalization of falsity meant a specific form of collaboration between law and medicine in early nineteenth-century England as 'experts defined rape as a moral problem which tainted its victim more than her assailant' (Clark 1987: 74). Clark contends:

> [L]egal reforms made it easier to convict rapists in the early nineteenth century, while the reformers themselves suppressed women's ability to protest against rape. Reformers viewed rape as a crime against public morality and decency, so they directed their most strenuous efforts at regulating women's sexual behaviour, especially that of working class women (1987: 74).

The colonial law on rape was modelled on such efforts to regulate the chastity of all women, which specifically acted to control the sexuality of working class women in England. Kolsky claims that:

> British presumptions about the frequency of false charges travelled to India where they combined with colonial ideas about Indian culture and made rape convictions examined by the high courts very difficult to uphold. Strict evidentiary requirements were established by the courts according to the presumption that the doubly doubtful complainant (the native woman) was a non-credible witness whose testimony could not be trusted. (2010: 123)

While colonial medical jurisprudence drew upon imperial patriarchies in framing all rape claims as easily fungible and positioned the native woman as a habitual liar, this was not a unidirectional story, as I suggest later.

The project of medical jurisprudence in colonial India was ethnological—it marked difference by characterizing the native as lying, licentious, seductive, malingering, or inherently criminal.[7] The stabilization of truth technologies accompanied the construction of the natives as inherently deceitful, with women being seen as devious enough to falsify signs of injury. This is best exemplified by citing Norman Chevers, a civil surgeon in the colonial administration who is often referred to as the father of medical jurisprudence in India (Kolsky 2010). Chevers' (1856) manual of medical jurisprudence was an enlarged reprint of a paper entitled 'Report on Medical Jurisprudence in the Bengal Presidency', first published in the *Indian Annals of Medical Science*. In the preface to the manual, Chevers specified that he intended the manual to be of use to judicial and medical officers in Bengal and North Western Provinces of the colony. His stated aim was to address medico-legal questions that arose in India '...which are not to be found in the works of our standard authority on the subject', that is, the corpus of works authored by Taylor (1856: iv). As a civil surgeon, Chevers felt the need for a 'treatise on Medical Jurisprudence' that would embody '... clear and practical expositions of the various and peculiar modes by which the natives of this country are wont to effect crimes against the person' (1856: 1).[8]

Chevers was of the opinion that the medical jurist 'should possess an intimate acquaintance with the dispositions, customs, prejudices and crimes of the people among whom his investigations are to be pursued' (1856: 2). Studying crime meant producing intimate or inner knowledge that would reveal how deceptive the exteriority of the colonized people was.[9] As Chevers extolled:

> [I]t is only by thoroughly knowing the people, and by fixing the mind sedulously upon the records of their crimes, that an European can learn how strange a combination of sensuality, jealousy, wild and ineradicable superstition, absolute untruthfulness, and ruthless disregard of the value of human life, lie below the placid, civil, timid, forbearing exterior of the natives of India. (1856: 8)

Colonial medico-legal discourse mapped different crimes on to specific religious communities—hence, it was believed that 'sexual jealousy is probably the most frequent cause of homicide amongst the Mussulauns; Criminal Abortion and Child Murder are rifest among the unhappy class of Hindu widows' (Chevers 1856: 11). The role of the medical expert in the colony was thus explicitly ethnological, desirous of revealing and displaying the 'real' nature of the native (Kolsky 2010).

The native rape victim became the object of intense suspicion as Chevers assumed that 'the belief in woman's virtue or man's honesty does not exist amongst' Indians (1856: 8). He opined that instances of rape 'appear to be of great frequency in India, and there is also reason to believe that persons are, by no means rarely, charged falsely with its commission' (1856: 460). Further, Chevers pronounced:

> There cannot be a doubt, however that, in many cases unusual and extraneous force is employed. I am informed by an eminent missionary, thoroughly conversant with the customs of the natives

in the neighbourhood of Calcutta, that he is assured that means are commonly employed, even by the parents of immature girls, to render them *aptæ viribus* by mechanical means, especially by the use of the fruit of the plantain! (1856: 480)

In 1865, Taylor cited the above illustration by Chevers to say 'it is scarcely credible that mothers should resort to such practices, nevertheless the facts are too well accredited to admit of denial' (1865: 993). Every significant medical jurisprudence textbook began with an instruction to the medical expert to look for signs of false cases of rape.[10]

The rather unfortunate remarks of Professor Amos on *Rape, Identity and Survivorship* delivered at the University of London in 1831 remain critical to these histories of the medicalization of falsity[11] in the Indian colony. Amos, who was cited in Taylor (1845)[12] and then verbatim, in Baynes (1854), began with the premise that the task of the expert was to separate real rapes from fake ones. Baynes, a civil and sessions judge of Madura who adapted English medical jurisprudence textbooks for judges and magistrates in colonial India, wrote:

[T]here is, however, one case in which medical evidence is of some importance, namely, where a false accusation is made. In some instances, as in respect to rape on young children, the charge may be founded on mistake: but in others there is little doubt that it is often wilfully and decidedly made from motives, into which it is here unnecessary to enquire. Professor Amos remarked some years ago since that for one real rape tried on Circuits in England there were on the average twelve pretended cases. (1854: 121)

To cite Amos:

[A] real rape is no doubt one of the most atrocious offences which can be perpetrated in society and when it is proved, and there is no pretence of any suggestion of concert, perhaps the judges are right in punishing it inexorably with death, whatever the ages or whatever the circumstances of the parties. But for one real rape that is met at the assizes a dozen or more sham ones are preferred. (1831: 34)

Alluding to Amos, Baynes notes that false cases of rape in India appear 'with great force ... as the experience of every Judicial Officer will prove' (1854: 121). The 1918 edition of Lyon's textbook on medical jurisprudence adapted for India noted that 'lying is one of the great difficulties with which the Medico-legal expert, in common with the Judge, has to grapple in Europe, and it is by no means less prevalent in India' (1918: 17). Referring to Manu,[13] the 1918 edition opined that 'the untrustworthiness of native evidence in India is notorious. In nearly every case in law, more or less false evidence is given, whether it be from fear, stupidity, apathy, malice or innate desire' (Lyon 1918: 21–2). Native women who complained of rape bore a double burden, suspected as liars being women, and presumed to be untrustworthy being native.

The paradigmatic statement that false charges of rape are not uncommon in India finds repetition in the various editions of Modi's medico-legal textbooks.[14] In 1922, Modi pontificated:

> [I]n the majority of rape cases of an adult woman the charge is made with the object of blackmail, or the act is done with the consent of the woman but when discovered, to get herself out of the trouble, she does not scruple to accuse the man of rape. If the complaint is made a day or two after the act, the case is probably one of concoction. It is also necessary to note the previous character of the female, and her relations with the accused. (1922: 253–4)

Modi cautioned doctors that fathers injured their young daughters sexually to foist a false charge of rape on their enemies (see Modi 1922, 1940).[15] As recently as the 2002 edition, we find the following declarations:

> False charges are not uncommon in India. Occasionally parents may induce chillies into the vagina of their female child to cause irritation and inflammation or may injure her genitals for the purpose of substantiating a false charge of rape brought against an individual with a view to take revenge or extort money from him, and may tutor a child to tell a circumstantial story of rape. (Modi 2002: 506)

Here we see a concern with simulation of rape rather than recognition of the act of inserting objects or chillies into the child's vagina as sexual violence.[16]

In the nineteenth century, medical experts created the concept of 'false assault' or 'simulation of venereal assault' and corresponding signs that would reveal 'fraud and lies' (Vigarello 2001: 145). Rape victims were believed to inflict injuries upon themselves to allege false complaints. These medical textbooks devoted a separate section to self-inflicted injuries. The persistence of such medico-legal categories is self-evident from the table of comparison given below, which places Modi's observations in the 1922 edition alongside the one published in 2002.

Modi 1922	Modi 2002
To substantiate false charges, marks of violence are sometimes self inflicted. Once I saw a young woman of twenty, alleged to have been raped by a man, who had several marks simulating scratches made with a *kankar* on the forearms and the chest, which could be wiped off by rubbing them with a piece of wet cotton wool. (Modi 1922: 248)	Modi saw a young woman of twenty years alleged to have been raped by a man. She had several marks simulating scratches made with a *kankar* (pebble) on the forearms and chest, which could be wiped off by rubbing them with a piece of wet cloth (Modi 2002: 502).

Rather than labour the point about the repetitive prose and the simultaneity of different temporalities in the manuals, I note that the construction of self-inflicted wounds embodied an inherent anxiety in colonial law. The position of medical experts was consolidated on the basis that only they could expose the trickery deployed by the victim, who was perceived to possess a cunning knowledge of criminal law.

THE ABLE-BODIED WOMAN

Early nineteenth-century British medical jurisprudence 'legitimized men's claim that women "consented" to violence, repeating the common belief that no man could rape a healthy adult woman by himself' (Clark 1987: 71). This proposition finds elaboration in colonial medico-legal textbooks about whether women can be raped at all, and if they can be, under which circumstances. Medical jurists discussed whether it was possible to rape a 'normal', able-bodied woman as opposed to a drugged, hypnotized, stupefied, sleeping, insane, or gagged woman who was divested of the normal or natural means to resist (see Taylor 1865). It is not surprising, then that one of the medico-legal propositions that has acquired an axiomatic status in everyday legal discourse is that an able-bodied adult woman cannot be raped by an unarmed man.[17]

Even today we find the inscription of difference whereby certain bodies are seen as *more* able-bodied than others. We find how social hierarchies such as class, which often coincide with caste, are elaborated in medico-legal textbooks. The measurement of what constitutes an able body is not measured through attributes of build, strength, nutrition, weight, disability, or medical history of the patient. As the 1969 edition of Modi declares:

> It is obvious that a woman belonging to a labouring class who is accustomed to hard and rough work will be able to offer a good deal of resistance and to deal blows on her assailant and will thus succeed in frustrating his attempts at violation. On the contrary, a woman belonging to a middle class or rich class of an educated family and not habituated to go about herself will not be able to resist for long and soon faint or will be rendered powerless from fright and exhaustion (1969: 344, also see Modi 2002).

Such statements in medico-legal textbooks were often repeated during my interviews with lawyers in the trial court in Ahmedabad. For instance, when I asked a public prosecutor in the Mirzapur trial court how he discerned false cases from true cases, he replied, 'There is one rule. An able bodied, healthy woman—not fat and fair body—cannot be forced to perform against her will. There must be some absence of injury in the absence of a weapon. If she throws a punch or scratches there must be some injuries on the chest, cheek, neck, knee—some kind of abrasions.'

Labouring bodies are strong and can resist and fight. Upper-class bodies are flaccid, educated, fair, and docile. The contexts of poverty, illness, and survival do not inform this characterization of the working-class body. In courts, the medicalization of falsity is used to organize difference on the grounds of age, marital and reproductive status, caste, tribe, and class in order to convert coercion into consent (see Chapter 6).

MEDICALIZATION OF CONSENT

Anna Clark's analysis of the rape law in nineteenth-century England reveals that British trials involving children, even those younger than twelve years, permitted evidence of their 'general indecency' (1987: 72). Newspaper accounts portrayed children's testimony as 'malicious' (Clark 1987: 68). Medical experts who medicalized falsity repeatedly maintained that working-class or poor parents, especially mothers, were the ones who injured and tutored their young children to levy false rape charges for the purpose of extortion. Clark points out that:

> Surgeons corroborated this notion of the wicked working-class child, sexually depraved at an early age. Dr Ryan declared that 'depraved mothers have induced their children to make accusations against innocent persons' and that gonorrhoea in children could result from non-venereal disease. His claims were influential in practice, for he testified in atleast one rape case invalidating the testimony of a young girl. (1987: 68)

Taylor (1865) thought that working-class children could fool medical experts into believing that symptoms of vaginal infections (*vaginitis*) indicated rape. He said that these 'children of scrofulous habit', especially 'girls up to six or seven years of age', had been 'tutored to lay imputations against innocent persons for the purpose of extorting money' (1865: 996). In his lectures on rape, French medical jurist Léon-Henri Thoinot instructed his students to 'remember, that every time you find yourself as an expert in the presence of a child supposed to be a victim of an assault, you should be on your guard; distrust should be, in cases of this kind, the first rule of the examination' (1911: 239).

During the nineteenth century, British medical experts debated whether rape, that is, complete penetration of the vagina by the penis, was possible by an adult man in the case of a girl child below the age of ten years. Surgeons testified in English courts that it was not possible for a man to rape a child; for instance, one surgeon, 'a Mr Leeson, proclaimed that it was "physically impossible" to rape a child and his testimony resulted in the acquittal of atleast one man accused of the crime. By 1844, Alfred S. Taylor found it necessary in his medical jurisprudence textbook to remind doctors that "it must not be assumed by medical witnesses that all these charges of rape on young children are frivolous, and that they impute an impossible crime"' (Clark 1987: 68–69). Taylor was one of the few experts to point out that the use of the term 'complete intromission' to define rape led to calling 'non-intromission' a non-rape (Vigarello 2001: 144). In 1845, Taylor wrote:

> Medically speaking, some penetration may take place without a necessary destruction of the hymen; and morally speaking, the crime must be the same, whether the membrane is ruptured or not, for how is it possible to repress what society agrees in regarding as a very heinous crime, if medical witnesses are to be allowed to dispute about degrees of penetration for its completion? It is doubtful whether in any case there could be complete introduction of the male organ into the vagina, without laceration and destruction of the soft parts: but are we to be told upon medical grounds, that no offence analogous to rape can be perpetrated on female infants, unless such marks of injury be present? This is making the proof of carnal abuse of such children to depend upon mere accident, it is laying down a rule that penetration to the vulva shall not constitute rape, while penetration to the vagina will be visited by the usual punishment. It is not supposed that the law would sanction this view; for on what pretence could a different punishment be assigned to the two acts. Is the moral injury to the female or to the laws of society, less in one instance than in the other? (1845: 459)

In order to demonstrate these arguments, Taylor's 1865 edition referred to Chevers' (1856) detailed analysis of rape on Indian children. Chevers (1856) argued that young female children could be completely penetrated, resulting in severe laceration as the Indian cases illustrated.[18] He recorded instances of the brutality and frequency with which rape was committed on children, especially concerning young girls during the 'in the first act of connexion' in India (1856: 479).[19] Chevers opined that:

> It is merely frivolous to argue, as a point of law, even that *complete vaginal penetration* is impossible in any infant however young, when it is certain, from numerous recorded instances, that such penetration has been effected in children of all ages—the fact that this penetration has, in very young girls, only been effected by severe laceration of the parts should, most assuredly, not be held as a mitigation of the atrocity. (1856: 472, emphasis in original)

The deaths of child-wives resulting from lacerated vaginas, fatal haemorrhage, and severe shock was used as evidence to establish that rape can cause death (see Lyon 1921).[20]

Among the cases and exhibits he cites, Chevers tell us that:

> [T]he museum of Calcutta Medical College contains a preparation, sent by Mr. G Evans, displaying the uterus, vagina and greater portion of the external parts of generation of a young Mahomedan female, showing laceration of the perineum, and a considerable portion of the vaginal sheath, the effects of violence done to the parts on the first act of copulation, by which a violent haemorrhage, to the destruction of the child (barely two years old) was occasioned. (1856: 481)

Colonial medical jurisprudence as an ethnological project treated raped bodies of native children as specimens in a laboratory. Resultant medico-legal knowledge that it was possible to rape a child in nature then circulated back to the metropolis. The emergence of partial penetration as a diagnostic category central to the rape trial occurred alongside the visibility of what Hyde (1997) calls the 'legal vagina'[21] of the colonized child, subjected to an ethnological clinical gaze.

The question of what constituted the proof of penile penetration had undergone a shift in England by 1831. Professor Amos' (1831) much quoted lecture (cited earlier) was delivered in the context of an amendment to the erstwhile rape law in England through Lord Lansdowne's Act, which held that it would not be necessary to prove emission to prosecute rape successfully in the case of a 'woman child' under the age of ten years, where consent was immaterial.[22] If penetration was proven—however slight this might be—it was sufficient to construe a crime of 'carnal knowledge'. Lord Lansdowne's Act now established that proof of penetration, even if incomplete, was sufficient without requiring proof of seminal emission. A sceptical Amos (1831) pointed out that this law meant that a 'eunuch' could also be found guilty of rape, since there were cases in which only evidence of emission could be found and not penile penetration.

Partial penetration acquired importance since this meant that the hymen might remain intact even though the offence of rape had been 'completed' in the case of children. Medical jurists such as Taylor (1866) repudiated the idea that an intact hymen be treated as physical proof of virginity, since this model was unable to account for rape on female children where the hymen may remain intact. Nor was it able to account for the absence of the hymen due to pathological reasons. In some cases the hymen may remain intact despite repeated instances of penile penetration, as in the case of prostitutes in Paris illustrated in Thoinot (1911). Lyon held that in rape cases virginity 'is not an essential question, seeing that vulval penetration is all that is necessary to constitute the offence of rape; and this may not be effected without destruction of signs of virginity' (1918: 261).[23] The 1918 edition maintains that 'as a general rule, when sexual intercourse takes place, the hymen is lacerated or ruptured. ... if however the aperture in the hymen is larger than usual or membrane itself be lax, repeated intercourse may take place without rupture or even laceration' (Lyon 1918: 262).

In the nineteenth century, we find that 'anatomical examination became more detailed ... the forms of the hymen, in particular, were definitely classified and sketched in the treatises in their labial, diaphlagmatic, half moon and annular versions' (Vigarello 2001: 142).[24] Not only do we find a taxonomy of different kinds of hymen—some normal and others pathological—but we also find that references to the medico-legal technique of inserting glass pipettes, measuring cones, and two fingers into the vagina. For instance, detailing how the medical examination of the victim should be conducted, the 1918 edition of Lyon's medical jurisprudence cites a case:

> [I]n 1901 a girl, aged 10, and her mother charged a wealthy old man with the rape of the former, and with infecting her with gonorrhoea. She was brought by the police for examination, by Dr A. Powell, three days after the alleged rape. The child is in a poor condition and very dirty. There is a slight muco-purulent discharge from the vulva and the vagina. The hymen is slightly swollen, of normal colour, circular with mesial oval opening. There is no tear or abrasion. The opening will not admit a 1/3 inch glass rod without tearing or duly stretching. (Lyon 1918: 302–3)

In this case, the child was found to be in poor hygienic condition and the charge, false. The insertion of glass rods, cones, pipettes, or fingers into the vagina of the raped survivor may be thought of as an early and enduring form of truth-technology (Lyon 1918; Modi 1922). This truth-technology was introduced in colonial India in the late nineteenth century along with newer forms such as 'criminal photography, fingerprinting and blood—and semen-stain analysis', which 'became increasingly significant in a wide variety of colonial criminal prosecutions and especially critical in rape cases' (Kolsky

2010: 112, see also Pinney 1998; Sengoopta 2003; Singha 2000a; 2000b).

THE TWO-FINGER TEST AS A MEDICO-LEGAL TECHNIQUE

Following Rabinow (1996), who has pointed out that the intensification of power-as-knowledge results from the shift from modelling culture on nature to the re-making of nature into a legal artefact through technique,[25] I argue that the hymen acts as a sign of the occurrence of rape retrospectively after the technique is deployed on the body. How is the woman's body re-made into a legal artifice through medical techniques? The elaboration of the two-finger test is found in the sixth edition of Modi's textbook, which was well established by 1940.[26] He says:

> In cases where the hymen is intact and not lacerated, it is necessary to note the distensibility of the vaginal orifice. The possibility of sexual intercourse having taken place without rupturing the hymen may be inferred, if the vaginal orifice is big enough to admit easily the passage of two fingers. In virgins under 14 years of age the vaginal orifice is so small that it will hardly allow the passage of one little finger through the hymen. (Modi 1940: 337)

Similarly, the 2002 edition of Modi holds:

> In cases where the hymen is intact and not lacerated, it is absolutely necessary to note the distensibility of the vaginal orifice, in the number of fingers passing into the vagina without any difficulty. The possibility of sexual intercourse having taken place without rupturing the hymen may be inferred if the vaginal orifice is capricious enough to admit the passage of two fingers easily. (2002: 503)

In the 2002 edition, the validity of the two-finger test in relation to children and young girls is presented in the following terms:

> [T]he circumference of the hymen can also be measured by a measuring cone. A circumference of 9 to 10 cm is considered the least necessary for coitus. In girls below fourteen years of age, the vaginal orifice is usually so small that it will hardly allow the passage of the little finger through the hymen. It is often difficult to distinguish between an indentation in a fimbriated hymen and a tear, unless the hymen is stretched by a finger tip, glass rod or Brittan's hymenscope,

which also give excellent transillumination of hymen when a tear is found to extend up to the vaginal wall. (Modi 2002: 503)

Irrespective of the age of the victim, medical jurists continue to uphold the validity of the two-finger test since the presence of the hymen is no longer considered a reliable indicator of virginity. Modi's 1969 edition promulgates the necessity for medical experts to determine the difference between a 'true' and 'false' virgin, since the hymen as a 'particular anatomical structure' was no longer considered an absolute proof of virginity.[27] Nature no longer provided a foolproof way of ascertaining virginity.[28] I quote:

It is seen that the presence of an intact hymen is not an absolute sign of virginity. With an intact hymen there are true virgins and false virgins. The necessary points for distinguishing between the two are as follows: If in a woman with an intact hymen, the edges of the membranes are distinct and regular, with an orifice of small dimension, which allows the terminal phalanx of a finger to penetrate and the hymen is well stretched, all the presumptions are in favour of non-penetration of the penis into the vagina. On the other hand, if in a woman who has an intact hymen, the hymeneal orifice lets one, two or more fingers easily, if the hymen is relaxed as to undulate and allow itself to be depressed, one can conclude that the woman can most certainly be a virgin, *but also that a body of the size of the penis in erection could perfectly well pass through the hymeneal orifice without rupturing it once or several times.* A true virgin or a false virgin, both are possible and one cannot be certain of either nor can one express such certainty. (1969: 319, also see Modi 1972: 305, emphasis added)

The passages cited above in the different editions of Modi's textbooks are reproduced from Thoinot's *Medico-legal Aspects of Moral Offences*, first published in French in 1898:

With an intact hymen there are true virgins and false virgins. How shall we distinguish them? Here are the necessary points in this respect:
   If, in a woman with an intact hymen, you find the edges of the membrane *distinct* and *regular*, with an *orifice of small dimensions*, which scarcely allows the extremity of the finger to penetrate; if, when the thighs are separated, the hymen is well stretched, *all the presumptions are in favour of a true virginity*, or, to express it better and not go beyond what ought to be stated, *all the presumptions are in favour of a non-penetration of the penis into the vagina.*

On the other hand, if, in a woman who has an intact hymen, the hymenial orifice lets one, two or more fingers pass through easily; if the hymen is relaxed in such a way as to undulate and allow itself to be depressed easily, you will conclude that the woman can most certainly be a virgin, but *also that a body of the size of the penis in erection could perfectly well pass through the hymeneal orifice without rupturing it, once or several times.* A true virgin or a false virgin, both are possible, and you cannot be certain of either, nor can you express such certainty. (1911: 55, emphasis in original)

It is stunning that the 1969 edition of Modi repeats Thoinot almost verbatim, as if repetition itself produces its own truths.

The two-finger test replaces the older notion that the presence or absence of the hymen can by itself signify virginity. It is technique that verifies whether the hymen is broken or not, and whether it is distensible or not. The relationship that is drawn between the clinical two-finger test and the erect penis is one of mimesis. The line between the two-finger test (as if it were a surgical procedure) and assault is a thin one, determined by whether the medical examination carried out with or without the consent of the patient, consent which she can only withhold at the risk of being presumed to be a liar. Lyon cautioned:

[A]s neither the complainant nor accused can be compelled by a Magistrate by anyone else to submit being examined (without being guilty of and running the risk of a charge for indecent assault), the medical man must invariably, and in the presence of witnesses, obtain the consent of the person in question to make the examination, and at the same time caution the persons that the results of the examination may be used as evidence against them. Where the victim is under age, the consent of nearest guardian should be asked. If a woman refuses to be examined it is probable that no rape has been committed. (1918: 295–6)

Consent, obtained under these straitened circumstances, then converts an assault into a medical test. That medical jurists have been aware of this mimesis is revealed in their emphatic recommendation that doctors secure the patient's consent for this test. Modi cautions that a rape victim:

[s]hould never be examined without her written consent taken in the presence of a witness if she is of and over 12 years of age and is capable of understanding the nature and implication of the examination, or

without the written consent of her parent or guardians if she under the age of 12 years or a feeble minded person. The examination of a female without her consent is regarded in law as an assault. It must be remembered that the police court has no power of compelling a woman to submit the private parts of her person to the examination of a medical man. (1940: 336)

Consent is an empty category from the point of view of the woman. It separates technique, the 'doing' of law, from sexual assault. The penetrative practice of clinicians escapes a charge of violence precisely because it is signified under another domain of scientific rationality sanctified by the state. State-sponsored medical jurisprudence invents such a clinical test precisely because it measures injury against itself, rather than injury to the victim. The object of diagnosis here is not the harm caused to the survivor of rape but how society is injured by the act of rape.

THE *HABITUÉ* IN INDIAN COURTS

So far we have concluded that while the natural state of the hymen is not reliable, it is technique which allows for a verification of the actual by substituting the penis with two fingers. In other words, the hymen can signify whether women are habituated to sex or not only after the technique is deployed on the patient's body. The word 'habituated' lies in the realm of interpretation, deriving its meaning from the medico-legal domain, for the word does not appear in any statute. The figure of the *habitué* is thus a product of technique, used to medicalize consent. Appellate courts routinely infuse life into the fiction of the *habitué* (HRW Report 2010).

The category 'habituated to sex' is not new to medical jurisprudence in India. It proliferates in medico-legal discourse from Chevers to Lyon. In one of his cases, Chevers concluded that although the woman's hymen was absent, presumably due to causes of diseases or other reasons apart from sex, the vaginal canal was narrow, indicating that 'she had not been habituated to sexual intercourse' (1856: 485). In the 10th edition of *Lyon's Medical Jurisprudence with Illustrative Cases*, we are told that 'closely apposed labia, even when the abduction of the thighs is extreme, indicate that the person is not habituated to intercourse' (1953: 445). The absorption of this category into legal discourse marks the beginnings of the medicalization of consent, since it now became possible to read alleged past sexual histories from medico-legal certificates.

In colonial courts, Kolsky notes,

> [B]etween 1904, when the Criminal Law Journal began recording all criminal cases reported by the High and Chief Courts, and 1947, there are seventy-five reported rape trials. In these cases, the high courts confirmed 37 per cent of the lower courts' convictions and either acquitted or reduced the sentences of defendants in the remaining 63 per cent of cases ... The high rate of reversal of convictions upon appeal may well be attributable to the fact that the colonial high courts established strict evidentiary requirements that made the truthfulness of a woman's charge dependent on a host of corroborating factors. By the 1920s, corroboration of a rape charge was recognised as a 'general rule' in the high courts. (2010: 115–6)

She further identifies 'four kinds of corroborating evidence' as 'central to high court case outcomes during the period under review. These were: class and caste status; prior sexual history; fresh complaint (the prompt lodging of a charge); and evidence of resistance on the body evidencing the crime' (2010: 116). It is not surprising to find that the figure of the *habitué* animates legal records during this period. *Garab Singh Gond* v. *Emperor*[29] observed that 'in November 1926 [P] was thirteen years and seven months old, but the Civil Surgeon, who examined her in connexion with this case, found that "the hymen had been ruptured long ago" and said: "the parts were so well developed that I think that the girl is used to sexual intercourse"'.[30] In *Siraj-ud-Din* v. *Emperor*,[31] the Lahore High Court observed that the hymen had 'old ruptures', thereby marking the distinction between old and fresh tears. How may we then read the intersection of law and medicine in rape trials today?

In the immediate aftermath of the partition, we find that the contestation between law and medicine was pronounced. *Anam Swain and Others* v. *State*[32] was an appeal in a gangrape case at a time when the jury system was still not abolished in India. The jury tried the charge against four men who were accused of the rape of a fifteen-year-old girl on 12 December 1951 in the village of Patkura (P.S. Tikhri) of Cuttack District. Upon hearing the evidence, the jury convicted the accused. However, the sessions judge recommended that the unanimous verdict of guilty returned by the jury in the rape case be set aside. One of the grounds cited in this reference was that the victim's testimony was unreliable and not corroborated by medical evidence, for 'the medical evidence was clear that such intercourse might have been as much with her consent as without her consent'.[33] Setting aside the reference, the high court said:

> The learned judge failed to see that no medical man could give any opinion as to whether sexual intercourse was made with consent or not. It was for the Jury to see, having regard for the circumstances and the evidence of the girl, whether she consented to the intercourse. This confusion appears to have been mainly responsible for the difference of opinion between the judge and the jury.[34]

The Orissa High Court, in its insistence that medical evidence could only be read in relation to the circumstances surrounding the particular case, argued against accepting the medicalization of consent by the session judge. To insist otherwise would imply that women who had been raped in the past would never be able to testify to the present.

Time and again judges have held that it is not the task of the medical expert to determine rape. Emphasizing the contention about the centrality of medicine in a criminal trial, courts have held that:

> [R]ape is a crime and not a medical condition … a legal term and not a diagnosis to be made by a medical officer … Medical opinion is only one amongst many bits of corroborative evidence to be weighed in deciding the case. Any conclusion on rape is not to be made by doctor or police. It is for the Judge to decide.[35]

It would be accurate to suggest that the nature and scope of medicalization of consent and falsity has expanded in rape trials. Today, the categories 'habituated', 'habitual', and 'used to sexual intercourse' continue to appear in appellate judgments and animate legal discourse in trial courts. The finding that a woman is habituated to sexual intercourse has been predominantly deployed to establish consent, subverting the legislative changes enacted after 1983.

TRUE VIRGINS AND LYING *HABITUÉS*

In rape trials today, the sexualization of women's bodies continues even though the past sexual history clause has been removed. In

2008, a woman who had been subjected to child marriage and thereafter deserted by her husband without consummating the marriage (*gauna*) filed a complaint of rape. The Madhya Pradesh High Court held that 'the Doctor ... has, however, opined that the prosecutrix was so habituated to sexual intercourse that it was not possible to ascertain as to when she had last been subjected to it'.[36] This excited declaration of extreme habituation, which makes medical determination of the last time the victim had sex impossible, is used to discredit the victim as a reliable witness. In a 2007 case, the Supreme Court acquitted the accused and observed that:

> [T]here was no injury on the body of the prosecutrix [A]. There was no sign of semen on the private part of the body. Neither her clothes were torn nor there was any presence of hair of the accused on the private part of the prosecutrix. The doctor after examining the prosecutrix deposed that the girl was habituated to sexual intercourse. In view of this evidence, we are of the opinion that the High Court as well as the Trial Court has not correctly appreciated the evidence and has wrongly convicted the accused-appellant. The accused who has been charged under Section 376 read with Section 511 IPC is entitled to benefit of doubt.[37]

In 2009, the Supreme Court set aside the conviction of the accused on the grounds that 'the prosecutrix appears to be a lady used to sexual intercourse and a dissolute lady. She had no objection in mixing up and having free movement with any of her known person [*sic*], for enjoyment. Thus, she appeared to be a woman of easy virtues'.[38] The *habitué* is thus characterized as loose, dissolute, and untruthful.

Equally, corroboration of virginity measured by hymeneal injuries remains a critical element in a conviction. In 2007, in *State of Rajasthan* v. *Munshi*, the court observed that 'the fact that the hymen was freshly ruptured and the vagina could take only one finger with difficulty shows that [RK] was not habituated to sexual intercourse and had been subjected to intercourse against her will more particularly as in a case of consent her underwear would not have been found to have been torn'.[39] Similarly, in 2008, the Aurangabad Bench of the Bombay High Court held that 'the version of the prosecutrix stands corroborated inasmuch as the hymen was found ruptured. Nowhere it is suggested by the defence that the prosecutrix was habituated to sexual intercourse. The medical evidence and version of the prosecutrix show, therefore, that she was virgin before the incident in question'.[40] Here, hymeneal injuries signify that the raped woman was not habituated to sex. The raped woman is positioned as a 'true' virgin in opposition to a lying *habitué*.

OF DUBIOUS CHARACTER: PRESUMPTION OF (LACK OF) CONSENT

We may recall that the amended law in 1983 held that in aggravated rape cases, such as gangrape or rape of pregnant women, when sexual intercourse is proven it would be presumed that the victim did not consent, unless the defence could prove consent, under s. 114 A of the Indian Evidence Act. I suggest that following the enactment of s. 114 A of the Indian Evidence Act, the reliance and centrality of the two-finger test has increased. The cases cited below show that the reversal of the burden of proof is successfully subverted since the manner in which medico-legal certificates are written provide grounds for the accused to establish consensual sex and not rape.

In 2004, *Revella Sivaiah* v. *State of AP*, convicting the accused for having raped a pregnant woman, noted that the medico-legal certificate declared that the vagina admitted '3 fingers loosely'.[41] The court did not pause to question why it was necessary to subject a married and pregnant woman who has been raped to the three-finger test in the first place. In 1986, hearing an appeal in a case of gangrape brought by a nineteen-year-old domestic worker, the Bombay High Court held:

> Thus when she was examined by Medical Officer he found an *old tear of hymen* and which according to the Medical Officer had not come into existence recently. ... He has also accepted that orifice permitted an insertion of two fingers and which again is a criteria to suggest that the girl was used to sexual intercourse. ... This is to be read in the context of positive assertion of the girl that it was her first experience when she was subjected to forcible intercourse meaning thereby that according to her she had no sexual intercourse previously at all. ... This is again to be read in the context of defence suggestion that the girl was habituated to sexual intercourse and was of dubious character and that is how the father was fade [*sic*, fed] up with her and that is how again she was forced to abandon father's house.[42]

An old hymeneal tear was taken to mean a past sexual history. This reading of old hymeneal tears as proof of habituation is haunted by Taylor, who said that the absence of a hymen does not provide proof of rape 'unless we find traces of its having been recently torn by violence' (1865: 993). The division between old tears and freshly torn hymeneal tears continues to act as a classificatory practice that separates the lying *habitué* from the raped virgin.[43] Similarly, *Kishania* v. *State of Rajasthan* pronounced an acquittal in a gangrape case while observing that the victim 'is an unmarried girl and the fact that her hymen had old tears and she was accustomed to sexual intercourse shows that she was a girl of easy virtues and scant reliance can be placed upon her statement unless it inspires complete confidence and is corroborated by direct or circumstantial evidence'.[44] It is evident that old hymeneal tears are treated as proof of premarital sex and further deployed to presume consent.

The medico-legal certificate thus provides a means for the defence to bring in past sexual history. The rape survivor is discredited once she is established as a *habitué*. Although the reversal on the onus of proof in gangrape cases puts the burden on the accused to establish consensual sex, the medico-legal certificate helps the accused to assert consent rather than lack of consent. The victim's sexual history as stated in the medico-legal certificate forms the basis of the defence's refutation of the presumption of lack of consent. It is, therefore, not surprising to note the increased reliance by defence lawyers on medical evidence. This trend continues in more recent judgments.

Such reliance is marked in *The Public Prosecutor* v. *Yejjala Ramaswamy*,[45] an appeal which resulted in the acquittal of the accused for having raped a pregnant midwife in her home. The medico-legal certificate recorded that the vagina admitted two fingers, confirmed the presence of spermatozoa and certified that the victim was five months pregnant at the time. The certificate stated that the victim was 'habituated to sexual intercourse' and that there was 'evidence of intercourse'.[46] The court held that 'the medical evidence does not show any injuries either on the private parts or notable injuries worth mentioning on the person of P.W. 1 to suggest the offering of resistance in any way during the alleged act of having sexual intercourse'.[47] This 2004 judgment is startling in its reliance on two infamous judgments that provoked protests—*Tukaram* v. *The State of Maharashtra*[48] and *Pratap Misra* v. *State of Orissa*[49]—to argue that there should have been marks of injury if the woman did not consent.

The court argued that as a midwife the victim would have resisted rape, knowing rape could lead to abortion. Surprisingly, the court held that 'it is not for the accused to take a specific stand of consent and the consent may be inferred from the facts and circumstances of the case also'.[50] This suggests that not only is the medico-legal certificate read to characterize a pregnant woman as a *habitué* and therefore a consenting subject, but further, it is also not incumbent on the accused to make the plea that it was consensual sex, not rape. Instead, the court reads the medico-legal certificate as providing evidence of consent without the defence specifically taking such a stand.

FLUIDS AND LIES

It is startling to encounter early colonial standards of proof which maintained that evidence of seminal discharge is necessary to constitute 'complete penetration' in judicial pronouncements even after the 1983 rape law amendment (see Clark 1987). The suspicion of adult women who are viewed as being in the habit of framing their lovers is found in *State of Rajasthan* v. *Hem Raj* (1986). In this case, the court acquitted the accused and declared that the married rape survivor was habituated to sex. The court held further that:

> If actually she has been forcibly raped, she should have raised hue and cry even during the time when she was being forcibly raped by the accused. Later she has stated that she did try to shout when she was forcibly raped by the accused but the accused put his hand on her mouth and thereby he muffled her voice. That explanation does not appear to be credible. Moreover, *it appears that she has enjoyed the cohabitation because she too discharged with accused.*[51]

The sexualization of the woman's body follows a standardized phallocentric imagination, which constructs a fantasy about the *habitué* as a pleasure-seeking, illicit body. To this imagination, it is necessary to perform the two-finger test on a married and menstruating *habitué*. The clinical impression that the victim 'also discharged with the accused' constructs women's sexuality 'as separate from women themselves' (Smart 1989: 30). The court assumes that 'women can enjoy sex "inspite of themselves" so this sexuality over which they have charge is constructed as essence which can bypass consciousness or which has a will of its own' (Smart 1989: 30).

As recently as 2007, the Bombay High Court accepted the defence argument that if a married woman testifies that there was 'complete penetration' then the accused ought to have ejaculated and leave forensic traces of semen. The court not finding any trace of spermatozoa was indignant and held, 'PW 1 ... is a married woman. She is used to, and is experienced in sexual acts. She did not face sexual act first time when the accused raped her. When she has described in First Information Report that the accused did act of complete sexual intercourse, it includes ordinarily the ejaculation and passing of semen.'[52]

The lying *habitué*, we are told, should have known that men ejaculate when they have 'complete' sex. The use of complete penetration as a diagnostic category reduces rape to a measurement of the degree and nature of penile penetration. An astonished court admonished the sexually experienced *habitué* for not knowing that seminal fluids, not her testimony, furnish proof of rape.

ALL *HABITUÉS* ARE NOT LIARS

If the fiction of a lying *habitué* organizes judicial interpretation, we also find judgments which hold that the clinical finding of a *habitué* does not lead to presumption of consent. These judgments do not reflect on the legality of the technique that produces the fiction of the *habitué* nor do they question use of the category of 'habituated'. The following judgments categorically assert that *habitués* are not liars, but none of them question the validity of the two-finger test. In *State of Punjab* v. *Ramdev Singh*,[53] the Supreme Court held that 'mere statement that according to doctor, victim's vagina admitted two fingers and she could on earlier occasions have had sexual intercourse five, ten or fifteen times rules out rape by accused once as alleged in no way casts doubt on victim's evidence'.[54] Further, the Supreme Court held:

> [A]nother factor which seems to have weighed with the High Court is the evidence of doctor ... that there were signs of previous sexual

intercourse on the victim. That cannot, by stretch of imagination, as noted above, be a ground to acquit an alleged rapist. Even assuming that the victim was previously accustomed sexual intercourse, that is not a determinative question. ... It is the accused who was on trial and not the victim. Even if the victim in a given case has been promiscuous in her sexual behavior earlier, she has a right to refuse to submit herself to sexual intercourse to anyone and everyone because she is not a vulnerable object or prey for being sexually assaulted by anyone and everyone.[55]

Vijay @ Chinee v. *State of Madhya Pradesh*,[56] a case about a young woman who was gangraped in Jabalpur district in 1988, records the medical expert's refusal to signify the findings of the two-finger test as presumption of habituation.

Dr Rupa Lalwani (PW-3) had stated that hymen of the prosecutrix was found completely torn and fresh blood was oozing out of it and she further opined that the vagina of a girl becomes loose even after one intercourse and two fingers can easily enter into her vagina. *She had further opined that loosening of vagina and entering two fingers into vagina of a girl cannot give presumption that the girl was habituated to sexual intercourse.*[57]

In this case, Justices P. Sathasivam and BS Chauhan further observed that:

[U]nder Section 114A of the Indian Evidence Act, 1872, which was inserted by way of amendment in the year 1988, there is a clear and specific provision that where sexual intercourse by the accused is proved and the question is whether it was without the consent of the woman alleged to have been raped, and she states in her evidence before the court that she did not consent, the court shall presume that she did not consent ... the prosecutrix had been consistent throughout in her statement that intercourse was against her wishes and that there was no consent as she had forcibly been caught and threatened and thereafter, she had been subjected to gang rape.[58]

While *Vijay @ Chinee* v. *State of Madhya Pradesh* points out correctly that the medico-legal certificate cannot give rise to the presumption of habituation, it does not question why the two-finger test is performed on each woman irrespective of her age, sexual, medical, or reproductive biography.

The answer is offered directly in a medico-legal certificate issued after a Dalit woman was brutally gangraped in Orissa (also cited in Chapter 6). In *Fanibhushan Behera, Jeet Shankar Bohidar and Dinabandhu Behera* v. *State of Orissa*, the medical expert testified that the following findings had been recorded:

1. There was no external injury on the body of the victim.
2. The hymen was not ruptured.
3. He could not give an expert opinion on whether the vaginal orifice was big enough.
4. He could insert his fingers into the victim's vagina up to two and half inches, and therefore *he could not rule out the possibility of a young man's penis entering into the vagina up to that extent.* His expert testimony was that no injury was caused to the girl when he inserted two fingers in the girl's vagina.
5. While he accepted the suggestion that medical opinion on the nature of vaginal injury depends on the nature of the hymen, extent of penetration, force used and size of the genital organs, he did not agree with the suggestion that the hymen is usually lacerated in the case of virgins.[59]

As a good student of Modi (1969, 1940) and therefore, Thoinot (1911), the doctor testified that the two-finger test mimics penile penetration and that a raped virgin's hymen need not be lacerated. The defence's suggestion that the doctor could have lacerated the hymen during the clinical examination betrays the public secret that a gynaecological examination cannot really prove habituation and the two-finger is state-sanctioned assault.

'THE RIGHT WORD SHOULD BE FOUND IN MEDICAL JURISPRUDENCE'

The use of the term 'habituated' prejudices the pre-trial proceeding. The medico-legal certificate comes to substitute the raped woman or child, since she need not be present in the court for her biography to be subjected to a sexualized reading. The naming of the *habitué* through the writing of the medico-legal certificate or in the judgment stigmatizes retrospectively. Yet prosecutors and defence lawyers know that categories like habituated are technical terms that do not exist in the realm of experience. For instance, in the words of Mr Mehta, a defence lawyer who had been practicing criminal law for over ten years in the trial court:

> Doctors give the certificate saying no sign of injury and write that she is habituated. The advantage of this goes to the accused. For an unmarried girl doctors write habituated. Habituated is an insulting word. It insults the woman. The right word should be found in medical jurisprudence. In reality, she would not be habituated—there may be other reasons.

Alternatively, as the APP said to me, 'the doctor gives evidence that she is habituated but intercourse may not have happened at all.' The prosecutor knew that the court feigns ignorance of the fact that habituated is a word that insults, and as a performative, it wounds.

While everyday legal discourse on rape in the courtroom breathes life into the figure of the *habitué*, medical experts deploy the category not merely in the courtroom or hospital but also in the morgue. Is 'habituated to sex' a clinical category? I posed this question to Dr B, a well-known forensic expert, his colleague Dr S, and Dr D, a student and researcher, at the V.S. Hospital in Ahmedabad.

> Dr B: I think no medical certificate will have that word. They will use 'used to sexual intercourse'. I think the term habitual partner is used in the Northern parts of the country even in medical certificates. That means the hymen is torn because of multiple sexual acts, consensual acts.
>
> PB: How reliable is the two-finger test?
>
> Dr B: It is not reliable. If she is habitual—habitual means she is married having regular relation [*sic*] with her husband, then whose semen it is cannot be verified. Supposing no injuries and is married, how can you prove it? It becomes very difficult to prove. Now change has come with the introduction of DNA. If there is a consented [*sic*] partner and an unconsented [*sic*] partner and if both have ejaculated then both the semen can be separated. That will take time.

Note that 'habitual' refers to women who are in the *habit of having sex* in marriage.

> PB: Don't unmarried women have sex in India?
>
> Dr B: In our society we are inhibited. In general, there is inhibition. We do not have sexual expression ... a girl usually has regular sex with

her married partner only—at least in most of the cases. Liberalization is slowly coming up. That's another area that we are working on now. We invariably do a genital examination of girls who commit suicide. Young girls who commit suicide for trifle reasons [*sic*]. To our surprise, we are getting some results. An eleventh standard girl had signs of regular sexual intercourse. It is very common. These girls hail from prestigious families and go to prestigious schools. We do this examination for academic reasons.

Dr D: We do not write these findings because these are embarrassing to the parents. There is already one trauma—the trauma of death. We do not want to increase that trauma into trauma of something else because these findings are our findings. We just avoid.

PB: What if she had been raped? Or, raped and blackmailed?

Dr B: We do not go into that detail.

PB: You use the category of 'used to sexual intercourse' but what is the way of ascertaining whether that was rape or not?

Dr D: If the girl is living then you can make out. After the girl is dead, who is going to say? Only God and that girl will know whether she was habituated or not.

Dr B: See our books say that these are the signs of virginity we always say that it is only the woman who knows whether she is a virgin or not. There is nothing by which you can say that she was virgin even if she has an intact hymen. If she has an intact hymen, hymen is elastic and permeable she can have sex with intact hymen.

Dr D: If hymen is there you cannot say she is a virgin and without hymen also you cannot say she is a virgin.

PB: Surely the two-finger test cannot discern whether the hymen was broken for other reasons?

Dr B: When a medical examination is done for this purpose, what is seen is whether the injury is fresh or not. If the allegation is old, then the difficulty persists.

PB: Because one assumes that habitual means habitual to heterosexual sex. Is this not technically misleading?

Dr B: The inference is that the hymen is broken.

Dr D: Only she can tell.

Dr B: Hymen can be broken for a number of reasons.

Dr D: Yes, the most common way of breaking hymen is when riding a cycle.[60]

The cadaver is analysed to bear signs of 'regular sexual intercourse', which are recorded and naturalized as evidence of an illicit sexual affair. Yet the 'research' is unable to tell us if the suicide followed continual sexual abuse and whether this is converted into a narrative of premarital sex. The slippage between the findings of the two-finger test and the characterization of the findings as 'habituated to sex' illustrates the attempt to translate and normalize moral categories into clinical categories. Hence, we are asked to believe that a *habitué* experiences frequent (hetero-) sexual intercourse and this sexual intercourse must be consensual. This complex transcription between body and discourse through technique describes the medicalization of consent. It reduces female biography to the production of a sexual history, available by reading the vagina as archiving the past for a possible reading in the future on a clinician's table.

Politics of 'Penistration'

I now describe the way the medico-legal textbook imparts structure to testimony. Below, I analyse the testimony of the gynaecologist who treated Noornissa, a child who was raped by her stepfather when she was ten years old (see Chapter 3). In the ethnographic vignettes that follow, I juxtapose excerpts from recent editions of Modi's textbook with excerpts from Dr Kadam's testimony, the gynaecologist who verified the injuries of rape inflicted on Noornissa.[61] I argue that medico-legal categories are treated as if these exist in the experience of the rape survivor. I maintain that underlying the statutory rape provision is an inherent anxiety that finds a clear expression when statutory rape is translated as 'technical rape'. Hence, Noor was constructed as a child-adult capable of inflicting injuries on her own body.[62]

I begin with an account of the prosecution's examination of the medical expert. The prosecution brought forth the case history narrated to the doctor by the patient. Following this the gynaecologist testified that Noornissa had suffered a number of injuries. Dr Kadam testified that he found a 7 × 1 × 1 cm abrasion on her chin, a bruise on the left side of her nose, a bruise on her right side of her breast, a 4 × 2 cm long bruise on her left hand and many long and thin scratches on both sides of her thighs. He testified that there was a

1 cm deep laceration in the six o'clock direction on her fourcette and on the left labia minora was a one-centimetre long cut wound. He testified that Noor could not be older than fourteen years at that time of the crime. Dr Kadam (referred to as Dr in the excerpts below) testified in Gujarati and English. The excerpts from the textbooks cited alongside excerpts of court proceedings illustrate how medico-legal norms frame courtroom talk. Consider the following excerpts from the examination-in-chief, which the defence lawyer constantly interrupted.

APP: In case of a girl of tender years the inner part (*referring to the hymen*) is higher—is that right?

Dr: Yes, it is higher.

DL (*interrupts*): The inner part.

Dr: I am saying that.[63]

J (d): In the case of a small girl the hymen (*yoni patal*) in the inner part is higher.

> The hymen is deeply situated, and as the vagina is very small, it is impossible for the penetration of the adult organ to take place. Usually the penis is placed either within the vulva or between the thighs. (Reddy 1990:298, also see Modi 1922, 2002)

If the law is clear that vulval injury is sufficient to establish the fact of rape, then why is it important that the hymen is deeply situated in the case of children? I argue that underlying this line of questioning is the assumption that a virile and young man should ordinarily be able to destroy the membrane. Taylor states:

In the case of an *old man or of weak virile power*, vulval intercourse might be had without destroying the membrane; but such a case could have only been decided by the special circumstances, which accompanied it. The presence of an unruptured hymen affords a presumptive but not an absolute proof that a woman is a virgin; and if of the ordinary size and shape, and in the ordinary situation, it shows clearly that although attempts at intercourse may have been made, there can have been no vaginal penetration (1866: 610, emphasis added).

I wish to draw attention to two important points from the excerpt cited above. First, when the child's body is distinguished from an adult body, it is read from the standpoint of ascertaining whether it is possible to penetrate the vagina without causing severe damage to or breaking the hymen. Second, the underlying assumption is that ordinarily a young and virile man would be able to destroy the hymeneal membrane. The defence sought to establish that Noor was not a child of 'tender years' and as a young and virile man, Shakeel, the accused, could not have raped her without destroying her hymen.

Consider the set of questions that followed as the examination-in-chief continued. In this excerpt, the defence lawyer attempted to characterize the doctor as unprofessional, embarrasing him for not being explicit enough. The words in italics were spoken in English.

APP: The injury in the *fourcette* and *labia minora* has happened due to *partial penetration*.

DL *interrupts*: (the answer was inaudible to me, hereafter inaudible.)

APP: He is shy? Why should doctor [feel shy]? *Penetration* and?

J *to* DL: Say, say, don't feel shy.

APP: Attempt.

DL: Attempt that is *penetration*.

J *to* DL: What is Gujarati for *penistration* (*pronounced in court and spelt as such in the Gujarati transcript*)?

DL: Due to *penetration* (*correcting the pronunciation*).

J (d): The injury on Noornissa's vagina (*yoni*) on seeing that according to my experience the injury is caused by the entry of the penis into her vagina and due to *penistration*.

We find here a slippage between penetration and 'penistration'—the latter combining into a singular category the meaning encased in the concept of penile penetration. The question about how to translate penetration in Gujarati is important. In the excerpt above, the word 'penetration', pronounced and spelt as 'penistration', is retained in the court transcript. I emphasize this usage since it vividly communicates how rape is defined in legal discourse. When penetration is translated in Gujarati, words like 'entry' and 'insertion' are used interchangeably. The objective is to establish that injury was caused due to the entry or insertion of the penis into the vagina. The language that translates penetration into the legal vernacular does not embody the idea that such an act is violent. It concentrates on the idea of entry (by 'penistration'), where lack of consent then is technically assumed.

The examination-in-chief continued to determine medical opinion on whether the hymen of a child who has been raped could remain intact. Note here the confusion between the judge, prosecutor, and the defence lawyer about which body part the question alludes to.

APP: *Aye*, Doctor, supposing there is partial penetration in vulva then can the hymen remain intact? If there is injury on the fourcette, can the hymen remain intact?

J: Which part?

APP: Hymen.

Dr: Hymen.

J: No, no. Hymen is intact.

Dr: Fourcette, labia majora?

J (d): If the penis (*ling*) enters partially then there can be injury on the vagina's fourcette and labia minora part and despite that the hymen can remain intact (*akhband*).

To constitute the offence of rape, it is not necessary that there should be complete penetration of penis with emission of semen and rupture of hymen. Partial penetration of the penis within the Labia majora or the vulva or pudenda, with or without emission of semen, or even attempt at penetration is quite sufficient for the purpose of law. It is therefore quite possible to commit legally, the offence of rape without producing any injury to the genitals or leaving any seminal stains. Rape is a crime and not a medical condition. Rape is a legal term and not a diagnosis to be made by the medical officer treating the victim. The only statement that can be made by the medical officer is to the effect whether there is evidence of recent sexual activity. Whether the rape has occurred or not is a legal conclusion, not a medical one. (Modi 2002: 495)

The medical expert's testimony defines partial penetration as vulval injury caused by forcible penile penetration and the presence of a wholly closed hymen. The experience of rape is translated as what the penis does to the vagina. It penetrates the vagina forcibly, leaving marks of injury, yet it is partial, for the hymen—which according to the medico-legal textbooks is situated higher in children compared to pre-adolescent girls—is not destroyed.[64]

The density of the category of partial penetration is not immediately apparent unless we refer to Noor's testimony during the cross-examination. Here, we learn that the category of partial penetration does not describe the experience of rape. Yet, the defence lawyer who subjected Noornissa to repeated questions asking her how she 'knew' that the accused had fully penetrated her, converted the medico-legal category into an 'experiential' category. I cite an excerpt here from Noor's testimony, which will be fully examined in the next chapter.

> DL: Look here you were lying down, then what did he do, how much did he do that you do not know. How much did he put his place of urination, half-full?
>
> N: Full (*akhi*).
>
> DL: How did you see, you were saying that you were lying down then how did you come to know?
>
> N: Blood came out.
>
> J: He inserted that's why blood came out?
>
> N: Yes.
>
> DL: How do you know that he had inserted?
>
> N (*quiet initially*): Because he penetrated me, that's why.

The word partial means unfinished, incomplete, limited, and half-done. It also means biased, one-sided, unfair, and inequitable. The category of partial penetration is translated here as placing half of the penis in the vagina. We have seen that partial penetration may mean that the penis has not been able to damage the hymen but nowhere is the suggestion made that partial penetration must be calculated in proportion to how much a penis penetrates a vagina. Yet questions about how deeply the vagina is penetrated animate the trial. In the phallocentric translation of the category of partial penetration as 'half' or 'full' penetration, the defence tries to introduce doubt that Noor did not actually know if she had been raped. Noor's insistence that she experienced full penetration is questioned over and over again.

From Noor, we learn that partial penetration is *not* an experiential category. Yet, the defence translates it as such. The defence lawyer, 'by his power to raise and enforce topics', leads Noor to accept the assumption that full or half penetration is relevant to the true testimony to her experience of rape (Taslitz 1999: 83), such that she has to insist that she *knew* that she was fully penetrated, showing how 'the rape trial silences and discredits the complainant's voice, using medical and legal discourses to distort their testimony' (Lees 1997: 84). The politics of 'penistration' encodes statutory rape as 'technical rape' in the defence lawyer's attempts to deny that Noornissa is a child, as we will see subsequently.

TECHNICAL RAPE

It bears repetition that 'technical rape' is a term used by lawyers to refer to statutory rape. The anxiety produced by the category of technical rape may be traced back to the construction of female children as seductive. According to Taylor, 'It may be observed, that the consent of the female does not excuse or alter the nature of the crime where she is under ten years of age, since consent at this period of life is invalid; and the carnal knowledge of the female is rape in law. Even the solicitation of the child does not excuse it' (1845: 458).

We are told that no matter what provocation the solicitation of a child may cause, it is the law that deems such expressions of consent invalid. I argue that the characterization of statutory rape as technical rape is not a simple matter of the use of folk categories in law. Rather, it masks the construction of the child as provocative and seductive to uphold the view that child witness is not actually a child, thus making a gesture towards the desires of the provoked. Moreover, the twin categories of false cases and self-inflicted injuries as a medico-legal norm naturalize the idea that it is possible to read signs of falsity from the feminine body. I show the centrality of these arguments by detailing the cross-examination of the expert witness below. I argue that the construction of the child as provocative and seductive underlies the defence argument that the child witness is not actually a child in a technical rape case.

Excerpt One illustrates the defence argument that Noor inflicted the external injuries on herself.

DL: Look here, injuries were ordinary. (*He reads out.*) Breast, hands, thighs, chin.

Dr: Chest/left arm, ordinary; Left thigh, multiple scratches, not ordinary.

The judge reads out the list of injuries from the medical report.

DL: If I do it myself then can I injure myself (*gestures*)? Judge explains the question.

To substantiate false charges, marks of violence are sometimes self-inflicted. Modi saw a young woman of twenty years alleged to have been raped by a man. She had several marks simulating scratches made with a kankar (pebble) on the forearms and chest, which could be wiped off by rubbing them with a piece of wet cloth. (Modi 2002: 502)

Dr: Multiple scratches are not possible, others are possible but multiple scratches are not possible.

J (d): It is true that the bruises on N's chin, the wound on her nose and bruise on the left side of her breast could have been self inflicted. It is not true that the multiple scratches on N's right and left thighs could have been self-inflicted.

Excerpt Two illustrates the defence argument that the internal injuries were superficial injuries. Note that the judge mediated the tension between the defence lawyer and the prosecutor in the exchange cited below.

DL: ...injury over labia majora; the skin had peeled?

Dr: No, there was a laceration ... in detail ... there was injury over the muscle.

APP: It had cut on the inside.

DL *to* APP: Do not speak.

J: I am asking.

Dr: The injury was more than the skin having been peeled off.

APP: It was in the muscle.

DL *to* APP: You hold your peace! Keep quiet!!

Dr: I did not answer well.

APP: You did not ask about the muscle.

J: I am asking.

APP: I did not cover it in the chief, that's why.

Dr *to* J: There was no CLW [cut long wound]—muscle too was injured. It is more than superficial, sir (*saheb*).

J (d): It is not true that on N's labia majora the skin had peeled off because of which there was injury but I am saying that the injury was more than the skin having been peeled off. And the injury extended to the muscle. Only the skin had not peeled off. And the injury was up to the muscle. It is not true that the aforesaid injury was not peeled off but I am saying that the aforesaid wound was peeled off and the muscle below the skin was also lacerated, which was more than superficial wounds.

Excerpt Three illustrates the defence argument that Noor had inflicted injury on her vagina by herself.

DL: Can she do it by herself, inflict the injury on herself by her nails?

Dr: No. She can cut herself superficially but inflict such wounds on herself—a child cannot do these.

DL: She is not a child (*balak*)!!

J (d): It is not true that the current matter is such that the injury could have been inflicted on the *labia minora* with nails. But I am saying that if nails inflict such injury then only the skin will peel and such deep injury cannot take place.

Excerpt Four illustrates the argument that the vaginal injury was caused due to the forcible insertion of a thumb.

DL: If thumb is inserted then?

Dr: No. I do not agree with you.

J (d): It is not true that the aforesaid injury on Noornissa's labia minora was such an injury that could have been caused by the insertion [*pravesh*] of a thumb.

Modi saw a case in which the father thrust his thumb forcibly into the vagina of his six-year-old daughter in order to bring a false charge of rape against his neighbour, who was his enemy and lacerated the posterior part of the vagina and the posterior commissure. (Modi 2002: 506)

Excerpt Five illustrates how an injury is differentiated from the psychological complications that follow rape.

DL: If there is no treatment then in this case can there be complications?

Dr: What complications?

DL: Greater bleeding, greater swelling.

Dr: Yes and psychological complications.

J: That depends on the person. Those [psychological complications] can happen even when according to her wishes [*iccha*], he is talking of injury.

Dr: There would be difficulty in passing urine, swelling on the vulva. Greater injury, person may also be in shock.

J (d): It is true that in this case on seeing the kind of injury on the vagina if there is no immediate treatment then other kinds of complication can take place. On the kinds of complications that can happen in that context I am saying that there can be greater bleeding and in the practice of passing urine pain be experienced.

Dr: I want to tell that such patients can contract AIDS.

Everyone in the courtroom laughed.

J to DL: Do you want to submit this?

DL: Patients can contract AIDS or gonorrhoea.

J: Sexual diseases [*Gupt rog*—literally, secret diseases].

Dr: Gonorrhoea.

J: Let it be sexual diseases [*gupt rog*], *yaar.*

J (d): And if the concerned person suffers from AIDS and sexual diseases [*gupt rog*] then the victim can also get such a disease.

Some victims may need professional psychological help. The medical officer should be ready to offer reassurance and advice to the victim or her parents. When there is a possibility of pregnancy resulting, imagined or real, the victim should be adviced to consult a gynaecologist for prevention of or later termination of that pregnancy. Rape Crisis Centres (as part of the nationwide anti-rape movements) have been established in the west, to provide counselling to rape victims, friends and relatives of the rape victim. The Ministry of Social Welfare in India is likely to consider setting up of an agency to deal with rape problems and other financial, legal and psychological services to rape victims. (Modi 2002: 507)

The relationship between courtroom talk and the medico-legal archive thus remains relevant to our understanding of courtroom talk in as much as the archive sets the limits on that which can be said in the courtroom. The first four excerpts cited above demonstrate how self-inflicted injuries or the medico-legal discussion on false cases structure the cross-examination. Modi's assertion that he examined a case in which the father had inserted his thumb in the child's vagina to lodge a false case has been generalized into a medico-legal norm. This norm is impervious to the public discourses on child sexual abuse that name such forms of forcible penetration as rape. The emphasis on falsity exists alongside the suggestion that the child is not really a child. In saying that Noor is not a child, the defence lawyer actualizes the implicit assumption that underlies the construction of technical rape. Technically, while consent of a child remains irrelevant, the idea of a solicitous child is actualized in the way the entire cross-examination is framed. It is the category of nature that is the unspoken category, evoked in the defence lawyer's continual assertion that Noor is not a child. The translation of statutory rape as technical rape marks this movement from the legal to the natural.

Such an articulation is expressed to the gynaecologist, suggesting that he cannot see the work of desire in the legal subject who is not really a child. By this argument, children cannot be raped, and those who are cannot be considered as children.

The excerpts cited above are instructive in understanding how the court denies the possibilities of therapeutic jurisprudence (Cattaneo & Goodman 2010). The court tells us that the category of psychological complications is not relevant, as they arise even in the case of consensual sex.[65] Dr Kadam's opinion that rape victims face psychological complications resonates with the discussion on rape trauma syndrome in the 2002 edition of Modi. The textbook clarifies that rape 'may lead to a wide variety of physical and psychological reactions' (Modi 2002: 507). The resistance to recognizing trauma indicates that the law annexes medico-legal techniques in order to advance the forensic aspects of law and pits it against therapeutic jurisprudence. However, as Cattaneo and Goodman point out, a growing literature on therapeutic jurisprudence 'advocates for laws and policies that maximize the therapeutic potential of the system, and minimize the negative' (2010: 482). When the humiliated, devalued, and insulted victim loses narrative control over her own story, she experiences severe psychological trauma. Therapeutic jurisprudence is broadly defined as those approaches to law which attempt to institute policies and procedures that do not re-victimize the victim. In Indian courts, however, the moment expert opinion leans towards therapeutic jurisprudence, be this in terms of treatment for trauma or other risks to health,[66] we find that the expert opinion is belittled and treated as if it were not relevant to the purposes of law. The adversarial trial represses any therapeutic potential by disallowing the creation of safer conditions for testimony.

'FUNNY REFERRALS'

The process of testifying itself reproduces trauma. It makes a rape survivor relive the rape and humiliates her.[67] The emphasis on annexing psychiatry for forensics ignores the production of trauma by the law, which severely compromises the mental health of rape survivors. How are symptoms of trauma expressed during the testimony represented in the writing of judgments?[68] In appellate judgments, we come across references to the trauma caused during testimony such as rape survivors weeping during the testimony, but such 'emotional turmoil too must be expressed in clearly recognizable ways' (Kannabiran 2002: 130). For instance, a trial judge '...found it unnatural that the prosecutrix should stop weeping on being consoled by one of the witnesses. He goes on to add that she could stop weeping only if she had cohabited with her consent' (Kannabiran 2002: 130). Or as a Gujarat High Court judge said to me, 'a judge must pay attention to the demeanour of the victim in the witness box. If she is a liar she will be conscious, perspiring, shifting, will not stand correctly and ask for water.' Emotional distress produced by the testimony is not recognized as sign of suffering but as a sign of complicity in a lie.

Troubled by the question whether the police referred rape victims for counselling or treatment for trauma, I found my way to the psychiatry department at the Civil Hospital in Ahmedabad. In 1998, I interviewed Dr RM at the psychiatry ward. She told me that the psychiatry ward had not received any referrals for treatment from the police. She had treated patients who had suffered sexual abuse and attempted to commit suicide, but these cases were not officially recorded as cases of suicide following rape. However, the emphasis on appropriating psychiatry for forensic purposes or aiding investigation had resulted in the police referring men who had been accused of rape to their department. In her experience, there had been five such referrals in six months (October 1997 to March 1998), specifically so that their semen samples could be collected for forensic analysis. I cite an excerpt from the interview below, originally in English.

> RM: Funny kinds of referrals especially in the emergency we get usually in the midnights—the rapists are referred. Ok? They are in the custody you know and the problem is that police finds a problem with extracting semen samples from these people. So they bring them here. And in six months we have got five such referrals ... We debated and debated that what can we do in such circumstances so ultimately we arrived at this strategy that when he comes we make him feel relaxed, you know, no harm from here, he should not be afraid of us, we are not people who doing any illegal procedure and one is motivated to be accommodating to whatever the person requires. If at all we give

them options. See the person is very much anxious and tensed [sic] so we tell them: 'if you want we can help you in imagining.' You know, if one is relaxed and one can be stimulated to imagine sexual fantasies and things like that so that it is easier for them to ejaculate. That much we do.

PB: So what kind of material do you have to use to stimulate the man?

RM: We give suggestions, you know, for the person to relax and he is just helped to fantasize.

PB: Would not the fear be that the doctor herself could become an object of the man's fantasy?

RM: That's the doctor's problem; a psychiatrist can manage that (*laughs*).

We see here an emergent practice that annexes psychiatry to aid the production of evidence.[69] The 'funny referrals' during emergencies at midnight have led to the invention of a method amongst the psychiatrists to use their expertise to aid police investigation. These relaxation methods and audio-stimuli describe the production of sexual fantasies in a clinical setting in order to help the patient ejaculate so that evidence can be collected. While there may be different ways to read the relationship between power, violence, and desire from the dense category of 'funny referrals', I suggest here that the law annexes medicine to expand the domain of forensics, while the emergence of the therapeutics remains nascent.

***

Thoinot's legacy continues to haunt rape trials in India. Despite several petitions by different women's groups to protest against the sexist and racist assumptions that underlie medical jurisprudence, change has been slow. It must be noted that the Centre for Enquiry into Health and Allied Themes (CEHAT), a NGO based in Mumbai, took the lead in developing a protocol for medical examination of rape survivors as well as an instruction manual, which has been adopted in three hospitals in Mumbai (also see Pitre 2005, HRW Report 2010).[70] Despite the stunning work by CEHAT in mobilizing doctors, public health officials, and the WHO, in addition to making numerous public appeals, Indian courts have been resistant to do away with the two-finger test. Even though many appellate courts have issued guidelines[71] to various agencies—including the police and hospitals—to deal with rape survivors with sensitivity and dignity, none of these judgments have focused on the legality and constitutionality of the 'two-finger' test. [72]

The Human Rights Watch Report (2010) tells us that whilst issuing guidelines on how forensic examinations should be conducted on rape survivors, the Maharashtra state government noted that the medico-legal report should specify the state of the hymen and how many fingers may be inserted in the vagina.[73] The office of the Director General of Health Services, Delhi, 'introduced a template for the forensic examination of rape survivors at government hospitals that seeks information about the size of the hymeneal orifice and asks doctors to comment on whether the victim is habituated to sexual intercourse' (HRW Report 2010: 9). No court objected to subjecting children to the 'one' finger test in contravention of WHO guidelines, which hold that '"most examinations" should be "non invasive and should not cause pain," and that "speculums or anoscopes and digital or bimanual examinations do not need to be used in child sexual abuse examinations unless medically indicated"' (cited in HRW Report 2010: 4). The guidelines further caution doctors to 'consider a digital rectal examination only if medically indicated, as the invasive examination may mimic the abuse' (cited in HRW Report 2010: 4).

In July 2010, Justice Kannan, who co-authored the 2011 edition of Modi's medical jurisprudence with Dr K. Mathiharan, named rape as an act of sexualized violence and a grievous crime. The infamous sections on false cases and self-inflicted injuries have now been removed. New case law has been introduced that will instruct doctors about the directions courts have taken in insisting that vulval injury is sufficient to constituent rape, and lack of injuries does not mean that the victim has not been raped. While this edition suggests that the two-finger test should not presume that women are habituated to sex, it does not prohibit the use of this test.

The two-finger test was excoriated as a colonial, sexist, and injurious procedure in the Human Rights Watch Report (2010) as this version of Modi went to print. Two months after the publication of the HRW report *Dignity on Trial* (2010) denounced the bimanual test as archaic, intrusive, and violative, Additional

Sessions Judge Dr Kamini Lau's now historic judgment challenged the medicalization of rape trials in India. In August 2010, Justice Lau expressed surprised concern in a Delhi trial court after noticing that medical examination of rape victims included the two-finger test and characterized the victim as habituated to sex. Making a distinction between a 'hymen test' and the two-finger test, Justice Lau opined that a limited vaginal examination in the case of unmarried women, which notes 'if the hymen cord is intact' and records the 'use of force' or 'any signs of tearing or bruising off and near the vagina' ought to suffice.[74] Apart from such 'hymen tests', Justice Lau was unable to 'understand why the Per Vagina (PV) test, which is normally called the Finger Test, is being carried out in routine on victims of sexual offences. This test only establishes whether the vestibule is congested and whether one, two or three fingers can be inserted.'[75]

The court ruled that:

> [T]he manner in which this medical test (PV Test) is carried out by inserting a finger inside the vagina of a women irrespective of age or marital status is violation of her body and in the absence of her consent would be violative of Constitutional dictates of right to Life as enshrined under Article 21 of the Constitution of India.[76]

This test, the court held, violates the woman's right to privacy since it makes her private sexual life public. The court futher noted that 'the PV Test/ Two finger test, medically has no scientific or conclusive basis and the opinion rendered by the doctor to the extent of congestion of vestibule is subjective'.[77]

The court observed that the extent, degree, and nature of such congestion could range from medical to sexual reasons and, in any case, pre-marital sex should not be held against an unmarried woman. Further, the court stated that 'once the character evidence of a rape victim is no longer admissible in evidence, how can [the PV test], which only permits the doctor to state if the woman is habituated to sex or not, continue to inform the rape trials'.[78] Finally, the court ruled that 'the PV Test which allows the doctor to state whether the woman is habituated to sex or used to sex is self incriminating as it is often used to disqualify the victim's testimony. This test shifts the focus of the investigations and the trial in sexual offences cases from the accused to the victim which is impermissible'.[79]

Holding that the 'two-finger' test is irrelevant to rape trials, Justice Lau remarked, 'state action cannot be a threat to the Constitutional Right of an individual. What has shocked my conscious [*sic*] is the fact that this PV Test/Finger Test is being carried out in routine on victims of sexual offences by the doctors thereby reflecting a rampant violation of the Constitutional Rights of such victims'.[80] This judgment marked an important yet early shift in the judicial interpretation of the two-finger test as unconstitutional.[81]

Yet these reports and judgments continue to overlook the call to apply this test to other kinds of brutalized bodies. The view that the body archives past sexual history is also deployed on sodomized bodies, wherein doctors insert two fingers in the anus to show marks of habituation (Gupta 2006; Narrain 2008; Modi 2011). The pathologization of homosexual and transgendered bodies in medico-legal textbooks, such as in Modi (2011), amount to degrading stereotyping of sexual minorities making it impossible to treat sexual assault of such victims therapeutically (PUCL Report 2003). For instance, doctors are directed to note whether there is a funnel-shaped depression of the buttocks towards the anus, which affirms whether the 'confirmed sodomite' is 'used to the act of sodomy' (Modi 2011: 682). Further, old lacerations in the rectum near the anus are noted as signs of past sexual history or evidence of a confirmed sodomite. The figure of the 'habitual sodomite' in appellate law narrates the story of 'the role of medicine lay in extending the understanding of sodomy from being a mere series of acts to "sodomite" as a species. The role of medical evidence in prosecutions under s. 377 lies in establishing that homosexuals have a variant anatomy, which becomes the basis for apprehending, in medical terms, who homosexuals are' (Narrain 2008: 58).[82]

The place of technique marks a critical aspect of the doing of law where the body is made to produce the signs of its own subjection. As protests against the medicalization of consent continue, the law is not concerned with the harm it causes to the rape survivor, but is solely concerned with proving how a phallocentric society is injured by the act of rape. The nature of injury produced during a *successful* rape trial that leads to a conviction is the subject of discussion in the following chapter.

NOTES

1. Standard medico-legal textbooks such as Modi, Lyon, or Taylor run into numerous editions, which are revised and updated by different editors but continue to be published under the name of the original author, even posthumously. Modi's textbooks are an authoritative source of medical jurisprudence in law courts today. The first edition came out in 1920. The instances of crimes cited in these textbooks are sourced from clinical experience, legal casebooks, medical journals, as well as newspaper reports (see Modi 1922, 1940, 1969, 1972, 2002).

2. In locating the formations of medicine and law we find that there are three kinds of modalities at work here. The statutes define who the expert is since not every medical professional is authorized to testify. Authorized doctors conduct clinical examination of rape survivors, and evidence collected thereafter is sent to state-run forensic science laboratories for forensic analyses. The third institutional site is the pedagogical one, where forensic science and its clinical practice is a specialization taught to students in medical schools. Doctors are called as expert witnesses by the prosecution in rape cases. Unlike British or American law, the defence does not hire doctors to give expert testimony or opinion in rape cases (see Lees 1997). However, it is accurate to say that often 'doctors play a crucial "expert" role in analysing women's responses and sometimes giving conflicting and distorting accounts of the "typical" bodily signs and symptoms of rape' (Lees 1997: 84). The law recently changed in 2013 by adding s. 357C, CrPC which holds that all hospitals whether public or private shall immediately provide first-aid or medical treatment free of cost to rape and acid attacks victims; and shall inform the police of such an incident.

3. As Foucault has famously said, 'power and knowledge directly imply one another; that there is no power relation without the correlative constitution of a field of knowledge, nor any knowledge that does not presuppose and constitute at the same time, power relations' (1977: 27).

4. In 2005, s. 164 of CrPc (Act 25 of 2005) was amended to insert a new section, s. 164A which held that:

(1) Where, during the stage when an offence of committing rape or attempt to commit rape is under investigation, it is proposed to get the person of the woman with whom rape is alleged or attempted to have been committed or attempted, examined by a medical expert, such examination shall be conducted by a registered medical practitioner employed in a hospital run by the Government or a local authority and in the absence of a such a practitioner, by any other registered medical practitioner, with the consent of such woman

or of a person competent to give such consent on her behalf and such woman shall be sent to such registered medical practitioner within twenty-four hours from the time of receiving the information relating to the commission of such offence.

(2) The registered medical practitioner, to whom such woman is sent shall, without delay, examine her and prepare a report of his examination giving the following particulars, namely:-

    (I) the name and address of the woman and of the person by whom she was brought;

    (II) the age of the woman;

    (III) the description of material taken from the person of the woman for DNA profiling;

    (IV) marks of injury, if any, on the person of the woman;

    (V) general mental condition of the woman; and

    (VI) other material particulars in reasonable detail.

(3) The report shall state precisely the reasons for each conclusion arrived at.

(4) The report shall specifically record that the consent of the woman or of the person competent to give such consent on her behalf to such examination had been obtained.

(5) The exact time of commencement and completion of the examination shall also be noted in the report.

(6) The registered medical practitioner shall, without delay forward the report to the investigation officer who shall forward it to the Magistrate referred to in s. 173 as part of the documents referred to in clause (a) of sub-section (sub-s.) (5) of that section.

(7) Nothing in this section shall be construed as rendering lawful any examination without the consent of the woman or of any person competent to give such consent on her behalf.

    Explanation. – For the purposes of this section, "examination" and "registered medical practitioner" shall have the same meanings as in s. 53.

5. Sakhare (1994) illustrates the semantic extension of the category of habituated to sexual intercourse in statutory rape cases. She cites a case of a fourteen-year-old girl who was raped by her fifty-eight-year old teacher at his house. Delay in reporting led to loss of medical evidence. The medical practitioner testified in court that there were no signs of injury or 'recent intercourse' and the 'finger-test' revealed that the girl was 'habituated to sexual intercourse'. In the instance of delay, the category of habituated is used to signify the presence of consensual sex rather than as evidence of the infliction of violence on the girl's body. Even though the survivor had

stated that the accused had inserted his finger in her vagina and then tried to penetrate her with his penis, her word was found to be uncorroborated because there was no evidence of physical injury. The Sessions Court acquitted the accused (*The State of Maharashtra* v. *Abdul Sattar* Sessions Trial No. 39 of 1985 cited in Sakhare 1994: 72).

6. We find a clear articulation of this category in a 1932 judgment, pronounced by the Allahabad High Court, wherein the court held that 'sexual intercourse in fact forms the principal part of the allegations made by the girl and there is no doubt that *technical rape* was committed' (*Abdul and Anr* v. *Emperor* MANU/UP/0111/1932, at para 3, emphasis added).

7. In the second half of the nineteenth century, Kolsky argues that 'medical jurisprudence emerges as a distinct form of colonial knowledge expressly committed to the service of the colonial state. The "rule of colonial difference", which consistently informed the processes of imperial law making, was also central to the formation of the field of "Indian medical jurisprudence"' (2002: 320). Pointing to the organization of otherness in colonial legal discourse on rape, Kolsky has argued 'while much has been written about the rule of colonial difference and the ways in which the colonisers adopted particular modes of governance to sustain control in the colonies, something akin to a rule of colonial indifference characterises the colonial criminal jurisprudence on rape. Ideas about Indian otherness certainly shaped the colonial rape case law but not in a manner that allowed white men to make any claims about saving brown women from brown men. In fact ... the colonial law of rape may have made Indian women increasingly vulnerable to rape by Indian men' (2010: 123). Kolsky further argues that the 'rule of colonial indifference', which manifested itself towards native women who had been raped had the effect of stabilizing the 'truth-technologies' of the medical jurist in the colonial legal system. While Kolsky's argument is persuasive, I believe that this analysis needs to distinguish between rape on adult women and children.

8. Chevers' analysis is based on the work of his colleague Dr Mouat, Chair of Forensic Medicine at his college, who collected copies of depositions in the Court of Nizamut Adalat made by surgeons in the Zillah Courts since 1840. These were cases relating to murder and wounding, wherein Magistrates had been directed to take the depositions of medical officers in Bengal. Chevers also bases his analysis on Macnaghetn's Reports of Cases between 1805 and 1826 in the Court of Nizamut Adalat, and for 1851–4 he refers to the Reports of the Nizamut Courts of Calcutta and North West Provinces. Additionally, he specifies that he 'made use of the records of the office of the Chemical Examiner to Government, which (together with a published report by Dr. O'Shaughnessay,) comprise details of all chemical

not only was the minimum mandatory punishment reduced but the court also took note of the victim's previous conduct, even though, as Dhagamwar points, out the woman's character was 'nowhere relevant in determining the quantum of punishment' (1992: 283).

Subsequently, the review petition filed by fifteen women's groups under the banner of Mahila Samyukta Morcha was dismissed, and the Supreme Court held that they had not relied on the victim's character or reputation while referring to her conduct. Terming the controversy over the judgment as 'unfortunate' the court clarified the scope of review of a judgment.[35] The judges found 'no error apparent on the face of the record necessitating review', but made the following observations in view of the elaborate submissions made by the counsel.[36] The court remarked:

> We have neither characterised the victim [SR] as a woman of questionable character and easy virtue nor made any reference to her character reputation in any part of our judgment but used the expression 'conduct' in the lexigraphical [sic] meaning for this limited purpose of showing as to how [SR] had behaved or conducted in not telling anyone for about 5 days about the sexual assault perpetrated on her till she was examined on … by the Sub Inspector of Police in connection of a complaint given against Ravi Shankar … we would like to express that this court is second to none in upholding the decency and dignity of womanhood and we have not expressed any view in our judgment that character, reputation or status of a raped victim is a relevant factor for consideration by the court while awarding sentence to a rapist.[37]

For the court, a 'reasonable woman' who has been gangraped by policemen (and has to fight false criminal charges against her partner) should immediately report the fact of custodial rape to the police. This judgment does not treat custodial rape as a hideous form of state violence, which further victimizes an already stigmatized and persecuted legal subject.

How, then, does the rape trial function as a symbolic vehicle of communication? Lees says:

> Rape trials today can be seen both as operating as a warning, and a way of restricting the activities of women through inciting the fear of public sphere, but also through punishing a victim for breaking the silence enforced by the emphasis on female respectability and

Yet, the emphasis on women's character often converts testimony of abduction into elopement, and testimony to elopement is open to being labelled as technical abduction.

CUSTODIAL RAPE: 'LASCIVIOUS' WOMEN

The judicial story of elopement is grim. Mody has argued that assertion of choice in heterosexual marriage creates a 'not-community ... because love-marriage couples neither did nor do constitute a community in the conventional sense of the word' (2008: 2). This does not mean that over time a couple cannot be 're-socialised into their communities and families' (Mody 2008: 5). Mody describes the inability of lovers to create communities of solidarity and identification, heightening their vulnerabilities as they risk danger and sometimes death. Families also make daughters who assert their right to choose their partners vulnerable to rape by policemen.[32] Since the Mathura trial, this precedent of injustice has found repetition.

Prem Chand and Another v. *State of Haryana* tells us that the victim, SR, had eloped with Ravi Shankar in 1984.[33] Her family filed a complaint of rape and abduction against Ravi Shankar. The police 'arrested' both of them and put them in different rooms, and two constables subsequently raped SR. Ironically, when the case came on trial, Ravi Shankar was tried alongside the two policemen who raped SR, and her testimony that Ravi Shankar did not rape or abduct her did not matter.[34] It was held that since SR was not eighteen yet, Ravi Shankar was found guilty of seducing her to illicit sexual intercourse and enticing her to leave the custody of her guardian under s. 366 IPC. He was sentenced to seven years rigorous imprisonment. The policemen were convicted and sentenced to ten years imprisonment.

The high court confirmed the conviction of the policemen, arguing that there were no adequate and special reasons to reduce the sentence. The high court acquitted Ravi Shankar on the grounds that it was not proven that SR was a minor, and that she had chosen to engage in a consensual sexual relationship with Ravi Shankar. When the two policemen filed separate appeals in the Supreme Court, the decision to convict the policemen was upheld, but the Supreme Court reduced the sentence to five years rigorous imprisonment. This judgment shocked the women's movement, for examinations made in the cases of poisoning, &c., from 1840 to 1844, from January 1849 to January 1851, and from May 1852 up to June 1854' (Chevers 1856: 2).

9. Chevers declared that 'theft, Perjury, Personation, Torture, Child–stealing, the Murder of Women and Aged Men, Assassination, Arson, the Butchery of Children for the sake of their ornaments, Drugging and Poisoning, Adultery, Rape, Unnatural Crime, the Procuration of Abortion, are among the leading villainies of these ingenious, calm-tempered, indolently pertinacious sensualists' (1856: 7–8).

10. This assumption that it is possible to deduce the experience of rape or consensual sex by locating the truth in the body finds precise articulation today in the use of newer forms of truth technology on raped survivors. When I conducted interviews with experts at the Forensic Science Laboratory in Ahmedabad, I was told that truth machines and lie detection tests could now measure falsity in rape cases. The importance of the lie-detection test was reiterated by Mr H, the City Commissioner of Police, who told me that 'scientific investigation is very important. Now we have polygraphy and narco-analysis. Give something to the individual, she automatically tells.' In March 1998, I interviewed a clinical psychologist, Dr V, who had been working in the FSL for fourteen years at that time. Dr V spoke of the use of lie-detection tests on raped women. She explained that they began using this technique under pressure from the police to solve cases. Referring to a much-publicized case of rape at that time, she argued that if the victim had been administered a lie-detection test, the accused could have been 'saved'. In some cases, she argued, this test is essential. The victim in this case had refused to take the test. She added, 'illiterate women are not aware of their rights and therefore submit to these procedures, else they too will refuse'. These new machines and technologies that medicalize falsity aim to deter women from testifying in courts rather than producing records with any evidentiary value. In contrast, Smart (1989) has shown how the discourse of psychiatry has been used to reduce consent to a state of mind. The psychologization of rape has been used to disqualify women's testimony to rape during trials in England.

11. Wigmore's contribution to the histories of the psychologization of falsity has been noted by many scholars. Famous for his canonical work on evidence, Wigmore was of the opinion that rape survivors should be subjected to psychiatric evaluations to evaluate their credibility. O'Neal (1978) reveals that in 1937–8, based on the recommendations of a committee which included Wigmore, the American Bar Association recommended that every rape survivor should mandatorily be subjected to psychiatric evaluation before the trial and such psychiatric certification

be admissible as evidence. Although such recommendations were not mandated as a rule for all rape survivors, we witness a painful history of case law in American courts, which allowed such evaluations, and also permitted the use of lie detection tests.

12. Taylor says, 'rape is defined in law to be the carnal knowledge of a woman by force and against her will. Medical evidence is occasionally required to support an accusation of this kind, but it is seldom more than corroborative because the facts are in general sufficiently apparent from the statement of the prosecutrix. There is, however, one case in which medical evidence is of some importance, namely where a false accusation is made. In some instances, as in respect to rape on young children, the charge may be founded on a mistake: but in others there is little doubt that it is often wilfully and designedly made for motives, into which it is here unnecessary to enquire. Professor Amos remarked some years since, that for one real rape tried on the circuits, there were an average of 12 pretended cases! In some few instances, these false charges are set aside by medical evidence—but perhaps in the majority, they are developed by the inconsistencies in the statement of the prosecutrix itself' (1845: 458).

13. The passages from Manu are cited in the section on *Falseness of Much Evidence Given by the Natives of India*. 'No crime causing loss of caste is committed by swearing falsely to women the object of one's desire, at marriages for the sake of (procuring) fodder to cow, or fuel (for oneself), and in order to show favour to a Brahman (Manu Code, II 26). Yet the disgrace of perjury is also insisted upon: "Naked and shorn, tormented with hunger and thirst and deprived of sight, shall the man who gives false evidence go with a potsherd to beg food at the door of his enemy" (Manu, 9, 235, 319, 325)' (cited in Lyon 1918: 21).

14. Modi's eighteenth edition asserts that 'adult females, who have been used to sexual intercourse, are known to have brought false charges of rape against individuals by staining their garments with a solution of starch or white of eggs to simulate seminal stains and with blood of a fowl or ruminant to show that the blood was due to the injuries inflicted on their private parts' (Modi 1972: 327).

15. Modi also stated that 'burns are sometimes self-inflicted for purposes of false accusation' (1940: 207). He illustrated this statement by citing the case of a Muslim woman who alleged that her husband burnt her partially but had actually burnt herself to get a divorce.

16. Similarly, Reddy says, 'parents may injure the genital organs of the child by introducing a blunt instrument or thumb into vagina or place irritants, such as, chillies, within the vagina to simulate rape, for the purpose of substantiating the offence' (1990: 300, also see Modi 1972).

17. This viewpoint continues to have immense valence among legal experts in Ahmedabad. A well-known male lawyer at the Gujarat High Court said to me during an interview, 'you try it with a girl friend. It is very difficult for an unarmed man to rape a woman single-handed. You try doing this with your friend and you will understand.' I was also told repeatedly in the trial court that women have the natural ability to resist rape by crossing their legs. The rapist's body is thus not thought of as aggressively intrusive, while women's ability to resist is seen as given in nature. Arguing that this viewpoint overlooks the way femininity and respectability are scripted in our society, a woman gynaecologist at the Civil Hospital said to me, 'We bring up our girls like lambs. And when they are raped, we expect them to fight back, no matter what.'

18. Chevers noted that 'the question has been mooted, in England, whether Rape, attended with Completion (i.e. Complete Penetration) can be perpetrated on a child of Ten by an adult man. The question is of some practical moment, and a careful investigation of some of the cases presented to the notice of Medical Officers in this country might help in elucidating it' (1856: 469–70).

19. Thoinot cites Chevers to make the point that in Hindoostan 'rapes committed on children are frequent and ordinarily produce grave lesions of the genital organs' (1911: 69).

20. The Phulmonee Dasi case, mentioned in the previous chapter, occupied a central place in Waddell's revision of Lyon's medical jurisprudence textbook in a separate section entitled 'may rape case death?' Such forms of death were distinguished from deaths caused by nervous exhaustion. 'On the question whether death may result from nervous exhaustion, the result of repeated intercourse, Chevers cites the case of certain Marquesan women, who boasted, apparently with truth, of having had intercourse with one hundred men in one night. The intercourse, however was voluntary; had it been otherwise, no doubt the exhaustion would have been greater' (Lyon 1921: 303).

21. Hyde (1997) has argued that the 'legal vagina' is the 'least private' and 'most spectacularized' body part that is fetishized and separated from the female body. He identifies four kinds of legal constructions of the vagina in American law. 'First, the vagina is constructed as a thing, a possession, a space that may be searched: the apartment vagina. Second, remarkably, the vagina, unlike any other bodily part is often represented in relationship to other people. Third, and related to the relational vagina, the vagina unlike any other bodily part, is the pornographic construction of the vagina on display, also searchable, open to gaze. Finally the vagina, as Freudians would predict, is often constructed as a lack, a gap, empty, an absence' (1997: 165).

22. Section XVIII of Lord Lansdowne's Act held that 'and whereas upon trials for the crimes of buggery and of rape, and of carnally abusing girls under the respective ages herein before mentioned, offenders frequently escape by reason of the difficulty of the proof which has been required of the completion of those several crimes; for remedy of thereof, be it enacted, that it shall not be necessary, in any of these cases, to prove the actual emission of seed in order to constitute a carnal knowledge, but that the carnal knowledge shall be deemed complete upon proof of penetration only.' In the case of girls between ten and twelve years, the Act held that 'it is in this case merely necessary to prove that the prisoner committed the offence in question upon a woman child under ten years of age, for consent is immaterial; and evidence of penetration is now sufficient, without further proof'.

23. In contrast, the issue of *virgio intacta* arose in law courts in cases regarding the nullity of marriage, divorce, defamation and allegations against women who were alleged to engage in prostitution under the Infectious Diseases Act. It was believed that the 'most reliable sign of virginity is an intact hymen' (Lyon 1918: 261, also see Modi 1922).

24. In 1866, Taylor devoted considerable space to a discussion of 'the signs of virginity' in his exegesis on 'rape on young women after puberty'. Arguing that the issue of medical evidence of 'defloration' is pertinent to civil law as much as to rape, Taylor proffered that 'the hymen may be intact, but this does not prove non-intercourse, because females have been known to conceive with the hymen uninjured; as an operation for a division of this membrane has been actually rendered necessary before delivery could take place' (1866: 608). He further remarked that the 'presence of the hymen is of course quite incompatible with the assumption that the female has borne a child' (1866: 609).

25. From Rabinow we learn of the 'shift from socio-biology, the social project of reengineering society on scientific principles (i.e. culture modelled on nature), to biosociality, a culturalisation of the natural, which in turn becomes artificial and is remade as technique' (cited in Franklin 1995: 177).

26. In Modi's 1940 edition, we are told that a glass rod of a pipette (ink pipette) should be used for collecting the mucous secretion of the vagina. The presence of the spermatozoa indicates a positive sign of rape. He says, 'in grown up married women it does not necessarily indicate rape, but it proves the occurrence of previous sexual intercourse' (1940: 337–8).

27. The 1918 edition of Lyon critiques the medical position that the hymen was frequently absent in women. It enumerates cases to indicate that the hymen is found frequently except in cases of congenital malformation. 'Practitioners often have the most vague conception of the hymen and mistake it for the margin of the fourcette' (Lyon 1918: 262).

28. Modi in his 1969 edition holds that 'a virgin is a woman who has had no sexual connection whatsoever at any time. The question of virginity is acquiring importance in cases of marriage suits like divorce, nullity of marriage etc. A virgin was once described by a judge as a *rara avis* and so far as medical evidence is concerned, the definition is almost correct. Certain signs in the breasts and the genitals, particularly the intactness of the hymen was always held to signify the physical virginity of a woman. But, in reality it is seen that this particular anatomical structure has limited value, since it happens that a single coitus is not necessarily sufficient to rupture the membrane. Cases are on record of women having regular marital relations, of pregnant women and even prostitutes in whom the hymen remained untouched' (1969: 319).

29. MANU/NA/0177/1927 at para 1.

30. In 1926, Maung Ba Tin was acquitted after the Rangoon High Court held that 'this conviction of rape rests on the evidence of the woman alone, without any substantial corroboration. ... The evidence of the Sub-Assistant Surgeon combined with the report of the Chemical Examiner, shows that she had sexual intercourse recently with someone, but shows no more than that. There were no signs of rape. No motive for a false charge is disclosed, but it is notoriously very unsafe in such cases to rely on the uncorroborated evidence of the woman alone, and to make it an exception to the general rule' (*Maung Ba Tin* v. *King-Emperor* MANU/RA/0031/1926 at paras 1 and 2).

31. MANU/LA/0231/1927.

32. *Anam Swain and Others* v. *State* AIR 1954 Ori 33.

33. Ibid. @ at para 7.

34. Ibid. @ at para 7.

35. *Fanibhushan Behera, Jeet Shankar Bohidar and Dinabandhu Behere* v. *State of Orissa*, MANU/OR/0255/1994 at para 14.

36. *Rajoo and Ors* v. *State of M.P.* MANU/SC/8353/2008 at para 11.

37. *Bibhishan* v. *State of Maharashtra* MANU/SC/7936/2007 at para 6.

38. *Musauddin Ahmed* v. *The State of Assam* MANU/SC/1126/2009 at para 7.

39. MANU/SC/8058/2007 at para 5.

40. *Balaji S/o Laxman Itkar and Suresh S/o Laxman Pawar* v. *The State of Maharashtra* MANU/MH/0310/2008 at para 14.

41. MANU/AP/1107/2004 at para 18. In this case, the defence relied heavily on Modi's twenty-eighth edition of *Medical Jurisprudence and Toxicology*. The defence arguments were resourced from the section titled 'Can a Healthy Adult Female Be Violated against Her Will?'

42. *State of Maharashtra* v. *Ravindranath Arjunsingh and Ors* MANU/MH/0359/1986 at para 14, emphasis added.

43. In *Jagannivasan* v. *State of Kerala* 'the doctor examining her found that no visible injuries were available on her person or her private parts. Her hymen was found irregular and her vagina admitted two fingers. The doctor preponderated that admission of two fingers in the prosecutrix suggested that she could be used to sexual intercourse and that otherwise there were no visible signs of rape or marks of violence' [(1995) Cri LJ 3229 cited in Kannabiran 2002: 139].

44. *Kishania* v. *State of Rajasthan* MANU/RH/0334/1987 at para 8.

45. MANU/AP/0964/2004.

46. MANU/AP/0964/2004 at para 8.

47. MANU/AP/0964/2004 at para 13.

48. *Tukaram and Anr* v. *State of Maharashtra* (1979) 2 SCC 143.

49. In *Pratap Mishra and Ors* v. *State of Orissa*, the Supreme Court held that 'in the first place, the admitted position is that the prosecutrix is a fully grown up lady and *habituated to sexual intercourse* and was pregnant. She was experienced inasmuch as she had acted as a midwife. The opinions of medical experts show that it is very difficult to rape single handedly a grown up woman and an experienced woman without experiencing the stiffest possible resistance from her' (AIR 1977 SC 1307, cited in Kannabiran 2002: 140, emphasis added).

50. MANU/AP/0964/2004 at para 13.

51. *State of Rajasthan* v. *Hem Raj* MANU/RH/0662/1986 at para 4, emphasis added. The court further stated that 'according to the doctor, she was habituated to sexual intercourse. She, being a married lady, she has been accustomed to sexual intercourse and the presence of blood was on account of the bleeding due to menstruation. He has further stated that on examination of her genital organs, he did not find any evidence of rape. Looking to these glaring facts and circumstances, we are persuaded to hold that the learned lower court was perfectly justified in acquitting the accused giving him benefit of doubt. The judgment of acquittal rendered by the learned Sessions Judge deserves no interference' (MANU/RH/0662/1986 at para 4).

52. *Hanuman Son of Mahadeo Kuchankar* v. *State of Maharashtra, through PSO, P.S. Gadchandur* (2010) ALL MR (Cri) 1499 at para 11.

53. MANU/SC/1063/2003.

54. Ibid. at para 11.

55. Ibid. at para 13.

56. MANU/SC/0522/2010.

57. Ibid. at para 33.

58. Ibid. at paras 34 and 35.

59. MANU/OR/0255/1994 at para 8, emphasis added.

60. The assumption that hymens are broken accidentally while riding a cycle is found in medico-legal textbooks. Yet, we know that even now it is not common for women to cycle in public spaces, either in rural or urban areas.

61. I use a later edition of Modi's textbook. While the changes in the editions retain the original emphasis on procedure, medical examination, and false cases in almost exactly the same words, the newer sections that have been added on in the recent editions are cited here to indicate that while recent additions have been made in response to the growing awareness about rape, such textbooks do not historicize medical conventions.

62. I draw attention to the fact that medical experts also face a hostile cross-examination. For women experts, the cross-examination is a humiliating experience. During a fact-finding enquiry, Dhagamwar learnt from a police officer that women doctors often refused to record rape 'in order to escape giving evidence; not only did this mean frequent attendance at courts and disruption of one's routine, it also meant being asked a lot of questions in "unparliamentary language", designed to shame and insult them' (1980: 3). During this investigation, the woman doctor stated that the victim was menstruating at the time of the incident and the menstrual blood would wash out the semen. The survivor told Dhagamwar (1980) that she was not menstruating at that time and she had begun to bleed so severely after the rape that her clothes had become heavily stained. The doctor did not verify whether the blood was a result of the injury. The structure of the trial thus disrupts the writing of medico–legal reports and compounds the difficulties for rape survivors to prove that they have been raped.

63. This means that the doctor meant to say that the hymen is situated deeper in a child's vagina.

64. In the case of rape of a twelve-year-old, the Supreme Court in *Wahid Khan* v. *State of Madhya Pradesh* held that 'it has been a consistent view of this Court that even a slightest penetration is sufficient to make out an offence of rape and depth of penetration is immaterial' (MANU/SC/1850/2009 at para 25).

65. Note the discussion on 'accidents following rape' in the Modi textbooks. We find here that convulsions, epileptic fits, mental derangement, and death are listed as accidents. The section on accidents that follow rape holds that 'convulsions, epileptic fits, and mental derangement have been known to follow rape. Death may occur as a result of rape from shock due to fright and mental emotion from injuries resulting from the assailants in an effort to overpower the victim, or due to excessive bleeding from severe injuries to the genitals and perinaeum, especially in children. These injuries, if not immediately fatal, may produce sloughing, and cause death due to septic

infections after several days or weeks. In some cases, death has resulted at the time of the perpetration of the offence from suffocation caused by covering the mouth and the nostrils with the hand or by thrusting a piece of cloth down the throat to prevent the female from crying for help. It is, therefore, necessary to examine the mouth for the presence of injuries or foreign bodies, when the body of a female, who is alleged to have died from rape, is bought for autopsy. Sometimes, a female is first raped, and then murdered to prevent the identification of the assailant by the victim' (2002: 508). The classification here between rape and its aftermath follows the logic that rape was the crime intended and its aftermath an accident that follows rape.

66.   In the 2002 edition of Modi, a new section on AIDS has been added. It follows the medico-legal discussion of unnatural sexual offences. Typically the textbook defines high-risk groups in the community as 'prostitutes both male and female, eunuchs, drug addicts and groups who may have sexual interaction with foreign travellers' (Modi 2002: 528–9). The official narratives of HIV/AIDS in India are repeated here as stigmatizing specific body populations while erasing the reality of AIDS within the heterosexual normativity of kinship and alliance. It is alarming that the research that has looked at the health risks flowing from rape does not find a place in this discussion.

67.   Arguing for a sympathetic attitude towards rape victims, a woman prosecutor at the city court said to me, 'there was this case where the girl was crying like anything when the cross-examination was complete. I did not know how to counsel the girl. I told her, "just forget about it. Concentrate on your studies. Nothing will happen to you." Justice BY handled the case beautifully. She counselled the girl. These gestures might help the girl. I told the parents do not remind her of the incident, don't discuss with any person, take her out, and concentrate on other things. We can only do these things. I don't appreciate such questions. How have you been raped? Describe? I oppose silly questions. Is it not enough that she has been raped? Can the defence ask any detail, the minute details? You can't ask. It reminds the whole shock to the girl. Some lawyers ask such questions of a girl of tender years. You can't do that. These are perverse persons. I told a prominent defence lawyer before you defend such type of cases; you must remember that you have a daughter. He didn't react. I always say to the defence lawyer just put your daughter in place of the victim girl and then cross.'

68.   Lawyers' perception of psychological effect of rape on victims is important to understand. For instance, a woman prosecutor practicing in the city trial court said 'rape victims are not sent to the psychiatrist. Psychological problems arise later on, not at the beginning stage, when she gets married. If this incident is in her subconscious mind it immediately bursts out, she might

be cautious, she does not want to react but her subconscious mind might. Such incidents happen when the girl is very sensitive. In case of such incidents in her childhood, she reacts when she gets married.'

69. Medical jurisprudence textbooks do not detail the procedures for collecting semen cases from men accused of rape and what should be done to secure such samples, when the accured cannot ejaculate.

70. In 2009, CEHAT's public interest litigation writ in the Bombay High Court (Nagpur Bench) resulted in the direction to the Directorate of Health Services (DHS), Maharashtra, to set up a high court committee to standardize a medical protocol which could be implemented uniformly in the state. The proforma and the manual was an outcome of this committee [Writ filed on 9 September 2010 by *Dr Ranjana Pardhi and Others against Union of India* in the Bombay High Court (Nagpur Bench)]. This ongoing litigation, which cannot find fuller exposition here, has marked one of the most important interventions challenging the medicalization of consent and demanding a therapeutic approach to rape survivors in recent times. Despite the massive protest against the use of the two-finger test (and the medicalization of consent more generally) in the aftermath of 2012, this test was not repeated by an act of law. While on going discussion between various ministries indicate that the formulation of the medical protocol is under negotiation, the fact is that consent continues to be medicalized.

71. *Hanuman Son of Mahadeo Kuchankar* v. *State of Maharashtra through PSO, P.S. Gadchandur* (2010) ALL MR (Cri) 1499.

72. In 2009, the Delhi High Court issued guidelines outlining the response from the police, medical experts, and prosecutors in rape cases. A committee was formed headed by Justice Gita Mittal to overlook the implementation of these guidelines. See *DCW* v. *Delhi Police*, Writ Petition (Criminal) 696 of 2008, order dated 23 April 2009.

73. An NGO based in Mumbai, CEHAT, opposed this move on the grounds that this test was neither legally admissible nor was it in keeping with international health norms on how rape survivors should be treated.

74. *St.* v. *Umesh Singh & Anr*, FIR No.1135/06, PS Uttam Nagar, Delhi, at page 23.

75. Ibid. at page 23.

76. Ibid. at page 24.

77. Ibid. at page 25.

78. Ibid. at page 25.

79. Ibid. at page 26.

80. Ibid. at page 27.

81. In 2013, the Supreme Court held that 'medical procedures should not be carried out in a manner that constitutes cruel, inhuman, or degrading

treatment and health should be of paramount consideration while dealing with gender-based violence. The State is under an obligation to make such services available to survivors of sexual violence. Proper measures should be taken to ensure their safety and there should be no arbitrary or unlawful interference with his privacy. Thus, in view of the above, undoubtedly, the two finger test and its interpretation violates the right of rape survivors to privacy, physical and mental integrity and dignity. Thus, this test, even if the report is affirmative, cannot ipso facto, be given (*sic*) rise to presumption of consent' (*Lillu @ Rajesh & Anr.* v. *State of Haryana* MANU/SC/0369/2013 at para 12–13). Although the Supreme Court named the two-finger test as unconstitutional, it was not banned.

82. Moreover, statements such as 'lesbian women can be so morbidly jealous of such woman with who they are inverted in love, that they are sometimes incited to commit even murder' are statements of prejudice, which medicalize lesbians as a 'criminal type' (Modi 2011: 684).

CHAPTER THREE

The Child Witness on Trial

Until very recently, the discourse on the rights of children did not influence juridical interpretation. The history of the rape legislation in India testifies to the suppression of the rights of female children in order to maintain the adult normativity of kinship and marriage. How does the child witness who testifies to rape[1] inhabit the juridical field when female childhood has not historically been the object of legislation on rape?[2] Surely the very definition of rape as forcible penile penetration of the vagina is itself an adult way of defining rape. In this chapter, I explore the effects of the failure to identify child sexual abuse as a distinct category of rape. While the first principle of statutory rape cases is that children below the age of consent are presumed not to have the capacity to consent to sexual intercourse, I show that if the law makes the courtroom habitable for female children, it does so by inscribing on their bodies the same conditions of testimony that apply to adult women.

I argue that while such testimonial conditions presume that the child must learn to gaze at her body as that of an adult, at the same time, the child witness must testify to rape in childlike categories, retaining suggestions of innocence. In court, the prosecution has to rely on the child witnesses' testimony to persuade the court that the accused is guilty. This description of facts must remain childlike, despite the evidentiary requirements of treating rape as an adult crime. We find that in such cases, defence lawyers use several strategies to establish that the child is not really a child, and in the ultimate analysis, the childhood of the legal subject is questioned.

Hence, on the one hand, the law assumes that the child does not have the capacity to describe what happened in adult terms, and on the other hand, the same standards that evaluate the testimony of adult women are used to verify that of the child. Courtroom talk that imagines rape as belonging to the realm of adult normativity operationalizes this rather fully.[3]

I address these issues through an extended case study introduced in the previous chapter. I met Hasinaben—whose husband raped her ten-year-old daughter, Noornissa—in the chambers of the additional public prosecutor, Mr Hirabhai, in the Mirzapur trial court. At this time, Hasinaben had already testified, and when I met them they were in court for Noornissa's testimony. The mother and child did not come to the court again. Although I interviewed Hasinaben twice in the court, I could not interview her after the testimony or go to her home. I did not conduct ethnographic interviews with child survivors in these kinds of circumstances for fear of causing distress to them; therefore, I recorded fragmentary conversations with Noornissa between hearings, when she wanted to speak. Subsequently, I followed the case over a period of four months. I sat through nearly forty hearings, some of which resulted in adjournments. I have combined my notes with the official transcript to narrate the nature of courtroom talk and its translation in courtroom records. This was supplemented with interviews of witnesses, experts, and lawyers who participated in this trial. I filed an application in the court requesting certified copies of the case papers. I have used pseudonyms throughout and have not specified the dates of the interviews with the witnesses and legal experts in order to avoid identification of the case.

THE CASE HISTORY

I reconstruct the case history from the interviews with Hasinaben, police documents, and court records. Hasinaben lived in a slum below one of the seven bridges in Ahmedabad city and earned her living by washing clothes in the houses of the well-off Muslim households in the neighbourhood. One evening in 1995, Hasinaben's husband Shakeel brought three friends over to their home. He asked her to cook some meat and the three drank till late in the evening. After his friends left, he told his stepdaughter Noornissa, who was ten years old at that time, to go buy him *bidi*s.[4] As Noornissa started to leave, he accompanied her. He took the child to an isolated place located at a distance from her house and raped her. After they had been missing for three hours, Hasinaben grew worried and began a frantic search for her daughter. Police statements indicated that her neighbours noticed her distress and suspected that the two had met with an accident. At midnight, Shakeel walked Noornissa home. Noornissa, who was severely injured, told her mother what had happened. Hasinaben decided at that moment to turn Shakeel over to the police, and with the help of a few other men, took him to a nearby police station. Shakeel was locked up there, but Hasinaben's complaint was not lodged, as this police station did not have the jurisdiction to lodge the complaint. In the meantime, Hasinaben took Noornissa to a local clinic in their neighbourhood to get her treated for the injuries on her feet. She did not get the 'internal' (gynaecological) examination done or tell the doctor that her daughter had been raped for fear of the word spreading in the neighbourhood. Next morning, she was sent to another police station. The complaint was lodged here.

The police subsequently took Noornissa to the civil hospital. She was in the hospital for three days. Hasinaben told me that she stayed at the hospital, but since she had no money, she did not eat until the third day, when a woman cleaner in the hospital gave her some food. Her older son, who made a living selling nail polish was with her when Noornissa was discharged from the hospital. They got on to a bus, asked for money from a co-passenger and walked the rest of the way home. Hasinaben moved out of the neighbourhood after lodging the police complaint, afraid that her extended family would come to know about what happened.

Two years[5] later, the case came up for hearing in the trial court, but the police failed to contact Hasinaben. When she finally went to the police station to enquire about the case, the police told her that they did not contact her because she had moved out of the locality where she had previously lived. They then asked her to contact the court constable[6] assigned to this case. It was two months after the trial had commenced that she first went to the court. She did not know that non-appearance in court could result in an acquittal. In the court, she met a lawyer who did not tell her that the case had been assigned to a prosecutor. She appeared three times in court. Finally, she met Hirabhai's junior[7] Beenaben, who told her that each time she came to court, she should first meet Hirabhai. Each time, it took her one-and-a-half hours to reach the court on foot as well as a day's wages.

Noornissa took the stand two months after Hasinaben had testified. Noornissa was twelve years old at this time. The verdict followed five months later, and Shakeel was sentenced to ten years rigorous imprisonment, the mandatory minimum sentence in statutory rape cases on children younger than twelve years of age. Subsequently the accused appealed the conviction in the Gujarat High Court. In 1997, the court turned down his plea for bail on the ground that Noor's 'evidence unerringly establishes that against her wishes and forcibly the appellant had sexual intercourse with her'.[8] The Gujarat High Court noted that the evidence of her mother and other corroborative evidence were reliable and trustworthy. The court also commented on the fact that the accused-appellant violated a fiduciary relationship by using a false pretext to lure the child to an isolated place to rape her. In 2002, confirming the sentence meted out by the trial court, the high court observed that 'the appellant being the father of the victim girl does not deserve any leniency as far as the sentence part is concerned'. To the best of my knowledge, this case was not appealed in the Supreme Court.

FROM COMPLAINT TO TESTIMONY

We know that the shame and stigma attributed to rape makes the decision to complain fraught with many social risks (Agnes 1983; Das 1996; Kannabiran 2002; L. Sarkar 1994). The police complaint in Gujarati is referred to as a *fariyad* (Farsi; feminine). Etymologically, *fariyad* means a cry—a cry of pain, one that protests injustice (*anyaya sammeno pukaar*)—or names a violation. It is also used to denote the first information report (FIR), which is the record of the first information of a crime often given orally to a police officer.[9] The police have been critiqued for routinely disbelieving complaints of rape and not reducing the first information into writing. Hence, a *fariyad* may not always be converted into an FIR. In cases of rape, the complainant (*fariyadi*) is not always the rape survivor. Even in the instance of adult women, the complainant is usually someone in the survivor's family. The relationship between the survivor and the complainant is a complex one, inflected by the subject position of the rape survivor in the family and by specific familial biographies. What did disclosure mean to Hasinaben, and how was her testimony framed in the court?

COMPLAINT AS A CRY: DISCLOSURE AND SECRECY

The nature of social sanction against reporting rape and the role of the law in deterring complaints has remained a troubled issue. Those who seek to assess the impact of public awareness against rape by analysing changes in rates of reported rape cases face the question of whether the changes reflect an increased occurrence of rape or a change in public attitudes to the stigma of rape. The social and legal negotiations of stigma and shame after the complaint has been lodged are a critical issue (Agnes 1983). In such cases, the complainant may engage in a series of social negotiations to separate the domain of the domestic from the extended family and the community. These negotiations attempt to block the knowledge of the reporting of rape against a family member from circulation in the wider networks of the family or community. Hence, the court or police station becomes a site of negotiations where such knowledge must remain a public secret. These concerns mark Hasinaben's narrative. I have translated the excerpts provided below from the interviews originally in Hindi.

> H: She was so small. She was only ten years old when all of this happened. I went to the police.
>
> PB: That was very courageous of you.
>
> H: What of courage? I had to do this. I thought if I do not do this, then he will come back. It will become a habit. Then when she grows up what will I do? Someone will pick her up from my cart [*lari*].[10] Lest this happens it is better that I don't let him off. Do men think that women will not say anything? But, when women start to speak out!
>
> Look at this child—she was so small then. If I had not complained, what else could I have done? (*Hasinaben was in tears.*)
>
> I have not told anyone in my family. It is a question of honour [*izzat*]. Only she and I know that we have to come to the court and

one or two other people who have to give their testimony [*jubani*]. And, if someone else comes to know the word will get out and they will talk amongst each other. I am alone in all of this ... I have a family but I have not told them either [*Noor looks at her crying*]. Sometimes I meet people like you with whom I can talk.

When I asked Hasinaben if Shakeel's friends asked after him, she told me that while his friends had come to know that Shakeel had been arrested for committing a rape, they did not know that he had raped her daughter. For Hasinaben, the complaint produced contradictory effects—while she took the help of men in her neighbourhood to bring Shakeel to book, after lodging the complaint she moved out of the neighbourhood in the hope that she could limit the circulation of rumours in her community.

Hasinaben critiqued the idea that the stigma of rape necessarily aligns it to the realm of the unsayable. Her narrative shows that the disclosure of and secrecy about the crime was achieved simultaneously by separating the sphere of the familial from wider kin and affinal networks. This precarious separation of the familial from kin and affines allows the domestic to move into the public in a distinct negotiation with the law. In order to protect Noor from repeated sexual abuse, Hasinaben filed the complaint; however, the legal complaint destroyed the public face of Hasinaben's marriage and risked her daughter's marital future. In a terrifying moment of remaking domesticity, Hasinaben was compelled into silence in order to hide the criminal complaint from her family and community. Hasinaben described the act of filing the complaint as an experience in abject aloneness and as the first reclamation of agency. For Hasinaben, the *fariyad* is invocatory, evocative of Poizat's description of the operatic cry when he says, citing Lacan, 'the cry is the abyss for silence to rush into' (1992: 90). Hasinaben perceived the *fariyad* as a cry that had the potential of destabilizing a male social order assured of its prowess by the assumption that women will not speak out against sexual violence.

For Hasinaben, the complaint was generative of a silence that neither the law nor the familial could address on its own terms. As we know, unlike other criminal complaints, a complaint of rape is pre-figured as a 'sign of conspiracy', and to occupy the subject position of a complainant in a rape case runs the risk of being named a liar. The popularity of the maxim first coined by Sir Mathew Hale that 'it is an accusation easily to be made and hard to be proved, and harder to be defended by the party accused' illustrates how the rape complaint is prefigured as an easy allegation (Hale 1650 cited in Cuklanz 1996:19). I quote Hasinaben below:

> Then I caught him; then his friends came, those who had come earlier that evening. They beat him and we handed him to the police. So then we went to the police. So I told the police inspector, and the inspector was drunk.[11] He started harassing me. 'Can anyone rape this girl?' he said. Then I told two to three other policemen. They said, 'what can we do, sister? Senior officer [*bade saheb*] says he [Shakeel] could not do this [raped Noor].' Then I left and the next day I went again to the police station. So then the policemen gave me money for *riksha*.[12] They said, 'You go to Y police station, you know the Y police station, don't you?' I went there and the inspector asked me some questions, and the case began.

Hasinaben points to the vulnerability of the child survivor in registering her 'presence' as a victim of sexual violence at the police station. 'Can anyone rape this girl?'—disbelief is anchored in a socio-legal theory of the improbability that young children could be raped. This delay in the writing of the FIR meant that Noor did not get immediate medical attention.[13]

I reconstruct what happened next in the words of the police sub-inspector (PSI) who had investigated this case.[14] The PSI told me that the police had detained Shakeel until he was charged under the offence of statutory rape under s. 376 IPC as they were certain that Shakeel raped Noornissa.[15] He said:

> He did it for sure. It does not matter from which place he was arrested. It may be illegal but it supports the case. I cannot say he was arrested at all. They detained him lest he would run away. The X police station [where the complaint was made initially] had no jurisdiction because this is a city police station. So, they sent the woman to Y [police station]. The complainant [*fariyadi*] delayed, waiting for her contacts [*jan-pahechan*]. I cannot say this in court—have to show as if … [he was arrested at Y police station]. That he raped; there is no question. The point is, there should be a conviction. I could tell … there were so many witnesses, how can it be false? She told the neighbours, who went looking for him. There was a police check post near the canal;

they went looking for him. He came back at midnight. His clothes were torn. The girl was injured. The X police station detained him so that his injuries may not be lost. The police while detaining him cannot fabricate the evidence. So many witnesses cannot lie. Salwar was found from the canal. The mother is illiterate; she would not be able to frame anyone to this extent. And the child would not be convincing. Even the biggest criminal contradicts while being crossed. If she had been tutored and repeated that like a cassette recorder in the stand, she probably would not be able to withstand the cross-examination.

After the PSI had testified, he granted me permission to interview Shakeel.[16] According to Shakeel, Hasinaben had filed a false complaint because he wanted to divorce her and she wanted all his property. He said he did not know who had raped Noor.[17] He described Hasina with contempt, calling her a fallen woman (*neech aurat*). He said he had married her to support her since she was a single mother. He said he was arrested not from his house but from another location in the city. I cite an excerpt from the interview below:

> I was arrested near S talkies.[18] ... What happened was that her daughter [Hasinaben's eldest daughter, D] and her husband got together and framed me. Ten to fifteen people beat me near S talkies. From there, I was taken to X police station and locked up. On 19th, I was attacked. They locked me up through 19th–20th September. On 21st, Wednesday, they took me to Y police station. Two policemen arrested me from S talkies and they did not write my complaint. Then when she [Hasinaben] came to X police station, then the policemen told her like this: 'don't you feel ashamed to say such things [that Shakeel had raped Noor]. Go to Y police station'.

The police officer's initial disbelief of the complaint and the illegal detention of Shakeel are erased from police documentation. Consider the following excerpt from the complaint.

> So that my daughter's honour [*izzat*] is not ruined I had not made a complaint [*fariyad*] at the police station but today I remembered if I let him go once then he will do *kharab kam*[19] again with my daughter.

The complaint tells us that Hasinaben 'remembered' that if she did not report rape, she would risk exposing her daughter to further sexual abuse. Yet, from Hasinaben's narrative, we know that she complained that very night. The *fariyad* is structured to account for the 'delay', and therefore, it is framed through the normative referent of honour that follows the stigma of rape.[20] By deploying this framing device, which re-inscribes the opposition between law and society, the police erase their role in the production of delay, and produce legality as that which is written.

The other police documents reconstruct the complaint similarly. For example, Noornissa's statement written by the police says that after Shakeel brought her back home, he ran away when Hasinaben confronted him. Likewise, the statement that the police elicit from Shakeel supports the rephrasing of the complaint.[21] The objective of this statement is three-fold. It establishes the story of the arrest and accounts for the delay. It establishes that the 'evidence' was not destroyed, as suggested by Shakeel's declaration that he did not change his clothes since the day of the incident. Finally, it establishes that Shakeel was not responsible for committing any crime other than rape, as he admitted to rape but denied beating the child. I cite the statement below (originally in Gujarati):

> My name: Shakeel. Caste: Sayeed. Age: 26. Occupation: Labourer. [Address]
>
> On being questioned in person, I hereby have it written that I live at the above stated address with my wife and two children. And I do construction labour work.
>
> On the past [date], I had gone for construction work labour and I came back home in the evening at around six thirty. At that time my wife, H and daughter N were present at home and after this, at around eight o'clock at night I had gone to the canal with my daughter N and there in the dark I did *kharab kam* with N. I did *kharab kam* and from there I went away and I did not go back home and on this day you sir [*saheb*] have caught me and I am wearing the same clothes which I was wearing during the event [*banav*]. I did not beat N.
>
> The facts written above are correct and true.
>
> In the presence of PSI, Y

The above documentation erases the effect of the detention, which resulted in a period of unaccountable custodial time when the *fariyad* was not accepted and Shakeel was detained without being arrested. Hasinaben's *fariyad* asserts that she was responsible for the 'delay' in lodging a complaint and Shakeel signed a written statement that he absconded after he raped Noor. Neither the initial disbelief nor the detention could be represented in the police documents. The translation of the *fariyad* into standardized writing practices of the police structures testimony in court and therefore the construction of 'discrepancies' between a witness' statement and police documents demands a nuanced understanding of practices of policing.

THE COMPLAINANT'S TESTIMONY

The complainant's testimony in statutory rape cases acquires significance for a number of reasons, although it has not received much attention in the existing literature on the rape law in India. Usually, it is the parents or close relatives who file such complaints. At times, complainants turn hostile in court, which means that they withdraw support to the prosecution's case and do not stand by their police complaint of rape in court. The testimony of the child witness is dependent on the capacity and interest of the complainant in pursuing such cases. For instance, a couple whose one-and-a-half-year-old daughter had been raped told me that they had decided to compromise the case because the child would have to come to court as she grew up, and this would not allow her to forget what had happened. Besides, legal proceedings would mean that everyone in their community would come to know and thus ruin her chances of her marriage. In yet another case, narrated to me by a public prosecutor, the child's father, who was an alcoholic, accepted money from the accused. At the behest of her father, the child witness testified in court that she had fallen on a branch and hurt herself.

   Appellate law reporters reveal that it is often the mothers who bear the burden of complaining against rape of their daughters.[22] In most instances, the complainant-mother is socially vulnerable, especially if she is a widow or divorced and therefore, economically, and socially disadvantaged. Unfortunately, statistical profiles that would reveal the percentage of cases that are filed by mothers, especially in cases of father–daughter abuse, have not been collated. Nor has sufficient attention been paid to the kinds of pressures brought against such women to change their testimony in court. This is an important issue for judges who have to decide whether they should rely on the complainant's testimony as clinching corroborative evidence. There have been cases where the complainant-parent may turn hostile to the prosecution case, or their testimony may show inconsistencies with that of the child survivor.[23] The complainant's testimony then may find alteration over a period of time, and hence, judgments often refer to the socio-legal processes that pressurize the complainant to assist the accused.

Justice Sharma of the Allahabad High Court directs our attention to this issue in his perspicacious interpretation of the testimony of a Dalit widow whose fourteen-year-old daughter had been brutally gangraped.[24] The judge did not rely on the mother's testimony to corroborate the victim's testimony. Arguing that the victim's testimony was credible and the medical reports showed compelling evidence of serious injuries, he noted that the manner in which the complainant,

> …as given her evidence indicates that she was deliberately trying to help the accused persons to escape from the charges. … The witnesses are subject to pressures of all kinds and the prosecutrix and her mother Smt. [D] were Harijans by caste and Smt. [D] was a widow having several minor children to bring up.[25]

In this instance, the Allahabad High Court rightly appreciated the vulnerabilities of a Dalit widow to compromise a case by turning hostile to the prosecution case.

While the place of the complainant's testimony in a rape trial may be significant to the prosecution's case as a source of corroborative evidence, for the defence the complainant's testimony may provide a motive for alleging a false case. In order to actualize this, the defence may rely on the medico-legal construction of parenthood, which naturalizes the proposition that parents forge injury on children's bodies to bring about false cases. Such injuries are constructed as falsities that can be detected by medico-legal techniques, as argued in the previous chapter. This category of falsity finds different interpretations depending on whether the complainant is the child's father or mother, and the relationship of the complainant with the accused.

Parents can be seen as using their power to injure their children's bodies in order to substantiate false cases of rape. This construction of parenthood naturalizes three propositions. First, this medico-legal norm naturalizes the idea that both fathers and mothers sexually injure their daughters for extortion and revenge. Second, in this narrative the injury inflicted by the parent is not constituted as sexual violence against the child, for not all forms of sexual assault are named as rape in law. Third, the idea that parents use children to bring false cases of rape for the purposes of revenge and extortion is naturalized. The notion that parents would deliberately ruin their daughter's chances of marriage by bringing about a false rape case has been challenged in appellate law.[26] However, during rape trials, the idea that parents sexually injure their daughters to bring about false cases recursively and heavily informs the grounds of the defence's line of questioning in a statutory rape case, where consent is not in dispute. It offers the defence a route to challenge the testimony of the complainant, child witness, and the medical expert.

This defence strategy makes the suffering of a mother unrecognizable in law. This is most clear in the paradigmatic case of a woman who brings a complaint against her husband for having raped her daughter. In such cases, the defence's attack on the mother-complainant's sexual and marital biography is made relevant to substantiate the category of falsity. In practice, the past sexual history clause is also extended to the complainant. This provides the defence with a ground to construct a fantasy which rests on the image of a malevolent sexually frustrated wife who wrecks vengeance on her husband by using her daughter in a rape complaint against him. Unlike other rape cases, since statutory rape technically precludes the conversion of lack of consent into a narrative of consent, the trial sexualizes the mother and creates a picture of matrimonial discord that then furnishes motive for a false case.

HASINABEN'S TESTIMONY

How then was Hasinaben's testimony constructed? I show here how the defence evoked Hasinaben's sexual and marital biography as grounds for establishing that she had a motive for making a false complaint against her husband.[27] Her testimony was subject to a line of questioning that portrayed her as sexually wayward and morally corrupt. She was represented as a malevolent mother who had overwhelming power in manipulating her daughter's speech. Mother and daughter were seen as collaborators in the conspiracy against the accused. As the complainant, Hasinaben was the first prosecution witness to testify in this trial. Her testimony had been heard before I started the fieldwork, and I base this analysis on the official transcript of her examination-in-chief and cross-examination, as well as interviews with Hasinaben. Hasinaben testified in the presence of Shakeel since the law accords the accused the right to be present during the proceedings to ensure a fair trial.[28]

The following excerpt follows her testimony, which stated that Hasinaben married Karim at the age of nineteen, lived with him for ten years and bore two children. After they divorced she married Jamal and gave birth to Noor. She was married to him for two years. Subsequent to their divorce, she married Shakeel.

Excerpt One

It has been two years after divorcing Jamal. It is not true that the divorce from Karim and Jamal happened at my demand.[29] But I am saying that the demand was his.

Excerpt one illustrates an indignant introduction of moral corruption. The defence constructed Hasinaben's marital biography as relevant to the motive. The suggestion that she initiated the two divorces introduced blame. It aligned itself to the stigma accruing from the idea that the wife who initiates a divorce must be morally corrupt. This is a normative picture that is not concerned with her subjectivity, the reasons for divorce, or the nature of the relationship, but frames these via normative referents for stability. It pictures divorce as the moment of instability. Hasinaben was forced to accept this framework of stability and deny any agency in the divorces in order to make her words count as testimony. This is what Taslitz (1999) has called semantic contagion. She could certify her speech only if she accepted the categories the defence introduced. We know, however, that 'the existence of violence in households as a measure of "stability" might yield a completely different picture of how stable married family life is' (Smart & Neale 1999: 29).

Excerpt Two

I got Noornissa's birth registered in the Municipality office. … But I am saying that by the *janampatri* I mean the birth that I registered.[30] It is true that while getting the birth registered I got my name registered as her mother and Jamalbhai as her father. ... I do not recognize or know Sharikh Mohammad. It is not true that Noornissa is Jabbar Mohammed's daughter. I have only one daughter by the name of Noornissa. None of my other daughters are named Noornissa.

Excerpt two directly introduces the idea that Hasinaben had falsified the facts of Noor's paternity. The defence suggested that she was in a relationship with a man called Sharikh Mohammad. One of the defence strategies was to create reasonable doubt about the identity of the man who raped Noor. The other strategy—questioning Hasinaben's character—was directed at establishing that she had a number of sexual relationships with different men in and outside of marriage, as the question about yet another unknown man named Jabbar Mohammed indicates. This is also clear when the defence suggested that Hasinaben had two daughters, each named Noornissa. The question was posed to raise doubt about the identity of the daughter. This question feigned ignorance of the convention that parents do not give two or more of their own children the same name. This feigned ignorance was directed towards proving that Hasinaben was morally corrupt and capable of forging paternity or the identity of her daughter to lay false claims on the state.

Excerpt Three

Last I married Shakeel. I have been married to Shakeel for two years. It is not true that I have been living with the accused since the last eight years or so. It is not true that when the incident happened I was divorced from the accused. It is not true that when the incident happened the accused didn't live with me. It is true that before the incident I had a quarrel with the accused. But I am saying that these are small fights and in the morning used to forget about this. It is not true that the accused used to drink everyday and on seeing that I was so cut up that I said, I do not want to live with you. It is not true that I wanted a divorce from the accused.

Excerpt three offers the motive for Hasinaben to lie. In this excerpt, we see that the defence introduced Hasinaben's marital biography as a referent to persuade the judge that she falsified the complaint, since the normative standards of a 'good wife' did not describe her. The blame shifted onto Hasina rather than act as evidence of Shakeel's abusive behaviour towards her and her children. She could not admit in her testimony that their marriage was troubled, as it could be translated as a motive for vengeance rather than evidence of the history of his abusive behaviour. The defence portrayed Hasinaben as a capricious wife, and deliberately overwrites her poverty and her responsibilities as a mother.

We find here that the defence deployed the history of matrimonial discord and her husband's alcoholism to construct the motive for falsity. From Hasinaben, I learnt that not only was her marriage troubled, but Shakeel routinely abused her as well. In the courtroom, the domestic was relevant only in so far as it established the motive to bring a false complaint against the accused. To admit the context of domestic violence would only serve to re-inscribe the defence argument that Hasinaben was a malevolent mother intent on taking revenge against her husband. I cite her words below:

> H: He did not do any work. He used to hang around doing nothing. Then he used to beat and yell. Then my children would start to cry. He used to beat me, grab my hair so she [Noor] used to cry a lot. He used to verbally abuse them as well. He would tell her [Noor], 'why are you crying? I will beat you a lot. You are like your mother.' Then the children used to quieten down.
>
> PB: Did he use force on you?
>
> H: Yes! He would get drunk, and then he used to fight and abuse, about everything—about sleeping and all. If I did not sleep with him, he would beat and abuse me. He was my husband [*admin*: literally, man] then what to go to the law for? They would say, 'this is your husband, so whatever he does at midnight you will have to do. So how can we write a complaint [*fariyad*]? If he is a stranger then tell us … This man is your husband.'
>
> PB: So you did not think of taking a divorce from him ever?
>
> H: No. If I had taken a divorce, I would still have been harassed. This world is like that. If you look at a mad woman also then even a mad woman has no peace. … That's why I thought that bastard [Shakeel] is lying there so let him lie there well fed. I have a protection [*saya*] on my head at least. Where there is no protection, there ten people raise their fingers and say, 'let us abduct that woman [*ye aurat ko apne utha le jate hai*]. If we do this to this woman then she will stay in our power.' This side[31] on seeing a single woman this is what happens.

This abject rendition speaks of how the horror of domestic violence and marital rape can neither be achieved nor verified in law. For

Hasinaben, the domestic subordinates conjugality as a relationship that is remade daily without public acrimony. When Shakeel raped her daughter, Hasinaben broke the 'habit of submission' by evoking legal remedies to prevent Shakeel from raping her daughter again (Hartog 1995: 66). However, her testimony repressed the narrative of domestic violence and the abuse against Noornissa prior to the rape. It repressed the identification of Noornissa with her mother as a victim of sexual and domestic abuse. The court was not concerned with the trauma of a wife seeking legal remedies against her husband for the rape of her daughter; instead, she was systemically blamed for breaking the habit of submission.

We may nonetheless ask that if the narrative of domestic violence is not admitted as evidence to indicate the guilt of the accused, why does it not inform the testimony to situate the child's experience of domesticity in the first place? I suggest that the dissolution of domesticity is irrelevant either as evidence of abuse or as context preceding the legal event for two reasons. First, the experience of the child witness counts as long as it verifies the sexualization of her body. Second, the socio-legal frameworks of rape on children constitute such crimes as a result of male impulse following the wife's inability to sexually satisfy the husband. Nor is judicial attention directed at how the child survivor may have experienced the dissolution of kinship and what the abuse entails. Hence, we find that there was no judicial concern with locating the legal event in the biographies of violence that situated Noor as both a witness and a victim to domestic violence and rape. Instead, the suggestion of discord or history of violence is used to discredit Hasinaben and Noor.

THE CHILD WITNESS IN COURT: HOW TO MAKE THE TESTIMONY COUNT?

We may recall that Noornissa was twelve years old when she was summoned to court to testify. She had to testify to something that is understood as an adult crime. At the same time, as a child her understanding of the crime is, by definition, considered insufficient. The anxiety generated by the idea that the 'child-woman' is innocent and yet not so innocent is constitutive of the structure of the child witness' testimony. I now look at how the prosecution makes the child witness' words count as evidence. Noor was prepared for giving evidence a couple of days before the testimony. The prosecutor considered the preparation of the child witness to be distinct from tutoring. Tutoring, disallowed in law, is seen as teaching a witness how to falsify facts.[32] Preparation, however, is seen as a pedagogy that teaches the child witness to represent what happened in ways that are relevant to a trial. The assumption here is that the child's testimony cannot be verified in the discovery of the nature of the child's words; rather, it is the tongue that must be taught how to utter specific words and phrases that would count as evidence. The child does not have and is not expected to have a composite understanding of the value of her utterances in court. Her utterances are simultaneously innocent and suspicious, for they are ill-formed. It is this ill-formed character of the child's voice that is taken for granted and made the object of the prosecutorial instruction.

Hirabhai left the task of preparation to the junior woman lawyer who worked with him, Beenaben. Over a period of time, I had observed that male prosecutors requested women colleagues to teach the legal subject (especially children) how to frame the testimony. Beenaben divided the preparation according to the three main stages of the testimony.[33] The first dealt with questions to determine if Noor was competent to testify and how to take the oath. The second addressed the kinds of questions that would be asked during the examination-in-chief by the prosecutor. During the examination-in-chief, the prosecutor is bound by the law not to ask the witness leading questions but to elicit the details of the event—what happened, when, and where. The third stage entailed an anticipation of the cross-examination. These legal categories and the structure of the trial testimony were not explained to Noor; instead, she was told what kind of questions to expect. I illustrate this by citing here an excerpt from the exchange in the prosecutor's chamber when Beenaben talked to Noor about how to depose in court. I have translated this excerpt from Hindi.

B: Then what did he do? He made you lie down.

N: He made me lie down and he climbed on top of me.

B: Then he put [*nakha*] his place of urination [*peeshab karne ki jagah*] into my place of urination. You will say this, *na*?

N: (*silent*)

B: What did his place of urination look like?

N: (*silent*)

B: For how much time did he keep doing like this?

N: (*silent*)

B: A lot?

N: A lot.

The attempt to subscribe this lesson in legal language to Noor's memory here communicates the importance of using specific words as evidence. It emphasizes sequential recounting, localizes injury, and specifies naming. In Noor's case, the police statement described what Shakeel did to Noor as *kharab kam*. I cite an excerpt from the police statement, translated from Gujarati, below.

> On the day of ... 1995 approximately at eight thirty in the night, I and my ma H and my father [*pappa*] Shakeelbhai were present at home. My father [*bapuji*] Shakeelbhai told me that come, child [*beta*], let us go buy *bidi*. He said this and for buying *bidi* took me to buy *bidi* and though my mother said no, still my *pappa* Shakeelbhai said that the *bidi* had to be bought. He took me out of the house and he took me to the wall of the pumping station, which is behind our huts and he made me climb the wall and then my *pappa* Shakeelbhai too climbed on top of the wall of the pumping station and after that in the dark, took me towards the canal and when we came to a thorny bush [*baval* bush] my *pappa* Shakeelbhai took off the *salwar* I was wearing and pushed me after stripping me naked. So, I started crying and he then covered my mouth. And lay me down on the sand and also started hitting me and threw my *salwar* on the thorny bushes and after doing *kharab kam* with me, this my *pappa* Shakeelbhai brought me home ... when I told the incident to my ma Hasinaben the incident that my *pappa* Shakeelbhai did *kharab kam* with me ... blood was also discovered on my private parts.

The representation of rape as an adult crime moves between a chronological account of rape and a metaphoric allusion to rape as *kharab kam* or to the vagina as private parts.[34] *Kharab kam* is an euphemism commonly used by the police in recording such complaints. In contrast, the description of the act of penile penetration as putting his place of urination in her place of urination acts as a rigid designator by which children are taught to describe the act of rape in words that are accepted by the court as a child's way of narrating what happened. Certain categories acquire the status of what Kripke (1980) has called rigid designators. Hansen follows Kripke when he says, 'for a name to become proper it must become a "rigid designator", a signifier that creates meanings but cannot be substituted by a set of descriptions' (2001: 2). Hansen has argued 'proper names do not describe objects or places. They create and fix those objects' (2001: 2). This reiterative practice of naming 'as a creation and fixation of identities, and of the use of names as claims to certain identities, properties, or entitlements' may be extended to the analysis of legal discourse (Hansen 2001: 2).

This pedagogy imagines a child's voice as innocent, one that is incapable of speaking adult words. Nor can the child be taught adult categories, for this would prejudice the testimony. Yet Beena could not bring herself teach a response to one of the questions she asked (as if she were a defence lawyer), 'What did his place of urination look like?' This limit marks a closure for the lawyer, for such questions are in the realm of the unanswerable. The lesson not only addresses the child witness to teach her how her words count as testimony, but also conveys to her that the lawyer may feign ignorance about what a penis looks like. It thus communicates to the child witness that the nature of cross-examination itself is marked with otherness and lies in the realm of that which may have no answers in a normative sense. This pedagogy operates within the force of law. Law names and thereby verifies rape through rigid designators. The survivor cannot name rape in her own words and thereby guarantee meaning recognizable in law. For meaning to be recognizable, it must be 'framed within the terms of the law itself, allowing protest only within the hegemonic categories of the law' (Merry 1994: 54). It is the naming process that is both constitutive and authorizing. I now show how this is verified during the trial.

THE CHILD WITNESS' TESTIMONY

During my fieldwork, I found that the Supreme Court guidelines on how rape trials cases ought to be conducted were not implemented in the trial court. In early 1996, *State of Punjab* v. *Gurmit Singh and Ors*[35] observed:

[S]ome defence counsel adopt the strategy of continual questioning of the prosecutrix as to the details of the rape. The victim is required to repeat again and again the details of the rape incident not so much as to bring out the facts on record or to test her credibility but to test her story for inconsistencies with a view to attempt to twist the interpretation of events given by her so as to make them appear inconsistent with her allegations. The court, therefore, should not sit as a silent spectator while the victim of crime is being cross-examined by the defence. It must effectively control the recording of evidence in the Court. While every latitude should be given to the accused to test the veracity of the prosecutrix and the credibility of her version through cross-examination, the court must also ensure that cross-examination is not made a means of harassment or causing humiliation to the victim of crime. A victim of rape, it must be remembered, has already undergone a traumatic experience and if she is made to repeat again and again, in unfamiliar surroundings, what she had been subjected to, she may be too ashamed and even nervous or confused to speak and her silence or a confused stray sentence may be wrongly interpreted as 'discrepancies and contradictions' in her evidence.[36]

The Supreme Court further said that it was incumbent on all high courts to ensure that all rape trials were held *in camera*, that the name of the victim was not published and, as far as possible, a woman judge should hear rape cases.

Critiquing the conduct of rape trials, a government pleader at the Gujarat High Court said to me (in English):

For a woman rape is a trauma: mental and physical. Even thereafter, she complains. She repeats the same story over and over again. The same story that she is hating [*sic*] the most, which she cannot make herself forget all her life. She has to tell this to the judge sitting on the dais. In our society where education is not so much, there is a fear psychosis. They fumble. They cannot narrate the story in the same manner in which it is narrated to their parents. There are in awe of the atmosphere. In that situation, the judge must take the witness in confidence. You have attended trials, have you seen any trial judge taking a witness into confidence? Do trial judges say, 'Do not have fear. You are like my child. Whatever you have to say is for the betterment of life of general public. No woman should be subjected to this. You give the complete statement without any fear.' Does the judge take the victim into confidence? Is this not the pious duty of the judge who is otherwise to hold whether the accused is guilty or not? By saying that the woman is not right in complaining against rape, is he not casting stigma on her?

Other high courts have developed guidelines from time to time on how rape trials ought to be conducted. In 1998, the Delhi High Court laid down guidelines on how trial judges should handle the proceedings in child rape cases (see Chapter 2).[37] The court lamented the fact that 'unfortunately much thought has not been given in our country to the plight of very young or seriously traumatized children required to appear as witness in open court'.[38] Arguing that 'the present system to which we are sticking and which is also as old as the hills, is highly unsatisfactory', Justice Jaspal Singh said, 'I feel it is time we in India give a fresh look and evolve some principles, which while protecting the child, do no harm to the defence'.[39]

The court points out that the traditional cross-examination in open court is unsatisfactory for the following four reasons: One, the cross-examination takes place a long time after the incident. The child is likely to forget the details relevant to proving a case for these may be peripheral to the child but relevant to the defence. Two, courtroom language is beyond the child's understanding and knowledge. Three,

> [That] leading questions tend to produce information which is inaccurate is something which psychologists have demonstrated again and again in a long line of experiments the first of which took place at the turn of the century. Recent works with children show, unsurprisingly that they are considerably more susceptible to this effect than adults.[40]

Four, the traditional cross-examination contains 'questions that cause emotional stress to the witness'.[41]

Justice Singh directed trial judges, prosecutors, and defence lawyers to conduct cases of child rape in the following ways:

> I hope that while the child is in the witness box every effort will be made to lessen her ordeal and that he will take care that nothing is said or done which causes unnecessary distress to her. The prosecutor in his zeal might undervalue the child's feelings. There is a need to keep a check on it. The defence counsel undoubtedly has a primary duty to their clients but they owe a duty towards the court and the

judicial system also. They are expected to avoid needless abuse and harassment of the witness. If the court notices any departure from this course of conduct, it should rise to the occasion promptly and effectively. Child sexual abuse being one of the most serious and damaging criminal offences, the trial judge shall handle the proceedings with considerable sensitivity and ensure that the trial is fairly conducted. He should take care that questions asked are not complex or confusing. Questions containing a negative or a double negative should be better [sic] avoided. The feasibility of giving breaks may also be kept in mind though such breaks need not be long.[42]

The court suggests that a screen be used in the courtroom but one that does not obstruct the gaze of the judge since it is important to observe the demeanour of the witness.[43] Further, in such *in camera* trials, the decision to allow child support persons, that is, a 'neutral' but supportive adult visible to the child in the courtroom, ought to be left to the trial judges. This judgment in a limited way questions the adversarial system, which 'assumes that trials achieve truth through the clash of equally matched adversaries' (Taslitz 1999: 81). Critics of the adversarial system have maintained that 'the adversary system of trial justice mirrors the male mode of dispute resolution' (Strier 1996, cited in Taslitz 1999: 81). Taslitz (1999) argues that rape victims face a harrowing cross-examination since lawyers, whether male or female, play by these male adversarial rules. He argues that American judges fail to see that 'the fundamental assumption of the adversary system that opponents are equally matched does not hold in rape trials. Victims are usually not practiced in the adversarial machismo of our system. Business as usual in the courtroom aids patriarchy, not justice' (1999: 99).

Adult women testifying to rape are not only unfamiliar with the conventions of the adversarial system, but when they adopt these conventions then they are constructed as 'loose' women and unreliable witnesses. For example, when a rape victim speaks with confidence or aggression on the stand, she departs from the expectations of what the demeanour of a rape victim should be. If she is able to name sexual parts, this is interpreted as a sign of 'looseness', and hence she is ascribed the capacity to lie about having been raped. If she is unable to cite the details of injury in forensic detail, her testimony casts doubt about the veracity of the complaint. As a public prosecutor who had defended rape cases in his prior career as a defence lawyer said to me:

> In sex offence, to establish that particular thing in court, you have to say that thing openly. Even in *in camera* trial she hesitates to answer. The defence lawyer keeps asking that particular question: for example, how do you know this particular part is known as this. Then he argues that her character is loose, how does she know everything. Generally the advantage goes to the accused. Defence lawyer asks questions which no one can answer. For example, no one can give answer to such questions. They get scared. She hesitates. She would not be able to answer in sound mind.

In other words, defence lawyers use linguistic and semiotic strategies to force the witness to adopt their categories, induce distress or hostility, and subsequently seek to establish her immoral character through her words and demeanour. I argue that the outcome of each case is underwritten by the conventions of courtroom talk, which systemically accrues blame, humiliates, and shames the legal subject testifying to rape, whether or not there is a conviction at the end of the trial. I suggest that such linguistic strategies are also deployed to disqualify the testimony of the child witness, even though here consent is not in dispute.[44]

The Delhi High Court judgment cited above does not address this fundamental issue at stake here as far as child rape is concerned. In its missive to trial judges not to cause unnecessary distress to child witnesses, it does not tell us what constitutes 'necessary distress'. The judgment retains the category precisely because the adversarial system systemically produces necessary distress. This discursivity authorizes the defence to impose systemic hurt on the child in the larger interest of proving guilt beyond reasonable doubt.

The judgment cited above aims to regulate the hurt caused to children within this system. For instance, while here the court advocates the use of words that are not confusing for the child, it ignores the question of the tone in which such questions may be posed to the child witness.[45] During the cross-examination, for instance, the defence converts questions into statements of fact, such as 'you are lying', which the child has to deny. While the judgment rightly points out that trial judges should intercede in preventing the defence from asking needlessly harassing and insulting questions or in limiting prosecutorial zeal, the adversarial system and the very evidentiary requirements of the law create a threshold of injury to the child witness. Noornissa's testimony provides a critique of appellate judgments by showing how legal discourse acts to injure the child witness.

CHILD AS A COMPETENT WITNESS

On the day Noor was to testify, she waited with Hasinaben outside the prosecutor's chamber. Hasinaben spotted six policemen escorting Shakeel into the court. She grabbed my hand and said, 'There he is. Look at him. He is the one. Noor was initially scared of staying here [prosecutor's office] alone. "Mummy has to stay with me", she used to say.' That day, Noor had no choice but to testify in his presence. We then went into the courtroom. I bowed to the judge as I entered, and sought his permission to sit at the table reserved for advocates at one end, near the witness box. The judge asked two lawyers not involved with this case and five of the six constables accompanying Shakeel to leave the courtroom. Two male defence lawyers, one male prosecutor, a female junior lawyer, a male bench clerk, a female typist, and a male peon (*patawala*) were present during the proceedings. Since it was an *in camera* trial, the door of the courtroom was closed and no one was allowed to enter the courtroom. Shakeel was accompanied by one constable and seated at the end of the courtroom. His handcuffs had been removed.[46] Noor stood near the witness box.

The proceedings commenced when the judge asked Noor in Hindi, 'you will not be frightened if your mother is here? Should she sit here?' These questions addressed to Noor were based on the presumption that her mother as the complainant was not a 'neutral' support person and could influence her testimony. After Noor indicated that she would like her mother to be in court, Hasinaben was allowed to sit in the court during the *in camera* trial. She sat in the first row of chairs reserved for litigants. The prosecutor called out to Noor and pointing to the witness box said, 'Come here.' Noor stood in the witness box.

The process of recording the testimony is time-consuming as the testimony is recorded on manual typewriters and the typist has to pause often to change the paper and carbon paper. The answers of the witness are often monosyllabic. The proceedings are not recorded verbatim. The judge rephrases the response to maintain a narrative record of the testimony.[47] In the excerpts below, only those sentences which are dictated by the judge, indicated as 'J (d)', belong to the written court record.[48] The court record was written in Gujarati. The questions to Noornissa were in Hindi, as were her responses. The lawyers and the judge switched to Gujarati and English during the testimony. I have indicated translations from Gujarati and English in the text. I have indicated English words in italics when these appeared in sentences spoken in Hindi.

The ethnographic account of the rape trial given below juxtaposes the oral script with the written transcript to make the following points. First, it details the linguistic strategies used to characterize the victim as incompetent. Second, it demonstrates how the lawyers ask unthinkable questions feigning innocence about the ordinary. Third, it illustrates how courtroom speech enacts domination by converting the rape trial into a pornographic spectacle. Fourth, it documents the humiliation, ridicule, and mockery that suffuses the trial but escapes the written transcript. Fifth, the juxtaposition of the oral and written transcript demonstrates the attempts of the victim to resist the linguistic domination in the courtroom that degrades and humiliates her. Finally, the rape trial is marked by a surplus, which is in excess of its value as evidence or fact.

Typically, the testimony is divided into three main stages. The prosecution asks questions from their witness—this is called the chief examination (also referred to as 'chief'). The defence lawyer follows with a cross-examination (also referred as 'cross').[49] The prosecutor is allowed to re-examine his witness, following the cross-examination. The examination-in-chief began with the prosecutor facing Noornissa. He rested his arm on the witness box leaning close to her. I have translated the following excerpt from Hindi.

APP: What is your name?

N: Noornissa.

APP: What is your father's name?

N: Shakeelbhai.

APP: What is your age?

N: (*inaudible*)

APP: Where do you live?

N: Near [...] society.

The answer was inaudible to the defence lawyer and he indicated the same to the judge.

J: Speak louder! That sir [*saheb*] pointing to the defence lawyer should be able to hear you.

J: How old are you (*in Gujarati*)?

N: Twelve.

J *to* APP: To see if she understands, to decide if she can testify, ask her important questions (*in English*).

The trial in its originary moments was not prefaced with explanation of its sequence or introduction of the actors to the child witness. Yet, the courtroom space and talk was structured such that the positioning of actors and the application of adversarial rules were quickly communicated to the child witness. Noor learnt that she must answer when spoken to. She learnt to speak loudly so that the defence could hear her, and that the defence could interrupt or object to her answers. She heard three languages that were spoken in court: Hindi, Gujarati, and English, each carrying a semantic load beyond the meaning of the words that were spoken. At times, the judge would switch to English, a language she did not understand. Her ability to answer important questions was tested; only she was not told she was being subjected to a test. These initial moments of the trial are crucial in setting apart this interaction from any other familiar social setting for the child.

The next set of questions determined the competency of the child witness to testify. In Indian law, a competent witness is one who is capable of submitting to a law higher than the courts, since the law is seen as mediating the relationship between the witness and God. Under s. 118 of the Indian Evidence Act, competent witnesses are all persons who are deemed competent to testify unless the court considers that they are prevented from understanding the questions put to them, or from giving rational answers to those questions due to tender age or old age, disease, or any other cause of the same kind (Ratanlal & Dhirajlal 1999). The competency of a witness to testify is a condition that must be fulfilled before she is administered the oath. The oath is therefore preceded by a series of questions that aim at establishing the powers of understanding rather than demonstrating the credibility of the witness. The law does not fix any precise age or rule to determine a child's competency to testify. In case law, however, it has been held that 'in determining the competency of the child witness the court will not enter into inquiries about the child's religious belief or as to his knowledge of the consequences of falsehood in this world or the next' (Ratanlal & Dhirajlal 1999: 401). The case law indicates that questions depend on the 'good sense and discretion of the judge' (Ratanlal & Dhirajlal 1999: 402).[50]

The following questions, asked in Hindi, followed after the judge had asked Noor her name, where she lived and whether she studied in a school.

J: Which religion [*dharma*], which community [*jati*]?

APP: Which community do you belong to—Muslim or Hindu?

N: Muslim.

J (d):   Q: Which community do you belong to?

    A: I am Muslim.

J *to the lawyers in English*: This [question] is prescribed.

J: Do you read the *namaz*?

N: Yes.

J (d):   Q: Do you read the *namaz*?

    A: Yes.

J: Do you go to the *masjid*?

N: No.

J: Have you seen a *masjid*?

N: Yes.

APP *to the judge in English*: Ladies are not supposed to go to a *masjid*.

J (d):   Q: Do you go to the *masjid*?

    A: No. I have seen a *masjid*.

J: Why do you read *namaz*?

N: To ask for blessings [*du'a*].

J (d):   Q: Why do you read the *namaz*?

    A: To ask for blessings.

J: Whom do you ask blessings from?

N: Allah.

J (d):   Q: Whom do you ask blessing from?

A: I ask for blessings from Allah.

J: Why do you ask for blessings?

N: It is a good thing that's why.

J (d):   Q: Why do you ask for blessings?

A: I ask blessings for daily bread and prosperity [*roji-barkat*].

J: If one lies what happens?

N: Crime [*gunha*].

J (d):   Q: If one lies do you know what happens?

A: If one lies then one commits a crime and is punished.

J: Who gives punishment [*gunha*]?

N: Allah.

J (d):   Q: Who gives punishment?

A: On lying Allah grants punishment.

J: If this Allah gives punishment, then what happens?

N: Leprosy happens.

J (d):   Q: What happens if Allah punishes?

A: If Allah punishes then leprosy happens.

At this point, a lawyer walked into the courtroom and the judge asked him to leave.

J: Swear, say that 'I swear by Allah that whatever I say will be the truth, I won't say anything but the truth.'

N *repeats*: I swear by Allah that whatever I say will be the truth, I won't say anything but the truth.

J: Say that: 'if I lie may Allah give me punishment'.

N *repeats*: If I lie, may Allah give me punishment.

Typist *types*: Witness sworn in.

The vivid picture of punishment that follows the utterance of a lie binds the child's speech and imbues perjury with a terrifying content. As a performative act, it emphasizes the place of testimony as carrying divine sanction, binding the child to obedience to the true account. The terror evoked by the image of being struck by leprosy on speaking false, re-iterated by the judge, is effaced from the written transcript, which merely records that the witness is sworn in. After she was found to be competent to testify, however, the issue of whether she could understand the questions posed to her was raised again during the examination-in-chief by the prosecution.

After she was sworn in, Noornissa was asked to identify Shakeel and point out to the judge where he was sitting in the courtroom. This was the only time Noornissa turned to look at Shakeel during her testimony. Hirabhai then asked her if she knew why she was in court. Consider the following segment from the transcript of the examination-in-chief translated from Hindi.

APP: Do you know why you are in court today? For what have you come here?

N: For rape [*balatkar*]. To testify to rape.

APP: Who was raped?

N: I was. (*Her voice drops*)

APP: At that time who all were at your home?

N: My mother [*ammi*] and my brother N.

J *turns to the lawyers and says*: Ammi? What is an *ammi*?

APP *to the judge in English*: In Muslim community mummy is *ammi*.

J (d): I was with my mother [*ammi*] and my brother N.

APP: At that time who else was there?

N: Shakeel.

J (d): My father [*pita*] Shakeelbhai was also there.

APP: At that time what was the time—day or night?

N: Night.

J (d): It was night time.

APP: What happened then?

N: *Abba* said, get some *bidi*.

J *to* N: *Abba*? Do you know Gujarati?

N (*nods*): Yes.

J *to the* APP (*in Gujarati*): Few words do come in, *abba–pappa*.

J to N: Do you understand Gujarati full?

N (*nods*): Yes.

APP *to* J *in Hindi*: After many days, a Hindi speaking witness has come.

APP *to* N: Then what happened?

APP: How much *time* [using the English word] has passed?

N: (*silent*)

J: How much time has passed since this incident?

N: About two years.

J (d): The incident took place approximately two years ago.

Here, we see the stereotype of a Hindi-speaking witness is deployed[51] to re-introduce the question of competency during the examination-in-chief. In determining competency to testify, the child witness must understand the function of stereotype in law, reflected in the manner in which Noor's responses are translated from *abba* to *pita* and *ammi* to *mummy*. The flow of the testimony is disrupted when Noor is asked again if she understands Gujarati 'full'. The performative use of the stereotype of a Muslim Gujarati as the 'Hindi-speaking' legal subject, in courtroom talk, posits Noor as alien and brackets off her competency in the everyday language and practice of law.[52] These categories are anchored to a political discourse that situates the Muslim Gujarati as the 'other'. Mehta insightfully describes the functions of a stereotype:

> First stereotypes establish a well-determined place for speakers and listeners by identifying Muslims as alien; second, in isolating Muslims, such speech puts them in an abstract space and characterises them as a coherent body beyond the limit of everyday practice. By being dissociated from daily life, the aggregation of micro decisions, the flow of everyday labour, stereotypes are separated from passing time. (2002: 222)

The function of the vernacular as a stereotype rests in the idea that the Gujarati Muslim is alien to Gujarati culture, and the vernacular becomes the site of intense identity politics. This must be understood in relation to the right-wing Hindutva discourse of *asmita*—a modality that seeks to articulate collective identity on Hindutva notions of cultural pride. The discourse of *asmita* functions by constituting the Gujarati Muslim as the 'other'. In this instance, the performative aspect of the stereotype communicates to Noor that for her to be competent to testify she must demonstrate an ability to use words that are divorced from her everyday life.[53]

EXAMINATION-IN-CHIEF

In order to make her words count in the trial court, Noornissa had to acquire competency in citing injury through the use of rigid designators. I have argued that for judicial verification of injury children are expected to narrate the sexual violence of rape in forensic detail. By this I mean that the repetitive detailing of the act of penile penetration or partial penetration is seen as necessary to verifying that the child had been raped. Yet the law requires that the testimony should be in the child's own words, even though we cannot map all the ways in which children may bring the experience of rape to language. To secure a conviction, however, it is important that the child be able to describe what happened in ways that are relevant in the law. Let us examine how Noor cites injury during the examination-in-chief conducted in Hindi.[54]

APP: Then what happened?

N: He took off my *salwar*.

J (d): And he took me near the bushes then my father [*abba*] Shakeelbhai took my *salwar* and threw it off.

APP: (*inaudible*).

N: [He] pulled my *salwar*

APP: Then?

N: *Abba* … (*inaudible*).

APP: Whose trouser [*patloon*]? Who took off father's trousers?

N: (*inaudible*)

J (d): Then my father [*abba*] took off his trousers [*patloon*].

APP: Then what happened?

N: (*silent*).

J: Took off his trousers, then what did he do to you?[55]

N: He climbed on top of me.

J (d): And then my father [*abba*] climbed on top of me.

APP: Then what happened?

N: Then he inserted his place of urination [*peeshab ki jagah*] into my place of urination.

J: What did he do?

N: Inserted.

J (d): And then he inserted his place of urination into my place of urination.

APP: Then what happened?

N: Blood came out.

APP: Where did blood come out from?

DL *to* APP *in English*: Do not lead.[56]

APP *to* DL *in English*: I won't, in such cases.

APP *to* N: You said, *na*, he climbed on you, what was he doing?

N: He was moving.

J (d): My father [*abba*] climbed on top of me and he was moving.

APP: Then what happened? He climbed on you, he sat, where were you?

N: (*silent*)

APP: Where were you, what was in the place?

N: Sand.

J (d): When my father [*abba*] Shakeelbhai had climbed on top of me at that place there was sand.

APP: Where you standing at that time?

N: I was lying down.

J (d): He climbed on top of me and was moving when my father [*abba*] Shakeelbhai climbed on me. He made me lie down.

APP: Were you wearing the *salwar*?

N: I was not wearing it. He had thrown it there.

J (d): When my father [*abba*] took me home then the *salwar* was left there where he threw it.[57]

The child must describe bodily parts and sexual injury without fully describing the designator. The court accepts the substitution of 'penis' with the 'place from where he urinates' and 'vagina' as 'the place from where she urinates' as a rigid designator. It creates a distinct mode of naming rape that is peculiar to a child. This reiterative practice of naming gives materiality to the sexualization of her body.

The use of rigid designators localizes injury to specific body parts. It elides the subjective experience of violence to sexualize her body and localizes the experience of violence to what is done to specific bodily parts. In this sense, the speech acts in the courtroom must mimetically perform what was done to specific body parts. The examination-in-chief is critical to the testimony as it provides the issues on which the defence can cross-examine the witness, and the categories used by the prosecutor become important to identify while analysing any cross-examination transcript. Both the prosecution and the defence operate within an identical framework of how to give materiality to injury, where the individual experience of the trauma matters only to the extent that it can be proved or disproved in language that has evidentiary value.

CROSS-EXAMINATION OF THE CHILD WITNESS

In statutory rape cases lack of consent 'is presumed by the law rather than disputed as fact during a trial' (Burgess-Jackson 1996: 164). Burgess-Jackson has argued that although statutory rape laws have been conceived of as 'philosophically barren', in fact these laws are 'a fertile source of conceptual and normative problems' (1996: 164). In fact, statutory rape trials are sites where the very childhood of the victim is on trial. The following excerpts demonstrate the various ways in which childhood is disputed during the trial. One of the ways is by characterizing statutory rape as 'technical rape', a phrase used routinely by lawyers in court, as described in the previous chapter. The idea that statutory rape is merely 'technical' rape demonstrates an anxious articulation of that which is legally disallowed and that which is actually possible in nature. This anxiety translates itself into the construction of the child as a collaborator, non-adult, child-adult and a child-liar. These categorizations shift swiftly throughout the testimony.

The cross-examination spilt over two days, lasting for over four hours. Initially, the defence lawyer questioned Noor about the school she went to, the language of instruction, and at the end of the first day's cross-examination, asked her how many times she had failed in school. Noor indignantly replied she had never failed. The defence hoped to establish that she was older than was claimed. Moreover, the defence lawyer communicated to Noor that he thought she was capable of failure, indicating his low opinion of her. Following this, for more than thirty minutes over the two days, the defence directed questions at Noornissa on the facts of her paternity and the relationship between her parents. This line of questioning challenged the assertion that Noor knew the identity of her biological father. The defence lawyer asked her the following questions about her 'natural' father: What was her father's name in the school records? Did she recognize her father? Where had she met him for the first time and was she with her mother at this time? For how many years had she known him? Did he still meet her mother and did the two spend time together? Did she went to go current school and live in her current home when she was raped?

We know that repetition and re-signification of answers are common defence strategies that aim to intimidate, confuse, and shake a witness into contradicting herself. These strategies are not abandoned in the case of a child witness. Rather, the defence lawyer aggressively sustained the line of questioning that linked her mother's marital biography to her being raped. The following excerpts indicate how Noor was constructed as a collaborator in a lie.

Excerpt One introduces the idea that Noor is illegitimate. This line of questioning was introduced on the first day, and follows the questions cited above. Raised voices are indicated in capitals.

> DL: Your mother told you that Jamalbhai is your father [*abba*], people told you that, mother [*ammi*] told you ... how do you know that Jamal is your father [*abba*]?
>
> N: (*silent at first*) I know.
>
> J (d): That Jamalbhai is my father [*abba*] was not told to me by my mother [*ammi*] or people told me, but I say that Jamalbhai is my father [*abba*] I know on my own.
>
> *Noor looked at the judge and averted her gaze from the defence lawyer.*
>
> DL: LOOK HERE! Does Jamalbhai come to your house?
>
> N: No.
>
> APP: No.
>
> DL *to* APP *in English*: Do not interfere.

APP *to* J *in English*: I have rights.

J *to* APP *in English*: I know him [DL]. He won't mislead.

J (d): It is not true that Jamalbhai used to frequent our house.

J *to* N: Speak with your mouth. I will explain four times if necessary. He [pointing to the DL] will explain, just tell me what you do not understand.

DL: Have you ever heard that your father's [*abba's*] name is not Jamal but is Jabbar Mohammed?

N: No.

Excerpt one illustrates how the defence dominates linguistic space by using repetition (Taslitz 1999). The effect of repetition is to suggest that Noor was unable to answer the question asked and had to answer 'forced-choice' questions, limiting the answer to a yes or no (Taslitz 1999: 90). The commands to look at the defence lawyer and the impatience at her silence increased Noornissa's anxiety. Her answers were not accepted even after her response to the defence lawyer's question about how she knew who her father was. Yet again, the defence deliberately feigned ignorance about everyday social conventions, pretending as if it were commonplace for mothers to furnish proof to their children about their paternity.

Excerpt two introduces the idea that Shakeel did not live with Hasinaben. This is how the cross-examination was resumed on day two.

DL: When the incident happened then Shakeel used to come and go to your house?

Noornissa did not answer. She looked at the judge.

J: He is saying that when the incident happened then Shakeel your father used to visit you or stayed at home? Did he stay at home? What?

N: No.

J: Where did he stay?

N: Outside.

J: Did he live outside or at home?

Hasinaben *to* N: Say that he stayed at home.

j *to* h *in gujarati*: I WILL HAVE TO ASK YOU TO LEAVE THE COURT. YOU CANNOT SPEAK IN BETWEEN!

APP: Sir [*Saheb*], the question is not proper, looking at the tender age of the girl. But look at the form of the question. It is difficult for her to understand.

J: Okay, okay. Listen, your father Shakeel used to live outside?

N: No, he lived at home.

J (d): It is not true that when the incident took place then my father Shakeelbhai used to visit the house. It is not true that at the time of the incident accused Shakeelbhai used to live outside. But I am saying that he used to live at home.

Excerpt two reveals that Hasinaben was fully aware of the normative referents being evoked here, and angry that the burden of interpreting the import of her marital biography fell squarely on the twelve-year-old. Comprehension of questions then entails competency to understand the normative. Noor is called on to act as a witness to her mother's life. The prosecutor asks the court to consider Noor's 'tender years' and reminds the defence lawyer to use 'comprehensible' language. Was this an objection to the line of questioning or merely to the way the question was framed? The question—whether Shakeel lived at home or not—required that Noor would have first have to comprehend that she was being asked whether they were indeed a stable family that lived together in a shared domestic place.

Excerpt three marks the competency of a child witness to offer resistance to the line of questioning. This segment followed the questions cited above.

DL: Look, when he lived with you how much *time*[58] did he live with you?

J: He is asking you that since how much time [*samay*] did your father Shakeelbhai live with you? He lived with your mother [*ammi*] for ten, fifteen days? One month?

N: I do not know.

J (d): I do not know since when the accused Shakeelbhai lived with my mother [*ma*] Hasinaben before the incident happened.

Excerpt three illustrates how Noor resisted the defence lawyer's control of the cross-examination by saying 'I don't know'. To confirm the defence's question on how much time Shakeel had lived with

Hasinaben would have meant agreeing with the assertion that Shakeel did not actually live with Hasinaben. To deny that he lived with her for ten to fifteen days or one month would have meant she would concede that the defence's question was important to prove what happened. Taslitz argues that to say 'I don't remember', or in this case, 'I don't know', is a strategy adopted by witnesses who struggle against the defence lawyer's control of the cross-examination, as witnesses 'don't want to confirm a detail's accuracy or concede that the point is important enough to remember' (1999: 95).

Excerpt four introduces the idea that Shakeel and Hasinaben did not get along. The defence lawyer was annoyed and raised his voice. This segment followed the questions cited above.

DL: Look, LOOK HERE! Between Hasina your mother [*ma*] and Shakeel your father [*bap*] there used to be words [*bolachali*], fights.

J: He is saying that there used to be fights between your mother [*ma*] and your father [*bap*]. When this incident happened then these two used to fight or there used to be no conversation between them.

N: No.

I turned behind to look at Hasinaben and saw that she was smiling.

APP *to* DL *in Gujarati*: The question is difficult. *Bolachali*? Just ask were they talking to each other?

J: Did they talk to each other?

N: They talked.

APP *to* DL *in Hindi*: Do not make meaninglessness out of meaning.

DL *to* APP *in Gujarati*: Whom are you teaching?

APP *to* DL *in Gujarati*: I can't teach you anything. I just have to be very alert with you (*laughs*).

J (d): It is not true that at the time of the incident accused Shakeelbhai and complainant Hasinaben did not speak to one another.

DL *to* N: Look daughter [*beti*], Shakeel is your father [*pappa*], right? And Hasina your mother [*ma*]? When the incident took place you saw him for the first time?

J: He is asking that when did you see your father [*abba*] for the first time?

DL: You saw your father [*abba*] for the first time…

APP *to* DL *in Gujarati*: Ask specific questions for specific answers. Just ask who took you away. This is a misleading question. Ask in question-answer form. In chief, it says that she was taken away from her father.

APP *to* J *in Gujarati*: How is he entitled to ask such questions?

APP *to* J *in English*: Misleading according to the Indian Evidence Act…

The judge asked the defence lawyer to rephrase the question.

DL *to* N: [You] do not understand a straight question! We are asking you so many times. When you went to take *bidi* from the house you had seen him earlier, where did you see him?

N: At home.

J (d): When my father [*pappa*] went out to buy *bidi*, I saw him at home.

By now, Noor was pale and obviously nervous. She continuously looked at Hirabhai and then at the judge. She crossed her arms across herself, hugging herself as she leaned against the witness box.

Excerpt Four exemplifies how the defence communicates blame to Noornissa. The resistance by the child witness is disciplined. When the judge upheld the prosecutor's objections, the defence lawyer directed his ire at Noor—'You do not understand a straight question; we are asking you many times.' She was told repeatedly that since she did not understand the questions, she was not a cooperative (read: good) witness. The defence lawyer's questions were deliberately calibrated to produce blame and signal disbelief.

The defence lawyer uses linguistic strategies that perform power by repetition (Taslitz 1999). The repetition makes alien a familiar world, where the ordinary trust a child has on her mother's word about the identity of her father, is questioned. Competency took on dual meanings here. First, it meant verification of her ability to understand a question. Second, competency must be understood experientially from the child's point of view since it also tests her ability to understand the questions normatively. Competency to testify in these circumstances required not just that she be legally qualified to take the stand, but that she understand that she was being told that she was an illegitimate child, her mother was immoral, and that she was lying. Noor denied any discord between her mother and stepfather. She grasped that dissolution of kinship and the violence that preceded this dissolution could not be acknowledged. Her childhood is not innocent but dangerous, as she is seen as capable of possessing knowledge of an adult mother's secrets. The child, then, not only carries the burden of moral corruption, which accrues to her mother, but is seen as her not so innocent collaborator.

CHILD AS A NON-ADULT

The victim's childhood itself is in dispute as far as the defence is concerned. The defence's line of questioning was consistently structured as if an adult witness was being cross-examined. At specific points of the testimony, the prosecution reminded the court that the defence lawyer was cross-examining a child. At other points of the testimony, however this was not in the interest of the prosecution, therefore it chose to remain silent. The following excerpts examine the moments during the cross-examination when the court was reminded that the subject was a child. The cross-examination regarding the determination of the time of the crime is an illustration of the manifold ways in which the court forgets that a child witness occupies the stand. To materialize injury, remembrance must be exacted and be exact. These questions followed the excerpts cited in the previous section.

DL: On the day of the incident, was it day or night? What was the *time*?

N: (*Silent. She looked confused. Her anxiety seemed to grow as the DL asked her about time*).

J: Was it evening or night?

N: Night.

J: Do not be anxious. Take your time in telling me. Whatever you don't understand I will explain. I already am explaining four times. Think carefully before speaking.

J (d): It is not true that at the time my father Shakeelbhai went to buy *bidi* it was evening but I say that it was night time.

DL: Do you know the *time*?

APP *to* J *in English*: She does not know how to read *time*, how will she say? Even in the chief, she has treated *time* like this.

DL: Do you know how to read *time*?

N: No.

J (d): It is true that I do not know what time of the night it was at that time.

Subsequently Noor was questioned repeatedly about the place of crime. Where did her father take her from—her home or from outside? Where was her mother at this time? The defence tried to shake her testimony by suggesting that at the time Shakeel asked her to go to the shop with him, Hasinaben was out washing clothes for her employers.

At this point the prosecutor turned to the defence lawyer to tell him that he appreciated his cross-examination. He said, 'In such type of cases, I must recommend your name. No problem, feel free to carry on with the cross-examination without any tension [*bindaas chaliye*].' There was laughter at this comment in the courtroom. The courtroom was marked with animated exchanges between the opposing lawyers, occasionally interspersed with laughter. Hirabhai did not object to the hostile cross-examination directly at all times but used humour to interrupt the flow. He excelled in courtroom performance and enjoyed the tension in the courtroom. His casual friendliness with the defence lawyer was markedly different from the latter's hostility during the cross-examination. Noor, however, remained unsure whether the laughter was provoked by her answers. The court was indifferent to the impact of the conversations between the lawyers on her, who seemed to understand that her words were the point of contestation between the opposing lawyers, now and hilarity amongst them, then.

The defence lawyer ignored the levity introduced by Hirabhai to proceed with the cross-examination. He continued to query Noor on whether Hasinaben had spoken to Shakeel at the time he asked her to go out with him, the presence of her brother, the location of the shop, its exact distance from her home in terms of kilometres, the number of footsteps and time taken, and whether (and when) she had passed the shop her father had purported to take her to. The defence questioned Noor relentlessly about her testimony that Shakeel had made her climb a wall to get to a canal which was deserted at that time. She was questioned about the height of the wall scaled, whether she had met anybody on the way, whether she had asked her father where he was taking her, and whether there were any police on the way.[59] She was expected to map the place in exact categories measured either by time taken or distance covered.

In the following excerpt we see that the court expects the child to know how to read time, and be able to testify to the exact duration of the rape. The description of the rape in her words is repeated over and over again in the questions posed to her during the cross-examination.

DL: When he lay you down, then a lot of *time* passed?

N: (*silent*)

DL: SPEAK UP! How much time?

N: A lot.

DL: How much *time*, a lot of *time*?

N: (*silent*)

J: How much *time* passed? 5 minutes, 10 minutes, 30 minutes?

DL: How much *time*?

N: (*silent*)

DL: How much *time*?

N: (*silent*)

J: When he lay you down, climbed on you, moved for how much *time*?

N: Six hours.

DL: Six hours!! Do you know the meaning of this? From morning to evening in school it is six hours, when you return home in the evening.

APP *to* DL *in English*: Do you think she understands what's the meaning of minutes? How it should be clear? You are wasting time.

J *to* APP *in Gujarati*: A twelve-year-old should know. Make her understand, *yaar*![60]

DL: I know before you told me I explained the meaning of six hours. I will explain. Do you know how much *time*?

N: I do not know.

J (d): That is how much *time* I cannot tell.

By the next question it seemed that Noor would burst into tears at any moment. 'That is, how much time I cannot tell' is how the court transcribed the oral script about what 'a twelve year old should know'.

Should Noor have known how much time six hours is? Or should she have known how to represent the duration of the rape in categories that are relevant to materializing injury? Even though it is totally irrelevant how long a survivor is raped to establish the crime, duration is used as a defence strategy to elicit remembrance in temporal exactitude. Nor does the court question this line of questioning. The question–answer sequence cited above deploys time in a mimetic relation to the act of rape. It forces the child to remember the sequence of the events in photographic detail, how each body part was assaulted, and for how long. It is almost as if she was called to testify to something she watched as a bystander rather than as someone who experienced the violence. Treated as a bystander at some points and as a not so innocent witness at others, Noor was characterized as a subject who did not fully understand what she was testifying to.

The court was not concerned with Noor's subjectivity or her experience of rape as unending, when time freezes. 'Six hours' addressed both the experience and the remembrance of violence, when neither the duration of the rape, nor the unfading nature of its memory could be captured in everyday categories of temporality. The value Noor ascribed to the duration of the violence was met with ridicule and annoyance in court. That she could not tell the duration of time was the only way in which she could testify to the way time freezes, and here her testimony met the limits of the legal evidentiary standards. Ultimately, she had to testify that she did not know the duration. 'I don't know' then functioned as a correct answer, since it was now infused with evidentiary value.

It was of no evidentiary value, however, that Noor was on the verge of tears after such an aggressive cross-examination. The written transcript does not record that the prosecutor intervened by asking the judge for permission to give Noor water. The judge looked doubtful and said, 'It has not happened till today that we have given water to anyone in the witness box.' The prosecutor replied, 'No, sir [*saheb*]. We give water to old people or those who are sick in the witness box.' The judge conceded. The court had literally forgotten that this was a child witness.[61] As in the police station, Noor found it difficult to presence herself as a child who has been raped. While appellate court guidelines cited earlier recommend that there should be reasonable breaks while taking testimony, in practice, providing a stool or water to the child witness was seen as a debatable issue in law, thus raising the question of what kind of body is ascribed to the child witness. Since rape is seen as an adult crime, it disallows the consideration of the witness's speech as being grounded in a child's body. From the child's point of view, competency to testify then requires not just the comprehension of adult normativity, but also the ability to embody the physical capacity of adults to withstand testimony.

CHILD-ADULT

Although the way 'time' was cited did not qualify as evidence of childhood, the citation of injury must retain the suggestion of an innocent childhood, even while naming and describing the violence graphically. The following excerpts demonstrate how the defence constructed Noor as a child-adult.

> DL: When he climbed on top of you, he put his urine [*peeshab*] into your urine then did you cry out?
>
> *At this point a young male lawyer walked into the court to talk to the prosecutor. The judge asked the lawyer to leave and said, 'this is a camera trial. You have to take permission.' The man replied, 'I thought I might learn something.' The judge said sternly, 'No, you have to leave'. By this time the glass of water was brought in for Noor and the lawyer left reluctantly.*
>
> J *to* N: He is asking that you screamed before or after inserting?
>
> N: After putting [*nakhane ke baad*].
>
> J (d): It is true that he lay me down and when he had inserted his place of urination [*peeshab ki jagah*][62] into my place of urination, I screamed only once.
>
> DL: Look here, you were lying down, then what did he do, how much did he do [penetrate] that you do not know. How much did he put his place of urination—half, full?[63]
>
> N: Full [*akhi*].
>
> J (d): It is not true that when I was laid down and climbed upon I did not know how much my father [*abba*] Shakeel inserted his place of urination into my place of urination. But I am saying that he put his place of urination full into my place of urination.

DL: How did you see, you were saying that you were lying down then how did you come to know?

N: Blood came out.

J: He inserted that's why blood came out.

N: Yes.

J (d): I started to bleed, on that basis I am stating that my place of urination was penetrated fully by my father [*abba*] Shakeel's place of urination. That my place of urination was penetrated fully by my father's place of urination that I did not know because blood came out but I am saying that I came to know that my place of urination was penetrated by my father's [*abba's*] place of urination.

DL: How do you know that he had inserted?

N: (*silent initially*) Because he penetrated me, that's why.

J (d): He inserted inside me, that's why.

DL: When he inserted, you screamed, then he lay down upon you, after that you kept lying and did not scream for a second time?

APP *objects*: [The question should be] did you cry at that time?

DL *to* J *in Gujarati*: He has taken it in the chief, else I would not have asked.

J: He is asking that when he inserted climbed on you, lay down then did you scream. You do not understand? [irritated] I explained four times. The faster you understand, the faster it will be over. You take your time and then speak.

N: I cried.

J (d): It is not true that I screamed once and thereafter I kept lying silently but I am saying I cried.

APP *to* DL *in Gujarati*: The style of questioning has to be different, if you ask small children as you would adults what will happen?

DL: When he climbed on top of you, he inserted his place of urination into your place of urination, then was his head moving or was he moving fully?

N: He was moving fully.

J (d): My father [*pappa*] Shakeel climbed onto me and moved, that is moved his head, that is not so but I am saying that he moved fully.

Hirabhai leaned across to whisper to me that Noor was answering very well, that her answers to these very questions would secure a conviction. Hasinaben felt differently. After the testimony, Hasinaben walked out of the courtroom in silence, her face set in silent anger. She said to me in a quiet tone of barely controlled anger, 'Does one ask children questions like these? Would these bastards [*haram ke*] ask questions like these to their own daughters or wives?' For Hasinaben, by the end of the trial, legal normativity appears illegitimate. We see here that in failing to narrate the stories of particularized injury, the law loses 'control of them on their own terms' (R. Ferguson 1996: 96).

The excerpts cited above demonstrate the conditions under which Noor's words count as testimony. Her experience of vulnerability is doubted. Her words are pitted against her experience. For her words to count as evidence she must cite injury over and over again. The repetitive questions construct a fantasy that pictures Noor as a child-adult, and as such she becomes an anomaly. Using Mary Douglas's (1970) identification of anomalies as integral to social order, James and Jenks argue that 'the stigma of anomaly works to explain how certain children are capable of actions which other, "normal", children are not: the system of classification stays intact by resisting the "defilement" of the abhorrent case' (1996: 324). Thus the normative assumptions of childhood as desexualised are reaffirmed.

Testimony is not possible without citing the injury for which the law is evoked. Rigid designators that name a sexualized body achieve this. However, this 'citationality of the performative produces that possibility of agency and expropriation at the same time' (Butler 1997: 87). On the one hand, the naming attempts to secure meaning and to guarantee that the child describes what happened. On the other hand, the 'linguistic display' does not 'overcome the degrading meaning' of the naming process (Butler 1997: 100). This degrading naming describes legal normativity as a field of force. Courtroom speech then becomes an object that is animated with the dual capacity to both injure and excite. As Butler puts it, speech is constituted as 'display, confession and evidence but not as a communicative vehicle having been deprived of its capacity to stake truthful claims' (1997: 85). The process of giving testimony displaces childhood. This is the effect of law's failure to name child sexual abuse—the story of children occupying a juridical field that deprives them of the capacity to make truthful claims as child survivors.

CHILD LIAR

In the following excerpts, I show how the defence lawyer characterizes the child witness' testimony as false. These statements by the defence constitute the last segment of the cross-examination following a standardized format where the defence lawyer states that the witness lied. The witness then is called upon to stoutly deny the defence assertion of falsehood.

> DL: Here the case has been going on, you have been coming here since three to four months, your mother and other women taught you what to say in court.
>
> APP: No, [she was] simply taught [that] if asked this, then say no.
>
> *There was laughter amongst the lawyers and the judge.*
>
> N: No.
>
> J (d): It is not true that during the period of this testimony, I have come to the court after that my mother [*ammi*] Hasinaben and other women taught me what to say and how to speak in the courtroom.
>
> DL: Your mother [*mummy*] Hasinaben, to give a false complaint against your father [*pappa*] Shakeelbhai asked you to say like this, that is why asked you to lie.
>
> N: No! (*rigorously shakes her head*)
>
> J (d): It is not true that between my mother [*ma*] and my father [*pita*] Shakeelbhai there existed a fight that's why my mother made me lie and because I lied a false complaint was lodged.
>
> DL: Nothing happened to you; [he] did not lay you down, did not insert, did not move.
>
> N: No!
>
> J (d): It is not true that my father Shakeelbhai did not do any *kharab kam* with me. Like this has happened.
>
> DL: You did not show the police the place of the incident nor could you show them the *salwar*.
>
> N: I showed it to them!
>
> J (d): It is not true that I did not show the police the place of the incident and the *muddamal*[64] *salwar*.
>
> DL: Police did not confiscate the *salwar* from the place of the incident.
>
> N: They did!

J (d): It is not true that the police did not confiscate the *salwar* from the place of the incident.

Noor reacted to being called a liar with anger. The child witness' voice is muted; her anger denied a rightful place in law.

The defence claimed that there was a conspiracy against Shakeel by Hasinaben and other women. The aggressive and repetitive statements made by the defence lawyer are a standardized way of closing a cross-examination. It marks a frontal attack where the child witness has to deny her part in the scenario of falsity that the defence creates. The materialization of injury that results in a conviction places her testimony at the limits of legal language. The cross-examination attacks the very foundations of kinship and its normative universe. It redefined Noornissa's subjectivity in ways that drew a complex relationship between words and objects.

Noor's Words

The introduction of blame creates pathos where the child's testimony in court is wrenched from her sense of the dissolution of the ordinary, the taken-for-granted knowledge about kinship and domesticity. Noor did not speak to me about what happened, but signalled the manner in which the legal discourse had inscribed itself on her subjectivity. This was conveyed to me during a conversation that took place between the testimony over two days. We were waiting outside the courtroom for the cross-examination to resume on the second day of the testimony. During this time, her mother had consented to a taped interview. Noor had been listening to us, when she shyly said to me that she wanted to wear my watch. When I gave it to her to wear, she wore it upside down. I taught her how to wear the watch so that she could learn to read time. She had not learnt how to read the digits.

'No, no,' Hasinaben protested, 'she will insist [on keeping it]. You keep wearing it. She has just lost her mind like that. The thing she desires she insists for it.'

'I do not know how to read time,' Noor replied.

Hasinaben admonished her, 'Why have you worn the watch if you cannot read the time?'

I insisted that Noor continue to wear the watch and began to teach her how to use it. She was subsequently called in for the cross-examination. She took the watch off and returned it to me before going into the courtroom to testify. She recognized the emphasis in the courtroom on time and perhaps anticipated the implicit blame that was to accrue to her for not being able to read time. The cross-examination constituted her now as a child, and then as a child-adult. The displacement of anxiety about the trial and her internalization of blame was concentrated on my watch. Her words were frozen, yet she indicated the effect of the testimony by finding a relationship of words to an object, perhaps one that pointed to her voice. Noor's words indicated her vulnerability and inability to remake her testimony within and outside the languages of law. As she left court that day, Noor shyly said to me that the pen I gave her as a gift at her request would be a *nishani*, an object that would remind her of me. She knew we would not meet again despite Hasinaben's promise to take me home.[65] In those brief hours, Noor and I were related to each other in remembrance through two objects, a pen and a watch—a complex relationship of words and objects that marked a present that was born in her knowledge that there was no future that could follow that moment.

***

In 1997, the Gujarat High Court refused to grant bail to Shakeel on the grounds that he stood in a 'fiduciary relationship' with Noornissa, and there was sufficient evidence on record to show that he raped her. Five years later, the Gujarat High Court upheld the trial court ruling dismissing Shakeel's appeal. The Gujarat High Court remarked that:

> ... regarding the actual act having committed by the appellant, the defence has not left out anything and has made all attempts by asking relevant and irrelevant and all sorts of questions. The Court has also permitted it. It is not necessary for us to appreciate each and every question being asked. While appreciating the evidence of the prosecutrix in the instant case, we have to bear in mind the fact that she is a victim of the incident and that she deposes against her own father and that at the time of incident, she was aged only ten years and that she is giving the evidence two years after. Even though time

has elapsed from the date of incident, she has still not come out of the shock and torture experienced by her.

At the time the judgment was recorded mass sexual violence against Muslim women and female children was reported in Ahmedabad, including in the very neighbourhood Noor had once lived in. In this context, it would perhaps have been a powerful move for the Gujarat High Court to evoke the Supreme Court's guidelines to indicate judicial intolerance of insensitivity towards rape victims. The Gujarat High Court, for instance, did not notice that as a Gujarati Muslim, Noor was forced to depose in Hindi even though she would have been more comfortable in testifying in Gujarati. The fact that the defence asked Noor 'irrelevant and all sorts of questions' met judicial disapproval, yet no directions were issued to the trial court to follow appellate judgments on the modalities of conducting rape trials, especially in the case of children. The Delhi High Court provides us a contrast.

In *Sheeba Abidi* v. *State & Anr*[66] the Delhi High Court held that it is the duty of the court to prevent the harassment of rape victims and other witnesses during cross-examination. Towards this, the Delhi High Court further stated that the defence lawyers should put down the questions they wish to ask a child witness to the presiding judge in writing and the judge would ask these questions in her own language to prevent any trauma to the child during cross-examination. Perhaps it is only fair to ask why the judicial interpretation of rape in courts in Gujarat has not taken a page out of these appellate judgments, since the Supreme Court ruled in the famous *Bharwad Bhoginbhai Harjibhai* v. *the State of Gujarat*[67] that corroboration is not necessary in rape trials. Instead we encounter a series of illegalities instituted at the heart of the rape trial—illustrated by the practice of compromise in rape cases in trial courts, although by no means only confined to courts in Ahmedabad. This is the subject of the next chapter.

NOTES

1. In this book, I am concerned with female children. The use of the category of child implies female children and any reference to male children will be qualified.

2. Julie Gammon's study of rape cases on girls below the age of fourteen that came up to the Old Bailey between 1734–94 reveals that 'each one

faced disbelief and censure in the middle-class courtroom in which the honesty of any female who claimed to have been sexually assaulted was questioned' (1999: 74–75). Further, 'for the story of a child above the age often to be given any credibility in a courtroom she was expected to undergo the same treatment as an adult victim on the witness stand. Yet it is evident from the difficulty in obtaining a child's testimony upon oath that it was recognized that her very young age did create a problem in understanding legal concepts applicable to adults' (Gammon 1999: 82).

3. The term 'adult normativity' highlights the normative between the testimonies of rape by adult women and children, while retaining the argument that in both cases the rape trial is constituted through phallocentric categories.

4. A *bidi* is a locally manufactured, inexpensive smoke made of tobacco rolled up in leaf.

5. The delay in law courts has been seen as a technique for denying justice to litigants and as a resource for litigants who use law courts for purposes other than stated in the law (see Moog 2003).

6. The court constable is entrusted with carrying the summons to the witness from the court and assisting the court.

7. 'Junior' is an abbreviation for a junior lawyer, an apprentice working with an experienced senior lawyer (or 'senior').

8. The two high court judgments regarding bail and the appeal hearing are on the author's personal file. The citation of the judgment has been withheld to maintain confidentiality.

9. The term 'first information report' is not mentioned in the CrPC. It derives its meaning from s. 154 of the code, which holds that 'every information relating to the commission of a cognizable offence, if given orally to an officer in charge of a police station, shall be reduced to writing by him or under his direction, and be read over the information; and every such information, whether given in writing or reduced to writing aforesaid, shall be signed by the person giving it, and the substance thereof shall be entered in a book to be kept by such officer in such form as the State Government may prescribe in this behalf' (Ratanlal & Dhirajlal 2002: 209). The section further holds that a copy of the information should be made available to the informer free of cost. In other words, the information regarding a cognizable offence has to be registered and the police have to initiate an investigation. It has been held by the appellate courts that the 'refusal to record an FIR on the ground that the place of crime does not fall within the territorial jurisdiction of the police station, amounts to dereliction of duty. Information about cognizable offence would have to be recorded and forwarded to the police station having jurisdiction' (Ratanlal &

Dhirajlal 2002: 211). The importance of lodging the FIR promptly follows the procedure to 'obtain early information of alleged criminal activity, to record the circumstances before there is time for them to be forgotten or embellished and the report can be put in evidence when the informant is examined' (Ratanlal & Dhirajlal 2002: 212).

10. This was a euphemistic way by which Hasinaben indicated her fear that Noor could be abducted for the purpose of prostitution when she grew up.

11. The sale or consumption of alcohol is prohibited in Gujarat. In this case, we find that Shakeel was not charged with violating the law prohibiting the consumption of alcohol. Similarly, we find that references to drunken policemen in police stations. The consumption of alcohol remains part of everyday life, so much so that encountering a drunk police officer in a state that enforces prohibition was seen as routine.

12. The word *riksha* refers to auto rickshaw. To travel in this motorized three-wheeler costs more than a public bus and less than a taxi. Hasinaben could not even afford bus fare.

13. In cases of rape, the police refer the rape victim to a government hospital, and the medico-legal certificate is a crucial piece of evidence. Such examinations are only carried out in government hospitals. In practice, doctors often refuse to examine a rape victim without police authorization. The Supreme Court has disapproved of such refusal to examine rape victims without police referrals, especially in rural areas (see *State of Karnataka* v. *Manjanna* [2000][6] 2 SCC 188). Following public criticism that the police do not register rape complaints and doctors do not examine the victim, the 2013 amendment introduced two new sections. Section 166A states that when a public servant disobeys a law by calling a person for the purpose of investigation into an offence, knowingly prejudices any person during the conduct of an investigation, and fails to record information given to him in rape and other sexual offences shall be punished for a minimum period of six months but may also extend to two years. Section 166B specifies that if any medical officer, in charge of public or private hospital, does not treat a victim s/he would be punished by imprisonment which may extend to one year and/or be fined.

14. I interviewed the PSI briefly in the courtroom while he was waiting to testify. By then, three and a half months had passed since Noornissa had testified. The investigating officer is usually the last witness to testify.

15. Section 57 of the CrPC holds that 'no police officer shall detain in custody a person arrested without warrant for a longer period than under all the circumstances of the case is reasonable, and such period shall not in the absence of a special order of a Magistrate under s. 167, exceed twenty-four

hours exclusive of the time necessary for the journey from the place of arrest to the Magistrate's Court' (Ratanlal & Dhirajlal 2002: 64).

16. I chose to interview Shakeel outside the courtroom rather than in the police van with other prisoners in the court compound. I interviewed him briefly in the presence of six constables and a few interested bystanders.

17. When I asked the court constable if he had spoken to Shakeel and how he had represented what happened, I learnt that Shakeel had denied raping Noornissa. According to the court constable, Shakeel maintained that he had raped his neighbour's daughter and he had been drunk that day.

18. 'Talkies' refers to a cinema hall.

19. *Kharab kam* or *jharkam* is a common metaphoric allusion to rape. It literally means 'bad deed', and has been translated as a wrong sexual act based on force or illicit sex depending on the context. I have hereafter retained this phrase in the translated excerpts.

20. One of the reasons for delay in registering cases of rape is that the police routinely refuse to believe complaints. Delay in rape cases compounds the difficulties in producing evidence, especially because the medical evidence is lost. Complainants may delay filing a case due to a number of reasons, mainly due to the adverse social consequences of reporting rape. Appellate courts have ruled that when the delay is on the part of the complainant, this does not necessarily signify that the case is false. This has been recognized as reasonable grounds by appellate courts to account for a delay in making a police complaint. For instance, in *Harpal Singh* v. *State of HP* (AIR 1981 SC 361), the 'court was satisfied by the explanation that since the honour of the family was involved the complaint was delayed' (cited in Ratanlal & Dhirajlal 2002: 213).

21. I came across the practice of recording such statements of the accused in other cases as well. While these statements confess to the crime, legally these do not meet the evidentiary requirements of an authentic confession.

22. See *Sudesh Jhaku* v. *K.C.J. and Others* 1998 Cri LJ 2428.

23. For instance, in *Sreehari Swarnakar* v. *Emperor* (AIR 1930 Cal 132 at para 9), the Calcutta High Court agreed with the findings of the jury who found the accused guilt of rape on a nine-year-old child. In this case, the mother testified that her daughter had told her that the injury was a result of a leech bite. The child denied this. The appellate judge noted that the testimony of the child should not be set aside merely on the grounds that the mother's testimony did not corroborate or contradicted the child's testimony. In this case, the judge ruled that alongside the conviction, whipping was an adequate form of punishment for rape on a nine-year-old child.

24. See *Ram Charan* v. *State of UP* 1998 Cri LJ 3368.

25. Ibid.

26. For instance, the Supreme Court held that the idea that the parents of the prosecutrix would have themselves caused injury to the prosecutrix by inserting fingers in her vagina, thereby rupturing her hymen, is not all understandable [see *State of HP* v. *Raghubir Singh*, (1993) 2 SCC 622].

27. This assumption may be traced to Taylor who cites a case described by Casper, where a ten-year-old girl's vagina had been dilated by the mother 'at first with two fingers into it, in order to fit her into intercourse with men' (1865: 993). In this case, we are told that the hymen was intact, yet the 'mucous membrane was reddened and painful to touch; and there was mucous discharge from it' (1865: 993). Taylor further adds, hypothetically, that if the mother had made an allegation of rape, from these symptoms a medical expert might have supported the claim. He cautions in such cases the truth could only be discerned by cross-examining the mother and child separately during the trial.

28. Section 273 of the CrPC makes it 'obligatory that evidence for the prosecution and defence should be taken down in the presence of the accused' (Ratanlal & Dhirajlal 2002: 435). The sessions judge, however, reserves 'the power to dispense with the personal attendance of the accused and to allow him to appear by pleader during the sessions trial' (Ratanlal & Dhirajlal 2002: 436).

29. Typically, the responses in a cross-examination that deny the assertion of the defence lawyer begin with the phrase 'it is not true that'.

30. The defence lawyer suggested that the term *janampatri* refers to its common meaning denoting a Hindu astrological chart. Hasinaben clarified that she meant that Noor's birth had been registered, and her parentage was recorded in a birth certificate issued by the state. The defence strategy often rests on a semantic exploitation of the words used in everyday life to establish the grounds of defence in the words of the prosecution witness.

31. By 'this side', Hasinaben refers to the walled city or the older part of the city, such as her neighbourhood, which was dominated by a Muslim population. In her narrative, the city was mapped in terms of Muslim- and Hindu-dominated areas. When she spoke of Shakeel's sisters who worked in a beauty parlour, she described that locality (not located in the old city) as a Hindu area.

32. Tutoring a witness to give false evidence amounts to an offence under ss. 192 and 194 IPC.

33. Section 137 of the Indian Evidence Act specifies that 'the examination of a witness by the party who calls him shall be called his examination-in-chief. The examination of a witness by the adverse party shall be called his cross-examination. The examination of a witness, subsequent

to the cross-examination by the party, shall be called his re-examination'
(Ratanlal & Dhirajlal 1999: 443–4). The object of re-examination 'is to
afford the party calling a witness an opportunity of filing in the lacuna or
explaining the inconsistencies which the cross-examination has discovered
in the examination-in-chief of the witness. It is accordingly limited to the
explanation of matters referred to in cross-examination. It partakes of the
nature of examination-in-chief in as much as no leading questions can be
asked' (Ratanlal & Dhirajlal 1999: 449–450).

34. The statement records the events leading up to the rape while
emphasizing that Hasinaben tried to prevent her daughter from going with
Shakeel. We see the implicit suggestion that Hasinaben did not trust her
husband with her daughter.

35. (1996) 2 SCC 384.

36. Ibid. at para 23.

37. See *Sudesh Jhaku* v. *K.C.J. and Others* (1998) Cri LJ 2428.

38. Ibid. at para 36.

39. Ibid.

40. Ibid.

41. Ibid.

42. Ibid. at para 38.

43. Section 280 CrPC provides that the sessions judge or the magistrate
records remarks that she or he thinks material regarding the demeanour of
the witness who is being examined. The judge's notes on the demeanour
of the witness are not made public and so I did not have access to such
material. Nor was it possible to interview the judge on the specific case
being heard at that time. By and large, judges are forbidden to speak on
matters before them and refuse to give interviews.

44. This is equally relevant in cases of rape of children younger than
twelve years of age, when the burden of proof is on the defence to disprove
rape once the fact of sexual intercourse is established.

45. Noornissa faced raised voices, anger, and jocularity that she did
not fully comprehend, and was often reprimanded for not understanding
questions during the testimony. She struggled not to cry at several points of
the testimony.

46. *Prem Shankar Shukla* v. *Delhi Administration* [(1980) 3 SCC 526]
and *Citizens for Democracy* v. *State of Assam* [(1995) 3 SCC 743] have
held that prisoners should not be handcuffed in the court. This rule is not
implemented uniformly. I saw prisoners (in other cases) tied to each other
by ropes on the court premises on more than one occasion.

47. Section 276 of the CrPC holds that 'in all trials before a Court of
Session, the evidence of each witness shall, as his examination proceeds, be

taken down in writing by the presiding Judge himself or by his dictation in open court or, under his direction and superintendence, by an officer of the court appointed by him in this behalf' (Ratanlal & Dhirajlal 2002: 437). The evidence 'may ordinarily be taken down in the form of a narrative, but the presiding Judge may, in his discretion, take down or cause to be taken down, any such evidence in the form of question and answer' (Ratanlal & Dhirajlal 2002: 437).

48. At times, police officers, forensic officers, medical experts, or the prosecutor dictate the response for the court record, or help the judge to do so.

49. The 'trend of the cross-examination is in most cases determined by the line of narrative unfolded in the examination-in-chief. It is usual to take each important item so deposed to and cross-examine the witness upon it. Its purpose is two-fold. First of all the cross-examiner tries to discover if the story told by the witness in examination-in-chief is tainted by exaggerations or falsehoods. Second, the adverse party can in some cases construct his line of defence from out of the mouth of the witness' (Ratanlal & Dhirajlal 1999: 447–8). During the cross-examination, leading questions can be asked, unlike the examination-in-chief.

50. In this case, we see that the sessions judge held that to determine competency, questions relating to religion are prescribed in law. The prosecutor accepted this interpretation and did not evoke appellate rulings on this issue.

51. As per s. 272 of CrPC, the state government determines the language of each court in the state other than the high court. Section 227 of the CrPC holds that a witness can give evidence in the language of the court or in any other language, and if the testimony of the witness is not in the language of the court, it must find true translation. In procedural law we find that 'the proper and convenient way of recording evidence is to take it down in the first person exactly as spoken by the witness' (Ratanlal & Dhirajlal 2002: 438).

52. As Mehta argues, 'the performative aspect of stereotypes is that they are magisterial and their function is to provide, in times of collective violence, a movement from the didactic to the practical' (2002: 233).

53. In the excerpts cited hereafter, I have retained in brackets the original words used to refer to her mother and father during the rest of the testimony.

54. Noor was queried about the time of the incidence. She could not tell the time as she did not know how to read time. The court accepted that she could describe time only as day or night. Noor did not name Shakeel either as her father or by his proper name but as 'he', but the judge translated her reference to Shakeel as 'my father', 'Shakeelbhai', or 'the accused' for the court records.

55. Note that the judge avoids using the honorific form of 'you' (*aap*).

56. According to s. 141 of the IEA, 'any question suggesting the answer which the person putting it wishes or expects to receive is called a leading question' (Ratanlal & Dhirajlal 1999: 451). Section 142 of the IEA specifies that such questions cannot be asked if the opposite party opposes these, unless the court permits it. In such a case, the court 'shall permit leading questions as to matters which are introductory or undisputed, or which have, in its opinion, been already sufficiently proved' (Ratanlal & Dhirajlal 1999: 451).

57. Following this, Noor testified that she did not know the time Shakeel took her home. She testified that she had worn a yellow-coloured *salwar* and a frock on top of *salwar* at the time. Shakeel dropped her home and stood outside the house while she went in and told her mother what had happened. We further learn that the police took her statements two days after the incident, and took her and Shakeel to the scene of crime. Noor led them to the place Shakeel had thrown away the *salwar*. Following this, the judge asked her to tell him her mother's name. Then the prosecutor showed her some clothes, which had been cut unevenly, presumably by forensic experts. She testified that these were her clothes, worn on the day she was raped. She was then asked whether she had been examined at the hospital. Noornissa testified that she had been admitted in the hospital for two to three days.

58. The defence lawyer used the word 'time' in English repeatedly, knowing she could not read time and did not understand English.

59. The implicit suggestion was that she did not make a 'hue and cry'—a legal doctrine explained in Chapter 4—when Shakeel was taking her away.

60. *Yaar* is a term commonly used to mean friend. The usage here denotes informality, which departs from received picture of courtroom proceedings based on formal, authoritarian distance between the judge and the lawyer at all times. Familiarity between the bar and the bench is a common occurrence during trials.

61. To take the stand is physically exhausting for a child. It was a hot afternoon and Noor had been standing for two hours facing a hostile cross-examination when the prosecutor intervened. He said to the judge, 'Sir, send for a stool. Her feet must be aching. Even ours ache—hers surely must be'. The judge said, 'I saw her shifting her feet. I thought it was itching her. She has been here for two hours.' A stool was brought in and placed in the witness box. Towards the end of the testimony, annoyed by Noor's silence, the judge directed her to stand and did not allow her to sit again until she answered a few questions.

62. The defence abbreviated the phrase *peeshab ki jagah* to *peeshab*, which means 'urine', thus emphasizing the filthiness of the act.

63. As we have seen in the previous chapter, by asking whether the penis penetrated partially or fully, the defence uses the medico-legal category of partial penetration as an experiential category. In this case, the medico-legal report stated that Noor's hymen was intact. It recorded medical evidence of partial penetration of the vagina and other injuries incurred on other body parts. Here, the category of partial penetration is misinterpreted as the length of penetration, rather than the fact that partial penetration is sufficient to constitute rape.

64. *Muddamal* literally means 'things of the case'. When clothes, a vial of blood, and other kinds of material evidence collected for forensic examination are preserved and produced in court for verification, they are referred to as *muddamal*.

65. After Noor's cross-examination, Hasinaben did not come back to the court to take me to her home.

66. (2003)(3) JCC 1216.

67. AIR 1983 SC 753.

CHAPTER FOUR

Justice Is a Secret
Compromise in Rape Trials

꒰꒱

The socio-legal process encapsulated in the word 'compromise' (or *samadhan*,[1] the coexisting Gujarati usage) is an exposition of how secrecy may be thought of as 'indispensable to the operation of power rather than as an abuse of power' (Taussig 1999: 57). Compromise as a form of public secret is not destroyed by its utterance before the judge but is subjected to a specific revelation in court (Taussig 1999). This specific revelation in a courtroom is actualized through the law of evidence when prosecution witnesses turn hostile to the prosecution case. Trial transcripts or trial court judgments do not record these as compromise cases except as a residue via the category of hostility. The ethnographic account of the way testimony is structured in a compromise case demonstrates how this effacement in law produces a specific revelation, which is perceived somehow to perform 'justice'.

Unlike other forms of out-of-court settlements described as mechanisms of alternate dispute resolution, plea-bargaining or mediation in courts of law, compromise is not legal in rape cases in India.[2] In Indian law, crime is classified into two categories: those that are compoundable[3] and those that are non-compoundable under ss. 320(1) and (2) of the CrPC. Rape is a non-compoundable crime, which means that opposing parties cannot bargain and settle out of court, thereby affecting the outcome of the trial. Such crimes cannot be compounded[4] or compromised between individuals, since state law is constituted as the sole arbitrator of the extent and nature of injury caused to society by a crime.

The power to reify society, act on its behalf, and to punish, incarcerate, or act in the interest of society must be conserved and continually reiterated. It is for these reasons that s. 213 IPC holds that it is a crime when there is an agreement not to bring the criminal to justice in exchange for some pecuniary or other gratification (Ratanlal & Dhirajlal 2001). The illegal gratification must actually (or promise to) conceal an offence, screen a person from legal punishment, or abstain from the criminal proceeding in exchange of any gratification or property.[5] Yet, I was repeatedly told in the trial court that most rape cases are compromised in trial courts. Intrigued by a practice that the law books clearly state as against the intent of law, I decided to pursue the story of compromise cases.

COMPROMISE AND QUASH

Although appellate judges have ruled that individuals cannot compromise rape cases yet the issue of compromise is routinely raised in appellate courts during sentencing, bail, or when a petition is filed for quashing (or making void) the criminal proceedings. In 2010, refusing to quash a complaint of repeated rape of a minor on the basis of a compromise the accused had contracted with the child's father, the Gujarat High Court held that 'statutorily as well as judicially, offence of rape is viewed as one offence where the Court should have no tolerance'.[6] Similarly, the Delhi High Court decried the legal strategy of appealing to the courts to quash a rape case after a compromise.[7] The Delhi High Court insisted that 'sexual offences constitute an altogether different class of crime which is the result of a perverse mind. By their very nature these crimes cannot be treated at par with economic crimes or the crimes such as causing grievous hurt or even attempt to commit murder'.[8] The court further held:

> [I]f the accused in such a case is an affluent person and the prosecutrix comes from a socially or economically weaker strata of the society, quashing in such a case would only encourage commission of such offences, as the accused, using his money power or otherwise, may be able to induce the prosecutrix to enter in to settlement with him and then seek quashing of criminal proceedings, on the strength of that settlement.[9]

The Delhi High Court rightly identifies that compromise negotiated between parties of unequal status is scripted by economic, political, or social dominance.

COMPROMISE AS A GROUND FOR BAIL

Even though courts have ruled that compromise would encourage men to commit rape with impunity, the acceptability of compromise in rape cases seems to have expanded in appellate courts, inaugurating new practices that often mask the violence underlying a compromise. It is indeed noteworthy that compromise is cited routinely as a ground for bail in rape cases.[10] In March 2011, the Patna High Court granted bail since other witnesses did not corroborate the victim's statement, and the victim also appeared (presumably before the court) to state that she had compromised the case with the parties.[11] In 2011, bail was granted after the counsel for the accused claimed that the rape victim and her grandmother had turned hostile following a compromise with the accused.[12]

Courts have also declined to grant bail on the grounds of compromise.[13] For instance, in a bail application in the case of the gangrape on a woman who was eight months pregnant, the Patna High Court rejected the bail application.[14] Similarly, in the case of the rape of a Dalit woman tried under the PoA Act, the defence counsel argued that this was a false allegation due to a dispute relating to wages, and sought bail on the grounds of compromise.[15] The bail petition was rejected, but the Patna High Court directed that the trial take place within six months. In these cases, whether bail (or anticipatory bail) is granted or not, the pressure to compromise is not seen as intimidation of witnesses.[16] In *Patu and Teerath Pal* v. *the State*, a ten-year-old victim's father testified that he resisted the pressure to compromise the gangrape of his daughter by the two accused.[17] While the High Court of Uttaranchal at Nainital upheld the trial judgment sentencing the accused to ten years each, the high court did not initiate legal action against the accused for attempting to force a compromise.

COMPROMISE DOCUMENTS AS EVIDENCE OF FALSITY

In courts, compromise documents are produced to introduce scepticism about the veracity of the victim's testimony, and to question her conduct or character. For instance, in the case of a fifty-year-old woman who was raped repeatedly by a younger man, the defence claimed that she had compromised the case with the accused for a sum Rs 5,000.[18] The accused's brother submitted an affidavit (Ex. D-1) ostensibly signed by the victim stating that she had not been raped and she had falsely implicated the accused. The rape survivor denied these allegations, testifying that the accused's brother wanted her to compromise the matter, but she had refused to accept his offer and the money offered was still with a local policeman. In this case, the Rajasthan High Court held that 'from Ex. D-1, no adverse inference can be drawn against the prosecution, rather it fortifies the case of the prosecution'.[19] This is one of the few cases where the court read the evidence of compromise as signifying the truth of the victim's testimony.

Defence lawyers generally argue that delay in registering a police complaint is caused by failed attempts to compromise the case, and therefore such cases are false.[20] In *Chamar Singh @ Raju Mahli and Paul Alexender @ Jendeer Minj* v. *State of Jharkhand*[21] it was alleged that the complaint of gangrape on a seven-year-old was false and it was filed only after the accused men refused to compromise the case with the child's family.[22] To indicate how compromise documents signify falsity in a trial, I turn to an appeal heard by a man convicted of raping a nine-year-old girl in the Rajasthan High Court in *Papuria @ Rajesh* v. *State of Rajasthan*.[23] The appeal challenged the Bhilwara trial court ruling sentencing the accused to seven years imprisonment. The Rajasthan High Court held that the child's testimony taken on oath was not corroborated.[24] The court noted that during the trial, five defence witnesses testified that the child had secured these injuries by falling on a fan. The defence produced the father's statement to the *panchayat*, executed on stamp paper which stated that the 'injury to the private parts of the prosecutrix was caused due to fall in the field while she was running away to escape thrashing by the accused for unauthorised entry of the cattle in the field of the accused'.[25] The trial judge had dismissed the compromise document on the grounds that the parents of the victim had not been cross-examined about the document, although the victim's brother, who had been cross-examined, testified that the father had compromised the matter before a *panchayat*.

The Rajasthan High Court ruled that 'the rejection of the document and other defence evidence by the learned judge appears to be incorrect and illegal, defence evidence cannot be rejected on extraneous consideration'.[26] The high court, unwilling to rely on the uncorroborated testimony of the victim, held that 'it appears to be a case of subsequent compromise, there is also reasonable doubt regarding the complicity of the accused and the fact regarding ravishing the prosecutrix. The possibility of her having been injured due to fall while running away cannot be over-Ruled [sic]'.[27] The compromise document executed in the presence of the *panchayat* was made to signify falsity. The court's acceptance of compromise statements executed on stamp paper before a *panchayat* marks the increasing reliance on compromise documents as a means to discredit the rape victim.

Children have no control on such transactions over their bodies. What happens when the child's parents turn hostile after negotiating a compromise, and the victim testifies to rape during the trial? In a case from Rajasthan,[28] a sixteen-year-old girl was returning home from a flourmill was accosted and dragged to a distance by the appellants. One of them pointed a gun at her while the other raped her. The eyewitness in this case turned hostile. The sixteen-year-olds' parents also turned hostile. The government pleader arguing on behalf of the state held that it was because the parents had entered into a compromise with the accused.[29] However, the court found this unbelievable. I quote:

> It has come in the statements of the parents that there was compromise between the parties. On this part of the statement, the PP [public prosecutor] argued that because of the compromise the parents have deliberately suppressed the truth. It has not been asked to the witnesses that there was incident of rape which was compounded. ... It can hardly be believed that the parents would compound the offence of sexual assault on their unmarried daughter of 16 years. There could not be any cause for the parents to come to the rescue of the accused in preference to the prestige and honour of their daughter.[30]

The court placed its reliance on the parents' testimony, dismissed the victim's testimony as unreliable, and acquitted the appellants on all counts except for the illegal possession of a firearm. In this case, the court believed that parents would rather go to a court of law than compromise a case of rape, and that the minor lied. When judges opine that parents would never compromise a rape case, they forget that compromise is a negotiation between adults where children's voices have no hearing.[31] The contestation over the monopoly to compromise suggests that a minor has little control over her own story of subjection.

COMPROMISE AND THE FICTION OF THE *HABITUÉ*

The culture of admitting written statements executed on stamp paper as defence evidence is bewildering. Why does a written statement on a stamp paper have legal validity when compromise in rape cases is illegal?[32] The Punjab and Haryana High Court rejected such defence evidence in the case of a thirteen-year-old Dalit girl who was gangraped by two men, one of whom was also Dalit and known to the victim.[33] In this case, the trial court in Jind found the two men guilty of gangrape and sentenced them to ten years of rigorous imprisonment.[34] On appeal, the counsel for the accused argued in the High Court of Punjab and Haryana in Chandigarh that the victim and her family members were 'habitual of levelling such type of allegations'.[35] The defence produced in court a male witness who testified that the victim levied similar allegations against his son, but compromised the matter for a sum of Rs 10,000.

The defence also produced a compromise document that stated the victim's name, her father's name, and address. It noted her caste as Harijan and age as fourteen. The document, labelled Exhibit Defence 1 (Ex. D-1), declared that the victim, accompanied by her parents and respectable members of the community, including the members of the *panchayat*, alleged at a police post that her uncle kidnapped and raped her. The document further stated that the father, when asked about the incident, admitted that the child in her immaturity had levied a false allegation of rape and abduction against her uncle without realizing the consequences. Such an allegation had been made in order to persuade the accused to compromise a pending court case against her family. This document, ostensibly signed by the victim's father and other witnesses, was registered at the police station as a daily diary report.

The court noted that a handwriting expert did not verify Ex. D-1. Nor was the mother cross-examined about this document, which the court inferred was a deliberate strategy. The court observed that rape is a non-compoundable offence, and therefore, the case could not be compromised by 'making a writing Ex D1'.[36] The court further held that even if 'Ex D1 is accepted without insisting for mode of proof, it is fraught with dangerous consequences, any rich and mighty [*sic*] may resort to this tactics and defeat ends of justice'.[37] This case indicates judicial concern about the creation of documents that allege compromise, unreliable witnesses who claim that the victim habitually compromises rape allegations, failure to lead evidence to 'prove' a document, and strategies of discrediting the victim as a means of discharging the burden of proof.

After the 1983 amendment, especially in those cases where the defence bears the burden of proof, such as in gangrape cases, defence lawyers seem to rely on compromise to establish the falsity of the complaint and to discredit the victim. The culture of compromise consolidates itself fully in the aftermath of the 1983 and 2002 amendments whereby the defence could not any more directly attack the victim on the basis of her past sexual history and the burden of proof was reversed in aggravated sexual offences. Defence witnesses who testify that the victim tried to exhort them on false rape charges are produced in court, or documents whose verifiability remains dubious are produced to indicate an amicable settlement or to serve as retractions of the complaint. This suggests to us that the figure of the *habitué* is manufactured through the fiction of compromise.

THIS IS A COUNTER CASE

Defence lawyers routinely argue during trials that the charge of rape has been filed against the accused to secure a compromise in another land dispute or other court cases between the two parties. The complaint of rape, then, is positioned as a 'counter case' in ongoing litigation between two parties. Consider the terrible story of abuse that unfolded in the Allahabad High Court in a bail petition in 2010.[38] The accused divorced his wife and gained custody of his daughter, whom he raped repeatedly. The child's complaints to her stepmother and other paternal relatives proved to be futile. She finally managed to complain to her maternal uncle, who rescued her from her father's home. When the father was tried, the defence alleged that the victim's mother had filed a compromise petition in a civil matter where she had not mentioned that her husband had raped their daughter. Thereby suggesting that the mother had tutored her daughter to lie in order to reach a favourable out of court settlement in the civil litigation against her husband. The high court denied bail, observing that 'the appellant has debased the relationship of father and daughter by committing rape on her. There can be no safer place than the house and custody of father to a daughter. Even if she kept mum for some time due to terror of the appellant, it does not amount to her consent for sexual intercourse by her father'.[39]

It is relevant here to recall *State of Punjab* v. *Gurmit Singh and Others*—a landmark case cited widely for evolving guidelines about how rape survivors should be treated in trial courts—concerned the brutal gangrape of a schoolgirl by three men.[40] The father brought the matter to the notice of the *sarpanch* of the village. The *panchayat* tried in vain to arrive at a compromise, and a police complaint was lodged. Challenging the defence argument that the victim's father initiated a false prosecution of rape in order to compound another civil or criminal case, the court held that:

> Even if it be assumed for the sake of argument that there was some such litigation, it could hardly be a ground for a father to put forth his daughter to make a wild allegation of rape against the son of the opposite party, with a view to take revenge. It defies human probabilities. No father could stoop so low as to bring forth a false charge of rape on his unmarried minor daughter with a view to take revenge from the father of an accused on account of pending civil litigation. Again, if the accused could be falsely involved on account of that enmity, it was equally possible that the accused could have sexually assaulted the prosecutrix to take revenge from her father, for after all, enmity is a double edged weapon, which may be used for false implication as well as to take revenge.[41]

The court departs from the standardized narrative of compromised false cases by pointing out that the victim could have been assaulted due to the enmity and rape itself is framed as a specific form of revenge.[42]

MONOPOLY TO SETTLE

We see time and again, that *panchayats*[43] attempt to appropriate the court's monopoly to adjudicate crime by treating rape as a social dispute that can be settled within a village or community. Further, the *panchayat* speaks the language of compromise as if it were representative of community consensus about how the victim should behave. Such settlements do not require the consent of the rape survivor or her family. The contestation over the monopoly to compromise rape cases suggests that the power to name the harm of rape is appropriated by the family or the community, wresting from the survivor her ability to prosecute rape as a crime against her body.

This is what happened to a twelve-year-old daughter of a gardener who was raped while cleaning a temple adjacent to their home early in the morning in Delhi.[44] Her mother found her unconscious soon after she was raped. When the parents confronted the accused, they were threatened that they would be killed if they went to the police. A *panchayat* was called in the neighbourhood (referred to as *gali panchayat* in the judgment) where the victim described what happened to her and the accused was also called. The *panchayat* decided to settle the case without the consent of the father.

The *panchayat* generated a compromise document. In this document, the accused 'admitted misconduct with the prosecutrix and also gave in writing that he was admitting his guilt. He assured (sic) not to repeat such an act in future and apologized for the mistake committed by him. This document also shows that a token penalty was imposed upon the appellant by the panchayat which then forgave him'.[45] In court, the defence denied that this compromise document referred to rape. Producing a defence witness, they argued that this compromise statement pertained to an earlier altercation between the victim's mother and the accused over water. It was this water dispute, they claimed, that the parents had framed a false charge of rape against the accused. Rejecting the defence arguments, the Delhi High Court observed that 'it is thus quite clear that the appellant had been putting pressure on the parents of the prosecutrix not to report the matter to the police, though they were not really willing to forgive him'.[46] It is apparent that the pressure to compromise is enforced through networks of powerful middlemen including lawyers, policemen, and local politicians who act on behalf of the accused. Refusal to compromise often results in tragic consequences.

COMPROMISE AS A TECHNIQUE OF TERROR

While we do not have any statistical accounts of how many murders or suicides follow the refusal to compromise rape cases, we must recognize that compromise masks annihilating violence. The violence underlying compromise does not emanate only from the accused or his family but also often gets articulated by functionaries of state institutions responsible for investigating the case, such as the police and other bodies like the Central Bureau of Investigation (CBI). Commenting on the CBI, the Kerala High Court observed that 'the investigators appear to be more interested in persuading the petitioner to settle and compromise the dispute rather than to ensure that the offenders are brought to book'.[47] The involvement of the police in pressurizing the complainant to compromise, as evident from these appellate judgments, illustrates the terrifying power of compromise as a public secret. In *Vijay Sood* v. *State of Himachal Pradesh*[48] the police put pressure on the complainant and her family to compromise the case, which they resisted. When press reporters showed up in their home to cover the event, her father was so ashamed that he committed suicide. Nor are rape survivors protected from threats and intimidation by the accused.

In a case from Agra, a young Dalit woman who was gangraped was terrorized by the accused after he was granted bail.[49] The family moved from Agra to Aligarh. The accused continued to intimidate the victim into compromising, threatening to see her raped again, and her father and brother murdered.[50] The victim subsequently committed suicide nearly one year after she was raped. While the court records the pressure to compromise as the context of the suicide, it does not consider punishing the accused for using compromise as a technique of terror. *Satyanarayan @ Chhinga* v. *State of Rajasthan* describes the terrifying story of a rape victim who was murdered at the behest of the accused when she refused to compromise the case.[51] Far from being an expression of collective consensus, compromise is predatory on claims to justice, and shadowed by violence or its threat. The normalizing function of the socio-legal category of compromise makes terror look like a social bargain.

COMPROMISE IS AN ADEQUATE AND SPECIAL REASON

We may recall that after the 1983 amendment it was legislated that courts may 'for adequate and special reasons to be mentioned in the judgment', impose a sentence of imprisonment for a term of less than the mandatory minimum sentence.[52] Over the last two decades, the Supreme Court has accepted compromise as an adequate and special reason to reduce the sentence to the period of incarceration already undergone in the interests of complete justice.[53] Although compromise is illegal, the judicial consideration of compromise petitions is made possible under the extraordinary powers vested in the Supreme Court under Article 142(1) to act for the achievement of complete justice.[54] In *Sukhwinder Singh* v. *State of Punjab* (2000), the Supreme Court heard an appeal directed against the judgment of the high court, which upheld the conviction of kidnapping, abduction, and statutory rape. In this case, the court observed that the girl, who was not more than sixteen years, had left her parent's home with the accused and was a 'consenting party'.

During the appeal in the high court,

> [t]he prosecutrix and the appellant appear to have compromised and a compromise petition was duly filed in the court. In the compromise petition, the prosecutrix has stated that she and the appellant belonged to neighbouring villages and that 'she does not want that she would be put to further ignominy on account of this episode. She wants to put an end to the matter and settle down happily with her husband'.[55]

For the Supreme Court, the compromise petition was a valid ground for reduction of sentence to the term served by the accused as an undertrial, since this was in the interest of the woman concerned. Now that she had married someone else, sending the accused to jail apparently endangered her 'happy and healthy' married life.[56] The court also clarified that as the case took ten years to traverse the courts it was in the interest of justice not to send the accused back to jail. The high court was chided for not considering the compromise petition an adequate and special reason to lower the punishment. This judgment marks an endorsement of compromise as a valid ground for mitigating a sentence in the interests of complete justice. This notion of complete justice, however, is not limited to statutory rape cases, where a court believes that the underage girl consented to sex.

It is stunning that the Supreme Court has extended such grounds of mitigation to aggravated forms of sexual violence such as gangrape. On 22 February 2011, a Supreme Court bench including Justices Markandey Katju and Gyan Sudha Mishra mitigated the sentence of three men accused of gangrape fourteen years before to the time they had already spent in jail.[57] The thin description of the facts in the Supreme Court order allows us only to note that a woman (presumably young and single at that time) was assaulted and gangraped by three men as she was returning home early at 6.30 after early morning ablutions. The three men were found guilty of gangrape and convicted to ten years—the mandatory minimum sentence for gangrape, and fined Rs 1,000 under s. 342 of IPC for wrongful confinement—again, the minimum sentence for this offence. The High Court of Punjab and Haryana confirmed the sentence. The Supreme Court then tells us that:

> [A]n application and affidavit has been filed before us stating that the parties want to finish the dispute, have entered into a compromise on 01.09.2007, and that the accused may be acquitted and now there is no misunderstanding between them. … Section 376 is a non compoundable offence, However, the fact that the incident is an old one, is a circumstance for invoking the proviso to Section 376(2)(g) and awarding a sentence less than 10 years, which is ordinarily the minimum sentence under that provision, as we think that there are adequate and special reasons for doing so. On the facts of the case, considering that the incident happened in the year 1997 and that the parties have themselves entered into a compromise, we uphold the conviction of the appellant but we reduce the sentence to the period of sentence already undergone in view of the proviso to Section 376(2)(g) which for adequate and special reasons permits imposition of a lesser sentence.[58]

The court enhanced the fine to Rs 50,000, to be recovered from arrears of land revenue if not paid within three months. The Supreme Court stated that although rape is not compoundable, yet it accepted a compromise petition because after all this while there was no 'misunderstanding' between the accused and the victim.

The impact of this judgment was swift. Following this judgment, the Gujarat High Court quashed a FIR (details of the case are not given in the order) in *Kulbhushan Kantibhai Patel and Anr* v. *State of Gujarat and Anr.*[59] The Gujarat High Court held:

The decision of the Apex Court in case of *Baldev Singh and Ors vs State of Punjab*, reported in *MANU/SC/0148/2011* and in view of the decision of this Court decided in *Criminal Misc. Application No. 2312 of 2008*,[60] I am of the view that though the offence is not compoundable and the reasoning adopted by learned Sessions Judge is also contrary to provisions of law, the complaint and the proceedings arising there from are required to be quashed for the sole purpose of avoiding untold hardship not only to the prosecutrix and her family members but their purpose of arriving at an amicable settlement so that parties may pursue their vocation and profession in life peacefully would be prejudiced. Filing of the affidavit by prosecutrix in the Court in unequivocal terms go to show that even in case if the prosecution is permitted to be taken to its logical end would not result into [*sic*] desired end and it would rather have adverse impact upon the parties lives which may not be in the interest of justice. Learned APP also in light of the observations of the Apex Court did not object to quashment of the complaint that may be passed by the Court.[61]

The appellate courts' picture of complete justice is tempered by the idea of what it calls giving the matter 'quietus', by accepting the idea that rape could be settled between the victim and the accused, and that what is crime in law is in fact a social dispute.

'SEX LIES HIDDEN LIKE FIRE IN WOOD'

The issue of the appropriateness of a 'prosecutrix' filing an affidavit in order to plea for the reduction of the sentence of the accused arose in the course of my fieldwork.[62] In 1996, the Gujarat High Court accepted one such affidavit. In *Dharmendra Dhirajlal Soneji v. State of Gujarat*, it was held that the victim 'has gracefully stated that she is already married and she has condoned the act of the accused as it happened on the spur of the moment because of tender age and immaturity'.[63] The facts of the case as stated in the judgment are as follows: On 6 April 1990, Dharmendra, a twenty-year-old man, raped a girl a little over thirteen years in her house in Ahmedabad. The Sessions Court found him guilty and convicted him to seven years imprisonment under s. 376 IPC (rape) and for two years under s. 452 IPC (house trespass for assault).[64] The state argued for enhancement of the sentence, while the accused appealed his sentence and conviction. The counsel for the accused–appellant argued that Dharmendra was very young and the sentence too harsh. He appealed to the court to reduce his sentence to the period undergone of one year and two months. He also produced the affidavit filed by the woman [A] (described as PW2 in the judgment) in support of his plea on the issue of the sentence. The Gujarat HC confirmed the conviction but reduced the sentence of rape from seven years to two years. It upheld the sentence for house trespass for two years.

Dismissing the plea of the prosecution that accepting such petitions would initiate an adverse precedent, the court stated that a matter of sentencing does not set a precedent. Admitting a petition like this, the court reasoned, would not mean creating a new socio-legal route for defence lawyers to pressurize rape victims to condone men who had raped them. In such cases, the court would ascertain whether the affidavit was filed under duress. Courts, we are told, are not like 'gullible children' and hence, the victim had been produced before the court at an earlier date to ascertain the contents of the affidavit.

The court clarified that it had not considered as a ground for mitigation the fact that Dharmendra, a married man, was the sole breadwinner of his family, and had a child to support. Rather, it was the woman's 'voluntary, true, genuine and graceful pardon' and her 'admission that the incident took place because of their immature ages' that mitigates the sentence.[65] Reading in between the lines unable to resist the interference, the court further held that 'perhaps she was a consenting party though undoubtedly the consent will not make any difference because PW-2 [A] was only 13 and half years of age. We wish we were wrong in drawing inference by reading between the lines, though it is difficult to resist the inference'.[66] The affidavit was converted into an admission of actual consent.

The Gujarat HC opined that Dharmendra was a victim of the 'psychic pollution' generated by 'obscene magazines', 'dirty obscene films' and 'foreign television channels' since:

> ... sex lies hidden like fire in wood. ... There are stories in our Puranic *shastras* where some Saints on merely seeing even the sex play of birds and fishes getting provoked were lured down to the sexual plane!! What we ultimately want to say and emphasise here is the fact that where the sex itself is the weakest aspect of human personality which

can be easily inflamed and set ablaze making a person to commit rape ... even on the slightest sexual provocation and further when this aspect is continually fuelled and inflamed by the continuously in flammable stream, rather river of obscenity all around, how are we to find fault with the girl of 13 years and a boy of 20 years, when they admit that whatever happened it happened because of their tender age and immaturity!! It's a known and accepted fact that the invasion of Satellite television channels and the resultant proliferation is spelling doom for the society!![67]

Obscene images were correlated with the increase in crime rates. Both the prosecutrix and the accused were constituted as victims. The court indicated that judicial wisdom lies in recognizing the 'victimizing conditions', which dissipates anger against 'indiscreet criminal acts'.[68] The judgment maintains that young men as victims of moral erosion should not be blamed.[69] The government, unlike in the case of defending territorial sovereignty, is unable to protect the youth from 'psychic terrorism' and prevent them from becoming 'sexual terrorists'.[70] These constitute adequate and special reasons to reduce the sentence.

The term 'compromise' is not found in this judgment. Nor is the plea to compound the offence. This judgment unequivocally holds that rape is a non-compoundable offence. The affidavit also recognizes this fact. However, the court endorses a new practice allowing defence lawyers to produce affidavits in order to plead for a reduced sentence. The high court could now ascertain whether such affidavits were true and voluntary on a case-by-case basis. A new socio-legal route is created through which compromise between the accused and the victim could be initiated after the fact of conviction in the trial court. This could be done without referring to such applications compromise petitions.

This judgment generated anxiety among lawyers in the trial courts and the high court during my fieldwork. In the opinion of a lawyer in the Gujarat High Court, accepting such affidavits goes against position that rape is an offence against society. I quote:

> It was absolutely wrong. I have never heard of such a thing. It [rape] is an offence against society and just because a complainant does not want to go to court, the court should not accept this. I mean now the court has done so, lower courts may follow, but a court should never

do this. The other thing in this case is that there is an attempt to draw a surmise the rapist watched some video film and therefore his mind was perverted. This kind of logic that leads to acquittal is without any basis. There is always a psychological factor for every act of crime, would you therefore not punish all the criminals?

Similarly, a woman APP in the trial court said to me:

The prosecutrix's writ was admitted in the High Court and the accused was acquitted on the ground that he might have been influenced by TV programmes. It is a kind of compromise. High Court is always ready to compromise. If both parties are coming with clean hand, ready to convince the court that we do not keep grudges with each other whatever happened then, even in those circumstances the High Court considers it a good thing and it is to be considered, court may acquit the accused. Never heard of it before. In this case, the accused's age was a consideration. In lower court, I do not think it is a good thing. It is in the interest of the accused. Court should see the age of the victim. It should not happen.

This viewpoint echoes the fears that the practice of filing petitions before the court to pardon the accused may initiate a new socio-legal practice in lower courts. It is perceived to be *like* a compromise. Although in a legal sense this judgment refers to an entirely different realm of sentencing, the concern here is not the *de jure* legal definition of what is a precedent, but the *de facto* sanctioning of a socio-legal practice that allows such petitions pardoning the accused. When a case is compromised to acquit the accused, it is seen as a compromise of the rule of law. If affidavits are filed at the stage of sentencing after the fact of guilt has been found, it is perceived to act in the interests of the accused. It is differentiated from the practice of compromise before the testimony.

When witnesses and accused seek a compromise after the conviction in an appellate court, the perceptions about the appropriateness of compromise change. In the case of the Gujarat High Court judgment cited above, the affidavit is not routed through the prosecutor's office even though it claims to represent the voice of the 'prosecutrix'. Once the trial is over, often the prosecution witnesses do not follow the case in the high court, which is sometimes far removed from the sessions court in the district headquarters. It is thus not difficult for the defence to secure an affidavit without the prosecution's knowledge. There is no shared notion of 'social justice' between the prosecution and the defence. The very socio-legal framework of rape is contested. The route to achieving acquittal at the appellate stage is not identical to the trial proceedings but is perceived as if this were a compromise, primarily since these are not seen as evolving from a consensus between the prosecution, the defence, or the accused, and the survivor's family.

THE CAREER OF COMPROMISE CASES IN THE TRIAL COURT

For the sake of clarity, I present two prototypical situations based on a reading of ethnographic vignettes that I documented in the trial court. One is the use of compromise as a tool in the hands of defence lawyers and the accused to pressure complainants and victims to change their testimonies in a courtroom.[71] The second is described in terms of love and elopement. In cases of female minors (those below the age of eighteen) who elope, I found that it was their families who filed complaints of rape, abduction, and kidnapping. The use of criminal law to discipline unmarried daughters points to the dissonance between what is legally constituted as rape and the social uses that rape law is put to. In either, the experience of the woman of consent or coercion remains opaque. The difference between elopement and abduction, rape and love is blurred.

Within the career of kidnapping, abduction, and rape cases, we find two kinds of standardized scenarios. Either the minor is coerced by the accused, in which case she supports the complainant's allegation. Alternatively, she elopes with the accused. In this case, she may be forced to support the version of the complainant, usually a parent, and return to her lawful guardian. In such cases, her parents then get her married to someone else, and compromise is seen as the only way of preserving her marriage. Alternatively, she may turn hostile on the stand by making a statement before a magistrate denying her earlier claim and stating that she was in fact not raped or abducted. The paradox is that while fifteen-year-old girls may be considered old enough to have sex in marriage as per the law, if they initiate pre-marital sexual relationships, state law is mobilized to punish them for their sexual choices. The police may file false charges that may be applied against her on the grounds of abetment to kidnapping, abduction, rape, and theft. Often these cases are registered when the man is from another community or from a 'lower' caste.

In the instance of love affairs referred to as rape, kidnapping, or abduction, typically the social use of the rape law is two-fold. The first imperative is to find the couple, leading to the arrest of the man. Second, the parents attempt to find a suitable husband for the girl even if she is below the legal age of marriage. After the marriage, the case is compromised. As a criminal lawyer who had practiced for fourteen years in the trial court told me, 'My father's brother's daughter eloped when she was fourteen years old. I myself filed the complaint and the man rotted in jail for three months. We got her married to a man in our own caste. The case has been compromised.' One of the additional public prosecutors at the Mirzapur court told me such cases are not restricted to minors. Sometimes, the age certificates of adult women are altered to make a case of statutory rape.[72]

Underlying these narratives, we find that the idea of social justice around which consensus evolves, centres around the re-insertion of the female subject in the structure of alliance. Once she is married within the community and the honour of the complainant is re-established, social order is restored.[73] The legal event must be effaced and the marriage protected from full disclosure of the events during the trial. This is the reason cited most often for compromise, and the consensus on social justice congeals in male-defined notions of honour. Compromise is an important site where the lines of power and authority are re-constituted through the re-insertion of the woman who experiences rape into the folds of familial, communitarian, and caste-based normativities.

The story of compromise must also be read alongside the socio-legal histories of the politics of honour in relation to rape and heterosexual love. I turn to Chowdhry's (2004) work on caste, sexuality, and violence to demonstrate how notions of social justice are framed by heterosexist norms of honour. Chowdhry (1998) details how the violence against those men and women who transgress either inter-caste or intra-caste norms take the form of terrible public spectacles in rural Haryana (North India). Since 'marriage provides the structural link between kinship and caste',[74] she argues that the control of female sexuality is central to the enforcement of caste norms, such that those who 'infringe caste and kinship norms in marriage are met with extreme violence' (1998: 332–3). Her research reveals that 'reported cases of kidnapping, rape and abduction are tabulated as sex crimes, and are even officially acknowledged to be "nothing but cases of love affairs with abducted women being the consenting party"' (1998: 336). She reports that most of these instances resulted in public killings of the couples. If the man escapes the retribution, the woman may be killed. Arguing that the enforceability of these notions of honour is not uniformly distributed among all men, Chowdhry claims that upper-caste men appropriate honour politics and lower-caste men are unable to enforce notions of honour especially 'in relation to the higher castes' (1998: 338). She argues that the politics of honour within the lower castes turns inwards, within their own caste groups, where the spectacle of violence finds terrifying consequences.

The severity of violence is most stark in hypogamous unions; that is, unions between higher-caste women and lower-caste men. In the event of consensual relationships of love and marriage between upper-caste women and lower-caste men, the distinction between consensual sex and rape is not socially intelligible. In state law, for instance, elopement is called abduction and love dubbed as rape. Chowdhry argues that there exists 'complicity between the perpetrators of violence and the police about the "justice" done for the sake of "honour"' (1998: 337). The public spectacle of violence that Chowdhry (1998) refers to in relation to Haryana must be read along with the case studies discussed herein, which suggest an increasing normalization of the politics of honour and notions of social justice in the field of criminal law.[75] The complicity of the law in normalizing social notions of justice entrenched in the politics of honour is constitutive of the socio-legal histories of the rape law in India (P. Baxi 2006, 2009).

THE CASE HISTORY

I met Purshottambhai Sadhu, the complainant in this case, in Hirabhai's chamber. The two interviews were conducted in the presence of the court constable, Ashokbhai, who had been assigned this case. These were carried out prior to the hearing. It must be borne in mind that the socio-legal process of compromise is shot through with anxiety, and in this case, the resolution of the case was not actualized until the day of the hearing. I indicate later how this altered my relationship with Purshottambhai Sadhu.

Purshottam Sadhu lodged a complaint of abduction and kidnapping against Daya. Daya, their neighbour, was a twenty-two-year-old married man and had fathered two children. The case papers do not reveal anything about Daya's wife. He belonged to a Scheduled Caste community[76] and Purshottambhai Sadhu described himself as an upper-caste Hindu.[77] Purshottambhai's daughter Sandhya had been missing for five days. When Sandhya disappeared from home, he had gone to Rajasthan to attend a wedding in his natal village and look for a groom for his daughter.[78] It was a neighbour, Jagruti, who broke the news to Sandhya's mother, Hansaben. Jagruti had seen Sandhya walking away with Daya near the railway tracks in their neighbourhood. When Hansaben could not find her daughter, she sent for her husband. It took Purshottambhai two days to return home. In the meantime, there was no word from Sandhya. Upon his return, Purshottambhai went to the police.[79] The police found them two days after the complaint had been lodged. Daya was then charged with kidnapping, abduction, and rape. He was not granted bail by the lower court and continued to be in judicial custody till the high court released him on bail. The case came on trial nearly two years after the case was registered. In the interim, Sandhya was married to a man who belonged to a sub-caste in their community. When she appeared in the trial court, she had borne a child. Daya was finally acquitted.

THANA: MAKINGS OF THE CASE

In order to examine the making of the case, I detail police records such as the complaint, the police statements, the *panchnamma*,[80] and the medico-legal certificate to describe the variegated nature of documents. I base my arguments on police records and ethnographic interviews, and I do not aim to fix a definitive interpretation to what happened. In fact, the police records show how different kinds of police statements are framed by a specific imagination of what kinds of futures are possible. The police record is prolific and addresses the changing relationship between the complainant, his daughter, and the police. In this case, where an upper-caste father is the complainant against a Dalit man, the incommensurability between the social imagination of such transgressions and the forensic descriptions in law produces an excited performance of the politics of honour.

THE COMPLAINT

I was working in Hirabhai's office one morning when Rajubhai, Hirabhai's junior, walked in with the court constable, Ashokbhai, and a tall, lean man who wore a red *tilak*[81] on his forehead and had red vermilion marks on his ears. Rajubhai greeted me. The court constable introduced me to the other man, 'this woman [*ben*] is from the government.'

> PB: No, no, I am not from the government.
>
> A: She is a lawyer. She will help you prepare your daughter's testimony.
>
> PB: No, I am not a lawyer. I cannot help your daughter. I am doing research on some cases that come to the court, of rape, abduction. I would like to know about your case, I am researching problems in the law.

Purshottambhai nodded. Ashokbhai[82] informed me that the girl's testimony was scheduled for the following day. They had been to the court earlier to see the prosecutor, but could not find him. On that day, the court had adjourned. Purshottambhai talked to me that day outside the chamber while he was waiting to meet Hirabhai. Initially, Purshottambhai and I conversed in Gujarati, and then in Hindi. Ashokbhai was also present during this exchange.

> PB: Your case?
>
> P: Daughter's abduction [*apaharan*], he threatened and took her.
>
> PB: Who was the accused?
>
> P: A boy named Daya.
>
> PB: Where did he live?
>
> P: In our neighbourhood.[83]
>
> PB: Did they know each other?
>
> P: They did not know each other. We are Maharaj and they are Senava.[84]
>
> A: They are Maharaj by caste and they are Senava.

P: We do not have any relationship [*sambandh*] with them, none of drinking their water or giving them our water to drink. No relationship. They are SC [Scheduled Caste], *na*.

P to A: What of the SC? They do black magic [*maulik kriya*]. They mislead you [*gumarahah karna*]. If you eat the *prasad*[85] they offer you then your mind can be corrupted [*kharab*]—you can lose your mind.

A: The difficulty is that the law is not established.

P: They are SC, *na*. They must have been given refuge wherever they went. They must have lived somewhere. I searched for five days, incurred so much expense. I contacted my relatives in villages.

   They must have taken money to meet the expenses. That's why we didn't think. We were so blind.

Purshottambhai evokes a specific picture of caste normativity[86] that rests on the idea that the upper-caste woman would maintain social distance from a Dalit man to anchor his complaint that his daughter was abducted. Such representations preclude the social possibility of any kind of consensual sexual alliances between an upper-caste woman and a Scheduled Caste man. Purshottambhai uses the metaphor of *prasad* to suggest that his daughter Sandhya had been enticed through corruption of the mind, because consent is not a socially intelligible category in this context. The word *prasad* here is animated with malevolence (as opposed to divine grace), luring away the upper-caste female subject from the *correct* path. Here, the word indexes zones of ambivalence, suggesting that the possibilities of inter-caste commensality and sexual desire are temporary aberrations caused by black magic. As Ashokbhai said, the law that is not well established to fully control inter-caste marriages. At the police station, Sandhya's statement affirmed the complaint. Purshottambhai said, 'We found our eyes. There was our daughter's statement. Her statement was that he forced her. The section was applied, and that's why bail was not granted.' For Purshottambhai, his daughter's statement gave him 'sight' again and allowed him to pursue the legal case against Dayabhai.

   How is the *fariyad* structured in this case? I cite from the complaint: 'This boy Daya since [*sic*] last one month used to frequently talk to my daughter and used to meet her and my wife had seen them and stopped them.' From the police documents of several other people whom the police interrogated, we find that

Daya and Sandhya knew each other before the incident. Sandhya's mother's statement to the police states that she had discouraged Sandhya from meeting Daya as he belonged to a Scheduled Caste community. Yet it is not these statements alone that revealed the ambiguity regarding Sandhya's wishes and desires concerning Daya. For instance, Jagrutiben, Purshottambhai's neighbour, states that she saw Sandhya leave with Daya wearing a new *sari*. The reference to the new *sari* appears in statements taken from other neighbours as well, and it is especially interesting that she chose to wear one in the middle of the hot afternoon—it signifies Sandhya's volition. Jagruti's statement that Daya took her with him is ambivalent in implying both the possibilities of elopement and abduction.

The records suggests that the precipitating moment for this event may have arisen after Purshottambhai went to his village to attend a marriage and to look for grooms in their community for the marriage of his daughters. The complaint reveals that he considered Sandhya and her sister to be of a marriageable age, although at this time Sandhya was legally a minor. I cite below an excerpt of the *fariyad* signed by Purshottambhai:

And while I was staying there my son Pappubhai came to the village and said, 'Pappa, Mummy is very ill'. That's why let us return to Ahmedabad. When I reached there it was dated [...] and it was [...] in the morning. At this time, I was brushing my teeth and washing up. Then the man who lives upstairs MS and his wife came and said your daughter has run away with a boy named *Senava*. So what should we do? So why have you closed down our *rickshaw* and *pan shop*? Saying this I said that I do not know anything in this matter and I have not shut down anything. At that time, MS' wife and he said to me that your daughter Sandhyaben was made to run off on [...] at approximately [...] by Daya, the resident of the *senavas* [*senava vasi*]. This was told and that it was wrong to have our *rickshaw* and shop shut down. About this, we did not know anything. In the meantime, my *dharmani*[87] daughter Jagrutiben w/o [wife of] B came home and said why are you fighting within? The girl Sandhyaben was seen being taken by our boy of [neighbourhood], the resident of the *senavas*, Daya Muljibhai Harijan on [date] at [time] morning on [...] Road and she was wearing a new *sari*. At which point to gather more information when I went to [...] also informed me that on [date] that Daya Muljibhai took the girl to [...] Road. It was afternoon during this time. At this time, the girl Sandhya was wearing a new *sari*.

I note two important points from this excerpt. First, there was tension in the neighbourhood over this episode, resulting in a shop and *rickshaw* being shut down. However, the reference to the tension in the neighbourhood is merely a trace in the police records. In disclaiming knowledge about the tension, the complaint suggests that Purshottambhai had not taken retaliatory measures in the neighbourhood. Second, although the reference to Daya as 'our boy' suggests that he belongs to a multi-caste neighbourhood, he is marked as one who resides in the dwellings of the Scheduled Caste group within the neighbourhood. The reference to Daya as 'the resident of senavas' (*senava vasi*) draws a referential relationship between his name and his caste, such that at times the caste name substitutes Daya's name. Other police statements also refer to Daya as Harijan.

The *fariyad* is powerful because, through it, Purshottambhai is able to translate the social notion of transgression into a penal offence. Although caste is not legally relevant to registering a crime in this case, it is constitutive in the writing of the police complaint. Moreover, we must also remember that the standardized frameworks of writing a police complaint structure the narrative as well as filter through it a certain idea of relevant facts in anticipation of a trial. This is done first by stating that Daya had an illegal intent prior to the incident—he had been meeting her for a month prior to the date of the crime—and by establishing that Sandhya was a minor. The *fariyad* concluded that:

> Therefore the abovementioned boy named Dayabhai Muljibhai Harijan, resident of [X], enticed and seduced my daughter Sandhyaben age 16 by [promising] to keep her well took her from my custody as her guardian and without my permission with illicit [*teerkarm*] intention. This is my *fariyad*, which I get written is according to the facts and true.

Subsequently, a warrant was drawn in Daya's name where ss. 366 and 363 IPC were applied and a search for the two initiated. Let us now turn to the account of how they were found. From Ashokbhai I learnt that the police got 'lucky' two days after the complaint was lodged when they received a wireless message from a police station saying that a couple had been spotted in the area. The PSI, Ashokbhai, and Purshottambhai set off in a jeep. It was late evening when the two were apprehended. On the way back, Daya was made to sit in the front, between the driver and Ashokbhai. The police officer had no spare handcuffs, so Daya's hands were tied with a piece of cloth. At one point, Daya suddenly grabbed the steering wheel in a bid to escape. The driver did not let go of the wheel; Ashokbhai overpowered Daya, and the accident was averted. What happened next is cited below (translated from Gujarati and the words in English have been italicised in the translated excerpt).

> A: We all got a new life. Behind us, there was a truck too. Today we would not have been alive. Then we got those two to the police station. Beat them [*mar peet*].
>
> PB: You beat both of them?
>
> A: Yes. Then the girl clearly said that I want to live with my father [*pitaji*]. We asked [Sandhya] whom do you want to live with? It was both their faults. They are children. At that time, the girl [*bebi*] had tremendous *mental effect*.
>
> P: Now it is all right. Now there is no effect. She is *fresh* now. After twelve months, when she came of age we got her married, for the last one-and-a-half years she has been in Ajmer. After marriage, she is happy.

This picture of a tremendous 'mental effect' on Sandhya at that moment coexists with the description that she was subjected to violence. We learn that Sandhya was positioned as a disobedient and lawless child. Her subject position as a victim (*bhogbannar*) was produced through practices of violence. It inflected the question of whether she supported the *fariyad* or not. It is clear that the movement when Sandhya shifted from accomplice to victim was accomplished at the police station (*thana*), a site where the power of the state and of her father came together in the *maar*, or beating, Sandhya experienced. Sandhya was then produced as a victim and a prosecutrix through these practices of policing, which effectively erased any record of the violence she experienced.

COERCION AND CONSENT: POLICE STATEMENTS (*JUVAB*)

The police records reveal three statements from Sandhya, two from Daya, and an additional statement from Purshottambhai. I suggest that the proliferation of records that exist side by side, not one after the other in a chronological arrangement, is indicative of an anticipation of different futures—as potentiality, which does not disappear, but 'on the contrary, it preserves itself as such in actuality' (Agamben 1999: 183). In this case then, the co-existence of police statements suggests that seduction is a dense category because it points not only to the potential of being raped, but also to that of love. Seduction poses a threat to the law precisely because it must always indicate a future—one that points to certain signs that have the potential of making law contingent. It is this threat to law that must be legislated and is indicated by this proliferate record.

Version One: Elopement

The following two excerpts cited below point to seduction as potential of love. The statements read as follows:

Excerpt One: Daya's Statement[88]

Last Tuesday, my lover Sandhyaben, and I both ran away from Ahmedabad. ... Then, on my way to my village, you sir [*saheb*] caught us. You recognized my lover Sandhyaben and I. With Sandhyaben, sex had happened. And I have received the information that Sandhyaben's father has lodged a complaint [*fariyad*] against us.

Excerpt Two: Sandhya's Statement

I have been in a relationship [*sambandh*] with Daya, who lives next door, since I was young ... We have lived together in Z for 2 days after that every day we had sex [*sambhog*] and with my consent [*marzi*]. I had the pair of clothes I wore when I left my home and did not take any jewellery or money.

Here, the *fariyad* is constituted as legal action against both of them rather than Daya alone. Sandhya is not only positioned as an abettor but is seen as potentially attracting the charge of theft. The statement indicates the loss of entitlement over her father's house and the police anticipate that her family could file a case of theft against her if Sandhya were to deny the accusation and repudiate her father's guardianship.

Version Two: Seduction and Force

The second statement taken from both Daya and Sandhya records force and love. I provide below excerpts from Daya's and Sandhya's statements to indicate how love frames seduction or inducement. This seduction is illicit when actualized through heterosexual penetrative sex and evidenced through medico-legal signs. It retrospectively allows for the production of the category of bad love (*kharab prem*) or illicit sex (*kharab kam*) that circulates during a trial. Let us consider Sandhya's *juvab* (police statement) first. The first segment I cite is foregrounded by her account of meeting Daya. He was one of the youngsters who used to play in her neighbourhood. One day, when her brother was screening a movie in their home, he came to their house, and sat beside her. The excerpts below have been translated from Gujarati and words in English in the original have been italicized.

Excerpt One describes how they met:

In the picture [the movie], *sexy* songs were playing, and Dayabhai got up and went to the bathroom, and seeing this, I followed him. And we both then *kissed* each other on the lips and then came back to see the picture. After this, he went home. Like this, we fell in love.

Despite my saying no, that I was too young, Dayabhai had sex [*sambhog*] with me. While doing this, he said, '*I love you, darling*'. He used to say this and would say, I am in love with you. Saying this, both of us used to love each other, and kissing each other on the lips we continued our love. We did sex [*sambhog*] secretly. I used to go to the temple every evening. Dayabhai used to come there. After that, we used to talk to each other. Perhaps this is where my mummy saw us and admonished me.

Excerpt Two describes what happened in the five days they were missing.

At that time, we had thrown our clothes from our body. Sometimes Dayabhai held his penis and told me to do this, and penetrated my vagina. This kind we had done earlier. Sometime at this point, I had said I am small for this, but he never heard me and used to have sex [*sambhog*]. So, we stayed like this for five days.

It is hard to imagine that a young woman under those circumstances could have recounted such intimate details in forensic precision to policemen. While insights into the documentary practices of the police remain a subject of future fieldwork, what is important here is how seduction is framed in these documents. Phrases in English such as 'sexy songs', 'kiss',[89] and 'I love you darling' in a *juvab* written in the vernacular suggest that the imagination of seduction is anchored in the normative discourse on love in popular culture. Love typically emerges as the normative discourse par excellence that contests social hierarchies and sovereign power, be it embodied in the paternal ruler, the masculine state or the authoritative upper-caste father. While the debates on sexuality in Hindi cinema have been a centre of feminist critique, the circulation of the cinematic idiom of love and sex in the contexts of policing remains to be explored (John & Nair 1998, also see Virdi 1999).

In this text, being in love and being subjected to forcible sex is seen to coexist within the ambit of seduction. For in law, a woman (read: upper-caste woman) is a potential target of rape. As we have also seen, the law blurs the distinction between rape and seduction. Sandhya, then, must be made to speak through the categories of whether Daya forced her or not, which are contingent on whether she supported her father's statement or Daya's. No licit category existed to describe her subject position as a lover, nor did any category exist to express the experience of violence in such an illicit relationship. Either she had to say that she eloped with him and was in love with him, or she had to say that he seduced her and forced her into an illicit sexual relationship despite her refusal. Could she have said that she was in love and consented only to a certain degree of sexual intimacy? What might constitute consent or violation for women is blurred to the extent that it is difficult to read Sandhya's subjectivity from the police records. Let us turn to Daya's *juvab*. I cite an excerpt:

> After which we used to meet regularly, say 'I love you darling', and used to *kiss* on the lips, and used to do love like this, and I told Sandhyaben that life is lived once, so one's first love must be for a lifetime. Then I told Sandhyaben to do sexual intercourse [*sambhog*]. She said that she is too young, but I forcibly made her lie down and did sexual intercourse. During sexual intercourse, she experienced difficulty. I did sexual intercourse gently-gently.

The mirroring of the description of events provided in Daya's statement with Sandhya's statement is puzzling. What is the sketch of illicit seduction provided here? We are told that the acts involved in seducing a woman—kissing her on the lips—rest on declarations of love. We get a picture of seduction as forceful, yet the act of penile penetration is framed as gentle, mindful of youth and experience. It is framed as sexual intercourse, not rape. Seduction is thus constituted as sexual intercourse with an admixture of force and gentleness. Force appears here as a form of persuasion, enticement, and gentleness that does not take refusal seriously and operates within the parameters of love. 'We did love like this' collapses the two—love and sex—within the category of the illicit. Love and seduction are expressed in the category of the illicit and the lawless simultaneously as a potentiality that law must legislate.

PRODUCING CONSENT AND CUSTODY

The law on abduction is clear that a girl ceases to be a minor at eighteen. In practice, the manipulation of age by citing documents such as the school leaving certificates brings into the picture other disciplinary bodies such as the school. Age is narrativized in a field of contesting claims. The police documents in this case show us that the case rests on the contestation of age and custody of a minor. The documents present a puzzle to us. The *fariyad* recorded Sandhya's age as sixteen. The date of birth in the school leaving certificate, however, declared Sandhya to be a few days younger than sixteen. The medical certificate showed her age to be seventeen. In the interview to me, Purshottambhai said that he arranged her marriage a year after she came of age, meaning that her age at the time of the incident to be seventeen. The police did not request age-determination tests.

These juridical records then address something other than Sandhya's subjectivity. They address the totality of the socio-legal crisis engendered by the event. The police record does not reflect how Sandhya may have framed what happened to her but the police reduce in writing Sandhya's consent to live with her father. I quote:

> On being questioned in person I am getting written in my statement [*juvab*] that on [date] you sir [*saheb*], took my statement in person. That statement is correct and mine. And today after my medical examination has been completed I have come to the police station and I with happiness and with my will and consent want to live with

my father Purshottambhai Sadhu. Because of which I am being sent with him. This is my reality [*hakikat*] and has been written according to me as correct and true.

Here, her consent to go with her father is recorded as an affirmation to her earlier statements and future course of action. On the same day, we find that Purshottambhai stated the following in writing:

> On being questioned in person, I state that I have got written in my statement [*juvab*] that my daughter named Sandhyaben on [date] was enticed and seduced [*lalchavi/fusalavi*] by Dayabhai. In this connection, I had got written a complaint [*fariyad*] in the [G] police station. And my daughter and this boy Daya were sent to the Civil Hospital for medical treatment. Now my daughter wants to stay with me with her consent, she is willing to stay. I am ready to keep her with me. I will not allow any kind of beating, pressure, or threat against this my daughter and will keep her well.

The word 'now' in Purshottambhai's *juvab* indicated a past in which implicitly there was a suggestion that his daughter did not want to live in his house. This shift then implies that Purshottambhai must take on a different subject position—as a complainant to a father who submits in writing to the police a promise to withhold violence towards his daughter in the future.

SEXUALIZATION OF THE FEMININE BODY: *PANCHNAMMA* AND THE MEDICO-LEGAL REPORT

Law's materialization assumes specific meanings when we turn our gaze to the circulation, examination, analysis, and preservation of material evidence called *muddamal*.[90] The things that are confiscated by the police for forensic examination may be classified into two categories: first, those extracted from the body of the victim and the accused, such as blood, hair, semen, and vaginal swabs; and second, the objects that may offer evidence of the crime, like weapons, clothes, letters, dirt, shoes, or other objects from the scene of crime. These are confiscated as the property of the state and subjected to forensic examination as samples (*namuna*) bearing traces of the crime. These are then sealed, certified, preserved, and stored, and subsequently produced in court as *muddamal*. The *panch*,[91] the lay presence in a criminal trial, are prosecution witnesses who examine these sites and objects to testify that such evidence was not tampered with. The *muddamal* is thus part of the performative aspects of the trial.[92] The *panchnamma* is a written statement by these independent witnesses who record the scene of crime and marks of crime on clothes or other personal belongings.

In the case of rape, the confiscation of clothes accompanies the production of a *panchnamma*—a written record of the observations by the *panch*. There are no provisions to provide victims with an extra pair of clothes. Dhagamwar (1980) recounts a case where a working-class woman was raped by a policeman, and could not even afford to buy a sari to replace the clothes confiscated as evidence.

Bhanwari Devi had to wear her husband's waistcloth since her clothes were confiscated as evidence, while he unfolded his turban and wrapped it across his waist (see Chapter 1). This transition between clothes as personal belongings[93] to clothes as the property of the state classifies an act of forcible acquisition as mere procedure.

What kind of record is created of the clothes? I turn now to the *panchnamma* of the clothes, which were examined by the *panch* and handed over for forensic analysis in Sandhya and Daya's case. One *panch* was a forty-three-year-old Bharward (caste used to refer to shepherds) man and the other a twenty-two-year-old Purohit (caste commonly used to refer to priests) man. They were not called as witnesses during the trial. I cite excerpts from the *panchnamma* below.[94] I have translated the *panchnamma* from Gujarati.[95]

> In this way, we, the above-mentioned *panch*, make our appearance on being called by you, [G] police station.
> And you, the police, have stated that in the [G] station, the woman witness [*sahedan*]—under crime [number] under the IPC Sections 363, 366 by the name of Sandhyaben, the daughter of Purshottambhai Sadhu, seventeen years old, is by caste a Sadhu. The accused in this matter, Dayabhai Harijan, lives near [...] in [...] next to [...].
> The woman witness [*sahedan bai*]—who lives in [...] near [...] Ahmedabad, who on [...] was enticed, seduced with the intent of illicit sexual intercourse, was taken from the custody of her father without her father's consent. And with the woman witness from [date] to [date] in different places and times the accused in this case

performed sexual intercourse. The clothes worn during the sexual intercourse [*sambhog*] by the woman witness Sandhyaben have been submitted to us.

The *panchnamma* is framed within the story of the crime as narrated to the *panch*. At this time, Daya was charged with the offences defined under ss. 366 (abduction) and 363 (kidnapping). The *panchnamma* clearly states that this offence was against the rights of her father as the guardian. It is illicit sex that is the object of criminalization. Sandhya, referred to as *sahedan*, a woman witness supplemented with *bai* (which also means woman like the suffix *ben*, but it is used in a more derogatory sense), was asked to submit her clothes to the *panch*. We are told that she submitted her inner garments, the underwear, and long skirt (*chaniyo*). The *panchnamma* holds that these clothes were the same worn during the time of the offence. We find description of the clothes by way of colour and cost.

That woman [*bai*] Sandhyaben submitted the underwear worn during the intercourse, which on sight seems to be blackish blue in colour. Along the waist and on the sides there is a white coffee border. Inside the underwear in the front side and on the backside that is above the vagina [*yoni*] semen spots can be seen. These have been circled with a red sketch pen and marked A1. Its cost may be approximated Rs 100 and there is one blue colour skirt [*chaniyo*], which has a white string. It is sewn in the front, that is, towards the front side—on being torn, with red thread. On seeing the back of the skirt, 10 cm below the waist can be seen stains of semen, which have been rounded off with a red pen as A2. With this, another semen stain can be seen. This has been circled and marked as A3. Below, that is, below the waistband [through which the string passes], 40 cm above semen stain can be seen. This has been circled as A4. And below that a semen stain can be seen which has been circled as A5. And in front of the skirt on the side of the left 20 cm and 15 cm above the waistband, a semen-like stain can be spotted. This has been circled as A7. And in the backside on the right 28 cm above the waist a semen stain can be seen, which is marked as A8.

Upon reading the *panchnamma*, we may paraphrase Hyde (1997) in stating that feminine underwear is the 'least private' and 'most spectacularised' clothing, fetishized and made to stand for the female body by training a voyeuristic gaze on them. The slippage from the functional descriptions of the underwear to 'above the vagina' constitutes the feminine undergarment unlike the other garments, allowing for the pornographic construction of the vagina on display. In examining the skirt not only are we informed that there are semen stains but the exact measurements are provided to indicate where these stains were found. Thus, for the purposes of the *panchnamma* the object of description is evidence of sex on clothes, which in turn stand for sexualized bodily parts.

This is brought out more clearly when we examine the counterpart—the *panchnamma* of Daya's clothes. I quote:

> And you police informed us that in the police station in crime [number] under s. 363, 366 IPC the complainant is Purshottambhai, Sadhu by caste. On [date] on [...] near [...] Ahmedabad from his guardianship his ward was enticed with the intent of illicit sexual intercourse [*jharkam*] without his consent as a guardian and in this case with the woman witness the accused had sex at different times and places. The clothes that were worn during sex the accused Dayabhai has submitted to us personally. The underwear which was worn during the sex, has been submitted. It is pink in colour. The waist has an elastic and black border. On the inner side where it is worn, there are semen stains, which have been marked as B1. On the backside, there seem to be semen stains which are rounded by red sketch pen as B2. And there is a jeans pant, which is black coffee in colour. On its hip pocket is marked 'outwear'. And in the front as well as in the back, there are two pockets. In this pant after turning it inside out near the chain[96] on the right side, there are semen stains. These have been marked with a red sketch pen as B3 and B4. These two clothes we the *panch* in person enclose in different envelopes, tied with thread with lac, sealed with the signature on the seal.

The jeans are described through categories that are unambiguously those of tailoring and dressmaking. Nor are the stains measured in centimetres. The *panch* do not say here that they found stains above the penis. A gendered gaze marks the difference in description. The derogatory reference to Sandhya as *bai* and the sexualization of her body through her clothes produces a document that tells a different kind of story. Here the issue is not so much about consent or custody. It is based on the naturalization of the idea that women's bodies can be searched for evidence of sex.[97] The female apparel similarly can substitute for the female body and allow the imagination of a mimetic relationship with the sexual act. The sexualization of women's bodies is thus part of the systemic legal process of giving materiality to injury caused to rape survivors, where the legal vagina can be searched and put on display. This is most perceptible in the medical examination of the body.

Sandhya was examined in the casualty ward where she was admitted for a day. Clinical examination in the hospital entails two processes, bringing together therapeutics with forensics. Bodily fluids are collected and sent for forensic analyses.[98] In this case, the medico-legal certificate declared that there were no marks of injury on her body. I cite the medico-legal certificate originally in English below.

1. Ext. genitals and breast well developed.
2. Pubic and axillary [sic] hair are well developed, black and not matted.
3. No external mark of injury over body and over clothes.
4. On P/V exam old hymeneal tear and two fingers admissible.
5. Urethral swab for genoccei [sic] and vaginal swab for spermatozoa are negative.

Thus far, Daya had not been accused of rape. The medical examination, which revealed old hymeneal tears, was important in the formulation of charges of rape against him. The prosecutor used the medico-legal certificate to infer that Sandhya was 'habituated to sex'. The effect of the complaint was the production of these documents, but their full disclosure would mean that Purshottambhai would never be able to marry his daughter within the community, nor would his honour be restored to him. Legality thus has the effect of disrupting caste sociality and its actualizations of social order.

THE SITE OF THE DOMESTIC: FATHERING A GOOD FUTURE

As a result of the police investigation and the charges drawn against him, bail was denied to Daya. In the meantime, while Purshottambhai's *fariyad* had the desired effect of gaining custody of his daughter, but now the very *fariyad* was animated with danger. I am concerned here with what it meant for Purshottambhai to father a good future for his daughter. The excerpts below are from an interview he allowed me to tape. Repeated throughout his narration is the English word 'feel', which he used to refer to 'suffering' or 'hurt'.

First of all, a person *feels*. I wear a *tilak*.[99] People think a thousand things—*sala*,[100] *tilakdhari* man is in court! People must be thinking because of this uniform [*vardi*] that he never went to the cinema! Even if they don't think like this, this is how I *feel*. My mind is not all right [*mera dimag thik nahi hai*]. I cannot drive on the highway. A film forms in front of my eyes. ... What anxiety happened! After this incident [*banav*] her mother had to be admitted to the hospital. I have aged. I am 55 years old.

He pulled out his wallet to show me a passport-sized photograph of himself. 'This was taken a couple of years back,' he said. 'I have grown old in these last two years.' Visually the change was indeed quite dramatic. He said:

I got a shock [*ahghaat*]. I didn't tell anyone about the incident. Not even my sons. It has an effect on the children. For 2 months, I have been selling tea and biscuits on a cart. I earn Rs 2,000. I don't want to have to take or give anything with anybody now. ... The results of this event [*banav*] are such that I am suffering to this day. I have a son aged 25 years but I thought of getting my daughters married first. Talk of the incident can leak [*baat nikal sakati hai*]. I do not have a daughter-in-law [*bahu*] in my house. This has caused their mother grief. We don't want to get them married in other castes.

The precedence of the marriage of his daughters over that of his son indicates the greater vulnerability of wife-givers than wife-takers. The effects of the legal event transform the domestic space as a very different, fragile interiority where caste, desire, and transgression are the running motifs. In this sketch of an inner life that suffers, the *tilak* is an ironic mode of speaking about caste as uniform. Wearing the *tilak* and being in court produces a complex interiority marked by shame, paranoia, and anxiety. The constant danger of word leaking out institutes structures of paranoia in the domestic.

The effects of the legal event render the domestic space as something that now must be secured. Fathering a good future for his daughter meant that if Sandhya were to marry after she turned eighteen, he had to ensure that the past remain a secret. It was to remain a secret from his extended family—from his brothers and his older daughter's affinal family. Nor was this a revelation that could be shared with anyone who married into the family in the future. The brothers were not involved in the marriage negotiations. Sandhya was married with the help of his sister's affinal family. He said, 'It is difficult to explain why we married her there. There is politics. However, I thought that my sister and my daughter, both would look after each other.' How, then, in this social matrix does Purshottambhai speak of Sandhya?

For now, the marriage negotiations were altered. Sandhya's consent was seen as important. Consent is no longer a category that animates the law alone.

> We selected the boy by talking to him ourselves. We also spoke to his father, mother, sister, liked them, then after the talks everyone agreed. The father and uncle saw the girl. It is a practical matter. The light which had been blown out lit again [*deepak band chalu ho gaya*]. It is her destiny. After such an incident has happened, we had to take the consent [*manzoori*] of the girl. That she likes him. The doctor said that it is not apparent how he seduced her.

We see how the re-insertion of Sandhya's position as a virgin to be gifted in marriage (*kuvari*) comes about by first manufacturing her consent within the structure of alliance in the Vaishanav Samaj. The alteration that found Sandhya was that she was seen as an adult between the categories of the *kuvari* and the *suhagin*,[101] indicating that she was marked by the experience of heterosexual desire—a category that has no name in the discourse on alliance and kinship in the Vaishanav caste, to which Purshottambhai constantly referred. It is a category that is indifferent to past experience of coercion or pleasure. The medico-legal reading of Sandhya's body was similarly indifferent to experience of pain or pleasure when it was declared that she bore old hymeneal tears. Yet, in the recapitulation of the category of a virgin, medical opinion does find a place, although this opinion is contrary to the findings recorded in the medico-legal certificate. Purshottambhai believed that it was not possible to read the consequences of the event from Sandhya's body. Medical opinion was folded into the realm of the intimate in the transformation of Sandhya from a victim of rape (*bhogbannar*) to a virgin (*kuvari*). Each attempt to perform normality led Purshottambhai to re-articulate the effects of the transgression into new limits of the normative.

MANAGING THE PUBLIC SECRET

In court, public records were seen as animated with danger and in need of a specific revelation. In taking the help of the police to recover his daughter, Purshottambhai now had to regulate the shame that would accrue to him on public exposure. How indeed was he to manage the case, especially now that Sandhya was married? Purshottambhai's engagement with the law was framed by the idea that Sandhya's life would be 'poisoned' if the secret were exposed. In his words:

> Her in-laws do not know that such an incident happened. If they come to know, then her life will be poisoned. She is married now; getting her from her affinal home [sasural] is out of bounds. We gave her life-essential [jeevan zarurat] things: sets of clothes, jewellery, and utensils. There was no demand. Otherwise, it would have been less for the boy's side. We have to live in the Vaishanav society [samaj].

The circulation of this knowledge could hurt the married life of his older daughter as well. He said:

> They [the accused] gave money to someone, sent a man to our house. They had their hand in this. They did this to put our position down. That man came to Ahmedabad. He said he had gone to my daughter's [Sandhya's married sister's] house. My knees went weak [dheela par gaya]. He said, 'she has been burnt with a primus [cooking stove]'. He spoke with this point. I rang up my third brother. He said 'everything is all right'. The manner in which they talk even after the incident: what's the point of talking? My older daughter was married. People from the community who came home after this incident gave this information to her in-laws. We told them that 'this is not true' ... We should bear the fruit. I did not compromise. I fed my daughter, raised her. I am in the driving line,[102] All India Tour, but I did not smoke nor drink tea. Now I don't drive. No shame remains of my grey hair [mere safed bal ki sharam nahi rahi].

The daughter's matrimonial home is haunted by the spectre of separation, indignity, violence, shame, rupture, and death. The possibility of violence, betrayal or abandonment within marriage is ordinarily only an issue when male honour is at stake. We know that when women testify to unspeakable violence in the domestic sphere, such experiences are denied or silenced (Karlekar 2003).[103]

Likewise, the everyday culture of domestic violence folds itself in the negotiations of arranged marriage to constitute marriage as containing within it the possibility of transgression and violation. It is this possibility that frames the narrative.

The circulation of talk thus needed to be regulated, for the public face of the law was now a danger to him. Ashokbhai, the court constable, remarked:

A: Now we have to see what the girl [*bebi*] says, whether she speaks according to the statement.

P: She will say so. She said clearly, 'I want to stay with my father'.

A: Yes. Police asked her that. She said clearly, 'I wish to go to my father's house.'

P: This was our duty, getting her married. It was a question of her reputation. We hail from Rajasthan.

A: My job is to prevent the witness from turning hostile. When I used to go to their house then I never went as a policeman. I used to go in civil dress; otherwise, people would ask why have the police come? Honour [*abru*] goes, whether I had to take his signature or summons.

P: If even by mistake he were to put on his uniform, her mother would fall ill.

A: We also have a caste society [*samaj*]. We have to behave similarly here too. We are also family people [*kutumb walas*]. If they come to know, her life will be destroyed. This even we [policemen] understand.

While Purshottambhai defined his duty as one that must guarantee Sandhya's future and his reputation, the court constable stated that his was to prevent witnesses from turning hostile, which to him meant ensuring that Sandhya would support the complainant-father. The shared discourse of honour and caste society (*samaj*) comes together in the performance of the uniform (*vardi*) of the state and the uniform of the caste. By dressing in plain clothes while on duty, the court constable keeps intact the duties of policing and the duties of belonging to caste society. The public face of the law materializes in plain clothes to maintain the uniform that symbolizes the public face of a family belonging to caste society. Appearances in court had to be regulated. For Sandhya to appear in court was difficult now that she was married. When Purshottambhai's son-in-law accompanied Sandhya to the city, he had to get an adjournment. He said, 'I could not bring him to the court. If they take the testimony tomorrow, I can dispatch her home. She is married now. Getting her from her affinal home [*sasural*] is out of bounds.'

At this time, rather than being structured as an exposure of the public secret the revelation in court was in need of a specific resolution via the process of compromise. One day before the hearing, attempts at compromise had failed. Purshottambhai said:

> A man from the accused's side had come. He did not give his introduction.
>
> He said, 'Is your name Purshottambhai? I have come for the case.'
>
> I said, 'I haven't given you an invitation. Do not come to my house. Climb down the stairs and don't come here.'
>
> I didn't ask him who he was. I was so angry when I saw him. There are twenty-four hours left and there is no chance of anyone else coming. Nor will my daughter agree to repeat that which anybody asks her to. I don't mention the name of the case in front of the children or guests. Is this any way to speak? Is this the time—in front of everyone?
>
> I said, 'Who called you?'

Compromise then had to be initiated in a 'proper' way. Who would approach him for a compromise? Was he a respectable man within the community? Where and how would the talks be initiated and in front of whom? How were notions of honour, caste, power, and respect to be performed? The process of compromise, in this case, had to have the effect of restoring normality. Having refused to participate in this mode of negotiation with twenty-four hours left for the hearing, Purshottambhai was desperate with anxiety when he met Hirabhai.

Hirabhai counselled Purshottambhai that compromise was the best solution. Once the case was compromised, said Hirabhai, 'if any one xeroxes [and distributes copies of] the testimony, no one would come to know anything.' Hirabhai's advice rested in the knowledge that the public face of the secret must be enacted in the courtroom because of the power of the judicial archive, which above all lays a claim to truth. The juridical archive appears as that which indexes the truth, and provides an authoritative and final account. In this sense, the judicial archive itself is a site of providing testimonial to the event. In effacing the archive, the testimony is emptied of the danger that animates it prior to the compromise.

After Hirabhai had left, Purshottambhai said to me:

I am in tension. How can I do it? Compromise? I will lose my face [*meri nak cut jayegi*]. They won't let us stay there. My sons will have to sell their land and go away. It belongs to the SCs now, people will say all kinds of things, I understand what he [APP] is saying but he should also understand what I am saying. I will not bring my daughter tomorrow. I will get something written that she cannot come, the train came late, has been stopped … I will bring her after two days. Now there is the case so I have to fight it out but I need time to think. I am tense. It is a matter of honour [*izzat*]. Someone should come from their side, some elder person; if they come to compromise, then something can be done.

The prosecutor was not concerned that a compromise entailed a dialogue between men of unequal social status in which the respectable men of the lower caste must script respect to Purshottambhai's caste status by requesting an audience at a proper time and place. We learn here that compromise is not only about removing danger to Sandhya but also has the effect of restoring social honour to Purshottambhai in the neighbourhood where his sons' future had to be secured. In the ultimate analysis, compromise would initiate a process of the effacement of the testimony to restore his name to him.

Equally Purshottambhai did not understand that Hirabhai could not guarantee a conviction. Hirabhai took me aside as if to explain why he counselled compromise. He explained to me that the prosecution's case was weak: 'She won't get a conviction. There are three reasons. One, she roamed about without raising a hue and cry. Two, [the] medical [report] will show she was habituated to sex. Three, she was above sixteen.'

In other words, he was saying that legally he would not be able to prove coercion beyond reasonable doubt. There was no evidence, according to him, of coercion or resistance. If she had been below sixteen, it would not have mattered whether she had consented or not as in law it would have counted as statutory rape. Apart from adducing consent from the category of the habituated woman, the prosecutor refers to the 'hue and cry' doctrine to assume consent. This doctrine has its roots in common law. Torrey tells us that the hue and cry doctrine was:

historically not limited to the crime of rape, but applied to all violent crimes. Victims were expected to alert the community in order to increase the possibility of apprehending the offender. However, although the hue and cry requirement has been abandoned for other crimes, it has persisted when rape is alleged. Initially, courts refused to hear a rape complaint unless the victim has raised a hue and cry immediately following the event. Later, this rule was modified: a victim's failure to immediately report the rape would not bar a prosecution but would still raise an inference adverse to the prosecution. (1991: 1041–2)

In Indian law, the hue and cry doctrine persists in rape, abduction, and kidnapping cases. I was repeatedly told that in such cases girls often roam about with the accused without raising a hue and cry. This reference to how rape, kidnapping and abduction judgments are indexed circulates as expert knowledge of the law and feeds into the context of compromise. The judicial archive itself is evoked as a deterrent to prosecution of the case. Rather than bringing Sandhya's testimony on record, the prosecutor encourages the production of its effacement. The law itself produces a reason not to prosecute the case. The prosecutor's advice does not only lie in the interpretations of the social implications of prosecuting for Sandhya (in terms of the effects on her marriage) but also in the knowledge that the prosecution would fail her.

THE PUBLIC FACE OF THE SECRET

A lawyer, Mr Desai, was then hired to fight the case with the prosecution, for Hirabhai did not want to argue the case after it had been compromised. I did not know the precise details of the negotiation the next day between Mr Desai and the defence lawyer, but the compromise was now underway. On the day of the trial, Purshottambhai was present with his family. He was scarcely recognizable. He looked younger, more like the photograph he had shown me earlier. His hair was now dyed jet black. His posture was upright and expression, tense. His *khakhi* attire, complemented by a red muffler, enhanced the impression that he had dressed up for a fight.

The witnesses had been waiting outside the courtroom for more than two hours. The judge sent out Dayabhai to look for his lawyer.

There was no sign of the defence lawyer. It was 1:15 p.m. at that time, and I had been sitting in the court for a couple of hours. I went to Hirabhai's chamber, and Mr Desai, the lawyer with the prosecution, came in. Beenaben and Desai asked me if I had interviewed Sandhya. On learning that I had not, before I could say anything, Desai had left the room and was speaking to her. I followed him and he introduced her to me. At that moment, I decided to speak to her.

> PB: I am a researcher. I am doing research [*abhyaas*] on cases such as yours. I will maintain your confidentiality in my writing. Do you mind speaking to me?
>
> S: It happened. In life. Such an incident. I want to remove the danger [*khatara*] itself. So that he does not look at me again. So that from next time he is on our side. I was a coward [*darpok*]. What did he gain, that he put me in disrepute [*badnami*]? I have a duty [*farz*] towards my parents. Mummy has a BP [blood pressure] problem. Tomorrow … I have small brothers; a sister who has a daughter old enough to go to school. I was naive [*naddan*]. Out of fear, could do anything … threatened … showed a knife.
>
> PB: Then?
>
> S: I don't remember… the incident that happened. (*Her eyes moisten, her voice drops.*) I am married now. I was married at eighteen, for the last two years. I live in Ajmer, Rajasthan. It is fine [*theek hai*]. I have two sisters-in-law. It is a small family. I have a good relationship with them. I feel for them as much as they feel for me.

A bright smile accompanied these words.

The legal present for her was primarily a way of removing the source of danger to her, for securing a future where Daya would not look at her ever again. At this point, Purshottambhai burst into the conversation, raising his hand to hit me, shouting, 'You will give this to the press, her life will be ruined!' As I stepped back to avoid the blow, his wife pulled him away from me and pacified him. She then turned to me and said, 'Do not worry, he is just angry because of the talk of compromise.' In midst of the process of compromise, Purshottambhai saw me now as a source of danger to his daughter—I was no longer someone who could be trusted not to expose his secret. I assured Sandhya and Hansaben that I would not go to the press and repeated the intent of my project. Sandhya's mother patted my arm and told me not to worry. Just then, Mr Desai called Sandhya aside to prepare her for the testimony, and I left. The process of compromise was finalized a few hours before the hearing. This is where I reached one of the limits of this research, where the secret was born with a public face.

I found that compared to other rape trials, this case was not held *in camera*. The testimony was recorded on a single day. The duration was also much shorter since expert witnesses such as medical and forensic experts were not summoned for the hearing. Their documentary evidence was accepted instead. After a few key witnesses were declared hostile, at the very end the police inspector in charge was examined. Ultimately, the court acquitted Daya on the grounds that there was not sufficient evidence against him. The testimony of the police inspector was found to be lacking in support from the testimonies of the other witnesses.

The hearing began with Purshottambhai taking the stand. The judge began to ask the questions. Usually it is the prosecution lawyer who begins the chief examination, but the judge reserves the right to ask questions as well. He then dictated the response to Faridaben, the typist.

J: What is the victim to you?

P: (*inaudible*)

J (d): This Sandhya is my daughter.

J: What happened on [date]?

P: (*inaudible*)

J (d): On [date] my daughter had gone to her maternal uncle's [*mama*] home. And my daughter went away without telling anyone. We looked around for her but we could not find her. That is why on suspicion I filed a complaint against the accused.

J: What is your name?

P: (*inaudible*)

J: Is this your signature?

P: Yes.

J (d): The complaint No. [...] is being shown to me. In that, I verify my signature. The complaint [*fariyad*] comes to be submitted as Ex. No. 11.

J: Your daughter has been kidnapped, abducted or made to run away [*bhagaviyu chhe*]—Has something like this happened?

P: No (*shakes head*).

J: When you found your daughter, did she tell you anything?

P: Yes, that she had gone to her maternal uncle's home.

J (d): 2. It is not true that my daughter went with the present accused or that the present accused took [*lai gayo*] my daughter. When my daughter came back, she told me that she had gone to my maternal uncle's home. Besides that, I do not know anything.

J: Anything else?

P: No.

At this point Purshottambhai was declared to be a hostile witness. The judge then began to dictate to Faridaben.

J: It is not true that in my complaint any such fact has been written that 'the present accused has made my daughter run away [*bhagari ne*] with him'. It is not true that I have written such facts in my complaint such as 'this boy Daya since last six months or so used to meet my daughter Sandhyaben occasionally and used to speak to her. The members of my family and my wife had seen this and stopped them.'

Desai: This case is with the prosecution.[104] Cross-examination? The accused does not have a lawyer.

J: Where is the defence lawyer?

D: Leave it.

J: No, call him.

D: He is on the third floor.

The accused went out to call him.

The judge handed Faridaben the papers to type. Purshottambhai continued to stand in the witness box. It was 4.20 p.m. now. There was no cross-examination although the judge had permitted it. It is here that the role of the prosecution becomes important. It would be difficult to actualize a compromise if the prosecution were to decide to cross-examine, although this in itself may not necessitate conviction. The record was dictated as follows:

My daughter's date of birth is from the [date]. To verify this I am submitting my daughter's school leaving certificate. It is not true that I am giving a false testimony in order to save the accused.

No cross-examination.

Purshottambhai testified to having filed a complaint. We are not told what prompted him to file the complaint or why Sandhya had left for her maternal uncle's place without informing her parents. Elaboration of these reasons could have meant acknowledging that his daughter knew Daya, imperilling Sandhya's marital future. The proceedings continued as follows:

J *to the court constable*: Send the girl's mother in.

He accompanied Hansaben to the witness stand. Purshottambhai sat in the back row. She took the stand.

J: What is your name?

Hansaben: (*inaudible*)

J: Where do you live?

H: (*inaudible*)

Farida types forty-eight against age.

J: What kind of work do you do?

H: (*inaudible*)

Faridaben types: House work [*gharkam*]. *The judge is interrupted by another lawyer.*

J: Keeping God as your witness.

H: (*repeats*)

Faridaben types: sworn in.

After the oath, the judge resumed questioning.

J: What happened to the girl?

H: She went away without telling us.

J: What is her name?

H: Sandhya.

J (d): My daughter [*chokri*] Sandhya went off without telling us to my natal home [*piyar*]—to her maternal uncle's house.

A lawyer interrupts the testimony. The judge then resumes the chief examination.

J: When did you come to know?

H: (*inaudible*)

J (d): We asked neighbours but we could not find her.

J: What did you do next?

H: We found her in my natal home.

J (d): And as we searched, we found her in my natal home.

J: You lodged a complaint?

H: No.

J (d): I did not lodge a complaint.

J: Has it happened that your daughter was abducted?

H: No.

J: Do you recognize him? (points to the accused)

H: No.

J (d]: I do not recognize the accused. That the accused abducted my daughter did not happen.

Hansaben's testimony that she did not recognize Daya not only strengthened the evidence of his not having abducted Sandhya but also supported the claim that Sandhya had indeed gone to her uncle's house. Hansaben's testimony indicates that Sandhya would not have any reason to know Daya, given the incommensurability of caste. Hansaben was declared hostile as well. She was not cross-examined by the prosecutor. The judge dictated the following before allowing her to leave the stand:

J (d): It is not true that I made a statement in person to the police that 'my daughter was abducted by the accused'. It is not true that I made a statement in person to the police that I got written in my *juvab* that 'I sent [my] son to fetch my husband and told him about the incident.' It is not true that I am giving a false testimony to save the accused.

It is here that we see how the transition between the *juvab* (police statement) and *jubani* (testimony) in this case is mediated by the compromise. Hence, courtroom talk effaces the socio-legal event that was referred to as abduction and rape at the police station and enters the record as a narrative of ungrounded suspicion against a man whom their missing daughter did not know. Next, it was Sandhya's turn to testify.

Judge: Girl [*chowkri*]!

Purshottambhai went out and called for her. She entered the courtroom and smiled at me. Her eyes were downcast eyes and hands entwined as she took the stand.

J: Where did you go?

S: Maternal uncle [*mama*].

J: Because? Why did you go because your parents quarrelled?

S: I went to my maternal uncle's place.

J: That you went but why did you go?

S: (*silent*)

J (d): I went to my maternal uncle's [*mama's*] place without informing my parents.

J: Do you recognize him? (*points to the accused*)

S: No.

J (d): I do not recognize the accused.

J: Did you have any relationship [*sambandh*] with him?

S: No.

J (d): I did not have any relationship with the accused.

J: That he took you somewhere, has such a thing happened?

S: No.

J (d): That the accused took me somewhere or I went with the accused did not happen.

J: Is there anything else that needs to be written?

S: (*silent*)

J: Has the accused done any *kharab kam* against your wish with you?

S: (*silent*)

J: That the accused has done any *kharab kam* against my wishes, such thing has not happened.

S: (*silent*)

J: Hostile.

Typist 2: Note: since it is made public that the witness has turned hostile, permission is granted to cross-examine.

The judge flips pages. It was 4:30 p.m. at that time. The defence lawyer stood in front of the witness box.

Typist: Is there a cross-examination?

J: No.

Typist types: No cross-examination.

Sandhya's silence was translated for the court record as a denial of previous statements made to the police that the event happened. The compromise meant that her speech in court itself must conceal whether she was abducted and raped or she eloped with Daya. Why, then, was the court record no longer dangerous? The official transcript of Sandhya's testimony, as dictated by the judge, did not mention the event. Even if it were photocopied and circulated, it would not amount to an exposure of the secret, because it was emptied of any reference to the event. This is an archive of effacement where hostility is the residue. However, we must first understand what a hostile witness is.

The hostility of a witness finds a complex rendition in case law. As Monir's commentary tells us, a hostile witness is not merely someone who makes a statement in court that differs from or is inconsistent with a previous statement, although this could be one of the factors in considering whether a witness is hostile or not.[105] Nor is a witness necessarily hostile 'if in speaking the truth as he knows or sees it, his testimony happens to go against the party calling him' (Monir 1989: 1601).[106] However, 'the witness must appear to be not desirous of telling the truth and it is necessary to regard him hostile for eliciting the truth' (Ratanlal & Dhirajlal 1999: 467).[107] Alternatively, when the 'prosecutrix' is perceived, in Monir's words, as expressing antagonism towards the prosecution and acts in favour of the defence, she may be called hostile. In such cases, s. 154 IEA[108] permits the prosecution to ask questions as may be put to her during a cross-examination. The permission to put such questions rest on the discretion of the court, and judicial restraint is advised in exercising his discretion.[109] Such questions are not only those that are directed at shaking the credibility of the witness but are also a way of eliciting suppressed facts.

Again, as a hostile witness Sandhya was positioned as a witness against the prosecution case and could be subjected to questions as if it were a cross-examination. The story of the hostile witness is inflected by public secrecy. As a residue, hostility is the 'unconnected moment, when the narrative could have taken a different direction. Even when a story is completed, the residue may become an important resource in memory for reopening the narrative' (Das 1995: 171). Yet, these

possibilities are what Koselleck calls 'the difference between vanished reality and its linguistic appearance, which can never be bridged' (2002: 37).

***

The laws on rape, kidnapping, and abduction situate violation in the realm of the collective rather than represent individual women's experiences of coercion or consent. I have argued that although the structure of the trial is altered in compromise cases, such that the trial does not constitute itself as a sexualized spectacle, however in doing so the potential of the trial to sexually humiliate the victim is not displaced. Hence, it is not enough to look at appellate judgments or even the records that we find in trial courts. For not only is the picture provided in the judgment isolated from its context, the socio-legal process that produces the acquittal is effaced from the written record. The court maintains the patriarchal authority of the father by reintroducing the practices fashioned outside the court and it is through these clandestine routes that the authority of the law is maintained. I show how the social moves into the legal to birth a public secret—one that severs law from its self-reference. It inserts contingency in the heart of state law. In other words, the case of compromise illustrates how legality is actually perceived as disruptive of sociality. In this instance sociality that is marked by caste-based patriarchies, and social justice in the domain of state law is possible only as a secret. In such cases, compromise is actively perceived, to put it in the words of a woman judge of a district court, as a mechanism for 'restoring social relations in society'. If hostility emerges as the residue in judicial texts, the ethnography of the trial remains complicit in the making of the public secret.

NOTES

1. The term *samadhan* in Gujarati means satisfied, peace, meditation, to finish. *Samadhan* when translated into English is defined as adjustment, compromise, reconciliation, settlement, and solution. People who speak Hindi and Gujarati also commonly use the English word *compromise*.

2. *Sreedharan T. and Ors* v. *Sub Inspector of Police and Anr* clarified that Lok Adalats cannot compromise rape or murder cases (MANU/KE/0402/2008 at para 27).

3. In such cases, compromise petitions may be filed in court before the sentence is pronounced.

4. The rules for compounding of offences provided in s. 320 CrPC specify that the composition of the offence under this section, 'shall have the effect of an acquittal of the accused with whom the offence has been compounded. Once a petition of real and genuine compromise is filed, composition is complete and effective, and will have the effect of acquittal though no specific order of acquittal is passed on the petition by the Court. The compromise petition on its being filed in court cannot be withdrawn. A case may be compounded at anytime before the sentence is pronounced' (Kelkar 1980: 224).

5. There are two interpretations to this section. According to the Calcutta High Court, this section applies only when there is actual concealment, while the Bombay High Court has held that a promise suffices for the application of this section (Ratanlal & Dhirajlal 2001).

6. *Dilipkumar Dhansukhlal Mehta* v. *State of Gujarat & 1* CR.MA/ 1004/2010 2/2, Order dated 03/02/2010, available at http://www. indiankanoon.org/doc/1320145/, accessed on 19 September 2012. At this stage the counsel for the accused–petitioner requested the court for permission to withdraw the application, and the court permitted him to do so.

7. *Narayani Gautam and Ors* v. *State AND Guddu and Ors* v. *State and Ors AND Than Singh and Anr* v. *State N.C.T. of Delhi and Anr* MANU/ DE/2794/2009.

8. Ibid. at para 46.

9. Ibid. at para 48.

10. Anticipatory bail on the grounds of compromise was granted by the Patna High Court in *Md Faiyaz @ Shabbeer Faiyaz* v. *State of Bihar*, Cr. Misc. No. 41875 of 2010, Patna High Court, dated 30.03.2011, available at http://www.indiankanoon.org/doc/270986/, accessed on 19 September 2012. Also see *Singheshwar Sah* v. *The State of Bihar*, Cr. Misc. No. 38319 of 2010, dated 10.03.11, available at http://www.indiankanoon.org/ doc/852004/, accessed on 19 September 2012.

11. See *Umrail Mian @ Umrail Ansari & Basir Mian* v. *The State of Bihar* [Cr. Misc. No. 42187 of 2010] dated 31.03.2011, available at http://www. indiankanoon.org/doc/1284313/, accessed on 19 September 2012.

12. See *Shesh Nath Choudhary* v. *The State of Bihar*, Cr. Misc. No. 1075 of 2011, Patna High Court, dated 22.02.2011, available at http://www. indiankanoon.org/doc/1122828/, accessed on 19 September 2012.

13. See *Jitendra Mahto* v. *The State of Bihar*, Cr. Misc. No. 6898 of 2011, dated 05.04.2011, available at http://indiankanoon.org/doc/1943508/,

accessed on 19 September 2012. In this case, the petitioner was charged with committing rape on a minor. As per the order, there were witnesses to the alleged crime and the medical report also corroborated rape. The counsel for the petitioner argued that the matter had been compromised between the two parties and that they were in a relationship, which the villagers who beat him up had disapproved of. The court rejected the bail application but urged the lower court to expedite the trial.

14. See *Jitan Singh S/o Sri Upendra Singh* v. *State of Bihar*, Cr. Misc. No. 33620 of 2010, dated 23.02.2011, available at http://www.indiankanoon.org/doc/1810200/, accessed on 19 September 2012. In this case, the counsel for the accused argued that a compromise had been reached between the two parties and a compromise petition had been filed in the court of Chief Judicial Magistrate, Nawada.

15. *Gajendra Kumar Rai @ Hiran Kr Rai* v. *The State of Bihar*, Cr. Misc. No.474 of 2011, Patna High Court, available at http://www.indiankanoon.org/doc/1378582/, accessed on 19 September 2012.

16. In *Sanjay Sharma* v. *State* (MANU/DE/0595/1995), the Delhi High Court did not grant anticipatory bail to a lawyer who was accused of having raped his landlord's wife and photographed her. He threatened to kill her son and husband if she did not compromise. The accused subsequently moved the Delhi High Court on the basis of the victim's 'statement under Section 164 CrPC, [which] completely exonerated the petitioner inasmuch as she has stated therein that she was having sexual intercourse with the petitioner out of her own free will, without any pressure and coercion' (ibid. at para 2). The Delhi High Court denied anticipatory bail after examining the case papers and the photographs, which seemed to preclude consent.

17. *Patu and Teerath Pal* v. *the State* MANU/UC/0065/2010.

18. See *Narain @ Naran* v. *The State of Rajasthan* MANU/RH/0230/2006.

19. Ibid. at para 19.

20. See *Lala alias Lal Chand* v. *State of Rajasthan* MANU/RH/0531/2003. In this case the defence asserted that the community was trying to negotiate a compromise, hence the delay in lodging the FIR.

21. MANU/JH/1235/2009.

22. See *Md Mahboob Ansari S/o Md Alauddin Ansari, Md Shamim Ansari S/o Md Amirruddin Ansari and Md Roshan Jamil Ansari @ Pinku s/o Md Amirruddin Ansari* v. *State of Bihar and Rabina Khatoon d/o Late Yusuf* MANU/BH/0591/2009. Also see *Aman Kumar and Anr* v. *State of Haryana* MANU/SC/0104/2004.

23. MANU/RH/0447/1995.

24. The medical evidence recorded that the child was injured, her hymen ruptured, and the injury was fresh, as evidenced by the bleeding. However, the doctor's testimony that the injury could have been caused by an erect penis or in other circumstances, by a hard blunt object, was interpreted to mean that medically it could not be ascertained that the child had been raped. Contrary to a number of other judgments, the court looked for corroborating marks of injury or resistance and the presence of semen. The court noted that despite the child's testimony that she was raped for two hours, she had no scratches or bruises on her body, nor did the vaginal smear indicate any presence of semen. Further, the eyewitness had turned hostile.

25. *Papuria @ Rajesh* v. *State of Rajasthan* MANU/RH/0447/1995 at para 2.

26. Ibid. at para 9.

27. Ibid. at para 9.

28. *Fota and Damra* v. *State* MANU/RH/0349/1999.

29. Fota was convicted of rape and sentenced to rigorous imprisonment for five years, with a fine amounting to Rs 1,000 by the trial court in Barmer, Rajasthan, in 1998. His accomplice Domra was booked under attempt to rape and also convicted for violating the Arms Act by carrying a gun. Domra was sentenced to five years rigorous imprisonment with a fine of Rs 1,000 and awarded one year rigorous imprisonment with the imposition of a fine worth Rs 100.

30. *Fota and Damra* v. *State* MANU/RH/0349/1999 at para 10.

31. In this case, a sixteen-year-old girl who was raped by the appellant while she was working in her parents' shop turned hostile during the trial, as did her parents. Her father denied the prosecution's suggestion that he had entered a compromise with the accused. The trial court convicted the accused to seven years imprisonment and the Rajasthan High Court overturned this sentence (see *Moola Ram* v. *State of Rajasthan* MANU/RH/0429/1999).

32. We know that several transactions enacted on the stamp paper that may not have legal validity are treated as if they are legal. As part of a larger legal culture, the writing on stamp paper infuses the compromise with the fiction of legality, as if the form infuses legality in the substance of the event. For analyses of the social life of the stamp paper see Dhagamwar 1992, Ghosh 2012, Holden 2008.

33. *Virender alias Bittu and Naresh* v. *State of Haryana* MANU/PH/0688/2010.

34. Additionally they were sentenced to one year rigorous imprisonment and Rs 500 as fine or rigorous imprisonment of six months for the crime of criminal intimidation.

35. *Virender alias Bittu and Naresh* v. *State of Haryana* MANU/PH/0688/2010, at para 21.

36. Ibid. at para 23.

37. Ibid. at para 23.

38. See *Mukhtayar Ahmad* v. *State of UP* MANU/UP/0147/2010. In this case, the Additional Sessions Judge, Saharanpur, convicted the accused for having repeatedly raped his daughter and sentenced him to life imprisonment along with a fine of Rs 5,000 and in default to undergo further imprisonment of six months. He was also convicted under s. 506 IPC and sentenced to one year rigorous imprisonment. The high court directed that the appeal be heard in three months while denying bail to the accused.

39. Ibid. at para 11.

40. MANU/SC/0366/1996.

41. Ibid. at para 13.

42. Similarly, the Allahabad High Court dismissed the defence's argument that the victim had filed a false case so that the accused would settle an ongoing court case with his opponent. The high court stated, 'morals have not gone down to this extent that the widow having grown up children will come to this extent to fabricate a false case ... It is unthinkable that one which will give false evidence due to enmity in order to settle the scores of others' (*Sushil Kumar Son of Deo Nath* v. *State of Uttar Pradesh* MANU/UP/1666/2007 at para 14).

43. Here, I am referring to both statutory bodies of local governance: the elected *panchayat*s and non-state *panchayat*s such as caste *panchayat*s. The leadership in these bodies may at times overlap. Caste or neighbourhood *panchayat*s are also found in urban localities. Moog says that 'while there may well no longer be any truly "traditional" panchayats left which are unaffected by the formal legal system, there still are tribunals of a traditional type in many areas. Panchayats are councils historically consisting of five members, although that number is by no means sacrosanct. Village panchayats ordinarily are made up of respected men from the village, especially from the dominant caste if there is one in that village. In some villages, and within certain castes, there are also caste panchayats, comprised members of one caste, which hear only intracaste disputes.' (1991: 550).

44. *Shanker Sahani* v. *State (Government of National Capital Territory of Delhi)* MANU/DE/0101/2010.

45. Further, the court noted that 'a token penalty was imposed upon the appellant by the panchayat which then forgave him. The appellant himself having filed this document, he cannot get out of it and it can definitely be read in evidence against him' (ibid at para 12).

46. Ibid. at para 13. In this case, the court dismissed the appeal while observing that it seemed that the child had been raped, although the accused had been convicted of attempt to rape. However, the prosecution had not challenged the reduced charge, hence all the court could do was to dismiss the appeal.

47. See *Sajina T.* v. *State of Keraia and Ors* MANU/KE/0041/2008 at para 4.

48. In this case, the high court convicted the accused.

49. *Sachin Verma S/o Cheetar Mal Verma Sachin Verma S/o Cheetar Mal Verma (in Jail)* v. *State of UP* MANU/UP/1487/2005.

50. This case also attracted the provisions of s. 3(2)(v) PoA Act.

51. MANU/RH/0668/2005. Her assailant was convicted for having committed homicide and sentenced to life.

52. *Mangilal* v. *State of MP* [(1998) Cri LJ 2304 (MP)] held that 'compromise cannot be a factor in reduction of quantum of punishment' (cited in Ratanlal and Dhirajlal 2011: 802). However, in the case where a four and a half year old girl was raped and the case was compromised, the sentence was reduced to the period undergone [see *Sadhu* v. *State of Bihar*, 2000 Cr LJ 4924 (Pat)].

53. See *Sukhwinder Singh* v. *State of Punjab* (2000) 9 SCC 204.

54. Article 142(1) states that 'the Supreme Court in the exercise of its jurisdiction may pass any such decree or make such order as is necessary for doing complete justice in any cause or matter pending before it, and any decree such passed or order so made shall be enforceable throughout the territory of India in such a manner as may be prescribed by or under any law made by the Parliament and, until provision in that behalf is so made, in such manner as the President may by order prescribe.'

55. *Sukhwinder Singh* v. *State of Punjab* (2000) 9 SCC 204 at para 2.

56. The Supreme Court opined that it was an adequate and special reason 'that the prosecutrix has since got married and she did not want the matter to be carried any further so as to lead a happy and healthy married life with her husband and had filed the compromise petition to that effect' (ibid. at para 4). This course of action would be the 'interest of the prosecutrix herself' (ibid. at para 4).

57. *Baldev Singh & Ors* v. *State of Punjab* MANU/SC/0148/2011.

58. Ibid. at para 2.

59. Special Criminal Application 954/2011, (Guj. High Court), Order dated 9 May 2011.

60. The Court of Ms Justice H.N. Devani of the Gujarat High Court in *Ayaben d/o Himmatbhai Mulji Bhai Rathod* v. *State of Gujarat*, Criminal Misc. Application No. 2312 of 2008, dated on 25 February 2008 quashed the charges of gangrape r/w the PoA Act.

61. *Kulbhushan Kantibhai Patel and Anr* v. *State of Gujarat and Anr*, Special Criminal Application 954/2011 (Gujarat High Court), Order dated 9 May 2011 at para 5.

62. See *Dharmendra Dhirajlal Soneji* v. *State of Gujarat* (1996) (2) GLH 727.

63. Ibid. at para 4.

64. S. 452 of the IPC holds that 'whoever commits house-trespass, having made preparation for causing hurt to any person or for assaulting any person, or wrongfully restraining any person, or of assault, or of wrongful restraint, shall be punished with imprisonment of either description for a term which may extend to seven years, and shall also be liable to fine' (Ratanlal & Dhirajlal 2001: 630).

65. 1996 (2) GLH 727 at para 8.1.

66. Ibid.

67. Ibid. at para 8.2.

68. Ibid. at para 9.

69. Ibid. at para 12.

70. Ibid. at para 13.

71. The relationship of compromise to truth or falsity is complex. Compromise was usually used to bolster the argument that most rape cases are false. Contesting this, a woman APP in the Bhadra trial court said to me, 'False cases? We believe the girl—it is our principle—Supreme Court and High Court Judges have abstracted one thing: no woman comes in court with false allegation to put her own life in tragedy. It is not always suited to say that every case is false. For the last one and a half years I have handled three to four cases of 376 [rape], and I have succeeded in getting two convictions. Other cases were compromised, which shows that the case is true because the accused was compelled to make a compromise. If the case is compromised, then she resists, and says, "This is not the person. I was at my uncle's place, nothing happened." There are ways of compromise.' The view that a compromise suggests the guilt of the accused is however, rare.

72. In some compromise cases, a lawyer may be engaged to work with the prosecution to actualize the compromise. In a rape, abduction, and kidnapping case, when Hirabhai was approached to compromise the case on the grounds that the victim did not want to testify because she had married in the meantime, he said, 'I am a PP. I cannot compromise. Engage a temporary lawyer. It would not happen for free. It will cost you a little something. You have to get the girl so that the lawyer can teach her what to say in court. If she utters as single wrong word then ... Bring the lawyer to me, I will teach him. Compromise is not our task.' However, this is not a consistent stance.

73. The discourse on compromise represses the issue of sexuality in marriage after a compromise. Likewise, once an adolescent initiates some degree of sexual intimacy, it is assumed that she consented to 'full' intercourse. The problems with naming sexual violence in relationships of choice are elided by the social and juridical discourses on sexuality and alliance.

74. This point has been argued by Dumont (1972), who provided a structural understanding of caste. He says, 'it is inaccurate to claim that kinship and caste are two utterly distinct domains; they are linked through the importance of marriage, an importance which is obvious in the case of caste, and which, in the case of kinship, is from the structural point of view sometimes explicit and sometimes implicit' (1972: 154).

75. One of the reasons for the complicity that Chowdhry cites is the belief that 'social issues must be resolved by caste leaders or caste panchayats and not according to the law of the land, which applies a different criterion of justice' (1998: 337).

76. Randeria (1989) describes the senava or cenava as amongst the lowest untouchable caste in North Gujarat. She says that among other such castes, the senava 'are considered permanently polluted because of their dual association with animal death, that is, through their caste-specific occupations and their consumption of carrion' (1989: 174).

77. The caste groups described as Sadhus are traditionally priests. K.S. Singh (2002) describes the Sadhus as disciples of Ramanand, a devotee of Vishnu. The Sadhus are strict vegetarians and prohibited from the consumption of alcohol. The Sadhus, we are told, were drawn from different caste groups to form an endogamous unit, and internal differentiation within the Sadhus arises from sectoral affiliations. Further, 'they rank themselves as Brahman in the *varna* order and claim an equivalent status to them. The neighbouring Brahmans do not attribute equal status to them. They enjoy middle order status in the local social hierarchy. … Community and division endogamy and clan exogamy are the customs followed while seeking marital alliance' (K.S. Singh 2002: 1216).

78. Amongst the Sadhus, 'girls and boys are married within the age of fifteen to twenty years and twenty to twenty four years respectively' (K.S. Singh 2002: 1216).

79. 'The Sadhus have a council of elders but not a formal caste *panch*. The council settles the disputes of intra-community matters. If they fail to solve the issue then they seek justice from the statutory panchayat. Statutory panchayat looks after the implementation of developmental programmes. To settle any inter-community disputes the statutory panchayat takes necessary steps. For any criminal offence … they appeal to a court of law' (K.S. Singh 2002: 1218).

80. The *panchnamma* is a written statement by independent witnesses called the *panch* who testify that the evidence confiscated during police investigation has not been tampered with.

81. *Tilak* is a vermilion mark applied on a devotee's forehead. In this context, it signifies caste identity.

82. While they waited for the prosecutor, the court constable Ashokbhai told Purshottambhai that the witness from Madhya Pradesh (MP) had been dropped. Ashokbhai later told me that the witness had given a false address and could not be traced. Her testimony was contrary to the prosecution case, claiming that Sandhya had eloped with Daya. Thus, it was good news that she could not be found.

83. I have not identified the neighbourhood to retain confidentiality.

84. The Senava, or Shenva also referred to as Chenva, Senva, Shema, Senwa, Sindhua, Sedma or Rajput are scheduled castes in Gujarat (see K.S. Singh 2002). K.S. Singh tells us that these caste groups are primarily rural communities, largely comprising landless labourers and workers engaged in other services. They are divided into different endogamous clans and at least 'three ascending generations from the mother's side are avoided while seeking a marital alliance. Divorce is permitted and remarriage after divorce or widowhood is allowed. … Intercommunity disputes are settled among themselves, or else are arbitrated by the Darbars in the village or by the gram panchayat representatives. Cases of divorce are settled within the community.' (K.S. Singh 1993: 1181–2).

85. *Prasad* refers to edible ritual offerings offered to deities and consumed by devotees. Refusal to eat *prasad* would be seen as offending the deity.

86. The Sadhus 'do not accept food and water from the Harijans, neither [do] they serve them. They accept *seedha* (raw food material) from clean castes' (K.S. Singh 2002: 1218–9).

87. *Dharmani* is commonly translated as fictive kinship. The term points to relationships made through choice. From the record, we come to know that Jagruti belonged the Pirat caste, and when she moved to this neighbourhood, she became a 'daughter' to Purshottambhai, indicating a relationship across caste boundaries by choice. Many anthropologists have pointed out that such relationships in the village often cut across caste boundaries. For example, Adrian Mayer shows how different castes are linked to each other as kin whereby 'ritual kin ties provides means by which differences of caste or ward membership can be bridged' (1960: 144). Mayer qualifies the description relationships across caste boundaries through ritual kinship or what he calls village kinship to point out that village kinship is not 'uniformly felt. … At the one extreme, the Harijans (especially the Tanners) have little contact with the rest of the village, and the use of kin

terms towards them is hardly stronger than their application to people of other villages' (1960: 145).

88. His statement reveals that he had been living in Sandhya's neighbourhood for seven years with his eldest brother and his wife. His brother was a peon at a school. His other older brother lived in N where he grew up with his family. His three sisters were married and the younger sister lived with his parents in N. At the age of seventeen or so he married and fathered two children. There was discord between him and his wife and they separated. She was living at her father's house at the time of the incident. Daya's wife is a silent figure in this story. No statement was taken from her. Police statements were elicited from Daya's family living in the neighbourhood.

89. Kissing on the lips cinematically indexes falling in love. For instance, in Hindi films, when a sex worker allows a man to kiss her on the lips, it signals that she has fallen in love with her client.

90. *Muddamal* literally means things pertaining to the case.

91. The relationship between the *panch* and the police is operative on the existent forms of local policing, which functions to implement surveillance on a body population and operates as a conduit of power to regulate a specific class of men who occupy the public space as rickshaw pullers, tea sellers, or local farmers. The constitution of such a network especially in and around police stations is an important factor in determining who is selected as a *panch*. Moreover, the *panch* I interviewed indicated their familiarity with police procedures. I was told that often the same people are produced as *panch* in different cases. One police inspector told me that while 'good' *panch* are selected in serious offences, in minor offences they do not bother as much. According to him, a good *panch* is one who would be able to speak well in the court. The police then interpret what is a serious crime, and anticipating the trial, select *panch* according to their ability to impress upon the court the veracity of police procedure.

92. Gell reminds us that 'it is a category-mistake to attribute dates to objects at all; because only events have dates. What objects have is *histories*, including many dated events, and we think that objects have dates only because we often identify objects by associating them with events surrounding their creation' (1992: 28, emphasis in original). *Muddamal* comprise objects that are said to bear histories and when these objects are produced in court for judicial verification, testimony is given to the histories that these objects bear rather than verifying that the object is the same. For example, Noornissa was asked to verify if the frock produced in clothes were the same as she was wearing at the time of the incident (see Chapter 3). The frock had been cut unevenly since the cloth had been analysed for forensic evidence.

93. We know from sociological and anthropological writings that apparel is intrinsic to social identities and the construction of the self. Clothing in cultural contexts such as those defined by caste-based sociality is centrally tied to social discourses of feminine chastity and shame (see Dwyer 2000; Tarlo 1996).

94. I was told during the course of the fieldwork that usually these documents are written by the police and the *panch* certify these documents by putting their thumbprints, for most of them are non-literate.

95. The *panchnamma* is written in a descriptive format. It details stains, marks, tears, and other identifying markers of the clothes such as colour, length, and cost.

96. The zip is commonly referred to as a 'chain'.

97. The male body is searched for marks of injury, especially to corroborate the victim's testimony. The genitalia centred examination looks at four aspects: (1) the development of the genitals and the man's potency, (2) whether the penis is injured, (3) whether there is any smegma formation (its absence confirms sexual intercourse except in the instance of circumcision), (4) the presence of vaginal epithelial cells, which can be located up to four days after the event. I cite from the medico-legal certificate, which recorded the findings of the Daya's examination: '1. Ext. genitals well dev. 2. Pubic and axillary [*sic*] hair; well developed and not matted. 3. No any [*sic*] stain over body, ext. genitals and over clothes. 4. No any [*sic*] injury over body and external genital. 5. Smegma over glans absent. Foreskin is circumcised. 6. Glans wash for vaginal epithelial cells is negative. The medico-legal certificate tells us that on examining Daya that no signs of injury were found on his body nor were any stains found. Daya's body was examined for evidence of sexual intercourse, indicated by the absence of smegma.'

98. The forensic analysis is broken up into two stages. The biologist determines whether or not the sample is from a human being and the serologist groups the samples. The stains found on other surfaces such as clothes are then matched with these samples.

99. *Tilakdhari* signifies a bearer of *tilak*, which denotes an upper-caste status.

100. *Sala* is a kin term used by a man to address his wife's brother. It is also used in a pejorative sense, as a term of abuse, as is the case here.

101. A term used to refer to married women, which also symbolizes Hindu women's sexuality within marriage.

102. By this, Purshottambhai meant that he drove buses on national routes.

103. The issue of dowry murders, cruelty or domestic violence remains entrenched in the coercive ideology of upholding the institution of marriage

(see Vatuk 2001). The reference to matrimonial discord arises when it threatens to shame the natal family, for families do not face loss of honour when daughters are burnt due to dowry demands. Honour is not threatened as long as women are 'good' wives.

104. Here, 'with the prosecution' means that a lawyer with a private practice was hired to work with the prosecutor to bring about a compromise.

105. Nor can a prosecutor declare a witness hostile because they have prior knowledge of this.

106. Hence, Monir (1989) says that an absent-minded comment by a witness on the stand that is unfriendly to the prosecution and effectively discloses the truth is not a hostile act.

107. 'It must be shown before a witness can be held hostile that there is good ground for believing that the statement that he has made in the favour of the defence is due to enmity to the prosecution' (Monir 1989: 1602).

108. When a testimony is declared hostile, s. 154 IEA permits 'the person who calls a witness to put any adverse questions to him which might be put in cross-examination by the adverse party' (cited in Monir 1989: 1599).

109. What this means is that the 'court may, in its discretion, permit the person who calls a witness to put any questions to him which might be put to in cross-examination by the adverse party, and this is different from requesting the Court to allow a party to cross-examine his witness on the ground of his having turned hostile' (Monir 1989: 1602–3). Monir adds, 'the discretion should not be exercised without sufficient reason and the reason should be stated; because by offering a witness, a party is held to recommend him as worthy of credence, and so it is not in general open to him to test the witness' credit or impeach his truthfulness. The discretion, when once, exercised by the first court, will not be reviewed by the appellate Court' (1989: 1603).

CHAPTER FIVE

Love Affairs and Rape Trials in India

Tracing the histories of 'minor jurisprudences' in European law, Goodrich (1996) says that the history of the jurisdiction of love reveals that with the hierarchical relationships between the sovereign and subject developed rules that confined relationships of heterosexual love to their function of reproduction.[1] Goodrich (1996) argues that the reproduction of social order traced through specific historically constituted, masculinist juristic genealogies erased minor jurisprudences in Europe that were premised on different conceptions of justice. He says that the courts of love established in the year 1400 by Charles VI of France are a good example of this erasure. The courts of love were constituted to hear disputes between lovers and were adjudicated by women selected by a panel of women on the basis of their recitations or written presentations of poetry. He argues that these were committed to a different vision of legal prose, predicated upon the 'existential commitments of writing', which constituted justice as desire and not law (Goodrich 1996: 4). Today, it is the 'negation of eros and of love to a space outside of serious social speech or law' that concerns social justice (Goodrich 1996: 5). In this chapter, I suggest that the jurisdiction of heterosexual love is made manifest in the domain of the law on rape, where love has historically been constituted as a function of social reproduction through what Goodrich (1996) calls masculinist juristic genealogies.[2] I depart from the doctrinal view of the rape law by arguing that the analytic of heterosexual love and heterosexual marriage in the field of violence assumes critical centrality to understand the social and juridical frameworks of rape in India.

For Borneman, the decline of marriage as a theoretical object of critique has accompanied the decline of interest in death as 'unpredictable and central to life in modern circumstances' (1996: 216).[3] Arguing that marriage and the symbolics of blood should return to anthropological analysis in relationship to death, closure, and exclusion rather than birth, life, and freedom, Borneman says that 'the project of putting oneself beyond risk through marriage will ultimately fail' (1996: 237). He argues that:

A 'symbolics of blood' is generative of a social formation whose authority is invested in a sovereign ruler ('Sovereign-Father'), in kinship relations based on a blood symbolism ('tabooed consanguinity' and the 'law of alliance'), and on the ability to 'take life or let live'. This blood symbolics is constitutive of a 'regime of power' based on both inheriting blood by descent and mixing blood by marriage, and is aligned with a particular configuration of power based on a 'sovereign's right to kill' or unquestioned ability to order or require someone's death. Alternatively, the 'analytics of sexuality' is a new mechanism of power generative of a social formation whose authority is invested in administering life by means of disciplining the body and regulating body populations. This new analytics of sexuality, then, is the basis for a regime of power that thematizes knowledge and the disciplines, the establishment of norms and rules, with a particular production and control of sexuality and the regulation of life itself. (1996: 216–7)

Although Borneman (1996) dwells on the silences within anthropological discourse on marriage in the context of AIDS, the relationship between marriage and death posited herein is provocative to the present analysis. It relates to the struggles of the women's movements in India, which have posited the relationship between heterosexual marriage and death by critiquing the normalization of violence against women within and outside marriage (see Das 2003; Karlekar 2003; Uberoi 1996). Feminists have linked marriage to exclusion, closure, and death by pointing out repeatedly that the opposition to heterosexual love as an expression of the positive right to marry signals the bloody terrain of the symbolics of blood. The blurring of love and rape, or consent and lack of consent has a specific manifestation when we look at the right of women to choose their partners.

I briefly explicate the judicial routes taken by the assertion of the right to choice.[4] A criminal complaint against the partner of the daughter charging him with statutory rape, abduction, or kidnapping is a stabilized legal strategy to 'recover' a daughter who enters into an 'improper' alliance. A *habeas corpus* petition claiming that the daughter is held in unlawful private detention may accompany a criminal complaint. The resourcefulness with which the natal family, in consultation with lawyers and police, deploys the laws on rape, abduction, and kidnapping then follows a rather efficient police procedure. The police hunt the couple down. After finding the couple, they are brought to the police station for questioning. If the woman states that she was not abducted or raped, she may face custodial violence, which is normalized by the category of police remand. If she is able to withstand the pressure and refuses to break off her relationship, she may be jailed on grounds of a criminal complaint brought against her, usually on grounds of having stolen some valuables from her parent's home before she eloped. Or, she may be detained in a state-run institution for women. Detention in state institutions of consenting adults follows a stabilized legal strategy. The woman bears the burden of proving that she was not raped, abducted, or kidnapped. She must now prove to the court that she is a consenting subject in a situation when she cannot appeal for resources for legal representation from her natal family (who initiated the proceedings against her), and all the resources for the legal dispute over her must flow from her affinal family, who bear the costs of legal representation for their son and his wife.

State law is also used to counter the criminalization of love. We encounter a bewildering number of petitions and counter-petitions filed in different courts by both parties. The appeals to state law range from petitions to quash the FIR, challenges to illegal detention and plea for personal liberty under the writ of *habeas corpus*, and filing collusive suits for the restitution of conjugal rights. Typically after the couple marries, the husband may file a case of restitution of conjugal rights against his wife.[5] The drama of restitution of conjugal rights is staged to establish the fact that the woman was not abducted or forced into marriage (see Chowdhry 2004). This sets the stage for the woman's consent to be certified. The performance of women's agency in court is grounded in the anticipation of police action; that is, fear of arrest, illegal detention, and custodial violence.

Arasu and Thangarajah (2012) argue that 'the institution of marriage is itself upheld as the only recognisable institution of partnership/intimacy in the context of heterosexual couples. Put simply, if a heterosexual couple were to counter a case of Habeas Corpus (or any other case) filed in the court by the girl's family they would have to be legally married' (2012: 421). Arasu and Thangarajah analyse *habeas corpus* petitions in the case of lesbian couples to suggest that unlike heterosexual women, lesbian desire is not named or recognized; a partner is named as a 'friend', pointing to a 'sanitization' of desire between women (2012: 425). The use of a series of laws to regulate lesbian relationships and force women to conform to heterosexist sexuality constitutes the unwritten precedent of injustice that underlies the criminalization of love.

In this chapter, I describe the risks heterosexual women experience whilst exercising their positive right to choose when, if, and whom to marry. The ethnography that follows shows how the power of state law stakes a hold over the life of a young woman, Chetna, who refused to say she was raped by the man she was in love with, and whom she ultimately married. In a sense, this narrative details the situatedness of the category of rape and the meaning of victimhood. I describe how this case was articulated at different sites such as the police station, the hospital, the jail, the state-run women's shelter, the prosecutor's chamber, and the courtroom. The journey that this case took helps us explicate the nature of regimes of legality and illegality that operate under the sign of the state law.

HABEAS CORPUS: CONSENTING WOMEN

Hussain's (2003) reading of the histories of *habeas corpus* in the colony demands a refusal to be surprised at the obvious awkwardness at finding the writ of liberty in regimes of conquest (also see P. Baxi 2006, 2009). He argues that the colonial history of the writ of *habeas corpus* in India must be seen as 'a history of increasing and ultimately complete legal institutionalization' that describes 'the disparate ways in which law posits legal subjects, and extends and consolidates state power' (Hussain 2003: 69–70). Citing examples from the Calcutta and Madras courts, Hussain observes that 'the court was even willing to use the writ to intervene in family disputes' (2003: 85). One such surprising circumstance is found in *The King* v. *DeUrilla*—a case published in 1814—where the Madras High Court held that the 'court will not, upon a habeas corpus compel a young woman that is marriageable to go home with her father contrary to her consent' (Hussain 2003: 85). Hence, 'the fact that the writ was petitioned for and granted in such instances suggests that habeas corpus had found a place in the social relations of early nineteenth century India' (Hussain 2003: 85). The use of *habeas corpus* petitions to contest marriages of choice is evidently not a new phenomenon.

One of the ways women's right to choice in marriage has been staged in courtrooms is through the evocation of the writ of *habeas corpus* against illegal detention by the state in everyday contexts (AALI 2004). The forms of state detention are varied. Women may be illegally detained in police stations, prisons, state-run women's shelters, or state-run asylums. Detention may be temporary or span longer periods—six months or more. When the woman refuses to go back to her natal family, the police and magistrates often consider state-run institutions to be the only spaces where the woman could be 'safe' from the struggle over custody between two 'parties'—her natal and affinal family. In other cases, the woman is sent to such homes for women to be free of pressures brought upon her; hence this space is constructed as a 'neutral' space that allows a woman to know her mind.

In *Chandrasinh K. Jadav* v. *the State of Gujarat & Ors*, for instance, we learn that the woman was sent back to the *nari gruh* (women's shelter) despite her stated wish to return to her matrimonial home, in order 'to enable her to disabuse her mind, if possibly under some threat or pressures she was not freely expressing herself before the court and further to coolly ponder over her fate embolden her and reassuredly [*sic*] telling us where she ultimately intended to return!'[6]

Women have also challenged state detention in women's shelters.[7] Kalyani Chowdhary filed a petition in the Allahabad High Court stating that she was illegally detained in a protective home for women in Lucknow.[8] The detention order followed a dispute between her father and her husband, or as the judgment says, 'a dispute between two parties'.[9] Clearly Kalyani's wishes were irrelevant in what came to be a battle for custody between two 'parties'. In court, Kalyani testified that she had married Vinod Kumar Chowdhary and wanted to live with him. Kalyani was allowed to leave after five days of illegal detention after the court determined that she had not committed any offence. The Allahabad High Court dismissed the arguments made by her father's lawyer maintaining that even a minor could not be detained in a protective home against her will or at the will of her father. Further, the Allahabad High Court noted that there is no law that requires magistrates to send such women to protective homes, which are meant only for women who are detained or rescued under the Suppression of Immoral Trafficking Act, 1956, Act no. 104 of 1956.[10] This judgment is important as it underscores how women caught in circuits of sexual trafficking are conflated with women who refuse to be exchanged in matrimonial trafficking, to paraphrase Gayle Rubin (1975).

Even though *habeas corpus* has been traditionally understood as a writ of right and not a matter of course, we find that there is a certain routinization of the use of the writ. For instance, Dwarka Prasad filed a *habeas corpus* petition in the Rajasthan High Court stating that his thirteen-year-old daughter Vedwati Kumari Sharma was missing since March 2001.[11] He filed a criminal complaint against Rajesh Sharma for having kidnapped his daughter and causing grievous harm to her. He then moved the High Court to trace his daughter. The court monitored the investigation such that the 'abducted' girl was produced before it within three days. Her statement revealed that Vedwanti was not a minor and had 'eloped voluntarily' with the accused.[12] She was nineteen when she married Rajesh Sharma and had given birth to a son who was three months old when she gave her statement in the court. The writ of *habeas corpus* was declared infructuous.

The court made two pertinent observations. First, the court emphasized that in *habeas corpus* petitions, it is not the High Court's place, '…to monitor police investigations … and the High Court is certainly not meant to be treated as an executing court for enforcing investigation of the cases which are registered by entertaining habeas corpus'.[13] Second, the Court remarked that the state—as the respondent—was at liberty to launch action against the father. This liberty was granted in order to check 'frivolous litigations which is [*sic*] repeatedly brought before this court in the form of habeas corpus'.[14] Cases that are falsified by the parents are rarely tried on grounds of perjury or contempt of court. Police officials, magistrates, and prosecutors do not usually see the father as a subject of perjury since the understanding of elopement as a crime against the father is often a shared discourse and therefore, 'voluntary elopement' becomes a marked category in legal discourse. Voluntary elopement is the counterpart to 'forced rape', a socio-legal category that seeks to fix the meaning of rape in legal discourse in India.

ELOPEMENT: WOMEN AS ABETTORS

The law on kidnapping of underage persons from lawful guardianship, defined under s. 363 IPC, is routinely evoked when an underage female subject elopes with a man without the consent of her lawful guardian.[15] This law does not include any exceptions such as when a minor is confined, sexually abused, beaten, or starved.[16] If an underage girl were to be rescued from domestic violence, her rescuer remains vulnerable to charges of abduction.[17] The rights of the lawful guardian are further protected in the case of female subjects under s. 366 IPC, which covers both kidnapping and abduction, the former category applicable to girls under eighteen years of age.[18] This law prohibits the kidnapping or abduction of any woman with the intent to compel her (or knowing that she will be compelled) to marry any person against her will, or to force, induce, or seduce her to illicit sexual intercourse (or knowing such will happen). Section 366 IPC positions men as potential seducers and women as potential victims of seduction outside marriage. Arasu and Thangarajah (2012) point out that this formulation does not think it possible to name women as seducers of other women.[19]

Tracing the development on the law around these crimes, Dhagamwar (1992) examines a complicated mass of judgments dating to the inception of the criminal law under British rule. She argues that in such cases, the perceptions of the woman's moral character influenced the judicial interpretation of the testimony to abduction, and further that such standards were extended to children as well. In the case of a twelve-year-old Muslim girl[20] who was abducted, kidnapped, and raped repeatedly, the court not only found her 'fast', but also dismissed her testimony on failing to uncover any signs of resistance or struggle (Dhagamwar 1992: 144). In this case, the medical evidence showed that the hymen had been broken.[21] This was then read to mean that she had consented to sex with the men under trial rather than proof of having been held forcibly in confinement and raped by them. Consequently, the very definition of seduction depends on the court's perception of what kind of female subject can be seduced illegally.[22]

The interpretation of seduction or coercion under s. 366 IPC has not been homogeneous. In a 1910 judgment, seduction was defined as that criminal act which induced 'the girl to surrender her chastity for the first time' (Dhagamwar 1992: 136).[23] However, in *Emperor* v. *Persumal* (1927), the court held that 'every time a woman surrenders herself to a lover whether it is for the first time or twentieth time, there is seduction' (Dhagamwar 1992: 137).[24] *Shaheb Ali and Anr* v. *Emperor* (1933) held that seduction is not limited to the first act of illegal sexual relationship with the girl.[25] In 1932, the Allahabad High Court had ruled that the term seduction could be applied to 'the first act of illicit intercourse' unless it could be proven legally that the 'girl had returned to a life of chastity or unless there was proof that the man intended her to be seduced by another man' (Dhagamwar 1992: 137).[26] The court further clarified that 'kidnapping a woman in order that she may be seduced to illicit intercourse is manifestly different from kidnapping a woman whom he has already induced to sexual intercourse' (cited in Dhagamwar 1992: 137).

While a husband cannot be convicted of kidnapping or abducting his wife, the seduction clause addressing illicit sex was seen to be a crime that resulted in the loss of chastity, but for chastity to be proven, the woman needed to be in a 'state of purity' before and after the incident. Dhagamwar is of the opinion that:

> [t]he interpretation of the clause 'to seduce to illicit sexual intercourse' appears to be an amalgam of the decisions arrived at in the two cases of *Shaheb Ali and Anr. v. Emperor* and *Emperor v. Baiji Nath*. While it is necessary for the girl to have always been chaste in order to bring the abductor's action within the purview of section 366 IPC, it is necessary to show that she had returned to a state of purity. If she had not given up her loose ways, her charge of being abducted with intent to seduce would lack credibility. (Dhagamwar 1992: 137)

The return to chastity then becomes an important consideration in proving what happened. Thereby, the time prior to the event and its aftermath must live up to the standards of chastity in the eyes of the law so that the testimony is believed.[27]

These laws were also used to contest the choices women made in terms of their sexual and marital futures. In *Chandgi* v. *Emperor*, a case from the Lahore High Court, Molia married his brother's widow S against her wishes. When she eloped with her lover, Molia lodged a complaint of abduction against him.[28] Mr Justice Broadway upheld the conviction of abduction, but lowered the sentence on the following grounds:

> In marriages of this sort, as pointed out by the learned Sessions Judge the woman has no say of any kind, and the result often is that she gladly goes off with a lover. It has often been held that when the woman is an active abettor in her own abduction the sentence should be a light one. In the present case in all probability *Musammat* [S] was by no means willing to marry the complainant and there seems every reason to believe that she actively abetted her own abduction. In these circumstances, ... I reduce the sentence accordingly.[29]

Here, we see that the judge could not interfere with the naming of elopement as abduction; hence, S was named as the active abettor in her own abduction. At the same time, the court recognized that families coerce women to remain in marriages against their own wishes, providing a basis on which the sentence could be mitigated.

In 1999, the Karnataka High Court framed cases concerning underage women as a 'delicate issue'.[30]

> The cases involving minors throws up delicate issues and a Court is required to take a very cautious as also a very realistic view bearing in mind the sociological consequences of the orders that a Court may pass. In a case where a minor is induced to leave the lawful guardianship, technically the offence of kidnapping would stand established and similarly, even if a minor girl voluntarily accompanies the accused and submits to sexual intercourse, again technically the offence of rape is committed. The Courts are however required to draw a distinction between instances where sexual attacks are made on minor girls, where force is used and where the act is atrocious, and the instances of the present type where the entire episode is a lover's escapade though it may technically constitute an offence.[31]

The anxiety between the 'technical' and the 'actual' rests on discerning between a lovers' escapade and acts of atrocious violence.

chastity. ... The rape trial retains something of the older notion of spectacle that Foucault saw as being displaced by disciplinary power and scientific reason, but a spectacle of degradation visited upon the victim rather than the offender. (1997: 73)

In this instance, the nature of warning is produced not only through the trial as a spectacle of degradation but also by the narratives of custodial rape that circulate as a warning to all women not to represent themselves as desiring subjects outside of social norms.

'HE HAS BACKING'

Referring to cases of love affairs framed as criminal complaints of rape, kidnapping, and abduction in the Mirzapur court, Hirabhai explained to me, 'It becomes a matter of honour [*izzat*]. In cases where the father is reputed, he does not accept easily if his daughter has run away. He has backing.' The father with 'backing' is reputed, powerful, and able to move state machinery, to stalk, monitor, incarcerate, charge, and punish his disobedient daughter. Hirabhai explained, 'The police initially book the person accused for abduction and kidnapping. Then they add rape—after taking her statement. So, if she says "yes" to the fact of sexual intercourse and is underage, then it is rape'. The documentary practices of the police are critical to the way such cases are framed. Citing an ongoing case of statutory rape that came up for a bail hearing in December 1996, Hirabhai exclaimed:

Look at this case, Baxi! A twenty-one-year-old man was accused of rape and abduction. The victim at the time of the incident was fifteen years old. The medical [medico-legal certificate] of the victim shows that secondary sexual characteristics are well developed. The hymen is ruptured. It indicates sexual intercourse. Her father was the complainant. The girl's [his daughter] statement clearly says that she was in a relationship with the man for the last three years. The police constable [*jamadar*] is very clever [Hirabhai read out from the police statement of the victim], 'I have had a relationship with him since many births.[38] It is an awakening of love [*prem ka ankur hai*]'.

Conversant with the police practice of signifying consent as the 'awakening of love' in statutory rape cases, Hirabhai was aware that the victim's statement was not a verbatim account of what she may have said to the police.[39] Rather, he subjected the case papers to a specific kind of reading to discern competing ways of framing what happened.

Hirabhai taught me that police documentation is usually marked with excess. For instance, police records usually comprised intimate photographs of runaway couples that were not relevant to the trial. Somewhat romantic at heart, he read out love letters and police statements to narrate tales of violent opposition to the lovers— accounts laced with an unspoken admiration for 'smart' women who defied their families—as is evident in his account of a love story of an 'upper' caste woman. In this case, her father, a Brahmin, had lodged a complaint against the man she loved and who belonged to the 'lower' Bharward caste (a shepherd caste). She met the accused, a driver from a neighbouring village, during the festival of *navratri*. After she eloped, her father also filed a *habeas corpus* petition in the high court. Since she refused to return to her father, she was sent to the *nari gruh* (state shelter for women). Ultimately, she married her partner and at the time of the hearing, their child was four months old.

In this case, Hirabhai explained to me, 'the marriage may be illegal as the girl is not eighteen yet. The girl is hostile. The father wants to do nothing with the girl. He does not come to court'. The police documentation revealed a consensual sexual relationship after the elopement, even though in law this consent was not relevant. At the same time, the police documents also characterized the woman as the agent of seduction by making it clear that it was she who decided to elope and refused to go back to her parents.

> Look, this is what her statement to the police says: 'During the time when our relationship started, we did not do any illicit act [*galat kam*].[40] The police statement states her age to be sixteen. She, in her statement says, 'I was in love [*mujhe prem hua tha*].' See, there is overwriting here to make fifteen look like sixteen. In her police statement, she says, 'we did *kharab kam* [illicit sex] once in one night. We did this seven–eight times over the next few days.' She did not say that she did not give her consent, but she is under sixteen, so it is rape.

Hirabhai further described the contents of the case papers.

> The girl wrote a letter to her parents telling them how the police tortured her and how she wanted her parents to stop looking for her

[a copy of the letter was attached in the case papers]. She also wrote to her parents saying that she was pregnant. She says, 'if you harm me, I won't come to your house.' This means that there were some other men in the village who desired her and were pressurizing the police to find them. She also said, 'I won't come to the village anyway, I will go to the women's shelter [*nari gruh*].' Somebody told her what to write. She uses the word *khichariya* several times—a word used by Bharwards, which means one who interferes, a nosy parker. She would not use this word herself being a Brahmin.

The police dossier was subjected to a specific reading to deduce love. 'She is a very smart looking girl—fair, short hair, plump. The accused did not turn up for the court hearing twice. The third time,' Hirabhai grinned, 'the judge sent out a warrant and sent him to Sabarmati [jail] for three days'.

Although he was now married to the purported victim, and the father who initiated the prosecution was no longer interested in pursuing the criminal complaint, the accused would be tried for statutory rape. Hirabhai urged me to recognize that 'there is nothing like the law of truth. There is something called the law of evidence. Law has nothing to do with justice or truth'.[41] I now turn to Chetna and Roshan's story to show how the value of evidence changes over time.

THE CASE HISTORY

When I met Chetna and Roshan in the trial court, I explained to them the nature of my research and asked them if I could interview them. Roshan laughed and said, 'Oh, we don't mind if you tape or give her name, our names. She will go on television'.[42] I visited their home one Sunday afternoon, where I interviewed both of them and Roshan's married sister Kumud, who was visiting them. The case history is based on police documentation, court proceedings, and ethnographic interviews. The translations are from Gujarati.

Chetna was seventeen and a half years old when her mother threw her out of her home after discovering her relationship with Roshan. Her parents opposed the relationship on the grounds that they belonged to the Patel caste and Roshan belonged to the Prajapati caste.[43] Chetna went to Roshan's house, but he was not home. He worked in a shop in the clothes market in the old city. When he came back from work, she recounted the entire incident to him. Chetna's mother subsequently went to the police and lodged a complaint stating that her daughter was missing and that Roshan had seduced and abducted her with the intent to have illicit sex with her. She further alleged that Chetna had stolen gold jewellery from her home. The night following this complaint, the police arrested Roshan and Chetna. Roshan, who was arrested on the grounds of rape, abduction, and kidnapping (under ss. 376, 366, and 363 IPC respectively), secured bail a week later. Two days after the complaint was lodged, the police also arrested Chetna for abetting rape, abduction, kidnapping, and theft. Chetna was sent to the central jail, and then to a shelter for women. After nine months, the police petitioned the court to drop the charges against Chetna since there was no evidence against her. After Chetna was released, she ran away to marry Roshan as soon as she came of age and by the time the case came to court they had borne a son. Her mother agreed to compromise and testified that Roshan had not kidnapped, abducted, and raped her daughter. Roshan was acquitted at the end of the trial.

IN THE PROSECUTOR'S CHAMBER

I heard of this case for the first time when Hirabhai drew my attention to the police papers that had been sent to him. Hirabhai shaking his head in disapproval said,

> Baxi, look at these papers! There is no reality in them. The medical shows the hymen was intact, yet the police said she was raped. Parents opposed the relationship. The girl is a Patel girl. The boy is Prajapati. She married him later. Has a child. Now the family wants to compromise. The girl is very smart. I asked her, 'Did you not feel scared as all this happened?' and she said, 'Why live in terror when one has loved [*pyar kiya to darna kya*]?'

The last phrase is a reference to a popular Hindi song[44] from a classic Hindi film, *Mughal-e-Azam*. It spans several contexts to give meaning to Hirabhai's reading of Chetna's life in categories of popular culture that re-articulates the legal framing of that which had happened. *Mughal-e-Azam,* a popular film made in the 1950s, is a story about King Akbar's son Salim (enacted by Dilip Kumar) who was in love with the beautiful courtesan, Anarkali (enacted by Madhubala). Akbar was enraged when he learnt of the relationship. In a performance in the princely court, the defiant Anarkali sings and dances to a song (composed by Naushad) to the lyrics 'Why live in fear when one has loved, one has loved; one has loved, not stolen; why should one sigh in secret' (*pyar kiya to darna kya, pyar kiya hai chori to nahi ki, chup chup ke ahe bharna kya*)? This song dramatizes love as resistance to the sovereign, declaring that sovereign power cannot dictate its will to the love that animates lovers, which defies the social chasms between a prince and a courtesan. The identifying marker of true love is thus one that does not know fear of the sovereign. Love is without guilt. It is posed in radical opposition to crime. Love is not theft. Love is not illicit. It is love that is all that law cannot be (see Raes 1998).

After he was acquitted, Roshan said to me:

Do you know what the prosecutor asked Chetna?
He asked her, 'You married in another caste, you are Patel and he is Prajapati, what is this?'
So she said, 'So what? Is he not a man? Is he not a human being? That is what she said.'
Then he said, *'Pyar kiya to darna kya?'*
If that is so, then where could he see caste?'
Chetna added, 'caste is always one. You are a woman. I am a woman.'

The evocation of a love song indicated that serious legal language could not communicate what Chetna sought to say about caste and love. She evoked the category of being human, where caste refers to the human species as a whole, while Hirabhai cited a love song that lies outside serious legal language (Goodrich 1996). He represented Chetna as an extraordinary woman whose story could only be framed through cinematic references.

THE SPECTACLE OF VIOLENCE

In the context of caste-based socialities that repress love, we find the narrative of repetetive violence. It is important to detail how legal subjects represent the repression of love and the repetitive narrative of custodial violence. I suggest that Roshan frames the story through a cinematic understanding of love, violence, state, and family, raising the issue of 'the very organisation of vision and its effects' (Doane 1987, cited in Pinney 1992: 47). Here, I am less concerned with the question about scopophilia or 'the pleasure of looking which causes libidinal excitation', and more with how the language of popular cinema provides a space for organizing elements of love and violence, separation and re-union of lovers, familial opposition, and state's compliance—a melodrama with a happy ending (Pinney 1992: 28). The re-telling of what happened in Roshan's words is a striking example of how the narrative is organized as if it were a story in a film.

The cinematic mode is not about the 'ordinary.' Roshan and Chetna told me that there had been many inter-caste marriages in the neighbourhood, including the marriage of a Brahmin woman with a lower-caste man. In none of these instances had anything like this ever happened. Chetna's mother opposed their relationship because, as Chetna put it, 'he was not from our caste'. The following excerpts are from a long interview in Chetna and Roshan's home. Chetna was nursing a young baby at the time. The excerpt given below, which I have translated from Gujarati, is in Roshan's words. Roshan's sister Kumud also recounted what had happened.

> R: Chetna's mother threw her out of the house. She threatened to go to the police, to the court. This 'story' started at 9.30 p.m. like a 'movie' and ended at 11.30 p.m. I came back at 9 p.m., then I came to know that her mother had thrown her out of the house.
>
> I explained to her [Chetna], 'We are not married and this will become a long *lafara*[45] [public brawl]'. So her mother brought about a long *lafara*. Then her mother phoned Chetna's maternal uncle [*mama*].
>
> K: He [Chetna's maternal uncle] is a goon.
>
> R: No, he is not a goon. But he goes to clubs, so he has contacts. He is quite old; he is forty-five years old. So, her mummy called the maternal uncle. Her [Chetna's] uncle's sons have a kite shop and there were many young men hanging out there. They all came here to beat me up. They told the neighbours, if anyone interferes then we will beat you up too. Everyone locked their houses and sat inside. Only one man—do you see that man who is wearing a white cap? [He

pointed towards the street, I saw a man pass by through the door.]
He took my father to the police station later. Anyway, then they really
beat us up, beat me. There were about ten–fifteen people. All the
people came to beat me up. Then her mother said, 'Come home',
and Chetna said, 'I will not come. You are getting someone's son
beaten up. Like you, he is also someone's only son.' Then Chetna
was also slapped a few times. Chetna began to say, 'It is my wish.'
Then everyone started beating me again. Then she said, 'Why are you
beating him up? Don't touch anyone.'

K: Her mother came with Chetna and shoved her and said, '*Challa
bharwa*,[46] keep the girl.' Her mummy called her uncle and everyone
else. Her mother did this—did a *danga*[47] with us. I was unmarried
then. I got married later. They said, 'let us abduct their daughter.' I
hid behind a gas cylinder for one hour.

R: They said, 'They did this to our girl, so let us abduct theirs.' When
Chetna refused to go with them, she was beaten up too.

Chetna's maternal uncle had three sons and no daughters, and looked
upon his sister's daughters as his own. Roshan explained, 'That's why he
came after us, like a villain her uncle [*mama*] came after us. That's why
his name does not appear in the court. He escaped.' Chetna's father
went along with the police complaint since, as Chetna explained, 'Papa
was scared: what if in the future my uncle got him in trouble?'

The villain in a Hindi film is one who typically escapes the gaze of
the police and law. The cinematic mode then offers a counter frame, as
if the cinematic can 'constrain the meaning through narrative chains of
signification' to situate 'otherwise undecidable images within sequences
that produce an argument and express intention' (Pinney 1992: 27).
The alliance between the police and Chetna's family to discipline and
punish is experienced as excess that could not be represented in legal
language. The incommensurability between experience and accusation
renders the spectacle of custodial violence as fantastical. It is fantastical
for Roshan, who insisted, 'Love marriages are not about being modern,
as a deviation from traditional Indian society; rather it is an ancient
practice, as traditional as tradition can be.'

THE *FARIYAD* AS CUSTODIAL VIOLENCE

Ordinarily custodial violence has been used to refer to police in
detention or in judicial custody. The struggle to retain a hold over an

unmarried daughter's sexuality is also a description of custodial power. When guardianship or the right of the father wears the terrifying face of custodial power, the father's home is often experienced as a site of custodial violence. A daughter who escapes the hold over her sexuality through a marriage of personal choice encounters a double articulation of custodial power at her father's home and in the police station, a site that also regulates the politics of honour. Chetna's assertion of her right to choice and refusal to renounce love provoked further custodial violence.

Chetna emphatically told her mother that she would live in Roshan's house. When her family realized that she was on Roshan's 'side', as the police put it, they left without her. Roshan and Chetna thought that they must have reconciled themselves to the situation and the matter would end there. Hence, they decided not to lodge a police complaint against the men who beat them up.

Besides, as Chetna said, 'if we had gone to get a complaint written then there may have been a problem.' They were afraid that the police would hand over her custody to her parents. Roshan continued to recount what happened afterwards. I quote Roshan and Kumud below:

R: Then we did not come to know. We were watching TV. We were sitting here [in the living room where we were]. She [*pointing to his sister*, Kumud] was in that room. The parents were also inside. We were sitting here and we had locked the door.

K: No, it was like this. When he was eating the food then everywhere there was blood even in the plate, there was blood and blood.

R: They beat me up so badly. There was blood.

K: They beat him up a lot, with a stick. The plate had

The *fariyad*

On learning that Roshanbhai Pannachand, living in our society bungalow [number], and my daughter Chetna have illicit relationship I scolded them both.

On [date] I and my daughter and my son Sameer were present at home. My husband had gone to work and on scolding my daughter there was an exchange of words. That night at 8.30 p.m. my daughter Chetna left without saying a word to anyone. When she did not come home we searched for her at our relative's home. On searching Roshan Pannachand's house too they weren't found. When my daughter cooked rice; soon it was full of blood. The police came in a big van.

R: Then they said, 'Who is Roshan Pannachand and Chetna Patel?' So she (Chetna) only opened the door.

Chetna said: 'you will not open the door, what if someone comes and beats you up?' So she opened the door and she said, 'come, I will go with you,' then they caught both of us and took us.

Chetna left home at that time she took from the locker the gold necklace and earrings kept there. Roshanbhai made my daughter run away with him with the intent of marrying her by enticing, bribing, and seducing her for the purpose of illicit sexual intercourse and that's why I give this *fariyad*.

On [date] at 8.30 p.m. from [place] Roshanbhai kidnapped my daughter with the intent of illicit sexual intercourse that is why I am getting this *fariyad* written down.

The police complaint lodged by Chetna's mother treads on the socio-legal route of compelling women to withdraw from relationships of love on pain of a criminal charge against the man and violence against the self. In Chetna's case, the law was used to coerce her to say that she was a victim of rape, abduction, and kidnapping. Chetna refused. It was at this point that the *fariyad* was written. Roshan was now positioned as a criminal who abducted and raped, with Chetna positioned as his victim.

The effect of the police complaint was to initiate criminal charges against Chetna. She was accused of stealing jewellery from her parents' house. As a transgressor of familial normativity when categories of impropriety were translated into categories of illegalities, there was a shift towards locating Chetna as a criminal, as Roshan recounted:

R: This story happened in [month] 1994. The policemen said, 'the girl is on his side so get a *fariyad* written.' Her mummy said that she has brought jewellery and all. Then the police asked her [Chetna about the jewellery], she said that 'I am wearing a jersey. I did not even wear slippers in my feet.' The police*walas* locked me in, then told her to go home. They did not want to write her complaint [*fariyad*]. She said, 'I won't go home, you release him.' The policemen said to her mummy, 'Your plan is not going to work [*apki daal galne wali nahi hai*]. The girl is on his side. So write a *fariyad* against the girl.' They applied penal sections [*kalam*] against her and against me, too.[48]

K: They [Chetna's family] bribed the police.

The narrative of custodial violence was erased from the police documents.

R: Then they took me in custody. Pappa was there. Mummy was crying. Then in the morning [they] took our remand—a lot. They told her to take her [Chetna's] remand. You know they have a women constable. She said, 'she is a small girl. I will not take her remand'.

The PI [police inspector] took us to the senior inspector and told him, 'He [Roshan] took the girl and raped her'. He said, 'beat him' and so, they beat me up really badly.

Then she [Chetna] felt, he is suffering so much beating for me.

K: The police used a stick [*danda*] to beat him.

PB *to* C: Did they take your 'remand' too?

C: Yes. They beat both of us.

Police violence is normalized by the language of remand so that it substitutes the category of custodial violence.[49] After the medico-legal examination, Roshan and Chetna were brought back to the police station from the hospital. Roshan was kept in the custody room overnight while Chetna sat outside the room in the police station. Until then, Chetna's statement was not taken. In Roshan's words:

Then they took me back. They kept me inside for one night and she was made to sit outside. The next morning, I was taken to Gaekwad Haveli[50] [crime branch]where they took my photograph and applied god knows what sections.[51] They took me to the magistrate's house. He was not there. It was a Saturday. All this happened on Thursday, Friday night. They took me to the Mirzapur court. I thought, being Saturday,[52] it would be a holiday. There they asked me if I had anything to say, I said, 'I don't want to say anything'.

That police inspector—he put pressure on me: 'if you speak then I will call you from the central jail to take your remand.' That's why I felt fear, that's why I said.

C: He said he would make him lie on a slab of ice.

R: He said [things] like this. That policeman—these people—say wrongful things, that we will take your remand like this or like that, make you lie on a slab of ice. That's why I did not say anything in court. I thought they would take a remand and get me from the central jail.[53]

Roshan was then taken to the central jail. On the same day, Chetna's statement was taken and she too was arrested. In the meantime, Roshan's brother contacted a lawyer who lived in front of his house in the city. This lawyer[54] helped Roshan get bail, and on 13 January 1994, he was released for Rs 15,000. Chetna remained locked up, as Roshan could not bail her out. The *fariyad* amounts to a specific form of custodial violence enacted by the family in collaboration with the police. The experience and threat of police violence remains erased from the legal documents but is constitutive in the framing of the legal event.

HOSPITAL NARRATIVES

The hospital narratives presented herein suggest that the averted gaze of the medical practitioner operates in a differential distribution of 'scandal and the light' (Foucault 1977: 9). The medico-legal gaze is arrested by specific body parts that correspond to the evidentiary sources for the purported crime. The medico-legal case is 'the individual as he may be described, judged, measured, compared with others, in his very individuality; and it is also the individual who has to be trained, corrected, normalized, excluded, etc.' (Foucault 1977: 191). The averted medico-legal gaze normalizing remand turns 'real lives into writing', as Foucault says, functioning 'as a procedure of objectification and subjection' (1977: 192). The scandal of remand, as narrated by Roshan below, does not meet publicity. The injured body in the aftermath of remand is not made visible by the medical gaze.

After the remand, Roshan was admitted to the civil hospital by the police and released from the hospital the following day. In Roshan's words,

> Then in the morning of the 7th, after taking our remand, the police put both of us in a *rickshaw* to take us to the civil [hospital]. Then my mummy told my brother and they were trying to get us released. But it took approximately eight–nine days. On 6th and 7th, I stayed in the custody room and on 8th and 9th, I was sent to the civil hospital. So, in the morning, they took us to the civil [hospital]. They did tests for both of us. Took the saliva and other stuff. They did this for her also. They brought me back from there.
>
> PB: Did they not record the marks of the beating?

R: They did not really examine me. They did the saliva-*valiva* [*sic*] test and did the test of below [genitals]. If they had examined my back then I would have told them. They did a very wrong thing by taking a remand. I told them I was sick. In the hospital, I vomited. She [Chetna] came there with a bowl. I could not even walk. She had to hold me.

The doctor did not record marks of injury apart from the abrasions on Roshan's cheek and neck. The medico-legal report attributed his symptoms of vomiting to jaundice, which he suffered from twenty-five days before, with no other diagnostic explanation or investigations indicated. The symbolism of the word 'patient' to describe Roshan brings forth an entirely different sketch of the doctor–patient relationship when subsumed under a medico-jural sign. The examination of Roshan's back is not a medical concern here; it is not a surface that arrests the doctor's gaze. The medico-legal certificate, released a month after Roshan had been examined at the civil hospital, is cited below:

Doctor's Remarks: History given by the patient himself

Pt (patient) well built, well nourished.

No external mark of any stain on the body.

Triple linear abrasion on right cheek and right side neck.

Secondary sex characters including external genitalia are well developed.

Patient is having vomit. Jaundice 25 days back.

Glans wash for epithelial shows no vaginal epithelium.

Smegma negative.

Sealed samples of blood and saliva handed over to the police.

The medical practitioner was concerned with injuries, stains, and the presence or absence of smegma or epithelial cells on specific body-parts. This reading of deviant body-parts had the effect of making invisible the evidence of violence incurred during the police remand.

Chetna was admitted to the hospital overnight and released on the following day. The medico-legal certificate in her case read as follows:

Doctor's Remarks: History given by the patient herself

Pt well built, well nourished

No external mark of injury on the body

No external mark of any stain on the body

Pubic, axillary [*sic*] hair black, not matted

Ext genitalia breast well developed

LMP four days back

Sealed sample of blood and saliva handed over to the [G] police station

Vaginal stains show no spermatozoa

Indoor findings (vaginal examination): P/S not possible, hymen intact, P/ V even one finger P/V difficult.

Comment: Clinical impression: Not habituated with sexual intercourse, probable she never had any intercourse.

Chetna told me that the several medical students who had accompanied the doctor while he was examining her later reassured her that medically the police could not prove that she had been raped. The medico-legal certificate would later act to certify—through so-called 'indoor' findings—that Roshan had not raped her. It is only when the matter came up for hearing in the trial court that the certification of the doctor that she was not habituated to sex acted to verify Chetna's statements. In a sense, the grounds of the failure of the case in terms of a conviction were generated within one month of the legal event. However, by this time, Roshan was released on bail and Chetna was jailed. The charges against Chetna are detailed below.

FROM VICTIM TO CRIMINAL

The normativity of the family lies in bringing together categories of love with power, and rights with obedience. In the absence of this normativity, no future could be imagined for the disobedient daughter within the family other than condemnation to inhabit the punitive institutions of the state. In this instance, the public complaint of rape or seduction is not considered stigmatic, for the identity of the family is traced through its capacity to bring punitive measures against an errant daughter. Failure to do so would be more threatening to normativity. The transformation of a victim (*bhogbannar*) into a criminal must be understood in the context of the family's decision to condemn Chetna to life lived in state institutions. This condemnation finds itself in the writing of police records. When Chetna refused to change her testimony following the remand, we find a statement by Chetna's father in the police records on the same date. I cite the statement below, originally in Gujarati:

> Today I myself the bearer of the signature below, M.R. Patel give the statement that my daughter Chetna Kumari Patel is in the possession [kabja] of and after today all the responsibilities of my daughter shall be borne by Roshanbhai Pannachand. She is in the possession of Roshanbhai Pannachand at this moment of time at present.
>
> Since this incident happened, despite our telling her, she did not stay with us and this Roshan Pannachand seduced her and took her and that is why she is with him.

The description of what happened is summarized by the use of the word 'possession'. Chetna's defiance of familial persuasion is seen as reason enough for her father to give up all his responsibilities towards her. Furthermore, it is the father who is seen as the natural guardian in law, with the authority to transfer the responsibilities. The police station is thus the site of betrayal for Chetna where, instead of gifting her in marriage to the man of her choice, her father chooses to write off his responsibilities. It is poignant because the consequences of the criminal charge brought against her by her own family now had to be borne by her alone. The law, then, is the site where the family articulates its power to discipline and punish Chetna. While Roshan was taken to jail, Chetna was questioned at the police station. She did not change her stance and the police recorded the following statement, which I cite below alongside Roshan's statement.

Roshan's Statement	**Chetna's Statement**
On being asked in person I am getting written that I live with my mother/father and sister and work in a clothes shop and earn approximately Rs 1,000 per month. My job timings are from 1 a.m. to 8 p.m. My date	On being questioned in person I am getting written that I live at the aforesaid address. I live at home with my mother and father and study in standard 12th. On this day you sir [saheb] have called me to the [name]

of birth is [date] 1969. On last [date] 1994 at eight thirty Chetna came to me and said to me, 'I was thrown out of my house and [told] go stay with Roshan'. Hearing this I said, 'you go back, don't come to my house.' Despite this, she did not go back to her house. During this time her family members came and after beating me up went away. After 10–15 minutes, the girl came back to my house with the desire to live in the house and her family members said 'you only keep her, we don't want to keep her with us'. I kept the girl in my house and at the time, she was in my house. I did not have any bodily pleasure [*sharirik sukh*] with her. During this time, her mother and father lodged a complaint with the police and took Chetna and me with them to the police station. After Chetna and I were introduced, we used to meet each other here and there, now and then. One year ago, I was married to Aruna who was from my caste. I terminated my relationship with Chetna. My in-laws said that Aruna wouldn't go anywhere. I got a divorce. A week ago, I got a cover [letter] from Chetna. 'I apologize for the trouble you have faced because of me and I want to live with you'. She sent one photo and proposed to marry in the court. When she came to my house then she was not carrying any jewellery and she was barefoot.

police station in connection with ICR [number] registered under IPC ss. 363, 366, 376, 380, and 164. I am getting written that in response to the questioning of the crime that Roshan and I both live in the same society near each other. Roshan and I have been in a relationship for the last four years and from then under some pretext or the other I used to go to Roshan's house. And for the last nine months this came to be known to my mother and father and we are four sisters and one brother.

On the day of [date] 1994, in the evening, a letter written by me to Roshan Pannachand found its way to my mother's hands and with mummy, words were exchanged, and she scolded me and told me to get out of the house. You don't have any right [*adhikar*] to live in this house and go manage Roshan's house and go now to Roshan's house. Saying this she pushed me out of the house and did not even allow me to wear my slippers [*chappals*] on my feet. At this at that moment I went to Roshan's house and went and told what happened, hearing which Roshan advised me to go back but I stayed at Roshan's house because mummy had asked me not to come back.

Chetna's statement cited above continues as follows:

> In the meantime my cousins [maternal uncle's sons] came and took me forcibly from Roshan's house but I came [back] to Roshan's house.
>
> At that time, I stayed at Roshan's house. Roshan has not had any body pleasure [*sharir sukh*] with me. After that the police came and arrested Roshan and took him to the [name] police station.
>
> A few days ago, I wrote to him asking him to marry me and sent him some photographs. For this reason, my mummy threw me out of the house and did not even let me wear slippers on my feet, and I have not taken any jewellery from the house. The fact of my having stolen jewellery is completely false and I don't know anything about the jewellery. This is my reality. It is true and factual and as I have got it written.

On the same day that Chetna's statement was recorded, the police sub-inspector wrote to the chief judicial magistrate petitioning the court to take Chetna into judicial custody. Chetna was charged with ss. 363, 366, 376, 380, 114 IPC. The chargesheet was not filed for nine months. During this period, the police received the age-determination test report, which concluded that Chetna's age was over eighteen and under twenty. Although the medico-legal report had been received, the police had not filed the chargesheet as they were waiting for the forensic science laboratory report to bring the investigation to a close. This they received nine months after the complaint had been filed. The forensic analysis did not reveal any evidence of what is referred to above as 'body pleasure'.

Nine months later, Roshan was chargesheeted on the following grounds:

> The accused on [date] 1994 at 20.30 hours made the daughter of the woman complainant (*fariyadi bai*) named Chetna age 17½ run away with him from lawful guardianship with the intent of illicit sex (*jharkam*) by enticing or seducing her did illicit sex with her. He was caught on [date] 1994 at 1700 hours.

While a chargesheet was filed against Roshan, the police sub-inspector wrote a petition to the chief judicial magistrate asking the court to release Chetna on the basis of lack of evidence. I reproduce the document, translated from Gujarati below:

> Subject: G Police Station under ss. 363, 366, 376, 380, 114 the accused named Chetna d/o M.R. Patel under CrPC 169[55] is being released.

With Hail India (*Jai Bharat*) the [G] police station's police sub-inspector Shri. Patel petitions in this honourable court this report that during the course of investigation no evidence was found against the accused in the matter in G police station under ICR no. [number] under ss. 366, 363, 376, 380, and 114. The accused girl Chetna, who is M.R. Patel's daughter by caste Patel, by age seventeen and a half, by occupation student, resident of [place] was arrested on [date] 1994 at 19.00 hours, charged with the above-mentioned crimes. Under s. 169 CrPC, it is our petition to free the above-mentioned Chetna.

Chetna was charged with the theft of jewellery under s. 380 IPC,[56] but there was no evidence to prove this.

This is a story of entitlements. By going against the wishes of her parents, Chetna lost all entitlements in her family, and to family property. This translates into a charge of theft whereby nothing truly belongs to her, to the extent that over and over again we are told that Chetna left with nothing, not even a pair of slippers. The accusation against Chetna repudiates the possibility of any kind of gift-giving, inheriting self-acquired property or receiving any form of material or symbolic gifts later as a bride. The alliance with Roshan symbolized a severance of all social relations for Chetna—no gifts would flow from the Patel family to the Prajapati family. It is not jewellery that is the object of contestation so much as her right (*adhikar*) to the family resources, which could not be devolved on her on marriage to a man of a 'lower' caste, and hence, a daughter becomes a thief.

The chargesheet also applied ss. 376, 366, 363, and 114 of the IPC against Chetna. Section 114 IPC states that when an abettor to a crime is present at the scene of crime, then they will be charged with the offence as if they had committed the crime themselves, like the principal offender.[57] When applied to Chetna, this section is confounding, for it describes Chetna not only as guilty of abetting the crime but by being present at the scene of crime as an abettor she is also charged with the offence as if she had committed it. Chetna was constructed as a victim, as an abettor to the crime (she was present while it was being committed), and her body constituted as the scene of the crime. This simultaneous positioning of the woman as abettor, victim, scene of crime, and accused is not a contradiction in law, for we are being told that the interpretation of the law makes it possible to frame a woman as abetting and committing rape, abduction, and kidnapping against herself. She is a victim since the offence is against the guardian. As the scene of crime, her body is constituted as 'evidence', devoid of subjectivity. As an abettor she instigates, plans, and influences someone to execute the offence against her guardian and on her body. She was present at the site of the crime as it is constituted on her body and she was found in the company of the accused. In other words, her decision to live with Roshan, despite the fact that she was a minor and could not legally marry him, when translated in these categories, amounts to the charge that she abetted her own rape, abduction, and kidnapping and she should be treated as if she were a principal offender since she was present at the scene of crime.

Chetna is a split subject for her body itself is constituted as the scene of crime and she, party to its violation. The fetishized female body exists as evidence of the crime, and injury against society is that which is incurred on this scene of crime. Crime against society refers to both the crime against the legal guardian and the crime against caste politics of honour. As the worst form of transgression in caste sociality, the minor upper caste woman's body enters the law as 'a scene of crime' where love can only be named as rape. Here, the social imagination of a lower caste man's love for an upper caste woman can only be exist in a mimetic relationship with upper caste imagination to substitute love by rape (see Rao 1999).

The consequences of this 'mistake in law' were severe for Chetna. She was taken to the Central Jail in Ahmedabad two days after Roshan and was brought to the police station. She was to spend two months there. Roshan recollected:

> I was in the Central Jail for eight–ten days. On the 14th, at 12 in the afternoon, I entered my house. They brought her on the second day to the central jail. I did not know this. And inside the Central Jail, a PI said to me, 'one girl has come, Chetna Patel, she is your *lover* isn't she?' I said, 'yes, sir.' I did not know that they had brought her in. Then she stayed there for two months.

The English word 'lover' is used derogatorily, increasing her vulnerability to the possibilities of violence that accrue to women when they are classified as 'lovers', or as 'bad' women, as we will see as follows.

PB: Chetna was in the central jail for two months?

R: Yes, for two months. I stayed there for eight–nine–ten days but she stayed for two months. Her mummy–pappa gave her up on her. 'We don't want the girl.' That's why no one went to release her. Her mother, two months later, sent her a message, 'Change your stance and we will get you released.' Her mother had gotten a lower age written down, so I could not get her released. I had come out, but I could not get her released. Our lawyer got her transferred to a state-run home for women [*nari gruh*]. There she stayed for four months. She wanted to take her twelfth exams [final year at high school] from there [*nari gruh*]. The police arranged that … then they would take her in the police van so that she could take her exams every day.

PB: How could you study?

R: There were all girls living there in the state-run home for women [*nari gruh*]. Then she wrote a letter to her uncle that it is not too good here—with the girls and all.

C: Those [police] inspectors used to come at night for the girls. They would knock at the door. I wrote saying: 'come and get me released from here.'

R: People make wrong use [*galat kam*], don't they? She wrote to her uncle: 'come and get me released.'

R: After three months, her uncle—her father's sister's husband—came to take her. After, which for two to three months, she lived with her father's brother.

The circulation of her story could have put Chetna at risk of sexual violence following incarceration. Chetna told me that it was fortuitous that she met a woman warden who protected her and allowed her to study. The warden allowed Chetna to have her meals separate from the other inmates and protected her from the men those who knocked at the shelter's doors at night. Her uncle ultimately helped her escape institutionalization. The story of custodial violence is thus dispersed at various sites: the family, police station, the hospital, the jail, and the state-run home for women. Chetna's story provokes us to re-think the category of custodial violence as the domain that simultaneously straddles the familial and the legal. With the exception of two women—a woman constable who refused to take her remand and the woman warden who protected her from custodial rape—the narrative of custodial violence that represses love is uninterrupted.

'HAPPY ENDING'

I describe here the narration of the 'happy ending', which brings a certain closure to the narrative. The closure describes the beginning of the compromise, for after the marriage the parents were forced to accept that there was no point in pursuing legal proceedings against Roshan. After Chetna's paternal uncle came to fetch her, she spent a few months at his home. Then she went back to her parents' house for two months.

> R: We needed the school-leaving [certificate] to get married. When she was staying with her mummy, she did not speak to her. She only used to talk to her two sisters.
>
> PB: Papa?
>
> C: Papa said later that if you want to marry, then marry that boy [referring to Roshan].
>
> R: He said that later, but in the beginning...
>
> PB: Then how did you spend those two months?
>
> C: My sister does beauty parlour work. I used to help her.

Chetna secured the documents that could get her married.[58] In the meantime, Roshan consulted the defence lawyer who fought their case till the day of the judgment.

> R: Near the collector's office. There is a temple near the court; at that temple Chetna came wearing a dress, like yours.[59] That temple's priest gave her a dress. He said that one girl had come to get married— wear those clothes. Then she wore the other dress. Many marriages take place there. This is the photo of the priest who married us [they showed me photographs].
>
> PB: You look very happy in these photographs.
>
> C: This is of the engagement, this is of the marriage, and the temple priest is sitting in this one. This one is of the court [laughs].
>
> R: We got married under the Hindu Marriage Act [HMA]; otherwise, we have to get our name written and everyone else comes to know. That's why we got married under the HMA. When her maternal uncle's son died, then there was no one at her house. Her elder sister

knew that she was going to get married. She [Chetna] reached before us [laughs]. I reached there with the lawyer. She got the ration card, school-leaving [certificate] because I had told her everything.

C: We had to do this [laughs]. Otherwise, if at home any problem cropped up again then I would become old just like this [as a single woman].

Chetna laughed mischievously at the thought.

R: Then she [Chetna] took a direct bus and came to the court. It took the entire day. We came back at six in the evening. Then when she went home, no one knew. The lawyer had said, 'don't tell anyone anything; tell them after one month that you have got married.' After one month, she woke up in the morning and told her mother. Mummy said, 'Go.' On Saturday the registry came. We had made a xerox of all the papers, three bunches, I said, 'Give the registry in your mother's hand'. Mummy started saying, 'This has happened and now, I can't do anything'.

C: It was a Saturday. Saturday is lucky. We got married on a Saturday. I was born on a Saturday. I was arrested on a Saturday [laughs].

Lucky on Saturdays is how Chetna constructs all the critical events in her life—her birth, marriage, arrest and declaration of her marriage. In constructing her arrest as a twist of luck, she speaks ironically of the helplessness of the family and law to discipline love and her prolonged laughter celebrated her luck to be with Roshan after all. I joined in the laughter as I looked at their honeymoon photographs in the album.

But a sombre note replaced the laughter. Chetna's older sister Deepika (whose statement we find in the police records) was not alive to witness the compromise. Chetna's marriage was followed by that of her sister. She was twenty-three years old when her parents married her to a man in their own caste. Chetna spoke of her sister with a deep sense of loss in her voice.

K: Her sister, no. 3—Deepika. She was like you—her sister.

R: She was murdered for dowry.

K: Her mother gave a lot of dowry.

C: She was married for two months, and then the neighbours told my mother that Deepika had put a noose around her neck.

R: She was going to do a PhD; she was going to go to Delhi.

K: She would have gone very far, wouldn't she?

C: Yes, she was not the one to sit idle, she would embroider, she wrote.

PB: Where was she married?

R: In the Patel [caste]. Not in another caste. Now if we sit with her mummy she never tells what the problem was. She lived with him for two months. Not much.

The loss then was magnified—having been punished for opposing familial normativity as well as experiencing grief at the murder of a sister. If we look at Chetna and Deepika's stories together, we find a sense of mourning about how parents conceive their daughters' future within caste-based patriarchal normativity. In Chetna's case, there could be no anticipation of a future within the folds of convention unless she agreed to the wishes of her parents. In the absence of her compliance, her future could only be imagined as one that lived in other disciplinary spaces of the state. The anticipation of future in Deepika's case was one which was controlled, planned, and projected within convention.

We know that the everyday violence of dowry folds into normativity of the heterosexist family. In Chetna and Deepika's case, the idea that daughters are a burden till they are married constituted the present lived in the spectre of dowry violence in the future. The control over the daughter's sexuality so that she is fit to be exchanged in marriage as a 'good' woman constitutes her present. The category of the 'good' woman is unstable, constantly in need of reiteration. It has to be continually proven that a woman is a 'good' wife. Part of the process of supplying such social proof is being able to meet dowry demands, failing which may result in torture and murder. Caste normativity and the family in this case authored two kinds of biographies for Chetna and Deepika. For both, kinship ties were enacted differently within and outside the fold of convention. Both were expected to conform to ordinary notions of parenting. Unlike the love affair, the dowry murder did not bring stigma to her parents. Stigma accrues to that which disrupts normativity. It is only when a daughter is a 'bad' wife that issues of honour and stigma may emerge. The possibility of rape, torture, or even murder is folded in heterosexist normativity; it is in its disruption that lies alterity or the asocial.

COMPROMISE: THE STRUCTURE OF TESTIMONY IN THE COURTROOM

We may recall that the case against Roshan continued after the marriage. It had dragged on in the trial court till Roshan appeared before the additional sessions judge. The APP at this time had decided that there was no truth in the charges of rape, abduction, and kidnapping. How then did the compromise come about? When I asked Roshan about this he replied,

> We got a date [for hearing]. We went in front of the magistrate [he named the additional sessions judge who heard his case]. He [the judge] said, 'Why don't you do a compromise [*samadhan*] with them? Call her [Chetna's mother] and go to their house.' I said, 'I cannot go, if I go then if they beat me up and you lock me up then?' He started laughing and said, 'I will send summons'. Then those people sent the summons.
>
> Chetna's uncle who had got her released then phoned her mother. Then he said, 'You are going to be called to the court and what are you going to do?' They replied, 'We are going to do nothing, now marriage has taken place and includes a child as well, now what will we do?'
>
> One and half years have passed since then and we have been getting dates.

Roshan communicated to the court the irony in the idea that he should initiate the compromise. He shifted the onus onto the judge to send the summons. Compromise thus appears as the shared vocabulary amongst the legal experts. Chetna's mother agreed to it. Chetna's family did not tell her maternal uncle about the compromise or about the hearing. On the day of the hearing, Chetna and Roshan were present with Roshan's brother-in-law. Chetna's parents were present as well. When I approached them for an interview, they refused to speak to me. I waited in the courtroom for the hearing to begin. It was nearly 12.45 in the afternoon. The courtroom was packed. The court was very busy that day; there were several cases to be heard, each with witnesses. Finally, at 1.05 the hearing in this case began. It was not held *in camera*. Other lawyers waiting for their cases to be heard were present, and there was a steady stream of movement in and out of the courtroom.

The proceedings cited below were conducted in Gujarati. Hirabhai said to the judge, 'in this case, compromise has taken place. There is only one certificate on evidence.'

J: What is the case about?

APP: This case … [G] police station

APP: Come on. Come on.

APP *to* Chetna: Call them.

APP *to* Roshan: You are the accused.

Chetna (*calls out*): Mummy, oh mummy (*subsequently, she stood near the witness box*).

Chetna's mother, Komalben walked in.

APP (*to the mother*): Come.

APP (*to* J): There are bundles of cases. There are witnesses in each case.

Komalben took the stand. Chetna stood next to the lawyers' table. Hirabhai asked Chetna to sit in the row of chairs reserved for witnesses.

Although the testimonies of the complainant and the prosecutrix were heard, all other expert witnesses, including the *panch*, were dropped. As the complainant, Komalben, Chetna's mother, was the first to testify. As she stood in the witness box, the typist was sent for.[60]

APP *to typist*: Write name.

Typist: I am waiting for the bench clerk.

The bench clerk told her the sessions case number, citation, and name.

J: Keeping God as my witness I state that I will speak the truth and nothing but the truth.

Komalben: (*repeats*)

Typist types: Given oath.

J: It is not *in camera*?

APP: No, Sir.

Chetna was sent out.[61]

APP: You have one son and four daughters?

K: Yes (*nods*).

J (d): Of my children I have four daughters[62] and one son.

APP: Third... (*inaudible*)

K: Yes (*nods*).

J (d): My third daughter's name is Chetna.

APP: The incident happened approximately three years and three months ago.

K: Yes (*nods*).

Typist types: the incident happened approximately three years and three months ago.

APP (d): during this incident Chetna was studying in High School.

APP: The name of the accused is Roshan?

K: Yes (*nods*).

J (d): I recognize Roshan Pannachand. He lives in our society.

The APP continued to question as the judge dictated.

APP: Look... (*inaudible*)

K: (*inaudible*)

J (d): After Chetna left then she and the accused have been married and at present Chetna has...

APP: Four months.

J (d): Has a baby of four months also.

Komalben did not deny that she went to the police.

PP: Did you give the police Chetna's school leaving certificate?

K: Yes.

J (d): I gave the police Chetna's birth registration xerox copy.

APP: When you found Chetna did you take her to the dispensary for medical examination?

K *laughs.*

DL: You don't know?

K: Yes (*nods*).

J (d): When Chetna was found then after that the medical examination was done.

APP: Got the medical examination done.

The judge signals the end of the chief-examination and turns to ask the defence lawyer if he had any questions to ask.

J *to* DL: Do you want to ask?

J: Do you have a *vakalatnama*? Check it.

A *vakalatnama* is a document in writing, which appoints and authorizes the lawyer to represent the client in a court.[63] The judge remembered the presence of the defence lawyer after the examination-in-chief was over and asked the bench clerk to check the record. Subsequently, instead of the defence lawyer, Hirabhai cross-examined Komalben. Hirabhai asked the judge whether he should question the witness about Chetna's age.

In the meantime, the typist typed: 'From the accused's side Shri Bharwad, cross-examination.'

> APP: When this incident happened had the accused come to your house?
>
> K: No.
>
> J (d): It is true that when the incident happened on that day during that time that the accused had come to our house that did not happen.
>
> APP: Chetna went out on her own?
>
> K: Yes (*nods*).
>
> J (d): It is true that Chetna went out of the house on her own.
>
> APP: And she used to meet him again and again?
>
> K: Yes (*nods*).
>
> J (d): It is true that we used to tell Chetna constantly not to meet the accused but she would not listen.
>
> APP: Enough. Go sit down.
>
> APP (*to* J): The entire case depends on the girl; otherwise, we will have to take evidence on injury. Drop the husband (*Chetna's father*). We do not need too many witnesses.

Subsequently, the prosecutor dictated the official transcript, instead of the judge, indicated as APP (d). The prosecutor did not ask Komalben if she threw Chetna out of the house, nor did he ask if her family members beat Roshan up subsequently. The aim of the cross-examination was to prove that Roshan did not coerce Chetna, and that it was Chetna who initiated the relationship. Chetna was called to the stand.

> APP: (*inaudible*).

C: (*inaudible*).

APP (d): The incident happened approximately three years ago.

APP: (*inaudible*).

C: (*inaudible*).

APP (d): During the incident the accused used to live in our society in front of our house.

Chetna's response in the transcript of the testimony is framed in the past tense, as if Roshan were the 'accused' for her and she does not refer to him as Roshan or her husband. Although the translation of her response is in the first person, it indexes a legal moment corresponding to the legal narrative when Roshan was named as the accused.

APP: Which standard did you study in then?

C: In 12th standard.

APP (d): during the incident I used to study in the 12th standard.

APP: (*inaudible*).

C: (*inaudible*).

APP (d): At that time, my age was 18 years.

Chetna testified that she was eighteen years old at the time of the incident. It is important that the evidence of her mother on the question of age was not taken except whether she had submitted the school-leaving certificate, which gave the officially recorded age as proof.[64]

APP: You had a relationship of love [*prem sambandh*]?

C: No, we used to meet in the society [society here means residential neighbourhood].

APP: You had love only ... not bad love [*kharab prem*]?

C: Yes (*nods*).

APP (d): I only had only a relationship of love [*prem sambandh*] with the accused. There was no bad love [*kharab prem*] between us.

Chetna construed the question regarding the love affair to imply that Roshan and she were in an illicit sexual relationship. She denied the suggestion: 'No, we used to meet in the society.' The implication is that they used to meet in public space of the neighbourhood and were therefore not in a clandestine sexual relationship. Hirabhai understood Chetna's meaning and rephrased his question. 'You had love only'. Bad love (*kharab prem*) was used as a euphemistic allusion to pre-marital sex. The shared discourse here does not name sex in an open courtroom. She was not asked very explicit questions, for now she was a married woman with a child, and the compromise altered the structure of the testimony such that sexually explicit questions were not posed to her in the open courtroom. The objective here was not to challenge her testimony by attacking her character.

We see here that the object of the crime had altered. Chetna was no longer required to say whether or not she had consented to sex. The medical evidence already available to the prosecutor made it clear that clinically she was not 'habituated with sexual intercourse, probable she never had any intercourse.' Chetna was not asked whether she was raped. Chetna testified to a relationship of love, which was then translated as love distinct from 'bad love', suggesting thereby that virginity purifies the experience of love, placing it in the moral realm that differentiates between the *good* versus the *bad*. These questions were articulated in the shadow of the compromise that had already taken place. In order to consolidate the legal narrative indicating what had happened, Hirabhai then asked her questions relating to the conditions under which she had left home. These questions were not posed to Chetna's mother since this distinction between good and bad love was not one shared by her. I reproduce these below:

APP: On the day of the incident mummy gave you a scolding, right?

C: Yes (*nods*).

APP (d): And my mummy gave me a scolding.

APP: And mummy said, get out of my house

C: Yes (*nods*).

APP (d): and mummy said that you get out of my house.

APP: Mummy said, get out of the house, go to Roshan's house. Saying this, she pushed me.

C: Yes (*nods*).

APP (d): You don't have any right [*adhikar*] to live with me. And you go to Roshan's house. And go to Roshan's house. Saying this she pushed me out.

After dictating (*the APP to Chetna*): Ok? Is this all right?

Chetna nods an affirmative.

APP (d): And didn't even let me wear slippers on my feet. That's how I went to Roshan's house. At that time Roshan was not at home. His mother–father [*ma–bap*] were there. I told them the above-mentioned incident.

Hirabhai referred to Chetna's police statement while framing his questions and dictating the testimony. Through this line of questioning, he established that Chetna was forced to leave her house without even being allowed to wear her slippers, highlighting the abjectness of her condition. Next, Hirabhai turned to the reason behind the quarrel between the mother and daughter.

APP: Did Roshan write you any letter?

C: No.

APP (d): And he did not propose to marry me.

APP (d): reads out from a statement the part on the letter.

J *to* C: Did you write him a letter? You marry me, sent him a photograph too?

C: (*inaudible*)

J (d): Some days ago, I posted Roshan a letter saying that I want to marry you and with it sent a photograph.

APP: Then the police investigation began.

C: (*inaudible*)

APP: Police arrested Roshan and me.

Having established that Roshan did not write a letter, rather that it was Chetna who not only wrote a letter but proposed marriage, the onus shifted. It foregrounded Chetna's desire to be with Roshan.

APP: And then the medical examination ... blood ... right?

C: Yes (*nods*).

APP (d): Then I was sent for medical examination to the hospital and my clothes were confiscated. A *panchnamma* was done.

APP: (*inaudible*)

C *laughs*

APP: She has a child.

APP (d): I have been married to Roshan and we have a four months old baby also.

We may note that while referring to the present moment, Hirabhai no longer referred to Roshan as the accused. He was now positioned as Chetna's husband and referred to by name. Subsequently, Hirabhai asked Roshan's lawyer if he wanted to ask anything. When Roshan's lawyer did not speak, the defence lawyer, Mr G, who had cross-examined Noornissa, asked him whether the question concerning age had been asked (see Chapter 3). He was in the courtroom waiting for the hearing in the case concerning Noornissa to commence. From the excerpt cited below, it is evident that for him age is reflected in the maturity of the subject testifying, rather than a technical application of number of years attained by her.

G (DL *in Noornissa's case*): Age?

APP: Seventeen and a half years.

G: Has to do with the maturity of the mind.

J: Age—take it [the evidence on age].

APP: Seventeen and a half. On the contrary, she has left her own house. The other witnesses have been dropped.

The issue of age is now dropped.

J (d): Police took my statement.

J *to* DL: Where is the IO [investigating officer]? If we can take the IO then we can finish this.

APP asked Chetna to leave.

The police officer who had arrested Chetna and Roshan, taken their remand, and was in charge of the investigation did not attend the next hearing either. He was finally dropped. A fortnight later, Roshan was acquitted.

I wish to derive two observations from the proceedings cited above. First, here the testimony to love is not effaced. Throughout this narrative we find that the burden of proving Roshan's innocence lies on Chetna. Chetna's testimony situated her as an agent of seduction and had the effect of establishing Chetna as a protector. Second, the structure of the rape trial was altered here. In the instance of compromise, when the woman is re-integrated within structures of alliance, the line of questioning is not against her honour. Categories such as 'bad' or 'good' love, which preserve gendered discourses of honour of men and modesty of women, inflect courtroom talk. This is in contrast to the routine sexualization of the testimony to rape, which sets out to defame the survivor of rape.

***

In constructing Chetna as a victim, witness, or accused, she was called to bear witness to something other than the experience of her subjectivity, and denied the possibility of testifying to custodial violence. The story of custodial violence narrated in this chapter is a revelation of the incommensurability between the legal subject's experience and the way she is named in law as a victim, witness, and accused in the crime of and for planning to kidnap, abduct, and rape her own body. This is a stunning illustration of what Lyotard has called 'differend' (cited in Davies 1996). As Davies argues, a differend arises when 'the parties are not speaking the same language—either literally or in effect, or if there is no rule which can be applied to them in common' (1996: 41). While the law always 'artificially sets up a differend between itself and both parties to a dispute, because it requires them to submit to its set of norms and speak to its language', in this instance the experience of the woman does not exist (Davies 1996: 41). It is this incommensurability that has been the object of ethnographic exploration in this chapter.

The competing accounts of rape show how, over time, the object of criminalization alters. Roshan and Chetna's marriage transforms that which was initially criminalized. Chetna was now reinserted in another kind of normativity. With the acquittal, it is this normativity that the judgment restored. In the ultimate analysis, the testimony to love succeeds after the compromise is effectuated, and only when Chetna is fully assimilated in another normative structure as a wife and the mother of a son, putting law beyond the threat of love. When love and law are pitted in such a radical opposition, public secrecy is not the socio-legal route to imagine a future. Rather, ethnographies of rape trials in India reveal how law fears love, how love finds justice, and how love mourns its loss. Reminiscent of Auden who says 'law ... like love we don't know

where or why, like love we can't compel or fly, like love we often
weep, like love we seldom keep' (1958: 77).

NOTES

1. Goodrich maintains that 'faith, fidelity and desire were alike to be
directed to the goal of reproducing the church, the ecclesial commonwealth
and the male line' (1996: 48).

2. We know that the laws of abduction in late nineteenth-century
Canada, for instance, were used by parents to punish a daughter and her
boyfriend for marrying against their wishes. Dubinsky (1993) suggests that
the English laws on abduction, which were applied in Canada in the 1840s,
expanded the criminalization of the abduction of propertied daughters to
include all women under the age of sixteen. She argues that the prosecutions
against consenting adults were scripted around those 'improper' alliances
between Canadian women and 'foreigners' from East or South Europe.

3. Citing Foucault's (1979) arguments in *The History of Sexuality*,
Borneman points out that for Foucault 'a discourse on sexuality and life has
replaced one centred around marriage and death' (1996: 216).

4. The recent literature on the right of women to choose marriage if and
when they want to has inaugurated feminist critiques of the techniques by
which a range of laws are used to criminalize love in plural legal contexts
in South Asia (see P. Baxi 2006, 2009; Chakravarti 2005; Mody 2008;
Welchman & Hossain 2005). While I do not wish to detail the many painful
instances where consensual marriages forged on love have resulted in extra-
judicial murder, in what has now come to be named as 'honour killings', I
wish to make a few brief points on this issue. First, state law exists in the field
of legal pluralism with plural structures of power (U. Baxi 1985). Second,
state law is often withdrawn when non-state law forces reconciliation on
an unwilling wife, violently recovers a consenting bride, or mandates a
spectacular death to lovers. Third, state law mimes non-state law by absorbing
notions of transgression that are mobilized by the apparatus normally seen as
the 'other' of state law. Fourth, state law allows the performance of different
kinds of discourses (for instance, rehabilitation and rescue) that address
the rationalities of state law and non-state law simultaneously through a
complicated circulation of categories, sites, and certifications.

5. Section 9 of the Hindu Marriage Act, 1955, holds that 'when either
the husband or the wife has, without reasonable excuse, withdrawn from the
society of the other, the aggrieved party may apply, by petition to the district
court, for restitution of conjugal rights and the court, on being satisfied of
the truth of the statements made in such petition and that there is no legal

ground why the application should not be granted, may decree restitution of conjugal rights accordingly'.

6. *Chandrasinh K. Jadav* v. *the State of Gujarat & Ors*, Spl. Criminal Application No. 356 of 1996, 10 April 1996.

7. Also see *Gian Devi* v. *The Superintendent, Nari Niketan, Delhi & Others* (1976) 3 SCC 234.

8. See *Mrs Kalyani Chaudhari* v. *State of Uttar Pradesh and Others* (1977) Indlaw 62. The inhuman and degrading conditions in a protective home in Agra were taken up in the Supreme Court for nearly twenty years after a public interest litigation was filed in the Supreme Court. See *Dr Upendra Baxi (I)* v. *State of UP & Anr* (1983) 2 SCC 308; *Dr Upendra Baxi (II)* v. *State of UP* (1986) 4 SCC 106. Also see the public interest litigation against a care home managed by the Welfare Department, State Government, in *Vikram Deo Singh Tomar* v. *State of Bihar* (1988) (Supp) SCC 734.

9. *Mrs Kalyani Chaudhari* v. *State of Uttar Pradesh and Others* (1977) Indlaw 62.

10. Also see *Payal Sharma alias Kamala Sharma* v. *Superintendent, Nari Niketan, Agra and Others* (2001) 3 AWC 1778.

11. *Dwarka Prasad* v. *State of Rajasthan and Ors* (2002) Cri LJ 1278.

12. Ibid. at para 3.

13. Ibid. at para 2.

14. Ibid. at para 4. See also *Mohd Ikram Hussain* v. *The State of UP and Others* AIR 1964 SC 1625 and *Smt Suneeta through Her Husband Tulsi* v. *State of UP and Others* (2003) (1) JIC 1027 (All). These cases arose when the father refused to produce his daughter after a *habeas corpus* petition filed by her husband.

15. Kidnapping is defined under s. 361, IPC which holds that 'whoever takes or entices any minor under sixteen years of age if a male, or under eighteen years of age if female, or any person of unsound mind, out of the keeping of the lawful guardianship of such minor or person of unsound mind, without the consent of such guardian, is sued to kidnap such minor or person from lawful guardianship'. The law specifies that the words 'lawful guardian' therein 'include any person lawfully entrusted with the care or custody of such minor or other person' (Ratanlal & Dhirajlal 2001: 490).

16. This law specifies that it does not extend to the 'act of any person who in good faith believes himself to be the father of an illegitimate child, or who in good faith believes himself to be the father of an illegitimate child, or who in good faith believes himself to be entitled to the lawful custody of such child, unless such act is committed for an immoral or unlawful purpose' (Ratanlal & Dhirajlal 2001: 490).

17. For example, we know from case law the instance when 'two girls ran away from their houses and remained for one or two days in the house of a woman of locality [*sic*] and no report was made to the police, it was held that the woman in whose house the girls stayed was guilty of an offence under this section' (cited in Ratanlal & Dhirajlal 2001: 504).

18. We must remember that 'the word "lawful" does not necessarily mean that the person who entrusts a minor to the care or custody of another must stand in the position of a person having a legal duty or obligation to the minor. The expression "lawful guardian" or a guardian may be lawful without being legal. The expression "lawfully entrusted" signifies that the care and custody of a minor should have arisen in some lawful manner so as to show as if the person having the custody of the minor has been entrusted with the care and custody of the minor' (Ratanlal & Dhirajlal 2001: 494). In such cases, the varying definitions of legal guardian under different personal laws assume a centrality.

19. The 2012–13 protest did not frame a critique of these laws nor any amendments to these sections were solicited.

20. See *Nura* v. *Rex* AIR 1949 All 710.

21. In legal discourse, a fast woman denotes a woman who does not conform to norms of chastity and modesty, or who initiates sexual relationships considered to be illicit. Here, the category of 'fast' is deployed to convert a testimony to repeated gangrape and abduction into a narrative of consent and volition.

22. The character of a woman is not based on ideas of courage or weakness, ability or competence, intelligence or compassion, but on the way her virtue is constituted in law. The determination of virtue is tied to sexual behaviour and existent notions of chastity. This is read from the circumstances under which she loses this chastity, as well as on the basis of her actions subsequent to the loss of chastity.

23. See *Rex* v. *Moon* 1 KB 818.

24. See *Emperor* v. *Persumal* AIR 1927 Sind 97.

25. See *Shaheb Ali and Anr* v. *Emperor* AIR 1933 Cal 718.

26. See *Emperor* v. *Baijnath* AIR 1932 All 409.

27. The law also requires that the intent of the accused be demonstrated and if the intent is not established the charge fails. Dhagamwar (1992) argues that if the woman gives her consent freely and intelligently it is relevant to determine the guilt of the accused if the prosecution holds that the woman was forced by the man to go with him. 'From her consent it would be wrong to infer that the woman had not been seduced although then it would be legitimate to conclude that she had been coerced' (Dhagamwar 1992: 156).

28. See *Chandgi* v. *Emperor* 28 Cri LJ (1927) 52.

29. Ibid.

30. See *State* v. *Raju*, Kar LJ. Short notes 24–5, Criminal Appeal No. 266 of 1999, High Court of Karnataka.

31. Ibid.

32. Male or female partners are usually referred to as lovers or paramours in judgments. I have not come across any appellate judgment where the category of boyfriend or girlfriend was used. I have used the word 'partner' while referring to relationships of choice.

33. See *Prem Chand & Anr* v. *State of Haryana* 1989 Cri LJ 1246.

34. The trial court tried the two policemen on account of custodial rape under s. 376(2) IPC, and tried Ravi Shankar for rape and abduction under ss. 376 and 366 IPC.

35. *State of Haryana* v. *Prem Chand and Anr* [1 SCC (1990) 249] clarifies that the Supreme Court is granted special powers to review its own judgments under Article 137 of the Constitution of India. Such power 'is exercised in accordance with, and subject to, the rules of this Court made under Article 145 of the Constitution of India. Order XL, Rule 1 of the Supreme Court provides: The Court may review its judgment or order, but no application for review will be entertained in a civil proceeding except on the grounds mentioned in Order XLVII, Rule I of the Code and in a criminal proceeding except on the ground of an error on the face of the record' [*State of Haryana* v. *Prem Chand and Anr*, 1 SCC (1990) 249 at 250].

36. Ibid. at 252.

37. Ibid.

38. The reference to many births may be understood by the idea in Hinduism that marriage is preordained and marriage is not limited to this life, rather it is a relationship experienced over several births.

39. As we discussed this case, the lawyer representing the accused walked in to ask Hirabhai whether the case could be compromised. In my presence, he said that the girl was willing to compromise for Rs 14,000. He was accompanied by the police officer on this case. The police officer also added that the case ought to be compromised as the man had been behind bars as an undertrial for one and half years. Declining this out-of-court settlement, Hirabhai told them that the judge would not allow compromise in a statutory rape case.

40. Literally, *galat kam* means 'wrong deed'. It also means 'wrongful sex' or indicates an illicit sexual relationship.

41. The passage of time further diminishes the possibilities of the woman's ability to speak out. In rape cases, Hirabhai told me, 'the girl's evidence is crucial. It must be reliable and the most material evidence is

of the girl. If she cannot speak, let her speak on video. The girl should be willing to speak. There should be a special court; an immediate court because delay benefits the accused. Otherwise, there will be no justice. In rape cases, unlike other kinds of crime, there is a lower conviction rate as compared to the number of cases that come up for hearing.'

42. Their names have been changed. Likewise, the names of the police officer and police station have been changed.

43. Prajapati, traditionally a potter caste, is listed as an OBC.

44. The lyrics translated from Hindi are: 'A human being loves someone in this world once, lives with this pain, dies with this pain. If one has loved, why fear? One has loved; it is not theft. Why sigh in secrecy, in hiding? The desire for him will remain in the heart; the flame of the light will live in the celebration. To live in love, to die in love; now what else can I do? Our love cannot stay hidden; his presence is everywhere. When there is no veil from God, why draw a veil from fellow people?'

45. *Lafara* has several connotations to it. It means affair, fight, brawl, trouble, and event.

46. *Bharwa* is used literally to refer to a pimp. Here it is used as a term of abuse, indicating that Roshan was not capable of being appropriate suitable partner in a marriage alliance and hence, he was insulted by being called a man in the business of selling and buying women in prostitution.

47. *Danga* is a word used to imply collective violence. It takes on a specific trajectory in relation to communal riots in India. In other contexts, it is used to refer to mob violence.

48. *Kalam* means a clause or a section in law as well as a pen or means by which writing is inscribed.

49. Remand here refers to the act of sending back a suspect into custody, especially in order to obtain further evidence on the charge. There can be a judicial or police remand; judicial remand refers to being sent to jail pending trial, while police remand is custody in a detention cell at a police station pending trial or an order for judicial remand or bail. The word is also used as a euphemism for police torture, which is designed not to leave obvious marks of injury on the body in custody.

50. The Crime Branch was located in a place known as the Gaekwad Haveli in the old city. It was first established in 1931 and has lately become infamous for police torture.

51. According to the police papers, Roshan had been charged with abduction, kidnapping, and rape under ss. 366, 363, and 376 IPC. At that time, Roshan said that he did not know which sections of the penal code were being applied against him.

52. The trial court is closed on two alternate Saturdays in a month.

53. From a police officer I learnt that the techniques of interrogation include a range of violent practices such as beating on the soles, making a person lie on a slab of ice, and beating with tyres.

54. The lawyer who helped Roshan get bail introduced him to Mr Bharward, who took up their case. We may note that both the lawyer and the client belong to the OBC castes.

55. Section 169 of the CrPC holds that 'if, upon an investigation under this Chapter, it appears to the officer-in-charge of the police station that there is no sufficient evidence or reasonable ground of suspicion to justify the forwarding of the accused to a Magistrate, such officer shall, if such person is, in custody, release him on his executing a bond with or without sureties, as such officer may direct, to appear, if and when so required, before a Magistrate empowered to take cognisance of the offence on a police report, and to try the accused or commit him for the trial'. This law allows the police officer concerned to petition for the release of the accused on the grounds that there is no evidence against her.

56. Section 380 of the IPC holds that whoever commits a theft in any building, tent, or vessel used as a human dwelling, or is used for the custody of property, shall be punished with imprisonment of either description for a term that may extend to seven years, and shall also be liable to fine (see Ratanlal & Dhirajlal 2001).

57. Section 114 of the IPC holds that wherever any person who is absent would be liable to be punished as an abettor, is present when the act or offence for which he would be punishable in consequence of the abetment is committed, he shall be deemed to have committed such an act or offence (see Ratanlal & Dhirajlal 2001). This section is stringed along with the other offences and does not specify if it is applicable to the theft charge alone. If this had been the case the charge of theft would have been read along with the law on abetting.

58. In her study on love marriages in Delhi, Mody (2002) says that the easiest way for couples who marry against the wishes of their families is to undertake what is commonly dubbed as the 'Hindu marriage.' This refers to marriage in Arya Samaj temples. The accompanying documentation includes photographic evidence of the ceremony and an affidavit signed by the couple, which specifies that the marriage is in accordance with Hindu customs, and that they are both Hindus or converted to Hinduism. The affidavit certifies that the woman is over eighteen years old and the man over twenty-one years of age. Mody is right in pointing out that the most important statement in the affidavit is the declaration that 'they have left home of their own free will, and that they have taken nothing from their homes except the clothes they are wearing' (Mody 2002: 245). She argues

that this declaration is critical since families file 'false' cases of kidnapping and theft against their children or their spouses so that the police can recover them, and they can pressurize them to break up (Mody 2002: 245). This marriage is then registered before the registrar of marriages. This route is preferred to civil marriage under the Special Marriage Act, 1954, (Act No. 43 of 1954) since it prescribes a different procedure: A notice of the impending marriage must be put up for a period of one month, and if after that period no one raises any lawful objection to the marriage, a civil marriage is permitted. Mody's ethnography provides a remarkable account of the way such marriages are negotiated in domains of law and within the domain of the familial. In this case, Roshan and Chetna relied on their lawyer to ensure that they were legally married and that this marriage was kept a secret until the time the marriage was registered.

59. Roshan meant that Chetna was wearing a cotton *salwar kameez* similar to the one I was wearing at that time.

60. In the transcript that follows later in the text, we will see that Hirabhai (referred to as APP) also questions the witnesses, although the case was with the prosecution (Mr Desai, referred to as D).

61. Chetna could not remain in the court to hear her mother's testimony since she was to take the stand next. Judicial objectivity demands that witnesses are not influenced by what is said in the court, and so they are not allowed to sit in the court until they have testified on the day of the hearing.

62. Komalben did not mention that one of her four daughters, Deepika, was murdered by the husband's family at the time the case was on trial. The question posed to her was based on the *fariyad*.

63. Unless specified in the *vakalatnama*, a lawyer cannot compromise the case, on behalf of the client without her consent or direction [see *Ramappaya* v. *Subanma and Ors* (1947) 2 MLJ 580].

64. The age recorded on school-leaving certificates, which is considered as evidence, may be different from the natural date of birth for a number of reasons.

CHAPTER SIX

On Interpreting Rape as/and Atrocity

❧❧

In 2003, nearly fourteen years after the enactment of the Scheduled Castes and Scheduled Tribes (Prevention of Atrocities) Act, 1989, (PoA Act), parliamentarians raised questions about how Indian judges distinguish between 'mere' rape and rape as atrocity during a discussion on the Act's dismal implementation. Dr Manda Jagannath, MP (Nagar Kurnool), for instance, pointed out that,

> …[I]n Andhra Pradesh a number of rape cases are committed. In one particular case, the Judge felt that the rape was committed because of 'lust for sex' rather than thinking that the woman was a dalit woman. Why are only dalit women chosen? Why are not women in one's family chosen for committing rape? They are also women. Be it a dalit woman or a woman in an upper caste family, the anatomy of their bodies is the same.[1]

The parliamentarian highlighted the fact that judges fail to recognize that Dalit women are not only stable targets of sexual violence, but also that there has historically been a widespread toleration of violence against Dalit women. In other words, judges do not acknowledge that men prefer to rape women belonging to specific classes or castes.

I begin with an analysis of appellate judgments to map the juridical discourse on rape as atrocity. I use Claudia Card's definition of atrocity in the context of Indian law, which distinguishes specific crimes as atrocities. Card has suggested that an atrocity, as a 'gross evil', is 'the widespread toleration of wrongfully perpetrated intolerable harm to individuals' (2004: 219). These atrocities which inflict 'intolerable harm' are not 'a matter of a large number of victims', nor are these a 'sum of assaults' (Card 2004: 217). Card believes that rape is an atrocity that communicates 'an immediate message to women and girls … that we will have in our bodies only the control that we are granted by men and thereby in general only that control in our environments that we are granted by men' (1996: 6). This violence is 'enjoyed for its own sake' and in this sense, is 'recreational'; yet it is also instrumental in 'sending a message' to all other women (Card 1996: 6–7).

I argue that in making a classification between lust and atrocity, judicial interpretation does not construct rape as atrocity, for such forms of sexual violence are seen as isolated crimes against individual women, irrespective of their caste or class. I contend that the judicial understanding of rape as atrocity is thin, and convictions of rape as atrocity are rare. However, we find some convictions in cases of rape that accompany other forms of atrocities. These do not always communicate the gravitas of the experience of rape as a form of tolerated 'intolerable harm' (Card 2004). This is an additive approach—it adds specific forms of atrocity to the crime of rape. In doing so, it does not necessarily alter the meaning of rape. For women, the PoA Act is hollowed out both at the level of naming and the doing of the law.

Protectionist laws such as the PoA Act aim to infuse criminal law with constitutional ideals of substantive equality by re-signifying previously stigmatized bodies as bearers of rights.[2] As a special law, the PoA Act mandates the institution of a governmental apparatus to allow Dalits and tribals greater access to courts. The PoA Act aspires to bring everyday and extraordinary violence against the Dalits and *adivasis*—to use the categories of self-assertion deployed by the Scheduled Castes and Scheduled Tribes—to challenge structures of impunity and immunity. In this chapter, I will argue that the exception is produced when the law institutes a series of hyper-technicalities to disarticulate atrocity.[3] Since the special apparatus exists in a field of power it is dismantled by the police, prosecutors, defence lawyers, and judges by deploying the rules formulated around the PoA Act. Far from withdrawing from or suspending law, there is a certain excess of technicalities that create and maintain exceptional conditions of impunity and immunity. The judicial archive then allows us to outline how caste or tribe gets occluded from the law as context, motive, intent, and evidence.

THE EMERGENCE OF ATROCITY AS A JURIDICAL CATEGORY

SR Sankaran suggests that 'perhaps the term "atrocity" was used for the first time by the Commissioner of Scheduled Castes and Tribes—a special officer appointed under Article 338 (1) of the Constitution as it originally stood—in his Annual Reports in relation to crimes against the Scheduled Castes and Scheduled Tribes' (2008: 128). Mendelsohn and Vicziany (1998) trace some complex narratives: as an administrative category, 'atrocity' was used as early as the Sixth Report published in 1956–7 when the Office of Commissioner for SCs & STs began to maintain a record of the complaints. By the 21st Report of 1971–3,

> ...perceptions had changed. The much larger complaints section was re-styled 'Cases of Atrocities and Harassment', a nomenclature which seemed to fit mounting concern about violence done to Untouchables. In the variant form 'Harijan atrocity', this was a term that quickly slipped into the vernacular of Indian newspaper reportage and official documents as an omnibus identifier of the frequent violence suffered by Untouchables. (Mendelsohn and Vicziany 1998: 44–5)

Mendelsohn and Vicziany argue that this evidence of atrocity, which was now part of administrative discourse, was also in response to the violence on Dalits due to their refusal to be 'passive victims', and 'as a reaction to the demands they are making or of their uptake of benefits provided by the state' (1998: 45). The category, atrocity 'was routinized and bureaucratized at a time when wider political developments suggested that India as a whole was an increasingly violent society and therefore that the Untouchables were not such exceptional victims' (Mendelsohn and Vicziany 1998: 45).

During the 1970s and 1980s, atrocities were documented as evidence of the systemic domination of Dalits, and over time the term came to be extended to include the crimes committed against the tribals as well. Studies such as the one conducted by the Indian Bureau of Police Research and Development (1979) held that 'in order to constitute atrocity, there must be an element of cruelty or brutality, or wickedness in the commission of a particular offence, or it should have the background of having been committed with the view to teach the Harijans a lesson' (cited in U. Baxi 1994: 137). A study on the basis of a systematic collation of police complaints led sociologist Kamble to argue in the 1980s that the law did not adequately address instances of violence against the Dalits. I quote:

> ...every offence stems from the inordinate lust for power that dominates the Hindu mind and vitiates the caste Hindu relations with the untouchables. The caste Hindu's mind is conditioned from early childhood by caste and the concept of untouchability. Therefore, in every offence committed by a caste Hindu against a scheduled caste person the practice of untouchability should be presumed and should be left to the caste Hindu to prove the contrary. (Kamble 1982: 147)

PS Krishnan, Special Commissioner for SC/ST, and Secretary, Ministry of Welfare, used the category 'atrocity' to pioneer the formulation of the special law (Krishnan 2009).

The PoA Act was introduced in the Parliament in 1989 in order to address 'the increase in the disturbing trend of commission of certain atrocities (against the SC and the ST). The normal provisions of the existing laws like the Protection of the Civil Rights Act, 1955 and the Indian Penal Code have been found to be inadequate to check these atrocities'. The Statement of Objects and Reasons of the PoA Act noted that:

> Of late, there has been an increase in the disturbing trend of commission of certain atrocities like making the Scheduled castes persons eat inedible substances like human excreta and attacks and mass killings of helpless Scheduled Castes and the Scheduled tribes and rape of women belonging to the Scheduled castes and Scheduled tribes ... A special legislation to check and deter crimes against them committed by the non-scheduled Castes and non-Scheduled tribes has, therefore, become necessary.

A perusal of the parliamentary debates[4] indicates that the bill was represented during these debates as a necessary and urgent legislation to address the growing atrocities against the Scheduled Castes and Scheduled Tribes as a result of social change engineered by governmental schemes and policies. The growing violence was framed as the backlash against new forms of social mobility and self-assertion. As Ganga Ram, MP, said, 'their women are raped and entire village is burnt'.[5]

The clubbing together of Scheduled Castes and Scheduled Tribes was seen as natural. Both were seen as potentially vulnerable to systemic domination by caste Hindus. Digvijay Singh, MP, pleaded, 'it is the responsibility of caste Hindus to see that atrocities are not committed against SC and ST people. We have to change our frame of mind and accept them as *brothers*'.[6] Or as Bajpai, MP, said,

> ...[I]n some unfortunate incidents the women folk of scheduled castes and scheduled tribes is [*sic*] sought to be dishonoured and assaulted with the object of teaching a lesson to that community. ... And this is the worst type of atrocities committed on SC people in dishonouring women. In tribal areas sexual exploitation is known to occur and the willingness of innocent tribal women is seared by exercise of authority or influence.[7]

The legislation sought to classify as atrocities those forms of sexual violence that overtly targeted Dalit and tribal women, which were performative, repetitive, and excessive. Hence, we find repeated allusion to the phrase, 'teaching a lesson', in legal and political discourse. Teaching a lesson means to put individuals and communities, in 'their' place—in the instance of women, their bodies literally forced under rapacious bodies—to transact power over despised and inferior communities. In this context, teaching a lesson becomes an operative term to distinguish rape as a crime from rape as an atrocity.

CLASSIFYING CRIME AND ATROCITY

The PoA Act introduces a series of new classifications that are relevant to understanding how rape is classified as atrocity. First, the Act 'uses the phrase "whoever, not being a member of a Scheduled Caste or a Scheduled Tribe",[8] to indicate that the provisions of the act come into play when the offender is not a Dalit or an adivasi' (Agrawal and Gonsalves 2005: 137). The victim must be classified as Scheduled Caste or Scheduled Tribe. Courts have held that a person belonging to the Scheduled Caste and Scheduled Tribe communities cannot be charged under the PoA Act rather such charges ought to be tried under the IPC (Naval 2001).[9] Moreover, courts have further clarified that in the instance of an offence by a person from a Scheduled Caste against a member of a Scheduled Tribe, 'the very opening words of Section 3 would show that the offence punishable under Section 3 of the Act can be attributed to only a person who does not belong to a member of the Scheduled Caste or Scheduled Tribe' (cited in Naval

2001: 75).[10] In other words, a Dalit man cannot be prosecuted for raping a tribal woman under the PoA Act and such a charge must be prosecuted under the IPC.

Second, a list of atrocities is provided under s. 3 of the PoA Act. Saxena clarifies, 'Though no conceptual definition has been attempted, S. 2 (l) (a) mentions that atrocity would mean all those offences, which are punishable under S. 3. Thus the definition of "atrocity" emerges by implication, i.e., actions covering various offences' (2004: 27).

Third, this does not mean that the offences under the IPC are excluded from the Act. Saxena notes with respect to offences covered under the IPC,

> ...[A]s per the clarification of the Ministry of Home Affairs the term implies '*any offence under the Indian Penal Code committed against members of Scheduled Castes by non-scheduled caste persons.* Similarly, all offences under IPC committed by non-scheduled tribe against members of the Scheduled Tribes are atrocities. *Caste consideration as a motive is not necessary* to make such an offence in case of atrocity... (2004: 27–8, emphasis in original)

Saxena also noted the clarifications offered by the Ministry of Home Affairs:

> It is further clarified that the term atrocity signifies 'crimes which have ingredients of infliction of suffering in one form or the other should be included for reporting'. This is based on the assumption that 'where the victims of crime are members of scheduled castes and the offenders do not belong to scheduled caste, caste considerations are really the root cause of the crime, even though caste considerations may not be the vivid and minimum motive for the crime' (2004: 27–28).

The language of atrocity seems to borrow from two sets of discourses—one from the existing definitions of crime and the other derived from the languages of suffering that are part of the repertoire of these targeted communities. The PoA Act then led to a new modality of speaking about sexual violence and a new apparatus to address the articulation of an atrocity.

The Act mandates the establishment of special courts, appointment of special prosecutors, and investigation of atrocities by police officers not below the rank of a deputy superintendent of police (DSP).

The special courts were mandated in order to minimize the delay in hearing these cases.[11] The state is thus obligated to ensure that the 'rights accruing from the abolition of untouchability are available to all concerned' (K. Sankaran forthcoming: 10). A special court is 'essentially a court of session and it can take cognisance of an offence when the case is committed to it by the Magistrate in accordance with the provisions of the Code of Criminal procedure' (Narayana 2011: 280, also see Saksena 2010). Kamala Sankaran further notes that a magistrate 'is not permitted to try a case arising under the PoA Act providing a further reason why the number of cases committed for trial in these cases are also relatively small' (forthcoming: 11). This process has also been critiqued for causing delay in the trials (see Agrawal and Gonsalves 2005).

The 1995 Rules, which operationalized the PoA Act, outline a number of features including prevention of atrocities by naming certain areas as atrocity-prone, granting power to the state to cancel the arms licenses of all non-Dalits and non-tribals, and if necessary, providing arms licenses to the members of the Scheduled Castes and Scheduled Tribes to ensure safety and protection of all tribals and Dalits. A new structure of review, monitoring, and awareness-raising is envisaged by the Act to prevent atrocities, such as the setting up of the Scheduled Caste and Scheduled Tribe cells to survey a locality, maintain public tranquillity, request police deployment when needed, and investigate causes of atrocities. It drew up rules for compensating victims of atrocity, including rape. For instance, women whose modesty had been outraged or those who had been sexually exploited are entitled to Rs 25,000 after the medical examination and Rs 25,000 after the trial. If the offence warrants a sentence of ten years or more, the victim would be compensated at least Rs 50,000. As per the Gujarat rules,[12] when a tribal or Dalit rape victim gets married, the government shall decree a sum of Rs 50,000 to the couple. Compensation would be available through specific procedures that now rest on proving the identity of the victim through governmental procedures of certification.

While the powerful victim blaming discourse that the PoA Act is misused in order to gain compensation circulates in courtrooms, in fact survivors find it hard to access compensation (see Agrawal & Gonsalves 2005). Delhi-based NGO, MARG, which conducted research on rape cases on Dalit and tribal women in Uttar Pradesh for the Government of India, revealed that irrespective of age, marital status, and circumstance, an overwhelming number of medico-legal reports read identically in Meerut District (Tekchandani 1995). Tekchandani says, 'largely the medical reports say that no marks of external or internal injury are visible, vaginal smear report is negative, hymen tear is old, there is no bleeding, victim is used to sexual intercourse and no opinion about rape can be given' (1995: 27). Each medical report disingenuously mentioned that all the victims have a mole on their cheeks as a mark of identification. Such practices of falsifying medico-legal certificates are not recognized as state forgery by our courts. The language of compensation, instead of reparation, brings the PoA Act closer to languages of damage. Equally the implementation of this regime of compensation oscillates between state practices of forgery and practices of illegibility as a mechanism of disarticulating atrocity.

CHALLENGE, QUASH AND DEFER: *SAHJAD ANSARI V. STATE OF JHARKHAND*

It may seem ironical that the constitutionality of the PoA Act has been challenged on the ground that it violates equality before the law and equal protection of the law. Indian courts have taken quite seriously the requirement that the fundamental right to equality disciplines the power of legislative action (see Appendix 3). I am interested in looking at the sociological impact of such constitutional challenges. I suggest that such challenges to the PoA Act became a routine defence strategy to defer or quash the complaint of atrocity. I base this argument on the basis of the observations of the High Court of Patna (Ranchi Bench) pertaining to a rape and atrocity.[13] This case, *Sahjad Ansari* v. *State of Jharkhand*,[14] describes a chilling account of gangrape, torture, and murder of a tribal young woman in November 1992 in Bihar (now Jharkhand).

On 5 November 1992, a young tribal woman boarded the Rajdhani Express bus at Ranchi to go to her sister's house in Giddi. Sahjad Ansari, a bus conductor, drove up to the bus on a motorcycle with two other men. They forced the victim to get off the bus and abducted her.

…the miscreants felled her down [*sic*] on the ground and committed gang rape on her. Thereafter, they took her forcibly to a coal mine at a distance of about one kilometer away from the house and on the way they threatened her with dire consequences if she reported the matter to any one and when she did not reply, one of them took out his belt and began lashing her with the belt. Later, the appellant Shahjad Ansari tied the neck of the prosecutrix with the belt and dragged her towards the coal mine and dumped her on the burning coal. Believing that she had died, the miscreants left the place. The prosecutrix suffered extensive burn injuries. Her clothes were totally burnt. Yet she was alive and by mustering courage, she walked towards a village located at a distance of about half a kilometer from the coalmines. She knocked at the door; the occupant of the house saw her and provided clothes to cover her body and took her to the nearest police station at Bhurkunda from where she was taken to hospital at Sayal and later she was shifted to Rajendra Medical College Hospital (RMCH) Ranchi … The prosecutrix in course of her treatment at the RMCH, died after about 35 days of the occurrence.[15]

The post-mortem report recorded the cause of death as resulting from the complications that followed due to the burn injuries. When she gave this statement, she could not sign the statement because of her badly burnt hands and fingers, a point that would be obfuscated by the defence during the trial, in a bid to question the veracity of the dead victim's unsigned statement treated as an F.I.R cum dying declaration. The trial court judgment was pronounced on 12 February 2002.

The delay was in part created by fact that the accused in this case moved the High Court of Patna (Ranchi Bench) to quash the FIR lodged against them.[16] The accused succeeded in getting anticipatory bail and a stay on the proceedings when the court admitted these applications for hearing—a fact that the bench noted with surprise. The petitioner claimed that the allegations made in the FIR do not constitute an offence under the PoA Act. The petitioner claimed that s. 3 of the PoA Act violated Article 14 of the Constitution since such acts of atrocities are not punishable when committed by the members of Scheduled Castes or Scheduled Tribes. Apart from this, the petitioner contended that s. 3(1)(xii) is 'incapable of being implemented inasmuch as it is not possible to find when a non-scheduled caste man can be said to be in a position to dominate the will of a woman belonging to Scheduled Caste or a Scheduled Tribe and then uses that position to exploit her sexually'.[17]

The court dismissed the application on the grounds that:

> Providing special courts, prescribing special procedure and special legislation to protect the weaker sections of the society from the exploitation of the vested interests cannot be held to be an Act of discrimination within the ambit of Article 14 of the Constitution. As the offences or activities are so heinous or serious then those offences can be treated as a class by themselves and a special procedure may be provided for dealing with them or for their investigation and trial. Article 14 of the Constitution prohibits class legislation and does not prohibit reasonable classification for purposes of legislation.[18]

On the issue of the quashing of the FIR, the court noted the tendency to file applications under Articles 226 and 227 of the Constitution for quashing of the FIR,[19] and rightly pointed out that the legal strategy to quash police investigation as the norm rather than an exception undermines the PoA Act. Justices G.B. Patnaik, CJ, and P.K. Deb strongly condemned the abuse of appellate process,

> We are indeed pained to find this sort of maneuvering [sic] and we have no hesitation to hold that the Court was not at all entitled to grant anticipatory bail even if it has entertained the application for examining the validity of the provisions of the said Act. This is a glaring example where the process of the Court has been abused and in such a heinous offence the accused persons are moving freely. The purpose of legislation enacting Act to prevent the weaker sections of the society from the exploitation by higher caste people will not be achieved if the Court entertains such applications and pass such orders, which emboldens the accused persons to commit such heinous acts. ... This case should be an eye-opener for future and the Court should be cautious in the matter of exercising jurisdiction under Articles 226 and 227 of the Constitution.[20]

When the case was finally heard in 2002, the trial court found Sahjad Ansari guilty of kidnapping, rape, murder, and atrocity crimes committed on the ground that the victim was a tribal. The court acquitted the other two men.[21] In 2007, the high court upheld the conviction and sentence meted out by the trial court. Although this case spans seventeen years, it is one of the few that names rape as an atrocity. We learn that for rape to qualify as an atrocity, judges do not need to deploy scale as a measure of an atrocity. Nor is an atrocity merely the sum of all assaults, rather what makes it atrocity is the intolerable and overwhelming harm that has historically been tolerated and even celebrated.

OUTRAGING MODESTY AS ATROCITY

Whoever, not being a member of a Scheduled Caste or a Scheduled Tribe assaults or uses force to any woman belonging to a Scheduled Caste or a Scheduled Tribe with intent to dishonour or outrage her modesty.

Section 3(1)(xi) as defined above is a new offence that may be punished by a minimum sentence of six months and a maximum of five years with fine. What does this offence signify, especially as Rege (2003) points out that rape is associated with the loss of honour in most vernacular languages? Historically, Dalit and tribal women have been perceived as inherently incapable of embodying honour, and hence, the social meaning of rape loses its power to describe the humiliation that Dalit and tribal women face. For instance, colonial law invested upper-caste women with greater modesty or honour as compared to Dalit women in the sphere of judicial interpretation and sentencing (see Dhagamwar 1992). While the use of modesty or honour re-inscribes a specific form of patriarchal control over women in which modesty or honour acts to both discipline and punish women, when used in this law it imbues Dalit and tribal women with modesty or honour as a virtue (*read*: patriarchal virtue) shared by all women. Hence, to name outraging modesty or dishonouring a Dalit or a tribal woman as an atrocity marks a discursive shift and imbues honour or modesty with a newer meaning. Section 3(1)(xi) may be added to a rape charge, since every rape outrages a woman's modesty and dishonours her.[22]

Mohammad Akhtar v. *State of Bihar* (2005) illustrates this additive approach. In 1994, Mohammad Akhtar raped a woman who was walking back from a paddy field in a village in Jharkhand.[23] The accused threatened her and told her, 'if you allow me to have sexual intercourse with you, you would not loose [*sic*] anything'.[24] Subsequently, the police complaint was registered under s. 376 IPC and s. 3(1)(xi) PoA Act. The trial court found the accused guilty of rape and convicted him for life under s. 376 IPC, and also found him guilty of outraging the victim's modesty and dishonouring her as defined under s. 3(1)(xi) of the Act, punishing him to five years rigorous imprisonment. One of the arguments put forward on behalf of the accused-appellant in the appeal to the High Court was that no case under s. 3(1)(xi) of the PoA Act 'is made out because the alleged rape was not committed considering the fact the victim lady belongs to the Harijan community'.[25] Dismissing this argument, the high court upheld the sentence under s. 3(1)(xi) PoA Act.[26]

Vidhyadharan v. *State of Kerala* (2003)[27] clarifies that a woman's modesty is outraged under s. 354 IPC when the assailant has 'mere knowledge that the modesty of a woman is likely to be outraged', wherein 'intent is not the sole criteria' (cited in Agrawal and Gonsalves 2005: 150). The Supreme Court held, 'the offence punishable under s. 3(1)(xi) of the Act is an aggravated form of an offence punishable under s. 354 IPC and therefore, no separate sentence for the offence is called for'.[28] I will return to this judgment in the analysis of the Khairlanji appeal, but for now we need to flag two points. One, the prosecution does not need to prove that the woman's modesty was outraged because the accused knew that she was a Dalit or tribal. Two, upon conviction under s. 3(1)(xi), no separate sentence under s. 354 IPC is required.

Sexual Exploitation

> Whoever, not being a member of a Scheduled Caste or a Scheduled Tribe being in a position to dominate the will of a woman belonging to a Scheduled Caste or a Scheduled Tribe and uses that position to exploit her sexually to which she would not have otherwise agreed.

Section 3(1)(xii) of the PoA Act, cited above, is a new offence, carrying a minimum punishment of six months and a maximum punishment of five years with fine. One of the interpretations of this offence is that the PoA Act criminalized the dominant practice, which constitutes tribal and Dalit women as 'sexually available' for men to exploit and abandon. For instance, in *Gujula Satyanarayana Reddy* v. *State of Andhra Pradesh*,[29] we learn that the complainant was an eighteen-year-old woman belonging to a scheduled tribe who used to work as a *coolie* (labourer) in the fields owned by the accused's father. The accused's family belonged to the landowning Reddy caste. The court tells us that the accused was in a dominant position and lured her into a sexual relationship by promising to marry her. The landlord's son lived with her for five months, and then abandoned her under familial pressure. Aggrieved, the woman filed a complaint against the accused under the PoA Act. The trial court found the accused guilty. Upon hearing the appeal filed by the accused, the high court confirmed the conviction but lowered the sentence. The high court reasoned that under s. 3(1)(xii) the accused was in a position to dominate the woman's will and he used his position as member of the Reddy caste to exploit her sexually by assuring her that he would marry her. However, the court noted that the accused wanted to marry the woman but his brothers would not allow him to marry her. Considering this, the court felt that the sentence of two years imprisonment was too severe and lowered it to six months instead. In this case, it is the subject position of the accused and not his intent that allows for a conviction. Such forms of sexual exploitation are now named as atrocity in the law.

Bharatsingh v. *Harijan Kalyan Vibhag*[30] clarifies whether rape can be prosecuted under s. 3(1)(xii) PoA Act. This was an appeal against a plea for anticipatory bail by one of the co-accused in a gangrape case. Anticipating his arrest, he moved to the court for bail. The victim was a thirty-five-year-old tribal agricultural labourer who was working in the outskirts of her village when four men from her village assaulted and raped her. The appellant, in this case, was charged with abetting gangrape. The Madhya Pradesh High Court held that it was not correct, however, to apply s. 3(1)(xii) as this assumed that there was some 'prior' association between the accused and the victim, and it called for evidence of the fact that the accused used his position to dominate the victim's will.

Further, the court clarified that rape is distinct from an offence punishable under s. 3(1)(xii), which '…contemplates the exploitation of a woman sexually by virtue of the position occupied by the offender with reference to the victim under a state of association between them. Illustrations come to the mind are the master and a female servant, a guardian and a ward, a teacher and a student, an elderly relative of the victim etc'.[31] The court held that s. 3(1)(xi), PoA Act should be read with the offence of rape, as defined by the IPC, as all forms of rape outrage a woman's modesty or dishonour her. The court clarified that 'the fact that these ingredients also form part of the ingredients of the offence of rape do not make out any case for the exclusion of the operation of the provisions' of s. 3(1)(xi).[32]

Sexual exploitation excludes rape by strangers whom a victim may not know, but whose identity the accused may know. This is made clear by a case from the Orissa High Court. In Orissa, a young tribal woman was brutally gangraped by three men while she was cycling back home one afternoon in the summer of 1992.[33] Her father and other villagers found the victim and caught the accused at the scene of crime. The accused were charged with the offences of gangrape and sexual exploitation under s. 3(1)(xii) of the PoA Act. Finding the accused guilty of the former, the trial sentenced the accused to life imprisonment, and sentenced them to five years of rigorous imprisonment under the latter. The court, however, acquitted them of the charge under s. 354/34 IPC (common intent to outrage modesty).

Justices Pasayat and D.M. Patnaik upheld the conviction of gangrape but did not find merit in the trial court's conviction on the grounds of sexual exploitation under the PoA Act. The high court reduced the sentence from life imprisonment to seven years rigorous imprisonment on the grounds that these young men were 'in pursuit of their first tests of sex without any violent intention'.[34] The idea that gangrape is devoid of violent intention is unintelligible, and equally, it is not clear why these 'first tests of sex' did not amount to outraging modesty.

Agrawal and Gonsalves (2005) are of the opinion that the application of s. 3(1)(xi) was either an error in law, or a typographical error in the charge sheet that was repeated in all the court documentation. It is indeed puzzling that s. 354 IPC was not applied with s. 3(1)(xi) PoA Act. What, then, are the stated reasons for setting aside the charge of sexual exploitation? The Orissa High Court held that:

> In the present case the offenders are not shown to have dominated the will of the victim girl. In order to attract application of the provision sexual exploitation must have taken place because of the

offender's position of dominance. The word 'otherwise' is significant, and clearly points out that the exploitation was with agreement of the helpless woman, which she would not have agreed but for the offender's position of dominance.

It is significant to note that the expressions used in Section 3(1)(xii) of the Atrocities Act are 'agreed' and 'exploit sexually' and not 'consent' and 'rape'. 'Consent' and 'agreement' are not conceptually and etymologically different…

Use of the expression 'would not have otherwise agreed' is intended to convey that the agreement would not have been there, but for the position of dominance. It is not a free and voluntary consent.

'Exploit' means to make an illegitimate use of, to utilise for one's ends, treat selfishly as more workable material person etc., to make capital out of. To have carnal knowledge of a woman by use of position of dominance, is sexual exploitation if the victim would not have agreed to the act, but for the position.[35]

Referring to the Prevention of Immoral Traffic in Women and Girls Act, first enacted in 1956, then amended in 1976 and 1986,[36] the Orissa High Court observed that:

In this, the old definition of prostitution, vide Section 2(f) which meant 'the act of a female offering her body for promiscuous sexual intercourse for hire' has now been changed to carry the meaning of 'sexual exploitation or abuse of persons for commercial purposes'. Promiscuous sexual intercourse, the important ingredient of prostitution stands replaced by the twin requirement of the exploitation or abuse of the person and secondly the abuse or exploitation should be for commercial purposes. The expression 'sexual exploitation' would include sexual intercourse without consent, which forms basis for conviction for rape.

Finally, the court tells us that the victim did not 'agree' to sexual exploitation because the rapists were not in a position of dominance.

For sexual exploitation to be an atrocity, courts have specified that the victim should know the accused or the accused should know that the victim is tribal or Dalit. In such cases, the burden is upon the prosecution to prove that the accused knew the victim. *Dilip Kumar Jha and Ors* v. *State of Bihar*[37] narrates the trauma of a fourteen-year-old tribal girl who was gangraped for seven hours in Dumka district in 1997. The trial court convicted the accused on the grounds of gangrape, sentencing him to rigorous imprisonment of ten years, and one year each for committing an offence under s. 324 (voluntary harm) and s. 342 (wrongful confinement) IPC. Additionally, the court found the accused guilty of the offence defined under s. 3(1)(xii) of the PoA Act and sentenced him to five years rigorous imprisonment for this offence. While the High Court upheld the conviction and sentence on all the counts mentioned above under the IPC, the court acquitted the accused of offence under s. 3(1)(xii) PoA Act on the following grounds.[38]

> …the appellants had no knowledge of the fact that the informant is a Scheduled Tribe girl. Furthermore to constitute the offence under Section 3(1)(xii) of the said Act, the prosecution has to establish firstly, that the appellants were in a position to dominate the will of a woman belonging to a Scheduled caste or Scheduled Tribe and secondly, uses that position to exploit here sexually to which she would not have otherwise agreed.[39]

However, when the prosecution is able to prove that the accused knew that the victim was Dalit, we are told that sexual exploitation must only be limited to unlawful sexual intercourse. For instance, when a Dalit woman lecturer's estranged partner threw acid on her face, the court held that this offence could not be classified as an act of sexual exploitation. Characterizing this as yet another misuse of the PoA Act, the court said, 'The law enforcing authorities must bear in mind that it cannot be misused to settle other disputes between the parties, which is alien to the provisions contemplated under the Act. … It is for the authorities to guard against such misuse of power conferred on them.'[40]

During this bail hearing, the court reading the victim's letters and stated, 'perusal of the letters go to show that she was bent upon taking revenge on the petitioner, she has stated that "99% she lives only to take revenge on him"'.[41] The letters are read as if these were confessions revealing the victim's motive to bring a false case against her estranged partner. Although the accused was granted bail, the judge observed that 'it appears that from [the] beginning there is something fundamentally wrong in this case', indicating deep judicial anxiety about the misuse of the PoA Act by vengeful women—a recurrent theme in the case law on atrocity.[42]

INSULT AND INTIMIDATION IN PUBLIC VIEW

> Whoever, not being a member of a Scheduled Caste or a Scheduled Tribe intentionally insults or intimidates with intent to humiliate a member of a Scheduled Caste or a Scheduled Tribe in any place within public view.

Rape may be read with s. 3(1)(x) PoA Act, as cited above. The offences defined in this section are punishable with imprisonment for a term not less than six months but which may extend to five years and with fine. It must demonstrate an insult or an act of criminal intimidation that is intentional in its aim to humiliate Dalits or tribals in public view. Hence, 'any place' indicates that the scene of crime may or may not be a public place rather it should be in public view (Naval 2001). Saksena (2010) has observed that this section acts like an 'omnibus clause' in Uttar Pradesh, whereby the police more often than not add this section to the crime without adequate reference to the context.[43]

In order to examine how judges read gangrape with atrocity as defined under s. 3(1)(x) PoA Act, I refer to a judgment from the Madhya Pradesh High Court. In 1992, a twenty-eight-year-old tribal schoolteacher took a bus to travel to teach in a school in a neighbouring village.[44] When she got off, three men followed her, caught her and threatened to kill her with a knife if she resisted them. She was stripped and raped by the three men. She was also warned against going to the police, or she would meet the same fate as a Madam R of Dhamoda village.

The trial court at Vidisa found these men guilty of gangrape and sentenced them to ten years rigorous imprisonment with a fine of Rs 2,000 and in default, one year rigorous imprisonment. They were also found guilty of criminal intimidation with the intent to impute unchastity under s. 506(2) IPC, and sentenced to one year rigorous imprisonment. The trial acquitted the appellants of the offence under s. 3(1)(x), PoA Act. No reasons were given. The high court upheld the trial court's verdict. The trial court ignored the fact that the accused threatened the victim with the same fate as another woman if she were to complain to the police. This threat minimally indicates two things. First, that the rapists conjured the image of a terrible fate that met Madam R who was possibly further victimized after having filed a police complaint. Second, it signifies that the victim's status as a teacher may have been known to the accused—just as the suffix Madam indicates. From the judgment, we also learn that one of the accused knew the victim's colleague and alleged that he did not get along with him, hence the victim, at his behest, had filed a false case. The structure of the defence argument, and the meaning of the threat provide us with the information that the accused may have known the victim. The court feigns ignorance about the fact that a tribal schoolteacher as a single woman and an outsider is especially vulnerable to sexual violence. We are not told if intent to insult or intimidate in any place in public view is an ingredient of gangrape. How would public view, which is any place the public can access, be defined in the case of gangrape?

ON THE GROUND OF

> Whoever, not being a member of a Scheduled Caste or a Scheduled Tribe, commits any offence under the Indian Penal Code (45 of 1860) punishable with imprisonment for a term of ten years or more against a person or property on the ground that such person is a member of a Scheduled Caste or a Scheduled Tribe or such property belongs to such member, shall be punishable with imprisonment for life and with fine.

The atrocities justiciable under s. 3(2)(v) cited above are punishable with imprisonment for life with fine. The feature critical to cases under s. 3(2)(v) of the Act (unlike the first two clauses cited above) is the necessity to prove that the woman was raped on the ground that she was a Dalit or tribal.[45] As a Gujarat High Court judge explained to me:

> When rape is committed, it is because of sexual perversion or blinding urge. He does not have in mind the fact that she is a Harijan lady. It is not proper to bring the Atrocity Act under its purview in this case. Only those cases when one class of community burn houses and rape women merely because they are Harijans, these are the cases that should come under the purview of the Act. When they burn Harijan houses. When a lady is in the forest, a solitary rape should simply figure under the IPC. The issue here is not that she is a Harijan lady.

One such case is exemplified by *Bijay Kumar Tiwary and Lalan Choudhary* v. *State of Jharkhand*.[46] In this case, we learn that on the night of 8 or 9 June 1999, in the village of Hasker, eight armed assailants attacked a cluster of houses occupied predominantly by Dalit families. The assailants knocked on the victims' door and when they did not open the door, entered the house through the roof. They assaulted the men and women in the house and stole their ornaments and money. After having looted the house, the men abducted three women—PD, GK, and SK—and raped them. From the judgment, it becomes evident that this brutal violence was in the context of a dispute over land with Shankar Tiwari, who along with his three sons and four others attacked the dalit families. The accused were sentenced to ten years rigorous imprisonment on the charge of gangrape and sentenced to ten years rigorous imprisonment for committing dacoity. The accused were sentenced to one year rigorous imprisonment for violating s. 3(1)(x) of the PoA Act and rigorous imprisonment for life under s. 3(2)(v) PoA Act, 1989. The high court upheld the sentence, dismissing the appeal.[47]

In order to understand *Bijay Kumar Tiwary and Lalan Choudhary v. State of Jharkhand,*[48] we need to uncover a labyrinth of cases and counter cases that indicates a pattern of attack and reprisal when Dalits go to courts. Noting that there was sufficient evidence to establish atrocity, the court tells us that 'the victim mostly *Dalit* were scared and subjected to indiscriminate assault being threatened at the point of annihilation. In that situation some of the male witnesses have (*sic*) taken shelter inside the house and females were subjected to robbing, assault in their presence'.[49] The court recognizing the pattern of attack and reprisal discards the governmental category of Scheduled Caste to describe the victims as Dalits—a political category of self-assertion—which names contexts of resistance. This indeed marks a discursive turn in naming the suffering of sexual violence as a form of caste violence.

'MERE' RAPE AND ATROCITY

This, however, is not a stable narrative—that is, not all forms of rape against Dalit or tribal women are classified as atrocities when they are read with s. 3(2)(v), PoA Act. In such rape trials, we find repeated acquittals on the ground of atrocity (see Mangubhai & Irudayam 2008). In these cases, although Dalit and tribal women remain stable targets of sexual violence, this is not the basis for classifying rape as atrocity. Furthermore, courts institute a distinction between 'mere lust' and 'atrocity'.[50] I list a few cases below to illustrate this classificatory practice.

Case One

Pappu Khan v. *State of Rajasthan*[51] describes the sordid story of a truck driver who raped one of the four tribal women who hitched a ride on his truck. A complaint was brought against the truck driver charging him of rape and s. 3(2)(v) of the PoA Act. The accused was found guilty of rape, but not of atrocity. Setting aside the conviction under the PoA Act, the Rajasthan High Court said, 'there is no evidence that he committed rape on her for the reason that she belonged to Scheduled tribe. He raped her without prejudice of caste to which she belongs only to satisfy his sexual desire.'[52] The Rajasthan High Court cites another case where the accused were convicted for having raped Dalit women on the ground that the Harijans must be taught a lesson. The latter has been described as *racial* prejudice in the judgment. From the perspective of the woman, however, these judgments de-sexualize caste or tribe as lived categories. For women, the experience of being raped is now further fragmented. Does a tribal woman experience rape as a woman or as a tribal? This additive logic acts on the totality of her social and experiential contexts to break it down into new categories—'mere' rape and atrocity.

Case Two

Hanamath and Ors v. *State of Karnataka*[53] upheld the conviction of the men who gangraped a Dalit girl of fifteen years. However, the Karnataka High Court held that the men who had gangraped the young girl did not commit the crime on the grounds that she was Dalit, rather the rape was 'a lustful act of misguided youth'.[54] By convicting the accused on the grounds of gangrape but not atrocity, the court seemed to believe that it was adequate to punish gangrape, since it was seen as a manifestation of sexual excess that exists in the nature of young men. The court splinters the meaning of rape here. On the one hand, the court acknowledges that rape is 'recreational'; that is, it pleasured the rapists. On the other hand, the court does not think that this case communicated a message to all Dalit girls, whether or not it signals an exchange between men of unequal status.

Case Three

Sukru Gouda v. *State of Orissa*[55] traverses many courts, displaying the judicial reluctance to believe a tribal woman's testimony against rape. The set of judgments discussed here reveal the plight of a tribal woman who was raped while she was collecting firewood from a jungle in Koraput, Orissa. The assailant, Sukru Gouda, was arrested after the victim and her husband lodged a complaint. In 1994, the trial court convicted Sukru Gouda of rape and atrocity under s. 376 IPC read with s. 3(2)(v) PoA Act and sentenced him to life imprisonment. On appeal, the Orissa High Court acquitted Sukru Gouda and observed, 'Admittedly P.W. 1 was an able-bodied tribal lady, capable of taking care of herself. It was natural that she would have resisted to the best of her ability if sexual intercourse was being committed on her against her consent'.[56]

The court added that the assailant had no weapon, nor did he threaten to kill her. The court further stated that the 'law is well settled that it is not possible for a single man to commit sexual intercourse with a healthy adult female in full possession of her senses against her will'.[57] The phallocentricism of the rape trial is attenuated in this special trial, and the stereotypes caricaturing Dalit or tribal women as wanting in morality found dramatization. The rape trial colonizes the meaning of atrocity, wherein notions of honour, dignity, or historic discrimination do not act to alter the meaning of rape produced during the special trial.

Nor did the Supreme Court inject new meanings, even though it found the judgment bad in law when the prosecution appealed. The Supreme Court said:

> It baffles us as to why High Court says that 'law is well settled that it is not possible for a single man to commit sexual intercourse with a healthy adult female in full possession of her senses against her will.' There is not even a single decision which says so. The presumptuous conclusion is that PW 1 was an able bodied tribal lady capable of taking care of herself. On that [*sic*] basis the High Court has come to this conclusion is not fathomable. To add to the confusion the High Court itself noticed that there were two contradictory stands.

One was that no such incidence had taken place and this was a case of false implication; other was that the act was with consent. Such irreconcilable stand should not have found favour with the High Court. ... To say the least, the conclusion is not only contrary to law laid down by this Court, but also shows scant regard to law declared by this Court.[58]

The Supreme Court remitted the case to the Orissa High Court to hear the appeal again.

In 2009, when the Orissa High Court heard the appeal upon remittal, it confirmed the conviction of rape but set aside the conviction under s. 3(2)(v) of the PoA Act on the grounds that 'it is the settled principle of law that mere fact that the victim happened to be a girl belonging to the scheduled caste or scheduled tribe does not attract the provisions of the said Act'.[59] The high court held that it was not satisfied that the prosecution had proved that the victim was raped on the grounds that she was tribal. It repeated the words of the Supreme Court in *Ramdas & Ors* v. *State of Maharashtra* (2006). I quote: 'The mere fact that the victim happened to be a girl belonging to a scheduled caste does not attract the provisions of the Act. Apart from the fact that the prosecutrix belongs to the Pardhi community, there is no other evidence on record to prove any offence under the said enactment.'[60]

Since the accused had been in jail since March 2009, the court determined that four years imprisonment met the ends of justice. These judgments reveal that the fact that Dalit and tribal women are stable targets of rape is not read as a form of historical discrimination. Instead we find everyday forms of gangrape are contrasted with stylized images of atrocity as sanctioning organized, mass-scale, and spectacular sexual violence calculated to send a message to men of unequal status.

IT IS REVENGE AND NOT ATROCITY

Yet even when the violence is collective and spectacular, judges make a distinction between revenge and atrocity. This distinction was dramatized in a special trial that recorded testimonies to the chilling violence that unfolded in Khairlanji, a village in Bhandara District, Maharashtra. By holding that this violence was not an atrocity, the

Khairlanji trial did not bring closure to the collective outrage. Rather the Bombay High Court created grounds for the dominant caste to hollow out the PoA Act in future. Hence, the account that follows is limited to the judicial narrative in the Bombay High Court when the case came on appeal.[61]

The Bombay High Court recounts eyewitness descriptions of what happened on that terrible evening on 26 September 2006. The eyewitnesses testified that thirty to forty people, mostly men, surrounded Bhaiyalal and Surekha Bhotmage's hut in Khairlanji. When Surekha Bhotmange tried to escape, she was chased by the accused. She was caught, beaten with chains, rods, and kicked to death. The men returned to hunt for her children—Priyanka, Roshan, and Sudhir—who were mercilessly beaten with chains and rods. Eyewitnesses saw their corpses being dragged to the road. Priyanka's naked body, along with the rest of her slain family, was hoisted to a bullock cart. There are eyewitness accounts identifying the men who gathered the corpses to dispose them in a nearby canal.

These accounts which draw a terrifying picture of men shooting, abusing, chasing, and killing the victims do not speak to activist reports of what happened to the victims. The charge of rape was not brought against the accused. It was local knowledge that the mother and daughter had been gangraped and paraded, and the genitals of the two young men crushed (Teltumbde 2008). It was also widely known that Priyanka was raped after she was dead. Yet a police complaint on the grounds of rape, stripping, and parading was not registered. It is commonly assumed that if a charge is not brought before the court, the violence did not happen. From cases reported in Gujarat 2002, we know that a large number of cases of rape were not brought to trial, and this became the grounds on which the fact of mass rape was denied. In the instance of Khairlanji too the fact that rape was not brought to trial does not mean it did not happen. Rather, the sexualization of the violence is a trace that haunts the testimonies of different witnesses.

The sole survivor in the family, Bhaiyalal Bhotmange, saw the body of his daughter 'which was in a naked condition with many injuries in the hospital'.[62] The post-mortem, conducted hurriedly by a junior doctor, did not investigate or record signs of sexual violence. The high court did not remark on the fact that a woman's naked body should have raised suspicions of sexual violence and an examination ought to have been done to determine internal signs of injury. Nor did it pass any strictures or guidelines, as in other cases, against the police or medical experts for failing to investigate the possibility of rape.

The case was handed over to the Central Bureau of Investigation (CBI), in the wake of angry mass protests by Dalits in Maharashtra (see Jaoul 2008). It is noteworthy that the CBI was unable to bring the charge of rape, parading, and stripping to the trial. The CBI charged eleven men for offences punishable under ss. 302 (murder), 354 (outraging modesty), 449 (house trespass), 201 (causing disappearance of evidence), 148 r/w 149 (rioting), and 120B (criminal conspiracy) of the IPC. Apart from this, the CBI charged the accused of committing offences under ss. 3(1)(x), 3(1)(xi), 3(2) (v), and 3(2)(vi)[63] of the PoA Act. The special court in Bhandara examined thirty-six witnesses. In September 2008, the special judge convicted and sentenced eight men for murder and rioting. Three were acquitted. The judge awarded the death sentence to six accused and life sentences to two accused. The eight men thus convicted were not found guilty of committing any offence under the PoA Act, nor were they found guilty for outraging modesty or dishonouring the women. The appeal against the death sentence was heard along with an appeal by the CBI against the acquittal of the convicted accused for the offences under the PoA Act. On 14 July 2010, the high court upheld the trial judgment but mitigated the death sentence to life imprisonment with the direction that none of the accused would be released until the completion of twenty-five years of actual imprisonment including the period undergone. The CBI's appeal failed.

The high court insisted that the mob who surrounded Surekha Bhotmange and her helpless children did not conspire to murder them on the grounds of their caste. Rather, the court held that the accused had a personal enmity against Surekha Bhotmange and her daughter for agreeing to act as witnesses in a criminal case of assault by the accused.[64] The court constructed the motive from the immediate provocation for the attack. Teltumbde (2008) has pointed out that the group of men who belonged to the dominant caste (mainly *Kunbis* and *Kalars*), led the mob targeted Surekha and her daughter for daring to act as witnesses against them in a criminal complaint of assault. Released on bail, they returned to Khairlanji, with their supporters, as Teltumbde (2008) narrates, in a celebratory mood, with the intention to teach the Mahar family a 'lesson'. Surekha and Priyanka Bhotmange were singled out since they had seen the assault on Siddharth Gajbhiye from a distance, and had rushed to take the severely injured man to hospital (Teltumbde 2008). They had identified the accused and were listed as witnesses against them. From Teltumbde (2008), we also learn that this criminal complaint was lodged after a period of harassment and intimidation of the Bhotmange family.

Teltumbde (2008) provides us with a poignant account of the history of the Bhotmange family, which I briefly summarize here. Bhaiyalal Bhotmange and his wife Surekha moved to Khairlanji in 1989 to cultivate a piece of land they owned in the village. They worked hard and supplemented their income by rolling *bidis* to make ends meet. Their eldest son Sudhir, who was partially visually challenged, helped them farm. Their younger son Roshan had enrolled in a computer class. Their daughter Priyanka, a school topper, cycled every day to junior college, where she had a promising future.

The dominant castes in the village, mainly belonging to the Other Backward Classes (OBCs) (such as *Kunabi, Teli, Kalar, Lodhi,* and *Vadhai*) resented the upwardly mobile and assertive Bhotmanges, who were one of the four Dalit families in the village. The dominant castes wanted to build a road through their land. When the Bhotmanges resisted the daily encroachment on their land, the destruction of their crops, and the trespassing, there were a series of complaints. Although the police did not support the Bhotmanges, they had an ally in the influential Siddharth Gajbhiye, who was also a village *patil* (which is an honorary post affiliating a villager to a police station). The criminal complaint against the accused for assaulting Gajbhiye must then be located within the circuit of everyday harassment, complaints, and reprisals.

A synchronic rather than diachronic understanding of the dispute frames the motive as individual revenge rather than collective revenge, which defines atrocity. The legal framing of the event in standardized legal formats, which sees motive in a single event as provocation to violence, elides a reading of the way caste materializes dominance over bodies, space, resources, memories, and affect. Hence, the court concludes that 'the incident had not occurred on account of caste hatred but the incident occurred since the accused felt that they were falsely implicated in the crime of beating Siddharth Gajbhiye by Surekha and Priyanka'.[65] The court does not recognize that the dominant caste's struggle to retain monopoly over the use (or abuse) of law is a feature of caste domination. Why was it difficult for the court to accept that the assailants sexualized revenge and found violence sexy?

When we read the judgment, we really do not get to see Surekha Bhotmange as an Ambedkarite. Instead she is positioned as Mahar woman who got *herself* killed due to a history of enmity that she created due to the force of her personality. The court seemed to believe that sexual violence as display of caste dominance could be scripted only between men of unequal caste status, transacted over objectified women's bodies. Do women who resist caste dominance, like Surekha Bhotmange, deserve the protection of law, given that in speaking out they stand outside male-defined notions of social order? The Bombay High Court seemed to think otherwise in its belief that 'the whole object was to take revenge against Surekha and Priyanka because the accused believed that they were falsely implicated and as such it is difficult to accept the prosecution version that offence under s. 3(1)(xi) of the Act is made out against the accused'.[66] The court was at pains to dissociate any suggestion of sexual atrocity from the framework of individual revenge.

The Bombay High Court accepted the prosecution's argument that since *Vidhyadharan* v. *State of Kerala* had held that s. 3(1)(xi) of the Act is an aggravated form of offence under s. 354 IPC, knowledge that a woman's modesty is likely to be outraged is sufficient. Yet the court states that since the prosecution did not appeal the acquittal under s. 354 IPC, it could not uphold the conviction under s. 3(1)(xi) of the Act. This is a perverse reading. The CBI did not need to appeal the acquittal under s. 354 IPC precisely since from *Vidhyadharan* v. *State of Kerala* it is clear that s. 3(1)(xi) is an aggravated offence. This perverse reading hollows out the stated objectives of the PoA Act. To name outraging modesty or dishonour would have meant acknowledging atrocity.

It was not as if there was no evidence before the court that the dead woman's body had been sexualized. This evidence is ironically used as one of the twelve aggravating circumstances against six accused that had convinced the trial court to award death penalty. We are told that the accused enjoyed the killings, were fearless in the mob's presence, and thought of the killings as acts of heroism. Further, the court notes that the 'accused Nos 2, 3, 6, to 9 removed clothes of Priyanka before disposing her severely injured dead body and thereby wanted to get satisfaction to their sexual eyes at such extreme circumstances'.[67] In constructing this case as rarest of rare, gender is deployed to argue for aggravating circumstances, whereas the mitigating circumstances efface caste, inasmuch as the trial court argues that caste hatred was not the ground of violence.

The Khairlanji trial tells us that even though the law maintains its monopoly to punish crime, it does not displace the monopoly of the dominant caste to rape, parade, and kill Dalit women. By not naming this violence as a caste crime, there are two messages—that the law will punish crime, but it will not displace caste domination in doing so. Sexual violence is central to caste domination, hence it is not even named. The trial is not a vehicle for communicating the violence of caste, but it becomes an occasion for de-politicizing caste violence as an act of personal revenge and re-inscribes the public secret by not naming what everyone knows (Taussig 1999).

DIVINE DISPLEASURE OR DEROGATION?

> Whoever, not being a member of a Scheduled Caste or a Scheduled Tribe forcibly removes clothes from the person of a member of a Scheduled Caste or a Scheduled Tribe or parades him naked or with painted face or body or commits any similar act which is derogatory to human dignity.

Section 3 (1)(iii) of the PoA Act criminalizes one of the most dramatized forms of atrocity, which is based on a series of abnormal inversions. This section, a most underutilized law, applies to both men and women by naming parading and stripping as derogatory to the dignity of Dalits and tribals. Stripping and parading of men and women creates a public in which the victim is put on display as a degraded object, where the victim is stripped literally and symbolically of all that is social. This form of bareness inverses in abnormal ways the means by which a person becomes social. Yet to enforce nudity on women in front of a sexualized public has a specific effect. It converts a public where women usually appear as regulated presences to a voyeuristic public where the nude body of the woman is made available in flesh, to sexually degrade. Stripping of women, in other words, not only literally strips them of all that it means to be social, but the victim is made to believe that she is to blame for this violence.

I turn to *Miss M.S. Annaporani* v. *State of UP*[68] to illustrate the legal rendition of the spectacle of violence that was enacted against a young Hindu widow in rural Uttar Pradesh for marrying a Muslim man (P. Baxi 2006). This case came before the Allahabad High Court when the court received a letter from the registrar of the Supreme Court of India. The letter arose from the *habeas corpus* writ filed under Article 32, Constitution of India, by an advocate, MS Annaporani, who was aggrieved by a news report in a local newspaper *Hitavada* on 30 July 1989. The newspaper report cited in the judgment detailed the violence suffered by a thirty-year-old woman (referred to as 'S') who was gangraped and paraded in a Sourana village near Gorakhpur (Uttar Pradesh), after she married a Muslim man. The facts of the case as gleaned from the judgment are as follows:

S was widowed for six years when she met Ali Raza. They married in the registry office in 1998. At first, no one commented on this alliance. Matters became contentious when the *gram pradhan*—Paras Nath Yadav, who according to the newspaper report, 'had courted [S]'s favour but without any success'—objected to this marriage and 'swore he would teach them a lesson'.[69] What happened next is best described in the words of the court:

> In the afternoon of June, Yadav barged into their house. In the fracas that ensued Raza was beaten up by the headman's Hindu supporters. The police arrived and removed the three protagonists to the Camporganj police station about 15 kms away. Raza was remanded to custody but [S] and Parasnath were released, contravening standard procedure, which requires all persons immediately connected with a case to be taken in for questioning. Worse the woman was handed over to the villagers, to be used as they saw fit.
>
> And then began the abominable outrage. [S] was taken to the house of one Badri Kiwat, one of the dadas [toughs] of Rampur. At

nightfall they entered her room. She was repeatedly raped till early hours. Everyone seemed to be waiting to have his fill. At dawn, after satiating half a dozen men, she made desperate bid to escape. But she could then hardly walk and was predictably captured and punished for her temerity.

A grand carnival of sexual insult was arranged. One Bijlee Singh, assistant pradhan and Parsanath's right hand man, and Phool Singh, another heavy weight, were placed in charge of special effects. They cropped her hair, garlanded her with a neck-lace [sic] of shoes. Painted half her face with black ink and half with lime, stripped her, smeared her body with red paint, sat her on an ass and paraded her four hours through every lane in the locality. The bizarre procession featured amateur music makers heralding the principal exhibit with drums and trumphets. The Pradhan's Bullet motor cycle, symbol of power in the outback, brought up the rear. At any given time, atleast hundred people were involved in the proceedings. [S] was stoned and beaten with lathis all along the 50 km route. She often fell off the ass, only to suffer the indignity of being hauled back by the breasts. Finally she was thrown out of the village and warned never to return.[70]

A local schoolteacher reported this case to the local newspaper after ten days.

This chilling account has been cited here to indicate the manner in which legal discourse discursively produces the abject body by anchoring terror in normative categories of the carnival, that is, bizarre processions, special effects, amateur music makers, and the participation of crowds in the proceedings. The genealogy of the description of women being paraded has been stabilized in law and popular discourse in India such that this violence is domesticated through the normalizing categories of 'parades', 'proceedings', and 'processions'.

The charge sheet is revealing.[71] Even though some of the men who orchestrated this terrible violence were subsequently charged, they were not charged on the ground of gangrape or rioting. Rather, they were with breach of public peace, for outraging a woman's modesty, and illegally detaining a married woman. The most telling evocation is the application of s. 508, IPC. Section 508 states:

> …whoever voluntarily causes or attempts to cause any person to do anything which that person is not legally bound to do, or to omit to do anything which he is legally entitled to do, by inducing or attempting to induce that person to believe that he or any person in

whom he is interested will be rendered by some act of the offender an object of Divine displeasure if he does not do the thing which it is the object of the offender to cause him to do, or if he does the thing which is the object of the offender to cause him to omit, shall be punished with imprisonment of either description for a term which may extend to one year, or with fine, or both (cited in Ratanlal and Dhirajlal 2001: 714).

The accused were charged for having forced S to do that which she was not legally bound to do, and by inducing S to believe that she will be rendered by some act of the offender an object of divine displeasure if she did not comply. It is startling that the police translated the spectacle of sexual violence as *legitimate* customary punishment. The evocation of the colonial law on divine pleasure assumes a shared discourse amongst the perpetrators, witnesses, and the victim about what constitutes custom and the divine sanction underlying custom. It positions the woman as a complicit subject in these sexual economies of power.

When the matter reached the trial court the victim turned hostile to the case and her application seeking permission to compound the offence was accepted.[72] We are told that S 'specifically stated on oath that nobody had done any insult to her nor had any offence been committed *vis-à-vis* her person nor was she mal-treated [*sic*]'.[73] On 27 September 1991, the accused were acquitted. Dismissing the *habeas corpus* petition, the court further held that:

It cannot be helped observing that from the judgment of the Magistrate it is apparent that the helpless woman has helplessly surrendered to the might of her adversaries. That alone might be the reason why no evidence was forthcoming in such an outrageous case. However, the type of evidence expected to come in such matters may never be forthcoming if normal mode of the role of evidence is followed. What alternative method of investigation or of recording of evidence in order to bring the guilty to book shall have to be taken requires immediate and serious deliberation by those who are responsible for making and enforcing laws and maintaining order in the society. Painfully and with a heavy heart, this petition is dismissed but with not too remote an optimism that necessity being the mother of invention, an appropriate law-net will be thrown to catch such rotten fish. After all, there is a silver lining to the blackest of the clouds.[74]

Judicial horror at the appellate level is displaced since it domesticates the violence in custom as if this were the natural habitat of this form of violence. The painful and heavy heart of the court beats in the patriarchal body of the law. It laments the patriarchy of customary punishment. The object of judicial horror is the failure of state law to preclude the formation of local publics that are embedded in the rule of law. The evocation of *habeas corpus* in this case points to those women who are made object and not brought within such circuits of power.

GENUINE AND FALSE CLAIMS: COMPENSATION TALK

By offering definitions of dignity, the PoA Act is directed equally at bodies and conducts, 'where rights may be understood as another resource that can be used to convince others how to behave' (Hussain 2003: 72). It is not surprising that the Act has become both the site of intense contestation and a site of a politics of resistance. We cannot therefore ignore talk about the Act in the courts, which is equally directed at bodies and conducts. This talk demonstrates a specific 'mentality' towards Dalit and tribal women, which aims to dismantle the govermentalization of access to courts of law. In Gujarat courts, it was commonly believed that Dalit and tribal women lie about being raped to gain compensation. As Hirabhai, the public prosecutor, said to me:

> In the lower communities such as Waghari, Bhangi, in such communities such kinds of cases have become the mother of all false cases. It does not become an issue of honour [*izzat*]; rape is not a big crime. They use rape to teach a lesson to the other person. The social welfare board for OBCs and SCs pay even in the interim. They make false claims to claim benefits. The government does not demand the money back.

Yet again we hear that Dalit and tribal women do not have any honour. The PoA Act itself has become a symbol of the very conflict that the legislation seeks to regulate.[75] When rape is affixed to atrocity, such cases are spoken of as 'the mother of all false claims'. In the words of a government pleader in the Gujarat High Court:

> The women from SC/ST, they come out with this kind of complaint for appropriating money or to take the advantage of the government

policy. The complainant gets compensation straightaway irrespective of what happens in the trial. Firstly, they get compensation and then settle with the one who has actually not committed the crime. They get money from both parties [state and accused]. This is one thing that has to be kept in mind.

Or consider the words of a high court judge:

What do you want to ask me? What kinds of cases or kinds of false cases are filed? Atrocity cases? Why are innocent people convicted because of hue and cry by women's organizations? … In one case, I ultimately acquitted the accused on the grounds that victim's statement was very doubtful—extortion was the sole motive. They are given *ex-gratia* compensation up to 11 lakhs. I even gave directives to the government not to give compensation until the trial is over. … Justice M.P. Thakkar in the Bhogin Bharward case says that once the lady [makes an accusation], it is enough, but in my opinion, these days, [you can] just hurl an allegation and run away with *ex gratia* compensation. It is not enough to rely on the girl's statement. Besides, there are anti-social elements that are taking advantage of this *ex gratia* compensation in the case of rape and get a percentage.

The reference to the *Bhogin Bharward* case,[76] where it was held that corroboration of a raped woman's testimony was not a necessary legal requirement, is now cited as a precedent that hampers justice. The court, in distinguishing between counterfeit claims and genuine claims, sees Dalit or tribal women as authors of extortion. Such a judicial stance was dramatized in a trial in Gujarat, as detailed below.

ATROCITY CRIMINAL CASE No 28 OF 1994

The definitions of dignity directed at bodies and conducts do not alter the structure of the rape trial. I argue here that defence lawyers use the provisions for compensation as a resource to attack the credibility of the victim.[77] *Mohanlal Amarji Marvadi* v. *State of Gujarat*[78] allows us to examine this modality in detail. Mohanlal Amarji Marvadi was convicted along with three co-accused by the city sessions judge in Ahmedabad for committing offences under s. 376 (rape), s. 342 (wrongful confinement), and s. 34 (common intention) of the IPC, and under s. 3(1)(iii) and s. 3(1)(xi) of the PoA Act. The four men were sentenced to suffer rigorous imprisonment for ten years and to pay a fine of Rs 3,000 or to undergo further rigorous imprisonment for six months; and rigorous imprisonment for one year and a fine of Rs 500 or simple imprisonment for one month for the two offences under the PoA Act, respectively. Mohanlal Amarji appealed to the high court, while the other three accused did not. The high court not only acquitted Mohanlal Amarji Marvadi, but also acquitted the three co-accused.

The prosecution's case was that two men who worked as watchmen requested a young Dalit woman to fetch water to their office in Dhaval Estate in Ahmedabad. When the victim arrived, the two men locked her inside the office. She was stripped, gagged, and then raped. The FIR states that one of the men raped her and the other molested her, although the victim testified in court that both the men raped her. The high court did not believe the testimony of the victim, characterizing it as exaggerated. The court excitedly proclaimed that the fact that she refused to undergo a gynaecological examination (the two-finger test) proved that she was fearful that 'her allegation of rape, much apart gang-rape would in that case would stand stripped naked and self-exposed as false!'[79]

Not only did the victim's father refuse to recognize the accused, but also stated that he was financially hard up, and 'he was fed up and tired' by his daughter's conduct. He told the court to release one of the accused, for 'his daughter has made a false complaint against him'.[80] When she was cross-examined, the victim, the court tells us, 'surprisingly admits that her father was very greedy by the nature in the matter of money. She has admitted that for making such a complaint, Rs 10,000/- are [sic] given to her. She has also admitted that to take the money, her father was pressurising her. However, she has stated that she has not received the said money.'[81]

The court then requested the prosecutor to file an affidavit to the district backward class welfare officer to find out how much compensation had been awarded. This officer filed an affidavit to state that no amount was paid to the victim. Accepting this statement on oath, the Gujarat High Court observed in dismay that the state government had increased the amount of compensation from Rs 10,000 to Rs 50,000. Rather than implementing the Act, the court questioned the rationale for 'awarding compensation and that too such huge astronomical amount' to a witness who was not 'dependable'.[82]

The court elaborated its concern that 'in a given case on the basis of totally false, frivolous and vexatious allegation, if so-called victims of rape are readily compensated', such cases will not only bring 'bad name to their entire community', but will simultaneously 'undermine public revenue'.[83] The court recommended that '1/10th of the total ex-gratia compensation as immediate relief' should be awarded and 'rest of the amount be put in any nationalized Bank for two or three years and the quarterly interest accrued thereupon can be given to the victim till the case is favourably decided in his/her favour!!'[84] The evisceration of the rule of compensation produces guidelines that enunciate hyper-technicalities, which make new distinctions between documented and undocumented victims.

DOCUMENTED AND UNDOCUMENTED VICTIMS

So far we have seen how the judicial interpretation of the PoA Act creates the very grounds on which the specificity of sexual violence as atrocity may be rejected. Now I turn to the question of evidence. How is the identity of the victim or the accused proved in the first instance? How can bias be determined through evidence, motive, context, and defence? One example of the techniques of disqualification is through the very certificatory practices of the state. In *Dasarathi Sahukan* v. *State*,[85] the sessions judge at Koraput had convicted the accused, finding them guilty of gangrape read with s. 3(2)(v) PoA Act, awarding rigorous imprisonment for life. The Orissa High Court confirmed the conviction of gangrape but stated that atrocity could not be proved on the grounds that the victim did not possess a caste[86] certificate to prove that she belonged to the Kondho tribe.

To further explore the question of certification, let us turn to a Supreme Court judgment delivered in January 2011 in the context of a stabilized and 'ritualized' form of punishing a woman for caste transgression.[87] This was a case involving a twenty-five-year-old pregnant Bhil woman (listed as a Scheduled Tribe in Maharashtra) who was assaulted, stripped, and paraded. We are told that she was in an 'illicit' sexual relationship with the landlord's son Vikram and that they had a child. Vikram's family, opposed to his relationship with a woman they considered socially inferior, arranged his marriage with a woman of their own caste. The four accused men, Vikram's relatives, went to her house to force her to break off her relationship with Vikram: they stripped her naked, abused her, beat her, and then paraded her. She was dragged before the shop of the Sarpanch of the village and was verbally abused—there were around hundred villagers at this time watching this spectacle. At this time, Vikram came and rescued her by giving her his *lungi* to cover herself. He then fetched her clothes and she covered herself by the roadside. Both of them went to the police to file a complaint. During the trial, almost everyone turned hostile except the victim. Vikram testified that he was in a relationship with the victim and that they had a child but denied knowledge about what happened in order to save his relatives.

The four men were found guilty under s. 452 (house trespass), s. 354 (outraging modesty), s. 323 (voluntarily causing hurt), and s. 506 (2) (criminal intimidation to impute unchastity to a woman) read with s. 34 (act done by several persons in common intention) IPC, and sentenced to rigorous imprisonment for six months and a fine of Rs 1,000. The accused were also sentenced to rigorous imprisonment for one year and fined Rs 100 for the common intention to outrage the modesty of the tribal woman. They were further convicted for violating s. 3(1)(xi) of the PoA Act and sentenced to rigorous imprisonment for one year and fine of Rs 100.

When the accused appealed their conviction, the Bombay High Court noted that they were powerful men in the village and it was not surprising that the witnesses turned hostile. The victim's testimony was found to be truthful and convincing. However, the Bombay High Court acquitted the accused of the charge of atrocity. It also set aside the trial court's ruling on the fine and ordered each of the accused to pay Rs 5,000 to the victim. The court believed that the compensation was inadequate 'considering that a lady was paraded naked on the village road on broad daylight. So, dishonour of a woman should have been taken seriously by the Additional Sessions Judge'.[88] It is a puzzle why the court did not minimally remark on the fact that the accused were not charged with committing an offence under s. 3(1)(iii) of the PoA Act on stripping and parading. In effect, the Bombay High Court did not recognize parading as atrocity but compensated the victim for the dishonour caused to her, by awarding her Rs 20,000—*as if* upper caste women are also punished for sexual transgressions through identical forms of sexual humiliation by tribal or dalit men.

Why did the high court not confirm the findings on atrocity? The court admitted that all the witnesses testified that the victim was Bhil and the cause of the violence emanated from caste norms, which forbade the alliance of a Dalit or tribal woman with an upper-caste man. Despite this evidence, the court said that the case for atrocity could not be made because the investigating officer did not procure a caste certificate. On appeal, the Supreme Court assailed the high court for setting aside the conviction under the PoA Act. I quote:

> We are surprised that the conviction of the accused under the *Scheduled Cases and Scheduled Tribes (Prevention of Atrocities) Act, 1989* was set aside on hyper technical grounds that the Caste Certificate was not produced and investigation by a Police Officer of the rank of Deputy Superintendent of Police was not done. These appear to be only technicalities and hardly a ground for acquittal, but since no appeal has been filed against that part of the High Court judgment, we are now not going into it.[89]

Such hyper-technicalities mark the distinction between an undocumented victim and a documented victim. It is the responsibility of the investigating officer to procure the *jati* (community) certificate,[90] which is issued by the government to citizens to establish their status as Scheduled Castes or Scheduled Tribes.[91] When the prosecution does not bother to furnish a caste certificate, an acquittal follows.[92] The court demands the prosecution prove that the victim is a 'documented victim'. A documented victim is a citizen who not only has to posses certification that she belongs to the SC or ST category but one whose documentary evidence is brought on record by a police, and authenticated in the courtroom. The evidence of caste domination must be materialized through the documentary practices of the state. The legal subject as dalit or tribal is a product of the politics of such documentary practices. This hyper-technicality is read as bias.

The Supreme Court further critiqued the very structure of the legal argument made on behalf of the accused on appeal as evidence of bias. The accused's counsel had argued that the victim's torn clothes produced as evidence ought to be disregarded since 'the people belonging to the Bhil community live in torn clothes as they do not have proper clothes to wear.'[93] The Supreme Court sharply castigated such an allegation and treated this argument as evidence of the 'mentality of the accused who regard tribal people as inferior or sub-humans. This is totally unacceptable in modern India'.[94] The court went on to script a history of dignity for the Bhils by asserting that the 'Bhils are probably the descendants of some of the original inhabitants of India known as the "aborigines" or Scheduled Tribes (*Adivasis*), who presently comprise of only about 8% of the population of India. The rest 92% of the population of India consists of descendants of immigrants. Thus India is broadly a country of immigrants like North America'.[95] The court further stated that 'despite this horrible oppression on them, the tribals of India have generally (though not invariably) retained a higher level of ethics than the non-tribals in our country. They normally do not cheat, tell lies, and do other misdeeds, which many non-tribals do. They are generally superior in character to the non-tribals. It is time now to undo the historical injustice to them'.[96] This promise to undo historic injustice seems to assure a radically new jurisprudence—in this case, we begin with the judges analysing the structure of a legal argument as evidence of a 'biased mentality'—and describing tribals as *adivasis*.

THE POLITICAL ICONOGRAPHY OF DIFFERENCE

The institution of 'hyper-technicalities' is constitutive of a political iconography of difference, as illustrated by a case study I documented during my research. The ethnography here is limited to interviews with the prosecutor, the survivor's father, and the survivor. I could not attend the trial hearings as I had to leave after eighteen months of fieldwork. I represent the case history on the basis of court documents alongside ethnographic interviews. This is followed by a brief account of what happened on appeal.

THE CASE HISTORY

Dhirubhai worked as a compounder in a government-run *ayurvedic* dispensary in a village, Doad, in Dhandhuka Taluka, Ahmedabad District. He belonged to the Vankar caste, which is a scheduled caste (Franco et al. 2000). Dhirubhai's father was a dealer in cloth in his own village, and died when he was young. Dhirubhai married after he got a job at the age of thirty-two. He had lived in Doad for ten months following his appointment in the government *ayurvedic* dispensary. At this time, he had two children: a ten-year-old daughter, Kavita, and a one-and-a-half-year-old son. Kavita studied in a boarding school in a neighbouring town. She returned to the village for an extended vacation during the festival of Janamashthami.[97] Kavita's friend Payal lived near her house. Payal's family belonged to the Koli Patel community. Her father, Jayantbhai Patel, was a carpenter by profession. In 1993, one afternoon she went down to Payal's house. Her mother was at home and her father at the dispensary. Kavita was hoping to go with Payal to watch the marriage procession of the groom on horseback (*var ghoda*) through the village that day. Payal was not at home. Taking advantage of the opportunity, Payal's father raped Kavita. When Dhirubhai found out what had happened, he went to the police station to file a complaint. Initially, the police refused to register the case. The prosecutor told me that the police later registered the complaint as an attempt to rape Kavita, and for outraging her modesty under the PoA Act. It was when the case was committed to the sessions court that the charge was altered to rape. The accused was tried for offences punishable under ss. 342 (wrongful confinement), 376 (rape), 506 (2) (criminal intimidation with intent to dishonour a woman) and s. 3(1)(xi) PoA Act. When the case came on trial, the accused had absconded. It was almost three and a half years since the complaint had been lodged.

THE PROSECUTOR'S BRIEF: A 'WEAK' CASE

It was late morning in March 1997 when Hirabhai's colleague, Mr Rajput, beckoned me into his chamber. He introduced me to the family as a researcher, and said to me in English, 'They are SC. A Patel man raped the girl.' I remember that Dhirubhai got up as I walked in and insisted that I take the chair he had vacated. He got himself another chair and sat next to his wife, who held a baby in her arms. Two children, a girl and a boy, sat besides their parents. Rajput began to speak to me in Gujarati,

> Look at these papers. They are so weak. They complained on the same day but the police did not note their complaint [*fariyad*] for three days. When they did, they did not even mention the fact of rape.

They have just said that when the man took off his *lungi*[98] and tied a cotton towel [*rumal*], she screamed and the mother came in … Preetiben Parmar [the woman prosecutor to whom the matter had come to] convinced the judicial magistrate about the offence, then the charge was framed. These were weak papers. There is no medical evidence. It was all lost. Police would not get her examined medically.

Dhirubhai described to me what happened at the police station that evening.

We all saw this so we went straight to the police station [*chowki*]. Our daughter has been raped in this way. No one listened to what we had to say. They said you should not make a false complaint. We went back in the night at 9 o'clock. They were engrossed in their party [*mehfil*]. Others came along too. 'Where should we go to search at night? Come tomorrow in the morning.' They found him the next day. They said: 'first, let your daughter identify him'. My daughter in front of everyone identified him: 'This man [*bhai*] raped me'. And the policemen started the case.

Why did the police bother to lodge a complaint at all when they refused to accept the complaint that the perpetrator raped Kavita? The police investigation, which the high court diligently reminds us that a Deputy Superintendent of Police (DSP) did not conduct, 'weakened' the case. We find that delay, and withholding of information from the complainant is deployed as a technique that weakens the possibilities of prosecuting rape, and simultaneously allows the police to maintain the appearance of investigating the crime.

I rely on Dhirubhai's account of Doad, the village where this case was registered. In his narrative, the two significant caste groups in the village were the Koli Patels, the 'hot headed' elements of the village, and the Darbars, who wielded political power through the local decision-making body, the *gram panchayat*. He said:

They could not appoint any nurse at the PHC [Primary Health Centre] for the last 15 years. They would call the nurses on the pretext of asking their assistance for deliveries and then rape them. Yes, in this PHC all this happens, that's why till date they cannot appoint any nurse there and the PHC runs without a nurse. Some eight to ten years ago, one PSI was even murdered in a crowded market near a crossroad. Even though he had been murdered, nothing happened to those people. These were Koli Patels [farming middle caste]. The

Darbars [Rajput caste community] have a very close relationship with the Koli Patels. If you were to go out after seven or eight in the evening, good staff [*karamcharis*] would not venture out. The Vaniyas [merchant caste] set up their shops elsewhere. The village started to empty out because of these influential and hot headed [*mathebhare*] elements. The village headman [*sarpanch*] of the gram *panchayat* is a Darbar. I went and spoke to the village headman when the incident happened. The village headman did not accept our petition.

How then did the prosecutor frame such contexts of policing? The prosecutor does not represent this as a terrifying situation of caste domination. Instead he said to me, 'Dhirubhai told me that Harijan women are really beautiful. They are locked up because Patel men rape and abduct them. It is normal.' For the prosecutor, it was the beauty of Dalit women around which the normality of rape is articulated, emphasizing the sexualized fantasies normalizing the rape culture of the dominant castes. In contrast, Dhirubhai named the systemic oppression of Dalit women and children by the dominant caste men belonging to the Koli Patel community as a context that explained the production of 'weak' papers and the abrogation of his legal rights as a complainant. Moreover, we must remember that 'law cannot be divorced from ideologies that make control of law a prize' (Nader 2002: 117). The *fariyad* is not a single accusation against a man but signifies an affront to an entire community. In Dhirubhai's words,

We were attacked two to three times. These were attempts to murder. The staff at the government's dispensary ran away. There was no one present in the clinic. Then I petitioned the government [*sarkar*]—'Sir, do what you have to but this job is my life'. The government then transferred me to Rajkot. The police said, 'write as we tell you to'. We were subjected to baseless abuse and threats. Then the *panchnamma* was done. They did not write anything. They came to our house. I had preserved my daughter's clothes soaked with blood for two days; no one came to collect the clothes. I showed them the clothes. They said 'you must not talk about all this'. ... The police did not write that rape happened this way. We really tried to register the complaint that such a thing has happened to our daughter but what did these people do? ... They submitted papers in which they have not mentioned a word like rape [*balatkar*]. [Dhirubhai fell silent.] Then they charge-sheeted. The case has not even come on remand, not on beating [*mar-jhur*]. The police protected him as if he was their relative.

Dhirubhai sent Kavita to her mother's sister's house after one attempt to kidnap her.

Dhirubhai's expectation that the accused would be beaten up rested on his knowledge of the techniques of policing. Dhirubhai constructs himself as a complainant by claiming knowledge of the techniques of producing evidence. We know that 'courts of law are spaces in which a victim becomes a plaintiff by acquiring the means of proving that damage has been done to him' (Lyotard, cited in Das 1995: 129). By this, I do not mean that Dhirubhai reproduces an accurate understanding of procedural or evidentiary law. Rather, he knew that it is necessary to produce documents as a means to prove injury. He articulated this poignantly when he talked about what happened when Kavita was taken to a nearby Government Hospital after a delay of thirty-six hours. It was middle of the night when the police escorted the father and child.

> I myself am in medical line. I know that there should be a PM [post mortem], a medical check up, its certificate, and the case is based on this. For the medical check up the doctor asked me for Rs 10,000. I did not have Rs 10,000. He said, 'I am giving a certificate like this.' I said, 'Give whatever you want to give. You are powerful. What you want to write you will write.' They didn't give us a certificate stating that she had been actually raped. We still do not know what is written in the certificate today.[99]

Dhirubhai's despair follows not knowing what was written in the medico-legal certificate (what he calls PM report), for the power to certify constitutes the means to prove injury.

THE POLICE STATEMENT

In a statutory rape case, the Supreme Court raised the issue of judicial trust in police documents.[100] I quote:

> We feel that it is an archaic notion that the actions of a police officer should be approached with initial distrust. We are aware that such a notion was lavishly entertained during the British period and policemen also knew about it. Its hangover persisted during post independence years but it is time now to start placing at least initial trust on the actions and documents made by the police. At any rate the court cannot start with the presumption that police records are

untrustworthy. As a proposition of law the presumption should be the other way around.[101]

It is noteworthy that the distrust in the documentary practices of the state is constructed here as a colonial hangover rather than seen as a systemic way by which the state produces practices of legality/illegality and legibility/illegibility (see Das 1995). By this, I also mean the practical operations of power that actualize corruption, political pressure by powerful offenders, and systemic bias. The issue of trust in police documents begs the question: what is the political economy of this trust? How do complainants read police writing? Kavita's statement provides us with some clues:

> My name: Kavitaben Dhirubhai's daughter Caste: Parmar; Age: 10 years; Occupation: Student; Res.: Doad
>
> On being questioned in person, I get written that I live at the aforesaid address with my mother–father. My father works as a compounder in a government dispensary. I study in 4th standard and my father [baba] has sent me to a village named [O] to study at the [S] School. There I live in a hostel. On the occasion of janamashthami, as holidays fell I came to [D] to my parent's house on [date] 1993.
>
> On [date] 1993 in the afternoon I went to call my friend, Payal, who lives behind the dispensary. Then while going to her house, her father caught hold of me by my hand took me into his house and closed the door of the house. At this time, there was no one in the house. And he said to me, 'Girl [chokri], lie down on this bed'. He showed me a knife. On being threatened, I laid down on the bed. And Payal's father was wearing a lungi. That he took off and wore a cotton towel [rumal].

The statement goes on to say that Kavita's mother heard her screaming when she was looking for her and found her before she was raped. The elements of coercing Kavita into the house are well laid out. However, this description falls short as the statement describes how the accused removed his clothes to wear a rumal (cotton towel) instead. As Dhirubhai said to me, 'Sister [Ben], it is so strange. Everyone knows that a full lungi when hitched up becomes a towel. How can they write a complaint [fariyad] like this?' Dhirubhai's sense of incredulity does not arise only from the fact that the police did not register the complaint of rape but how they wrote it. While the Supreme Court advocates trust in police documents, it does not deliberate on how police documents are written and how police documents can inspire trust.

BIG MEN: PICTURES OF CHILDHOOD

I return to the prosecutor's chamber now. To prepare for the trial, Rajput interviewed Kavita. After Kavita left, he called me to his chamber and said to me,

> It was *Janamashthami*, she was going to fetch her friend when the man pulled her in and raped her. She was not saying the proper words, said, and took off clothes, and climbed on top of me, and started to move. I asked a lady advocate to tutor her to say the exact words, otherwise the definition of rape, the act of rape is not covered.

What are these 'exact words'? I reproduce below an account of Kavita's conversation with me to indicate the linguistic burden she must carry, for later in the trial, her words would be characterized as 'exaggerated'. I have translated the following excerpt from Gujarati.

> PB: You have come earlier for the case? Do you want to talk about what happened?
>
> K: I had gone to call her [Payal] to her house. I knocked at the door at that time [he] pulled my hand and pulled me inside and showed me a knife and then [he] made me lie on the cot and took off my clothes and then he took off his *lungi* that he was wearing, and after that slept over me and then you know the place from where [they] urinate, that inserted in my place of urination. So I started screaming a lot. So he put his hand on my mouth and then it started to pain a lot and ... Then I came to consciousness. Then my clothes were soaked with blood and then he said 'don't tell anybody, I will kill your papa and your mummy and your brother'. Said like this—'You and your mother and you come back tomorrow' and said like this then.[102]
>
> PB: Did you tell your mummy?
>
> K: When I was beaten then I told my pappa. Then took me to his house. He was not there; he had run away, there was a lock on his door, then [we went to the] police. Then the police did not take the petition [*arji*].[103] Got the medical investigation [*tapas*]. We had gone to the hospital in the night; there we had done the medical investigation.

Pauses.

PB: Did it pain a lot?

K: Yes, I was in a lot of pain, after they took me to the hospital they gave me medicines and it became better.

PB: Now do you feel better?

K: Yes.

PB: Do you go to school? Which standard?

K: Sixth.

PB: And what all do you play?

K: At home, I do house work—utensils and clothes.

PB: Do you have friends in Rajkot from school? Do you play with them?

K: If they come home, then I play. Otherwise, I stay at home and wash utensils.

PB: Do you feel scared here?

K: Yes, everybody is so big.

PB: Do not be scared. If you feel afraid I am here, come to me, ok?

K: Okay (*smiles*).

Kavita's experience of pain was relevant as long as it caused her to scream. Her fear was pertinent as long as she mentioned the knife. Coercion, then even in the case of a child is made to appear realistic, if the knife and scream as signs of force and resistance are emphasized. That the man was much bigger and stronger than her was not elicited as an aspect that could be made real in law. Kavita's awareness that men in the court were big, powerful, and influential, and that this scared her, brought to language her experience and the way it related to the world around her. It was the bigness of men that stood out in her expression of what caused her terror.

The picture of childhood that emerges is one that is lost. Play was banished. She could not say that she had played even the most common games children play at her age. She drew images of listless disinterest about school. She was straddled into adulthood by helping her mother with housework and with her siblings. The event folds into her sociality that she bore witness to the despair experienced by her parents as well as the cross talk between adults about the case. Never quite treated as an adult, she nonetheless carried the burden of behaving like an one. Her silences and her attempts to represent her experience in language fell by the wayside of the crosstalk of despair that gripped her parents. Although the prosecutor was sympathetic, empathy was not a mode of address. The law does not address trauma directly and on its own terms, but acts upon it in its categories to make it real or unreal.

POLITICAL SUBJECTIVITY: PROMISE OF JUSTICE

The process by which law conserves itself is founded on a different order of violence against litigants, which Dhirubhai experienced when the defence lawyer asked him to compromise the case in open court. Compromise is quintessentially what Philips calls 'spoken law'. Philips has argued that it is a mistake to think of judges as mere implementers of the law. The source of this misrepresentation, she argues, 'begins with the equation of law with written law' (Philips 1998: 123). Rather than thinking of judges as 'mere conduits of written law', their speech in courtrooms and outside remains central to the interpretation of law and judicial outcomes for 'spoken law has a life of its own, logic and rationales of its own that are separate from and cannot be found in written law' (1998: 123). Consider Dhirubhai's words:

> Those people had even come to compromise. The next day his party came to compromise. I said I do not want to compromise, for my daughter. I want to fight the case. I have been fighting the case till today. There is no question of compromise. In the presence of the judge, the lawyer [*vakil*] said to me, 'Why don't you compromise?' I said to the judge, 'In your presence, is it right of him to talk of compromise?' The judge scolded him. 'This is a court; in a court you cannot use such words, go out and talk.' Then he came to talk to me. I said, 'If it were your mother, sister or daughter, would you talk of compromise in the court?' When I used these words, he looked at me and went inside. I said 'no' to the judge, 'We are not going to reach a compromise of any sort'.

It was Dhirubhai's evocation of kinship that silenced the defence lawyer, and not his reminder that it is not permissible for the defence lawyer to talk to him about compromise.[104] Here, I wish to evoke Strathern's (1992) argument that the 'very desire to put facts "into their context" is a merographic move. The context, by virtue of not being equivalent with the thing put into it, will illuminate the thing from a particular angle' (Strathern 1992: 73). Thus, using kinship to illuminate the wrongs of the defence lawyer in suggesting compromise is a merographic move. Yet one may ask why is kinship deployed? Why is it a culturally effective linguistic strategy? The defence lawyer is silenced by the argument that his gaze does not see the raped survivor *as if* she were his daughter. He is critiqued for adopting a distanced professional stance as a lawyer and therefore, a voyeuristic model of upper-caste masculinity, which affirms rape. The merographic move is productive of shame and silence as the defence lawyer is reminded of his membership to society *via* kinship, as a father.

In narrating how Dhirubhai invested his desire for justice in the trial, we may ask, what did the disclosure mean to him and how did law re-define his subjectivity? The disclosure, Dhirubhai insisted, must be read in a context of threat and fear. Here, we find that the concerns about stigma and its disability do not frame disclosure. 'I have not thought about it. I often feel like this, that we, our family, should simply commit suicide… We have not met one person who has had a sympathetic word for us.' It does not pave way to a socio-legal route where the effects of stigma as social death can be negotiated or managed in the future. The effect of the police 'weakening' the case, by not writing his complaint, denies him the possibility of imagining a future for his daughter and his family. Rather the brute here-and-now tarries with finding death.

Merry rightly observes that 'despite a rich literature on rights in social movements, we know relatively little about why and when a person adopts rights talk' (2003: 346). She argues that:

> The adoption of a rights consciousness requires experiences with the legal system that confirm this subjectivity. Rights-defined selves depend on encounters with police, prosecutors, judges, and probation officers that reflect back this identity. Indications that the problem is trivial, that the victim does not really have these rights, or that the offender does not deserve punishment undermine this subjectivity (Merry 2003: 344).

Dhirubhai's encounter with the law does not mirror the political subjectivity promised by the PoA Act. His encounters with the law redefine his subjectivity in deeply wounding ways where the making of subjectivity through law enters the terrain of the abject; the voice of caste substitutes the desire for life.[105]

> D: I have been coming here hearing [*muddat*] after hearing (*said in utter resignation*).
>
> PB: You have shown a great deal of courage.
>
> D: Many a times I feel that I should with my family commit suicide, really, swear by my mother. [He was in tears]. I have to endure a great deal to come here. I have come since yesterday. Yesterday I left in the morning at six. I reached here with these children at nine in the night. This is my state. Every other day, there is an adjournment. I don't even get a travel allowance from the government. I have petitioned every director, chief minister, people in the government, everyone. It was the Congress government in power at that time. I have given written petitions of this incident. I have given one to the Crime Branch as well.

Dhirubhai tells us (not unlike Hasinaben) that as a complainant, he should not have to bear the burden of being courageous. The loss of faith in justice folds into Dhirubhai's inner life like a wound.

The accused had absconded and did not appear for the hearing on that day either. After we had waited the entire day for the case to be heard, Dhirubhai learnt at 4.30 in the evening that the accused, on bail, had not made an appearance. The court issued a warrant for the accused. Dhirubhai was advised not to bring his family on the next adjournment. I did not meet him again. Upon my return to Delhi, I wrote to Dhirubhai including in my letter the names of lawyers who could help him. His reply found me after I finished fieldwork. I reproduce excerpts from his letter below, translated from Gujarati.

> Sister, after my daughter's case I am shattered mentally. I filed my daughter's case in Doad but ever since then until this day it is as if I have witnessed some scenes enacted by a theatrical company. I have lost faith in justice completely. When my case was first opened at the hands of the judge at that time I witnessed [*darshan*] the first rays of dawn. And, I experienced a surge of joy and happiness or so I thought I felt. But, after P. Judge was transferred, some other judge came. I could not foresee that I would get any kind of help in this case.
>
> My wife, my daughter, and I were present. And our testimony was taken. We were asked extremely obscene questions. At the time of my testimony, whenever I uttered a word they refused to write what I said. But, when the other lawyer asked anything then interpreting this

as the truth this was noted down in the judge's record. I did not feel that the judge sir [*saheb*] had any time to take notice of the complaint in our tears and our poverty.

To this day, we have built this hope that in the court we will get true justice and I knocked at the doors of the court so that those demonic men who exploit people as poor and naïve [*seedhha*] as me no longer do so. Despite this, I felt that the result was zero. I keep thinking day and night that if this is the state of India then I wonder till how long the country will stay together in one thread in unity? Even after one month since my wife's, my daughter's, and my testimony was taken. There is no news of what the court's justice is. I am completely exhausted mentally and have become a debtor.

Many a times at time the thought of committing suicide crosses my mind, that this world is only full of hypocrisy. What does one get—disrepute and disappointment?

Did I understand what the quest for justice could mean for someone who was denied the means to prove injury? The first judge who heard his hearing before being transferred brought him hope that they would get a just hearing. He describes this as a sacred vision (*darshan*) and an experience of happiness. In the court of the next judge, Dhirubhai experienced despair when the lawyers and the judge did not seem to hear his words, or write what he said. The impress of the legal process marks his subjectivity. The suspicion they are held in, further marked by what he called 'obscene' questions, converts the law into a Kafkaesque experience. Making their suffering seem unreal, the court appears to be like a theatre company, and the law stages his punishment. It puts him on trial. The experience of justice in its otherness is absolute. The evidence of his suffering is not recognizable in law.

The trial court repeatedly echoes the argument of the defence that the charge of rape was retrospective, exaggerated, and false to enhance the seriousness of the offence. The trial court found the accused guilty on the following counts. The first ground was outraging the child's modesty under s. 3(1)(xi) PoA Act, and the accused was sentenced to rigorous imprisonment for four years and a fine of Rs 500 or imprisonment of thirty days. He was also found guilty of violating s. 342 IPC (wrongful confinement), sentenced to rigorous imprisonment for one year and fine amounting to Rs 500 or imprisonment of thirty days. Finally, he was found guilty of violating the offence under s. 506 IPC (criminal intimidation), sentenced to rigorous imprisonment of one year and a fine amounting to Rs 500 or imprisonment of thirty days. For violating s. 354 IPC (outraging modesty), the accused was not given a separate sentence as he was punished under s. 3(1)(xi) PoA Act. This judgment was pronounced in 1998.[106]

The appeal was filed in the Gujarat High Court in 1998. The accused was in jail for nine months before he was let out on bail. The appeal was listed thirty-five times in the Gujarat High Court from 1998 to 2011. In 2011, the Gujarat High Court in its oral order quashed and set aside the charges under the PoA Act while upholding the charges of criminal intimidation and wrongful confinement under the IPC. However, the sentence was reduced to the imprisonment already undergone by the accused. The court observed that in this case the police investigation was carried out by a police officer, below the rank of a DSP. The court held that the trial judge committed a 'grave error' in not appreciating the rules for investigation as defined under the PoA Act Rules. Hence the judgment holding the appellant-accused guilty of atrocity was quashed and set aside. The conviction of wrongful confinement and criminal intimidation was upheld but the sentence was mitigated to the term of imprisonment the accused had undergone.

The routinization of such forms of judicial interpretation in the Gujarat courts allows us to make two observations. First, this insistence on correct police procedure is selective. In the 2002 cases, the Gujarat judiciary did not accept that the police procedure was vitiated due to procedural lapses or evidence of bias (see Grover 2002). Yet in reference to the PoA Act, the Gujarat courts quash or dismiss the conviction of atrocity on the grounds that the police investigation is biased since it is not supervised by a DSP. In other words, if exception was marked by the suspension of procedure in the context of the mass rape during 2002, it must be read alongside the institution of hyper-technicalities in everyday contexts of rape of Dalit and tribal women in Gujarat. Hyper-technicality itself suggests excess, which manifests as a specific form of marking exception. Second, the politics of producing a 'weak' case, which implicates the police, is obfuscated by such hyper-technical readings of the PoA Act. The courts do not recognize the fact that when a case is not investigated by the DSP, it may be read as evidence of a biased mentality and policing be understood as the means by which the governmental apparatus permitting Dalits and tribals to access courts of law is systemically disarticulated.

***

I have argued that the implementation of the PoA Act leans heavily towards dismantling the governmental apparatus that the Act brings into force through the routine refusal to name sexual violence as atrocity. I have identified several strategies by which the PoA Act is hollowed out. Standardized judicial narratives distinguishing between mere rape and atrocity rest on stylized pictures of atrocity. Yet, collective and spectacular violence, attendant on a series of attacks, reprisals and complaints, have been classified as revenge rather than atrocity. Far from converting 'the Dalit's structural negativity within the caste order into positive political content, and to make historic suffering and humiliation—the experience of being "ground down" and "broken"—central to the identity of Dalit', policing and prosecuting atrocity by and large is invested in denying political subjectivity to dalit women' (Rao 2009: xii). When women like Bhanwari Devi or Surekha Bhotmange are identified as political subjects who author change, they are situated outside male-defined social order. The denial of political subjectivity finds dramatic performance in the special trial, communicating symbolically the inability of law to protect the rights of sexually brutalized Dalit and tribal women. The historic forms of discrimination against tribal and Dalit women have not inaugurated a new jurisprudence by treating women's trauma on its own terms. Instead, the constitutional meanings ascribed to atrocity are inverted by instituting a series of hyper-technicalities. It is these hyper-technicalities that create an exception, instituting conditions of impunity and immunity.

The rape of all female children does not produce judicial horror, for some children are seen as occupying the space outside the normative. This has a further implication—the assumption that these women and children deserve the violence of rape, for they blur the very point at which difference is located. As Parker et al. (1992) have pointed out, the efficacy of such an iconography of difference lies in the fact that these are actual experiences of women and children. Dhirubhai correctly recognized that in making his daughter's rape unreal, the iconography of difference gains its efficacy. The political iconography of difference is authored violently by the law's broken promise. The legal discourse on rape as/and atrocity then scripts a conversation between men of unequal status, wherein rape as sexualized dominance is enacted, displayed, and communicated to the men considered inferior among other men.

Notes

1. Lok Sabha debates, Short Duration Discussions (RU: Regarding Atrocities on Dalits), 12 March 2003, p. 29, available at http://indiankanoon. org/doc/452722, accessed on 12 October 2011.

2. The opposition to the PoA Act is extremely complex, ranging from the Hindu Right's refusal to implement the law in Maharashtra, a distrust of all special laws as diminishing the rights of the accused to a fair trial, to the argument for amending the PoA Act, making a case for caste neutrality in the Mirchpur trial in 2011. For instance, 'in Maharashtra the Shiv Sena, which represents the Brahmanical ethos par excellence, made it an election issue in 1995 to recommend to the Central Government to repeal the Act. True to its promise, after coming into power, it began withdrawing over 1,100 cases registered under the Act alleging that these cases were false and were registered out of personal bias' (Saxena 2004: 113). As distinct from this position, we often meet the argument that all protectionist laws allow for the abuse of power. This argument often derives from the experience of anti-terror laws. I believe that the commonplace characterization of the PoA Act as an exceptional law on the same register as anti-terror laws produces incommensurable comparisons. True, protectionist and security laws mark a departure from routine law in being characterized legally as special legislations. Here, the similarity falters. Anti-terror laws 'interlock' with ordinary criminal law, as Ujjwal Kumar Singh has argued, which leads to the 'withdrawal of existing safeguards and dilution of evidence, decreases the threshold of proving guilt, encourages shoddy investigation and tilts the trial disproportionately in favour of the prosecution' (2006: 123). The anti-terror apparatus is thus deployed to identify, stigmatize and target 'suspect communities' (see U. Singh 2007).

3. Rao believes that 'exceptionalism is written into the Indian Constitution', which scripts Dalits and *adivasi*s 'as exceptional subjects' and 'legal exception … as a form of political inclusion' (2009: 24). She derives her understanding of exception from Giorgio Agamben, for whom 'the state of exception is thus not the chaos that preceeds order but rather

the situation that results from its suspension' (1998: 18). Agamben further states that 'since "there is no rule that is applicable to chaos", chaos must first be included in the juridical order through a creation of a zone of indistinction between outside and inside, chaos and normal situation—the state of exception' (1998: 19). Critiquing this view of exception, following Michael Foucault, Hussain argues that emergency or exception institutes a series of hyper-legalities marking 'the proliferation of regulations tactics that characterize the governmentality of the modern state and the operations of modern power' (2007: 734). Hussain argues that 'the difficulty in using the theoretical paradigms of the state of exception is that its specific substantive and connotative associations are ones of decision and declaration, abeyance and suspension and an emptying out of set of rules from the governance. Even at Guantánamo, which seems such a clear example of a camp that is an extra-legal zone, subject only to executive decree we find not only an emptying out of law but an abundant use of technical distinctions, different regulations and multiple invocations of authority' (2007: 740).

4. Dr Rajendra Kumari Bajpai introduced the Bill. She was then Minister of State of a new Ministry of Welfare introduced during the Rajiv Gandhi led government.

5. Lok Sabha Debates 1994: 78.

6. Lok Sabha Debates 1994: 101, emphasis added.

7. Lok Sabha Debates 1994: 62.

8. Section 2(1)(c) of the PoA Act specifies that SCs and STs shall have the meanings assigned to them respectively under clause (24) and clause (25) of Article 366 of the Constitution.

9. Saksena (2010) shows that in Uttar Pradesh Dalits are charged by the police for offences under the PoA Act, especially when such offences are committed by a group of people cutting across caste groups.

10. See *T. Taranath & Anr* v. *State of AP & Ors* (1999) (1) Crimes 188 (cited in Naval 2001: 75).

11. Take, for example, the struggle to set up a special court in the aftermath of the mass murder of Dalits by upper-caste men belonging to the Reddy caste in Tsundur, Andhra Pradesh, in 1991. Balagopal notes that this is in sharp contrast with the implementation of the Terrorist and Disruptive Activities (Prevention) Act, 1985 (TADA), an erstwhile anti-terror law, wherein the state designated special courts 'within two *months* of the passage of the act by parliament, and upwards of 15,000 persons have been sent to jail for TADA offences' (1991: 2403, emphasis in original).

12. Scheduled Caste and Scheduled Tribes (Prevention of Atrocities) Gujarat Rules, 1995, available at http://www.sje.gujarat.gov.in/showpage.aspx?contentid=1630&lang=English, accessed on 20 August 2011.

13. See *Banshilal Madholal Sarpanch* v. *State of Madhya Pradesh and Anr* MANU/MP/0242/1990. This was a constitutional referral that clarified whether an accused could use the provisions of the Criminal Procedure Code relating to anticipatory bail when charged with offences under the PoA Act, including rape.

14. MANU/JH/0200/2007.

15. *Sahjad Ansari* v. *State of Jharkhand* MANU/JH/0200/2007 at para 2.

16. *Kamal Nayan Narsaria alias Kamal Narsaria* v. *State of Bihar and Ors* MANU/BH/0145/1995.

17. Ibid. at para 2.

18. Ibid. at para 4.

19. Ibid. at para 5.

20. Ibid. at para 10.

21. The accused was found guilty for violating 'sections 366, 376, 302/34 IPC and section 3(2)(v) of the PoA Act. While sentence of rigorous imprisonment for life was awarded for the offence under Sections 302/34 IPC read with Section 3(2)(v) SC/ST Act, sentence of ten years for each of the offences under Section 366 IPC and 376 IPC was awarded besides sentence of seven years rigorous imprisonment under Sections 201 IPC. Two other co-accused who were also put on trial, were however acquitted of the charges' (*Sahjad Ansari* v. *State of Jharkhand* MANU/JH/0200/2007 at para 1).

22. The application of this section, however, is not standardized and uniform. Other sections in the act may be used with a rape charge instead of this section.

23. *Mohammad Akhtar* v. *State of Bihar* MANU/JH/0376/2005.

24. Ibid. at para 2.

25. Ibid. at para 10.

26. The high court further upheld the conviction under section 376 but reduced the sentence from life to twelve years as the accused had already undergone more than nine years imprisonment, which was the time it took the case to traverse to the High Court.

27. *Vidyadharan* v. *State of Kerala* MANU/SC/0918/2003.

28. Ibid. at para 10.

29. (1997) Cri LJ 948

30. MANU/MP/0180/1992.

31. Ibid. at para 10.

32. Ibid. at para 12.

33. *Fanibhushan Behera, Jeet Shankar Bohidar and Dinabandhu Behere* v. *State of Orissa* MANU/OR/0255/1994.

34. Ibid. at para 17.

35. Ibid. at para 18.

36. The court specified that 'the amending Act of 1986 has changed the title of the Act from "Suppression" to "Prevention"' (ibid. at para 18). We may note that substantial changes were made to the Suppression of Immoral Trafficking Act, 1956 (Act no. 104 of 1956) when it was replaced in 1978 by the Prevention of Immoral Trafficking (PITA); and in 1986 by the Immoral Traffic (Prevention) Act (ITPA). In this judgment, older definitions of sex work are evoked.

37. MANU/JH/0099/2004.

38. The court further opined that ten years rigorous imprisonment was not too severe for rape of an unmarried girl, a student of class ten.

39. MANU/JH/0099/2004 at para 12.

40. See *Jones* v. *State* (2004) Cri LJ 2755 at para 16. The complaint was registered under ss. 328, 352, and 506(1) IPC and 3(1)(x) and 3(1)(xi) PoA Act.

41. (2004) Cri LJ 2755 at para 13.

42. Ibid. at para 14.

43. Additionally, s. 506 IPC was made cognizable and non-bailable in Uttar Pradesh *vide* Notification No. 777/VIII 9-4(2)—87, dated 31 July 1989, published in UP Gazette, Extra, Pt A, Sec. (kha), dated 2 August 1989. In other states, it is non-cognizable and bailable.

44. *Malkhansingh S/o Ganpat Singh and etc.* v. *State of Madhya Pradesh* MANU/MP/0588/2002.

45. We must note that the cases of gangrape cited earlier could have been prosecuted under s. 3(2)(v) of the PoA Act, which enhances the punishment, if it can be proven that the victim was raped on the ground of her identity. However, in cases where there is no prima facie evidence of targeted violence on the basis of identity or where the prosecution finds it difficult to prove this, those forms of rape which attract a minimum of ten years punishment are read with these different provisions under s. 3 of the act.

46. MANU/JH/0899/2006.

47. The high court also found that the testimonies of the two victims were credible since they sustained a lengthy cross-examination. The medical evidence sustained the allegation of gangrape.

48. MANU/JH/0899/2006.

49. Ibid. at para 10, emphasis added.

50. Mangubhai and Irudayam tell us that a district judge in Andhra Pradesh dismissed 39 rape cases read with s. 3(2)(v) PoA Act on the grounds that they had been committed not on the basis of caste, but for reasons such as 'sexual lust' or 'revenge' (2008:152).

51. *Pappu Khan* v. *State of Rajasthan* (2000) 1 Rajasthan Law Weekly 551.

52. Ibid. at 556.

53. See *Hanamath and Ors* v. *State of Karnataka* MANU/KA/0600/2005.

54. Ibid. at para 17.

55. MANU/OR/0077/2004.

56. Ibid. at para 11.

57. Ibid. at para 11.

58. *State of Orissa* v. *Sukru Gouda* MANU/SC/8415/2008 at para 6.

59. *Sukru Gouda* v. *State of Orissa* MANU/OR/0814/2009 at para 10.

60. *Ramdas & Ors* v. *State of Maharashtra* MANU/SC/8626/2006.

61. Several appeals were jointly heard: *Central Bureau of Investigation through DSP, CBISCB* v. *Sakru Mahagu Binjewar (Original Accused No. 2) and Ors* AND *Shatrughna S/o Isram Dhande, Vishwanath S/o Hagru Dhande, Ramu S/o Mangru Dhande* and *Shishupal S/o Vishwanath Dhande* v. *The Central Bureau of Investigation through its Dy SP, CBI, SCB* (Along with Criminal Appeal No. 763/2008) AND *Central Bureau of Investigation, Special Crime Branch* v. *Gopal Sakru Binjewar and Shishupal Vishwanath Dhande* (Along with Criminal Appeal No. 171/2009) MANU/MH/0893/2010.

62. Ibid. at 32A.

63. The section reads: 'Whoever, not being a member of a Scheduled Caste or a Scheduled Tribe knowingly or having reason to believe that an offence has been committed under this Chapter, causes any evidence of the commission of that offence to disappear with the intention of screening the offender from legal punishment, or with that intention gives any information respecting the offence which he knows or believes to be false, shall be punishable with the punishment provided for that offence.'

64. MANU/MH/0893/2010 at para 34 D.

65. This is also suggested by the defence argument that Surekha Bhotmange 'used to threaten people would be falsely implicated under the Atrocities Act' (Ibid. at para 26).

66. '[T]he whole object was to take revenge against Surekha and Priyanka because the accused believed that they were falsely implicated and as such it is difficult to accept the prosecution version that offence under s. 3(1) (xi) of the Act is made out against the accused'(MANU/MH/0893/2010 at para 43 C).

67. Ibid. at para 45.

68. (1993) Cri LJ 487.

69. Ibid. at para 3.

70. Ibid. at 489.

71. Charges were framed against the accused subsequently for offences under s. 294 (obscene acts or songs), s. 342 (punishment for wrongful confinement), s. 354 (assault or force with intent to outrage a woman's

modesty), s. 498 (enticing or taking away or detaining a married woman with a criminal intent), s. 504 (intentional insult with intent to provoke breach of peace), s. 508 (act caused by inducing a person to believe that he will be rendered an object of divine displeasure) and s. 509 (word, gesture, or act intended to insult the modesty of a woman).

72. Section 354 and s. 509, IPC can be compounded, with the permission of the court, by the woman against whom the criminal force has been used or who has been insulted or whose privacy has been violated. Under s. 342, which defines wrongful restraint, the person restrained can compound the offence. Likewise, s. 498 allows the husband of the married woman who has been detained with criminal intent to compound the offence since the offence is seen as being against the husband rather than the woman.

73. (1993) Cri LJ 487 at 489.

74. Ibid. at 490.

75. See *State of Gujarat* v. *Farukhbhai Ahmedbhai Shaikh* (1997) 2GLR1400.

76. *Bharwada Bhoginbhai Hirjibhai* v. *State of Gujarat* AIR 1983 SC 753.

77. In *Ramdas & Ors* v. *State of Maharashtra*, the victim was accused of lodging a false complaint 'since the Pardhi community has an Association which a sum of Rs 40,000/- to the victims of such offences' (MANU/SC/8626/2006 at para 5).

78. MANU/GJ/0405/1995.

79. Ibid. at para 14.

80. Ibid. at para 16.

81. Ibid. at para 12.

82. Ibid. at para 21.

83. Ibid.

84. Ibid. at para 22.

85. MANU/OR/0254/2007.

86. We are assuming here that jati is translated both as caste and tribe in English.

87. *Kailas and Ors* v. *State of Maharashtra* T.R. Taluka P.S., MANU/SC/0011/2011.

88. Ibid. at para 11.

89. Ibid. at para 10.

90. The community (*jati*) certificate is often translated as caste certificate in English from the vernacular, even when the case refers to tribals.

91. In other cases, courts have not placed their reliance on community certificates. See *Paranjothi* v. *State*, Crl. A. No. 30 of 2003, Madras High Court, available at http://indiankanoon.org/doc/1663679/, accessed on 19 September 2012.

92. In *Purno* v. *State of Madhya Pradesh* charges of atrocity under s. 3(1)(xi) were dropped by the high court since the prosecution did not produce a caste certificate to prove that the victim was a tribal (MANU/CG/0087/2010).

93. *Kailas and Ors* v. *State of Maharashtra* T.R. Taluka P.S. MANU/SC/0011/2011 at para 16.

94. Ibid.

95. Ibid. at para 19.

96. Ibid. at para 39.

97. This is a festival to celebrate the birth of the Hindu God Krishna.

98. A lungi is a long piece of cloth worn by men that is tied around the waist and extends to the ankles.

99. The medical certificate is important for the purposes of claiming compensation.

100. See *State, Govt of NCT of Delhi* v. *Sunil and Anr*, (2001) 1 SCC 651.

101. Ibid. at 662.

102. Kavita did not name the rapist or tell me her friend's name. This did not mean that she did not know who he was. The dissociation between Payal's father and the pronoun 'he' reveals the trauma. However, in court she would have to point to him and identify him, just as she had to identify him to the police earlier.

103. Kavita meant that the police did not accept the complaint (*fariyad*).

104. In his provocative study of the role of Dalit lawyers in the implementation of the PoA Act in courts in Uttar Pradesh, Jaoul (2011) indicates how compromise is enforced routinely. Jaoul says, 'the use of justice seems to be favored by Dalit activists only, and initially at least by the victims, while the judiciary institution itself seems committed to extra-judicial means of conflict resolution. Ambedkar's portrait in the Dalit lawyer's room, as against Gandhi's in the courtroom definitely meant something. Paradoxically, the judiciary abided to [sic] the unofficial conception of Gandhi, while Dalits struggled for the implementation of the law that incorporates the official conception of the struggle against untouchability' (2011: 12).

105. Dhirubhai's narrative is instructive in suggesting that the analytic of 'sanskritization' that sociologists use as an index to social change resulting in the adoption of upper-caste norms needs to be attentive to the formation of subjectivities that link humiliation, shame, and powerlessness in complex ways (see Srinivas 1996).

106. The orders and judgments are on the author's personal file. The references of the orders and judgment have been withheld to maintain confidentiality.

Conclusion

It is my hope that *Public Secrets of Law* has succeeded in bearing witness to the struggle against the widespread tolerance of the intolerable harm of sexual violence (see Card 2004). By focusing on the violence that underlies the socio-legal processes constitutive of the rape trial, I have questioned the widely prevalent view that the normative and philosophical exegesis of law is best executed by analysing judgments of courts of appeal. Since court officials, like legal academics, construct a hierarchy of what is 'real' law, they too consider appellate law as worthy of jurisprudential comment and research, distinct from the cases archived in the record rooms of trial courts. I am reminded of the words of an official in the records room who said to me, 'You should look at Supreme Court cases. The rest are useless *compro* [read: compromise] cases, and those which secure a conviction result inevitably in an appeal. There are not many interesting conclusions to draw from *compro* cases except that these result from economic deprivation.' Such evaluations of compromise cases as 'useless' or 'trash' cases that do not offer serious ground for asking normative and jurisprudential questions, indicate a hierachization of juridical knowledge routine to lawyerly ways of constructing what is law.

Moving away from the view that appellate law is real law, I privileged the trial court as a site of enquiry to elucidate how law can be localized such that it bears little resemblance to the rule (or the doing the rule). Those aspects of trial that do not enter juridical records detail ways in which the violence of state law is written on women's bodies. It is in this basic sense that the ethnography of the rape trial departs from the social and juridical frameworks of rape that we glean from appellate law. Lawyer's law, then, is not exhausted by legal norms provided in law books and published judgments, or by describing a gap between the law and its implementation.

It is far too easily assumed that law reform is comprehensive if informed by appellate law or its implementation. Law reform does not really redress the injuries of spoken law. Nor does it address the manifold conventions of law in different sites. I have highlighted the criminal trial as a site where different kinds of expert knowledge converge to produce different effects of power and knowledge. While it is never easy to bring about legislative changes, the changes that are demanded need to be further grounded in an understanding of the practice of law as it is dispersed over different sites. Outside this endeavour, we may end up normalizing and even exacerbating the categories of legality (or illegality) that hide from public view the injury caused to survivors of rape.

PUBLIC SECRECY

It remains a public secret that rape trials inscribe extreme indignity and humiliation on women's bodies. Such 'active not-knowing' describes the operations of public secrecy that fail to do justice to rape survivors when they are revealed in courts of law (Taussig 1999: 6–7). Rather than think of courts as public theatres that annihilate secrets, I have suggested the manifold ways in which law is invested in the operations of public secrecy. I have indicated that state law devises its own forms of customariness, which compete with, complement, or substitute the legal norm. In other words, the juridical field is not only dispersed at different sites and articulated by different temporalities (sometimes simultaneously), but it is also constituted by its customary practices, which shadow, compete with, and contest its norms. Doctrinal law is born out of such processes—repressing the violence that underlies a landmark trial, which repeat over and over again.

The repetition of precedents of injustice in landmark trials indicates why—notwithstanding the Supreme Court's repeated verdicts naming rape as an infringement of the right to life, exhorting courts to treat rape survivors with dignity, and instituting guidelines for the conduct of trials—testifying to rape continues to be a Kafkaesque experience. More than thirty years after the Open Letter protests against the Mathura judgment, this precedent of injustice still echoes in our courtrooms. The cacophony of cross-examinations that divide the body into sexual parts, calibrate duration, map ejaculations, chart marks of resistance, and choreograph postures resounds in our courtrooms. The judicial gavel is not always raised to regulate these ways of talking to rape survivors.

The architecture of doctrinal law is built on the scaffold of courtroom talk, which situates humiliation at the heart of testimony. To illustrate the contemporaneity of such an argument we simply need to read the case law, which holds that slight penile penetration is sufficient to proove rape and proof of ejaculation is not necessary to establish rape. In June 2011, the Bombay High Court observed that the accused 'inserted his penis in her vagina 4 to 5 times' but noted that the victim 'has not stated where the semen was discharged. She has not stated when the sexual act was completed. She is not cross-examined on this aspect at all despite her otherwise lengthy cross-examination. This is the most material sentence in her evidence'.[1] The court speculates that 'if the Appellant No.1 had penetrated her 4 to 5 times it would mean that there was no discharge of his semen except on the last occasion. On the last occasion he could have ejaculated either inside her vagina or after withdrawal, outside it'[2]. However, the court held that it 'makes no difference to the act of penetration. Even slight penetration is sufficient to constitute rape. Ejaculation in the vagina is wholly irrelevant to the offence of rape'[3]. Finally, after observing once more that the defence lawyer did not gather material information about where the semen fell, the court held 'the fact that the penetration took place not once, but 4 to 5 times makes it (a) more dastardly act, which constitutes a gross violation of human rights. It matters not whether the semen of Appellant No.1 was discharged'.[4]

The court speculates on where the ejaculation fell and suggests that the defence lawyer should have asked 'when the sexual act was completed', even though it was irrelevant to the norm being laid down. It was perfectly compatible for a defence lawyer to ask questions about ejaculation even if doctrinal law declares it irrelevant. In other words, doctrinal law does not displace courtroom talk; rather, it is necrophilic in relation to such forms of humiliating questioning. Similar courtroom talk is evident in Gujarat courts too.

In an appeal heard in July 2012, it is evident that the victim had been asked irrelevant and humiliating questions about the duration of rape, whether or not the accused ejaculated, where he ejaculated, and whether she bit the accused, grabbed his hair, or kicked him.[5] In the end, however, the Gujarat High Court was sceptical of the victim's claims as there were no marks of resistance. One of the other grounds on which the rape survivor was disbelieved was that she had typed her complaint and had gone from police station to police station to file it. Rather poignantly, women's awareness of their rights or the legal process is constructed as a sign of immorality.

Likewise, a thirty-five-year old Dalit woman who had complained that a doctor raped her in his clinic on 23 May 1991 was discredited for being aware of the law.[6] In July 2012, the Gujarat High Court held,

> [T]he conduct of the prosecutrix is not believable as she did not inform her husband for two days about the serious incident which took place in broad day light in a clinic of a Doctor. It is proved in the deposition of the Investigating Officer that she had lodged the complaint as per the advice of her husband, so that she can get Rs. 10,000/- from the government.[7]

The positioning of Dalit or tribal women under the PoA Act as *extortionists*, rather than legal subjects aware of their rights, implies an investment in conceiving of Dalit and tribal women as sexually immoral subjects. Such precedents of injustice systemically disregard the use of rape as a means of domination, especially of young, working-class, poor, Dalit, tribal, and Muslim women.

JUDICIAL HORROR

The jurisgenerative potential of law is stultified by the disciplinary discourse on shame and stigma, which acts as a resource for the defence to enact a specific disqualification of the testimony to rape. The defence deliberately feigns ignorance and asks questions that are unanswerable within given normative frameworks.[8] The defence's line of questioning actively shames and re-stigmatizes the legal subject by deploying customary forms of lawyering. In a very basic sense, cross-examination is perceived by defence lawyers as a method of deterring women from testifying in courts of law. Judicial horror leading to convictions is produced after these processes of verification, which deploy shame and stigma to demonstrate rape.

The way records are written and questions are framed during the trial convert it into a pornographic spectacle. Yet such sexualization is not limited to one fragment of the testimony or one set of documents. Rather, the sexualization of women's bodies is performed over and over again. Even documents such as the clothes *panchnamma*, which serves as a record of seized evidence, sexualize the woman's body. The production of judicial horror rests on such repeated sexualization of the raped body, and demands the excited performance of the rapist's intent in a court of law. Judicial horror is thus not given; it is achieved within the law. It is not a state of mind, mentality, or mere function of judicial sensitivity (or insensitivity). Rather, it stands produced through legal discourse such that some forms of rape generate judicial horror, and not others. Jeganathan's (1998) concern about the use of the analytic of horror as a response to the incomprehensibility of violence in anthropological discourse is also pertinent to understand the systemic production of the conditions of horror in legal discourse on rape. The processes that produce judicial horror need to be re-examined lest we always place the burden of courage, as Hasinaben and Dhirubhai remind us, on those testifying to the violence of rape.

CRIME AGAINST SOCIETY

It is a public secret that while rape survivors are forced to bear the burden of courage against the widespread tolerance of intolerable sexual harm, the law exacts a cost from the survivor who speaks out against rape. The construction of rape as an offence against society in law books and appellate judgments hides the processes by which law's injury to rape survivors is manifested. In other words, the production of such injury is conceived as the cost of administration of criminal justice, which remains unproblematized at least from the perspectives of violated women and children. Law assumes that once the female subject is constituted as a desiring subject, a different order of evidence is required to prove injury against society. Hence, courtroom talk demonstrates that to materialize injury, the injured witness must mimetically reproduce the act of rape. Such injury inflicted by law is deemed necessary for a crime against society to be proven, in the process eliding the injury caused to the individual testifying against such a crime.

Notions of social order, morality, or society are further illustrated by the judicially sanctioned—whether constitutionally or otherwise—jurisprudence of compromise. In compromise cases, we find an active construction of the role of law as restoring rather than disrupting social relations, often rendering invisible, inaudible, and even unnameable the terror, deprivation, or intimidation that underlies such out-of-court processes. Testimony is constituted as disruptive of social order and inimical to the interest of society.[9] The notion of social order or social justice remains phallocentric, for the monopoly over compromise remains contested and the survivor's voice muted.

In fact, the more we speak of compromise, the more shadowy the figure of the woman becomes. The shadowy figure of the rape victim who turns hostile begs our attention. Indeed, we have before us a few cases where women face the threat of perjury when a compromise fails.[10] Do we need to situate a compromise, often brokered on behalf of the victim, in the context of the contestation over the monopoly to compromise? Should judges minimally examine the imbrication of the legal subject in structures of power which script her story, and what it means to produce such scripted statements in court? Should there not be modes of innovation in procedure, practice, and courtroom speech, such that the conditions of testifying against rape find radical alteration? Surely to refuse a compromise should not invite censure, boycott, shame, or even risk one's life. Put another way, compromise does not necessarily signify that the woman was not raped; rather it may signify the social or legal pressure to desist from speaking against the violence of rape. Further, is judicial discipline not required to control the production of compromise documents as a route to construct the rape survivor as a lying *habitué*, and therefore, prejudicing her testimony?

In everyday and extraordinary contexts, however, the culture of compromise that underwrites rape prosecutions has not been sufficiently discussed either within the women's movement, or by legal academics. Can the amendments we seek of the rape law be effective without reflecting on the cultures of compromise that constitute rape trials? We need to think of the entire process from complaint to trial as a field of contestation where social, economic, and political dominance scripts the legal outcome. Unless the victim is provided safe conditions of testimony, compromise as a tool of terror, bargain, inducement, and domination promises to defeat well meaning measures of reform.

INCOMMENSURABILITIES

Juridical categories incommensurable with the survivor's experience, deployed during the rape trial, convert rape into sex and sex into rape. I have noted, for instance, the incommensurability between Chetna's experience and the way she was named in law as a victim, witness, and accused for planning to kidnap, abduct, and rape her own body. I have also argued that juridical and medical discourses collaborate to obfuscate the meaning of rape from the point of view of the survivor. The raped body is made to speak the truth by the deploying the technique of the two-finger test, and in this sense constructed as an archive that can reveal past sexual history. We have encountered the arguments of the defence lawyer who deployed the medico-legal category of partial penetration *as if* it existed in Noor's experience in order to discredit her testimony. We may recall here that the defence lawyer suggested that Noor was a lying subject when she testified that she experienced the assault as *full* penetration. Not only was she constituted as a child-adult but the idea that a diagnostic category could exist in her experience was also naturalized.

The law—whether legislative or adjudicatory—does not allow experience of abuse and violation to find representation in languages in intimate familiarity with a survivor's everyday world. The ethnography of evidence presented in this book describes how the child comes to learn that certain words have value as evidence, while other words are wasted in the court. We have seen how Noor and Kavita learnt to use rigid designators naming sexual parts or penile penetration to communicate the experience of rape. Since adults constantly talk past the experience of the child witness, Kavita could not impress upon the prosecutor that 'big men' caused her terror. She was expected to emphasize that she resisted by screaming and the man who raped her threatened her with a knife. Even though consent is immaterial in a statutory rape trial, judges and lawyers forget that a child does not need to be threatened with a knife or demonstrate resistance. Yet, these elements of force highlighted and her experience of coming to the court to testify and her terror of big and powerful men were elided.

The anxiety, shame, blame, and fear experienced by a child during a trial are not accessible to judicial imagination. The judicial confusion about whether the law allows a child to sit in a witness box or drink a glass of water betrays its limits. Scolding and even shouting at a child for breaking down and not answering questions in midst of a hostile cross-evidence is seen as effective courtroom practice. Asking a child questions about time when she did not know how to read time to answer a question most would not be able to answer—i.e., duration of rape—is classified as evidence.[11] Noor's conversation around my watch, far from a childish fancy for an unobtainable object, reflect how she blamed herself for not being able to answer the questions put to her. This conversation signalled how Noor had internalized feelings of inadequacy, blame, and humiliation.

While for Kavita play was banished, her childhood was suffused with witnessing her parents' suffering. For Kavita's father, the encounter with the law did not validate the political subjectivity promised by the PoA Act. Dhirubhai's encounters with the law redefined his subjectivity in deeply wounding ways, where the making of subjectivity through law enters the desire to take life—his own along with his family's lives. The complaint is a cry. It is an invocation to the law to punish the accused. As the already uncertain promise for justice further recedes, so does the will, or the capacity, to live. Hence, it is important to remember that the child's subjectivity is not inscribed by the legal processes in a court of law but simultaneously also through the act of witnessing her parents' suffering, or being subjected to the power of their care.

TECHNIQUES OF CERTIFICATION

The medico-legal certificate occupies a central place in the trial, for it imparts structure to the cross-examination. By recording whether or not two or more fingers could be inserted in the vagina, the medico-legal certificate provides lawyers with the technique to characterize women as lying *habitués*. One of the central arguments of this book is that consent and falsity have been medicalized through medico-legal techniques. The *habitué*, who is constructed through the two-finger test, exists in a mimetic relationship to determine whether an erect penis could penetrate the vagina. While the natural state of the hymen is not considered to be reliable, this technique supposedly allows actual verification by substituting the penis with two fingers. In other words, the hymen can signify only after the technique is deployed on the body of the violated, or the proof of injury is localized to what the vagina reveals to the medical expert. The figure of the *habitué* is thus a product of technique, which is open to semantic exploitation. The body of the law thus wounds when it is named as the wounded. Phallocentric law must mimetically do to a woman what the particularized aggressor did to her in order to *know* that she was raped and to declare that society has been injured by the act.

The tremendous psychic costs inflicted on survivors by these violent techniques of gathering evidence are fully ignored. Bearing the brunt of curious and lewd eyes at the police station and the hospital, the rape survivor experiences humiliation over and over again. The number of people present when rape survivors are examined is not limited to the necessary few. From Chetna, we learnt that interns were present at the time of her examination in the hospital. We know from rape survivors' accounts that they are not reassured, comforted, or informed about the medico-legal process. They are not made to feel that they are in control of what is happening to them in the aftermath of a police complaint. It is truly appalling that rape survivors are not even given a pair of spare clothes to change into when their own are confiscated as evidence.

Nor do indigent families in police stations and emergency wards find solace, or even food to eat. We learnt that Noor's mother did not have food to eat for two days in the hospital, nor the money to travel back to her home with Noor after she was discharged. She then had to bear the costs of moving out of the neighbourhood where she lived. Khyati's father had to travel to the court from another city with his entire family for each hearing. Yet, though survivors are offered paltry amounts of compensation under the PoA Act, they are accused of levying false cases. Surely when a rape survivor is provided a nominal amount of money under the PoA Act the state acknowledges that it also imposes financial costs of testifying to a crime committed against society.

The very courts that have been quick to allege that women lie about rape in order to get meagre sums of compensation do not point out that the accused often purchases impunity and compromise. Surely the culture of compromise is founded in an economy that traffics in inducement and terror? Central to such forms of trafficking is the role of policing. In the police station, rape survivors routinely face disbelief, humiliation, intimidation, and delay. The FIR in a trial remains foundational. Naming violence as a crime, in the first instance, is determined by specific techniques of policing that describe the way sociality enters interpretation and recording of rules. I have shown how class and caste inflect techniques of policing to *weaken* a case of atrocity and rape. Delay produced by the police is a technique for weakening a case. Disbelief at this stage denies the complainant the means to prove injury and forecloses the possibility of emergency medical assistance to the victim. Police pressure to compromise the case produces yet another kind of emergency for the victim. Appellate law indicates tragic consequences that follow compromise resulting in annihilating violence, such as murder or suicide.

The imbrication of the police in cultures of compromise has meant a specific form of documentary practice where prolific police records address different futures and conserve the potentiality of these futures in the present. In Sandhya's case, the police records two versions of what happened. While one stated that Sandhya and Daya had eloped, the other said that she had been abducted and raped. Here, the police already anticipate different socio-legal routes by speaking to the law as well as to the familial normativity at the same time.[12] Such techniques simultaneously act within the law and suspend it in order to gain legitimacy by upholding local economies of social order, such as the one based on familial and caste-based normativities.

Yet even when rape is named as atrocity, judicial discourse refuses to acknowledge systemic and targeted political violence by making a distinction between atrocity and mere lust. The dominant view that abnormal sexual lust causes men to rape women does not account for repeated and performative sexual humiliation such as stripping and parading.[15] Judges routinely occlude caste or tribe as the context of the violence. In the rare instance when rape as atrocity is recognized, it is seen as exchange of violence between men of unequal status, rather than leading to an understanding of what it means to be raped as a Dalit or tribal woman. The Khairlanji case illustrates the painful pitting of caste and gender against each other to deny the grounds of atrocity. The governmentalization of access to courts itself is used against Dalits and adivasis to hollow out the PoA Act of its substance such as the insistence on caste certificates as a means to prove atrocity. Sexual violence then must be seen as vital to understanding the politics of law and governance.

JURISPATHIC GOVERNANCE IN THE TIMES OF MASS SEXUAL VIOLENCE

Although the ethnography presented in this book features rape trials in Ahmedabad courts in everyday contexts prior to the terrible mass violence in 2002, it allows us to reflect on how everyday contexts of rape cultures are mobilized to silence voices of protest. It is not my argument that there is a seamless continuity between everyday rape trials and the special techniques of disqualifying women's testimonies in the aftermath of mass violence. Rather, the almost heroic labour in bringing these voices to courts of law makes a compelling argument to recognize an extraordinary routinization of jurispathic forms of governance. I argue that the specific form of governance that characterized the immediate aftermath of the events in Gujarat 2002 was marked by what may be called jurispathic governance, to use Cover's (1995) term, such that it attempted to eradicate the possibility of a sensitive and responsive jurisprudence to redress sexual violence (see IIJ 2003). Cover has famously said that 'judges of the state are jurispathic—that they kill diverse legal traditions that compete with the state' (Cover 1995: 214). For Cover, the jurispathic tendencies in law always exist in 'a state of tension' with the jurisgenerative capacity of the law or 'a world of meaning in which justice is pursued' (Sarat 2001: 5). I extend Cover's meaning of jurispathic to those forms or tendencies of governance that hollow out state law of its normative content. Specifically when the conditions of adjudication are such that judges of the state cannot breathe life into constitutional law, or when state judges kill those forms of state law that guarantee constitutional safeguards to those who are systemic targets of mass violence.

The publicity given to the mass violence in Gujarat 2002 recorded the angry and traumatized narratives of Muslim women who spoke about how they barely survived targeted, systemic, and lethal forms of mass sexual violence. Regulated, censored, and silenced over time, these voices did not find a hearing in courts of law (T. Sarkar 2002).[14] In 2002, the claim to a distinct Gujarati identity based on the discourse of *asmita* (literally 'pride') as a political claim to difference acted to repress everyday forms of violence against women while celebrating the systemic genocidal rape of Muslim women and children during the violence in Gujarat. Discourses of *asmita* produced rape cultures that expanded and even celebrated the threshold of toleration of intolerable forms of sexual and reproductive violence (U. Baxi 2005).

Numerical narratives were mobilized by *asmita* discourses, enabling the representations of organized and targeted mass violence as an aberration (U. Baxi 2005). *Asmita* discourses structured the denial that mass sexual violence occurred, asserted that such violence was exaggerated, and positioned those who spoke on behalf of rape survivors as authors of propaganda against Gujarat. Such 'rape culture signifies ways of doing competitive party politics and managing governance *in which brutal collective sexual assaults on women remain enclosed in contrived and escalating orders of impunity*' (U. Baxi 2005: 342, emphasis in original). Such escalating orders of impunity inflected judicial discourse as well.

The Gujarat judiciary seemed to have absorbed *asmita* articulations almost fully. In the aftermath of the 2002 violence, witness testimony was challenged on the ground that as Muslims they did not understand Gujarati, and signed documents in Gujarati were therefore false. Gujarati Muslims like Noornissa were positioned as Hindi-speaking witnesses.[15] The language in which a traumatized survivor may scream in her nightmares was divested as the medium of expression in court. In contrast, the trial court in the Bilkis Bano case in Bombay observed that 'naturally, in the given circumstances, the prosecutrix was likely to express the facts in her mother tongue i.e., Gujarati'.[16] Further, notions of Gujarati pride were now aligned to the trope of the 'independence' of the Gujarat judiciary. When the Supreme Court transferred the Best Bakery and Bilkis Bano trials to Maharashtra, the Gujarat Government claimed that there was 'no aspersion much less a whisper of lack of faith in the judiciary of the State of Gujarat' and the case for the transfers was 'a clear-cut attempt ... made by the

Petitioners to undermine the majesty and dignity of the entire judicial system of the State of Gujarat'.[17]

Protests against the government were read to signify disloyalty and activists were positioned as anti-national subjects (U. Baxi 2005). This form of jurispathic governance constructs activism or critique as a form of defamation of all Hindu Gujaratis and those who raised their voices against the state as anti-Gujarat and anti-national. The Gujarat High Court caricatured activists—and by name, Teesta Setalvad and Mihir Desai (Citizens for Justice and Peace)—as 'super investigators', 'anti-social', and 'anti-national' elements.[18] Passing judicial strictures against the Gujarat judiciary, the Supreme Court gave Setalvad and Desai a hearing on this issue and ordered that the Gujarat High Court expunge the paragraphs for castigating 'serious aspersions' on the petitioners.[19]

In the aftermath of 2002, compromise meant further exposure to conditions of terror, threat, penury, boycott, sanction, and inducement. The culture of compromise was mobilized to justify the threat, intimidation, and terror used against Gujarati Muslims to force witnesses to settle, withdraw, and turn hostile in criminal cases against the perpetrators. Grover (2002) documents the *mafipatrak* (letter of apology) that Muslim survivors were made to sign in Gujarati. Likewise, the circulation of the word 'compro'—an abbreviation for compromise, implied that Muslim men and women were forced to withdraw complaints from courts of law in order to return to their neighbourhoods (see IIJ 2003). The IIJ report reveals survivors were able to return to their homes on condition that they compromise. The blurring of terror as 'peace', and compromise as 'justice' was central to the work of *asmita* discourses. Further, courts were reported to have actively compromised cases, thereby marking the continuation of jurispathic governance, by positing the exception as the rule (Jha 2011).

The Gujarat police refused to register the FIRs, carry out test identification parades[20] and omitted the names of the perpetrators. Grover says,

> ...the police adopted an innovative and illegal method of registering FIRs. Instead of registering a separate and distinct FIR with regard to each and every cognizable offence, a single omnibus FIR is recorded. The contents are general, vague and bereft of details. The incidents

reported therein relate to different places, time and accused persons. Some FIRs have been registered where the accused are both Hindus and Muslims and have been booked as part of the same mob. In one FIR, totally unconnected events are clubbed together. The events are spread over several places and at times over several days. (2002: 363)

Among scores of other survivors, the police refused to record Bilkis Bano's complaint of gangrape, instead the police wrote an omnibus FIR that did not even mention that she was raped. Bilkis Bano had to fight a long and terrifying legal battle, making history as perhaps the only woman in independent India who secured a conviction under the existent riot and rape laws (see Nampoothiri and Sethi 2012). It is therefore fitting to conclude this book with this brief for justice.

THE STATE OF GUJARAT V. JASWANTBHAI CHATURBHAI NAI AND 19 ORS

Bilkis Bano, whose case was summarily closed by the Gujarat police, petitioned the Supreme Court of India with the help of the National Human Rights Commission (NHRC) to bring to trial the men who gangraped her and murdered her child along with other members of her family. In 2003, the Supreme Court handed over the investigation to the CBI and transferred the trial out of Gujarat to the adjacent state of Maharashtra. The decision to transfer the trial did not rest only on assessing whether there was a public perception of lack of safe conditions to testify. At issue in transfer always is the question of securing the integrity of the narratives of the accused and witnesses free from local intimidation from hostile elements. Never has the integrity of state judicial system served as a ground for transfer but if there ever was a situation in which that integrity was in doubt, it was in this case. The decision to transfer the trial to a special court in Bombay indicated judicial recognition of the jurispathic forms of governance in Gujarat that annihilated the material conditions necessary for testifying against mass sexual violence.

To narrate what happened, I rely on the judgment delivered by Justice U.D. Salvi in *The State of Gujarat* v. *Jaswantbhai Chaturbhai Nai and 19 Ors*.[21] In court, the prosecution opened the case by foregrounding the political context to the violence:

[L]arge scale communal riots resulting in genocide erupted in the State of Gujarat following the call for Gujarat Bandh given by Vishva Hindu Parishad (VHP) in conjunction with Bajrang Dal on 28.2.2002. Apparently the immediate reason for this call was death [*sic*] of Hindu Kar Sevaks in burning of Sabarmati Express at Godhra Railway Station on 27.2.2002. Bhartiya Janata Party (BJP), which had close links with VHP and Bajrang Dal, was in the seat of power in the State of Gujarat at the material time.[22]

On 28 February 2002, arson and looting overwhelmed the village of Randhikpur. At 10.30 in the morning, many people gathered, shouting 'kill, butcher, and burn the Muslims' ('*Musalmanano maro, kapo, salgao*').[23] The violence was systemic, planned, and targeted.

On this painful day, Bilkis was visiting her father in Randhikpur with her daughter Saleha. Her father, Abdul Issa Ghanchi, sold milk in the village. Married to Yakub Rasool Patel, Bilkis was in the fifth month of pregnancy. When the violence broke out in the village, Bilkis and her family decided to flee. As they ran towards the fields behind their homes, they could see their homes being burnt. At midnight they reached the village of Kuwajar and took refuge in a mosque. Shamim, Bilkis' cousin, was in labour. Bilkis, her mother Halima, her aunt Sugraben and a few others went to fetch the village midwife, who helped Shamim give birth to a baby girl. By next afternoon, they had to flee Khundra. On their way they met a man belonging to the Nayak tribe who was moved by the sight of Shamim struggling to walk with her newborn baby. He gave them refuge for two days in his house.

The terrified family seeking refuge in this man's home included Bilkis; her daughter Saleha; her mother Halimaben; her sisters Mumtaz and Munni; and her brothers Aslam and Irfan. The stranger also protected her uncles; Majidbhai and Yusuf Musa Patel; her aunts Sugraben and Amina; her cousins Shamimben, Mumtazben and Madinaben; Hussain, the son of her cousin Shamimben; Sadaam, the son of her aunt Amina, and Shamim's newborn. When it was no longer safe for them, they left early in the morning for the village of Sarjumi through another village, Chhaparwar. They walked past the main road through the fields of the village by a bylane that led to another village, Panivela. This place was marked by a couple of *kuccha* houses on one side and on the other, a jungle alongside hillocks. Camouflaged in the clothes their tribal host had lent them, they hoped that they would escape the men who sought to kill them. That was not to be. Two white vehicles driving down from Chhaparwar bearing around thirty men armed with swords, sickles, and sticks stopped in front of them shouting in Gujarati in unison: "'*Aa rahya Musalmano, emane maaro kaato*" (these are the Muslims, kill them, cut them).'[24]

As the men began to attack them, Bilkis and her family tried to run in different directions in a desperate bid to save their lives. Bilkis was cornered. Shailesh Bhatt (accused number 4) snatched her daughter Saleha and smashed her to death on the rocky ground. Jaswant Nai, Govind Nai, and Naresh Modhiya then stripped and gangraped Bilkis. As she tried to plead with these men to spare her, she knew that no one could come to her rescue as other members of her family were also being assaulted. The special court noted that,

...Jaswant Nai did foul act of rape despite her pleading not to do such foul act as she was carrying a baby in womb and he was like her brother or uncle. Thereafter, she deposed, the A/2-Govind Nai and the deceased A/3-Naresh Modhiya raped her in succession; and her hands were held by the A/1-Jaswant Nai and the deceased A/3-Naresh when she was raped by the A/2-Govind Nai. She further deposed that she became unconscious and her assailants left her believing that she was dead.[25]

A couple of hours later, when she came to consciousness, Bilkis found that her family members, her daughter, Saleha, and Shamim's newborn had been killed. She looked for her clothes among the slain corpses of her family to cover her naked body and then climbed a hillock where she hid herself the entire day and night. Bilkis then climbed across and down another hill to find some water to drink—where an *adivasi* woman helped her by giving her clothes to wear. Eventually, she spotted a policeman, to whom she narrated what had happened to her. She was then taken to the Limkheda police station, where she narrated the terrifying facts of her family's murder and that she had been gangraped and left for dead. She also identified the accused since they were from her village.

Bilkis was to testify in court later that the police officers threatened her for revealing the names of the accused. They warned her that a poisonous injection would be administered to her in the hospital where she would be taken for a medical examination. The police did not record her complaint accurately. In the FIR, they wrote that a mob of five hundred people had attacked her family, and did not list the names of the accused as revealed by Bilkis. Nor did the FIR mention that she had been gangraped. The FIR was not read out to her, although her thumb impression was secured.

At the Limkheda Hospital she narrated what had happened to her to the medical officer, but she was not given emergency medical attention. When she was brought back to the Limkheda police station, she met her father, who told her that her family members, including her daughter, were lying dead at the scene of crime, and that he had identified their corpses. By now totally distraught, Bilkis lost consciousness and was sent to the Godhra Refugee Camp. It was at the camp that she met her aunt, Sugrabi, to whom she narrated what had happened to all of them since they fled the village. At the camp, Bilkis Bano also met Jayanti Ravi (district magistrate and collector of District Panchmahal) and repeated the horrifying account to her.

A number of witnesses testified in court collaborating Bilkis Bano's testimony, including the social workers who had met her in the Godhra Relief Camp, the district magistrate and collector, the women who saw her in the police station, and other survivors in the camp. In court, Jayanti Ravi deposed that Bilkis 'had mentioned the names of the offenders, whom she had identified, and the FIR given by her was not lodged as per her narration'.[26] At her intervention, Bilkis was treated at the Godhra Civil Hospital and her statement recorded at the Godhra police station. Bilkis was in the camp till May 2003, now joined by her husband, who reached the camp seventeen days after she had been sent there. Madina Patel, also a survivor from Randhikpur, who learnt that her son had been killed when she reached the camp in Godhra, testified that she had heard Bilkis describe what had happened to her to the Limkheda police, upon which the police verbally abused her.

On 4 March 2002, five police officials visited the place where the corpses were lying. They took photographs and left the site unsecured, without conducting an inquest. On 5 March 2002, under the supervision of police officers, the corpses of Bilkis' family—four women, two boys, and one girl—were buried in a pit in Kesharpur jungle.[27] Nearly ninety kilograms of common salt was added to this pit to assist early decomposition of the bodies. Not only was there an attempt to extinguish any evidence, but the inquest *panchanama* of the dead bodies also made false claims: it recorded the presence of a fictitious woman *panch*. The inquest *panchanama* did not record that the body of Bilkis' daughter had been found. The two doctors, according to the prosecution, conducted perfunctory post-mortem, did not collect vaginal swabs from the female bodies and maintained incorrect post-mortem notes,[28] hence bringing to record the precise forms of erasing evidence of targeted mass rape and murder.

The doctors who examined Bilkis in Godhra testified to injuries on her body and that she was twenty weeks pregnant at the time she was assaulted. The court observed:

> [T]he fact, therefore, cannot be ruled out that the prosecutrix was terrorized by display of deadly weapon/s so as to bring about her unwilling submission to intercourse without offering physical resistance. If there is sexual intercourse without any physical resistance, it would be like any other normal sexual intercourse. It is not shown from the medical works that a pregnant lady carrying 20 weeks fetus in womb would suffer abortion if she has sexual intercourse once, twice or thrice in succession.[29]

During the cross-examination, further injury was inflicted on a survivor who had endured intolerable sexual violence, lost her child, and watched her family die. As the court noted, Bilkis was 'cross-examined at a [*sic*] considerable length till, perhaps, the defence exhausted itself of all its ammunition'.[30]

The court observed that 'it is also unlikely that the persons in the mob intoxicated with a desire to kill and ravish women would have spared the prosecutrix in response to her pleas to spare her as she was pregnant. Killing of Saleha, daughter of the prosecutrix, shows the mood of the persons in the mob'.[31] The men who gangraped Bilkis Bano were sentenced to life. The court held that 'evidence shows that Hindus and Muslims, including the accused and the victims lived together without noticeable disharmony over generations at village Randhikpur till Vishwa Hindu Parishad gave call for Gujarat Bandh following the Godhra Train Burning Incident, and ferment of communal hatred sparked off the riots'.[32] Further, the court observed that:

[A]n individual has his secret agenda in joining the riots. Many join for looting the properties, some join for satisfying their lust and few join the riotous mob for killing and more often the religious fervour is merely a cover for their secret agenda. In the instant case, evidence shows that the A/l- Jaswantbhai Nai and the A/2-Govindbhai Nai committed rape in succession on the pregnant prosecutrix despite her pleadings [*sic*] to spare her. After satisfying their lust they did not bother whether the prosecutrix was finished or not.[33]

The man who murdered Bilkis' daughter was sentenced to life. The court was to determine later that Radheshyam @ Lala Vakil, Bipinchandra Joshi @ Lala Doctor, Kesharbhai Vohania, Pradip Vohania, Bakabhai Vohania, Rajubhai Soni, Mitesh Bhatt, Ramesh Chandana and others had raped and killed Bilkis' family members.[34] The court observed that 'as regards multiple murders and gang rapes of Halima and Shamim, it is not clearly understood from the evidence as to who gave the fatal blows or actually committed the rape on Halima and Shamim. Culpability could be fastened on the accused by means of the principle of constructive liability in law'.[35]

The court found that Somabhai Gori, a police head constable on duty at Limkheda Police Station, 'did not record the complaint of the prosecutrix as per her narration and proceeded to register an offence ... against unknown persons'.[36] Instead, 'the FIR recorded carried incorrect narration, purportedly made by the complainant, the prosecutrix, that a mob of 500 persons, not known to her, carrying sticks, gave stick blows on her head and left leg, and the mob was shouting in Gujarati "Tamara Muslim Manas Hoye Hamara Hindu Manas Mari Nakhe" (you Muslim persons killed Hindus) and when she told them that she was pregnant she was left alone, and as the result of the assault she felt unconscious'.[37] The FIR was typical in that it did not record the names of the accused, directed blame at a large crowd of strangers, and specifically refused to record rape. The court held that 'there is convincing evidence of the fact that he refused to record the FIR as narrated by the prosecution and framed it in the manner which he knew to be incorrect with an intention to save the accused involved in the crime from legal punishment.'[38]

The trial court observed that 'apart from this, it needs to be observed that the protection to the public servant u/s 197 of CrPC.,

1973 extends to the acts done while acting or purporting to act in discharge of one's official duties and not otherwise. Framing of false record was certainly not an act, which could have been committed by the A/17- Somabhai Gori while acting or purporting to act in discharge of his official duty. No exception, therefore, can be taken on the ground that the prosecution of the A/17- Somabhai Gori was bad for want of valid sanction to prosecute him.'[39] Gori was convicted for offences under ss. 217 (a public servant who disobeys law to save a person from legal punishment) and 218 IPC (a public servant who frames a record incorrectly to save a person from legal punishment) and sentenced to two and three years of rigorous imprisonment respectively. The other police officials and the two doctors accused of falsifying post-mortem reports were acquitted.[40]

In this case, the structure of the rape trial, although read with the riot provisions, maintains strong continuities with everyday rape trials. The trial was marked by routine arguments about whether the victim resisted, allegations that a pregnant survivor who has been gangraped would miscarry, and a lengthy cross-examination about how she was raped until 'the defence exhausted itself of all its ammunition'.[41] The routine defence arsenal, as this book demonstrates, injects immense humiliation into the experience of testifying. Not only does rape and riot trial not displace the structure of the rape trial, the judicial explanation of why the accused Jaswant and Govind raped Bilkis is resourced from everyday legal discourse on rape. Jaswant and Govind's 'sexual lust' is regarded as a 'secret motive' for joining the riotous mob.[42]

Here, rape is not seen as political violence which specifically targeted Muslim women. The court does not recognize that men do not rape to satisfy their sexual lust rather rape is a preferred tool of sexually humiliating the 'other'. To gangrape a pregnant woman during a pogrom is a form of systemic and deliberate sexual and reproductive violence. This motive remains a public secret even while individual culpability is recognized and punished. Just as we see in the instance of atrocity, here too we find that judicial discourse on rape is saturated with the language of male lust now attracting punitive gaze for its excess. It follows an additive logic where rape is added to riot without changing the meaning of rape as commonly understood in everyday contexts, making it difficult to introduce new meanings of rape as systemic, targeted, and mass violence.

This case poses a challenge to jurisprudential thinking on how to record, examine, and frame women's testimonies to mass sexual violence. Even though law writes history out of the context of mass sexual violence, Bilkis Bano's testimony creates legal history. With the important exception of this trial, Indian law has unfortunately failed to prosecute mass sexual crimes. The absence of prosecutions of rape in the context of mass crimes such as those recorded during communal riots suggests that the rape law systemically prevents women's sexual and reproductive histories from entering court records and denies acknowledgment of the historical wrongs inscribed on their bodies (Das 2006; P. Baxi 2007). Bilkis Bano's testimony and the activism that created the conditions for her testimony is historic precisely for defying those rape cultures that make mass sexual crimes illegible in judicial discourse.

Justice Salvi's court witnessed remarkable courage by survivors and witnesses who testified despite the threat, intimidation, and penury that pursues them even today. The fear of political persecution, lasting grief of the dead, and politics of speaking against targeted mass rape haunts the text of this judgment. The immense labour that underlies preparing such a brief for justice weighs down on us as we read each page of the judgment pronounced by Justice Salvi. Although the Supreme Court's decision to transfer the Bilkis Bano trial created the juridical conditions to testify, it was the work of activists and lawyers that sustained the material conditions of testimony, ranging from meeting legal costs to providing emotional support and legal advice. Such phenomenal activism reflected a complex understanding of the trauma involved in such a difficult legal and political challenge. The collaboration between the survivors, activists, and lawyers marked a stubborn refusal to accept the operations of public secrecy.

The Bilkis Bano trial compels us to question the infliction of an enormous burden of courage upon survivors of sexual violence, not to further mention the difficulties imposed variously upon human rights and social movement activists. As the jurisgenerative promise of this trial gestates, many lessons have yet to be learnt about transforming social, juridical, and political discourses on rape in everyday and extraordinary contexts. These lessons, surely not confined to Gujarat, have yet to find actualization in projects of legislative and juridical reform. It is clear though that we may identify the relegation of the troubled issue of sexual violence to the margins of social, political, and legal theory in our academia as the work of public secrecy. To position this book as an entreaty to research, theorize, and protest the formations of rape cultures is to make a plea to take the suffering of rape seriously. Until then, we remain complicit in the normalizing power of rape cultures.

NOTES

1. *Satish Gayaji Gaikwad* v. *The State of Maharashtra* on 13 June 2011, Bombay High Court, at para 26, available at http://www.indiankanoon.org/doc/383849/, accessed on 22 September 2012.

2. Ibid. at para 26.

3. Ibid.

4. Ibid.

5. *State of Gujarat* v. *Jumma Husain Sindhi*, Judgment dated 9 July 2012, CR.A/361/1994 6/ 6, The High Court of Gujarat at Ahmedabad, available at http://indiankanoon.org/doc/54569421/, accessed on 22 September 2012.

6. This was an appeal by the State of Gujarat challenging the additional sessions judge Vadodara's verdict on 23 February 1993, acquitting the accused from charges under s. 376 IPC and s. 3 and 7 of the PoA Act, 1989. See *State of Gujarat* v. *Dinesh Ramanlal Pathak*, judgment dated 20 June 2012, Appeal No. 726 of 1993, The High Court of Gujarat at Ahmedabad, available at http://www.indiankanoon.org/doc/19580500/, accessed on 22 September 2012.

7. Ibid. at para 4.

8. There is hardly any debate amongst defence lawyers or in the Bar on what could constitute a fair defence without converting the rape trial into a pornographic spectacle.

9. We have seen how legal discourse on rape is concerned with the marriageability of the rape survivor. The aftermath of sexual violence is a life that is constructed, as devoid of the possibility to rejoin society.

10. In early nineteenth-century England 'rape victims whose prosecutions failed could actually be tried for perjury. ... Even though prosecutions for perjury often failed, the imprisonment and humiliation suffered by these women could effectively deter many victims from prosecuting rapists' (Clark 1987: 69).

11. Agnes points out that 'the Bombay High Court in a recent decision has held that the degree and depth of penetration are irrelevant' (2005: 1860, see *Sidharth Atchutrao Sawant* v. *State of Maharashtra* [2000] [3] MhLJ 46).

12. Such documentary practices source their inventiveness in different ocular fields. Rather than constrain police documents to a lawyerly one, I suggest that police documents are inflected by a cinematic imagination—be this in the weakening of Khayati's police complaint, or framing Sandhya's statements.

13. We have no alternative feminist vocabulary to name such forms of sexual assault—the word 'parade' emerges from the experience of the spectator who is invited to participate in the spectacle from the point of view of the perpetrator.

14. Several fact-finding reports had reported extensive sexual violence. One of the first reports, *Survivors Speak*, documented how women in camps reported systemic, targeted forms of sexual violence (Hameed et al. 2002). Women's complaints of rape to the police were not recorded, they were not given emergency medical treatment nor were they able to escape continued intimidation and terror. After the violence, the condition of women in camps was appalling. Women were not treated for trauma or vaginal infections, STD, HIV/AIDs, abortions, or pregnancies in the camps. The rhetoric of denial accompanied testimony after testimony of the most chilling accounts of sexual violence, as the mass rape was denied as a lie in the parliament. Few cases of rape were registered.

15. See *State of Gujarat* v. *Rajubhai Dhamibhai Bariya*, 2003, in CR. A / 956/2003, Before the High Court of Gujarat, judgment dated 26 December 2003.

16. *The State of Gujarat* v. *Jaswantbhai Chaturbhai Nai and 19 Ors* Sessions Case No. 634 of 2004, Before the Court of Special Judge for Greater Mumbai at Mumbai, Judge Shri U.D. Salvi (Courtroom No. 49), judgment dated 21 January 2008 at para 305.

17. Counter Affidavit on behalf of State of Gujarat, 21 November 2003 at para 23. Mukul Rohtagi, Additional Solicitor General, appearing for the State of Gujarat, filed a counter-petition to the application for directions dated 21 November 2003 and the Note of the Amicus Curiae dated 12 October 2003 and 21 November 2003 on 18 December 2003.

18. See *Teesta Setalvad & Anr* v. *State of Gujarat & Ors* Criminal Appeal Nos. 443-445 [Arising out of SLP (Crl.) Nos, 530-532/2004].

19. Ibid.

20. In the absence of the test identification parade (TIP), no evidentiary value accrues to a witness identifying an accused for the first time in court. In relation to the 1984 anti-Sikh riots in Delhi, Grover (2002) cites the instance of Harbhajan Kaur, who could have identified the perpetrators if the police had carried out the TIP. After eleven years, she could not identify the perpetrators in court. In the 1984 trials, the lack of TIP led to the

dismissal of cases since the benefit of the doubt went to the accused (see Grover 2002).

21. *State of Gujarat* v. *Jaswantbhai Chaturbhai Nai and 19 Ors*, Sessions Case No. 634 of 2004, Judgment dated 21 January 2008.

22. Ibid. at para 3 (1).

23. Ibid. at para 15.

24. Ibid. at para 3. Bilkis identified the men in the vehicles as Shailesh Bhatt, Mitesh Bhatt, Govind Nai, Jaswant Nai, Baka Khima, Keshar Khima, Lala Doctor, Lala Vakil, Raju Soni, Naresh Modhiya (deceased), Pradeep Modhiya, Ramesh Chandana and others from Randhikpur.

25. Ibid. at para 197.

26. Ibid. at para 246.

27. The court also heard the testimony of a dalit witness, Mukeshbhai Harijan, who stated that 'days after Godhra riots, the police took him to one Kotar (ravine) at the outskirts of village Kesharpur at about 12.30 p. m. where he and other neighbours had dug a waist-deep pit, and 7 dead bodies—4 females, 2 boys and 1 girl were buried in the pit dug by them' (Ibid. at para 309). Mavsi Mulabhai Patel, who had sold the ninety kilograms of salt in three gunny bags to two policemen accompanied by three men, including the deputy *sarpanch*, turned hostile to the prosecution case.

28. The prosecution argued that the identification of the bodies was incorrect; the notes stated that the bodies had decomposed and although no post-mortem examination was performed nor the bodies dissected, it was maintained that viscera was ruptured. The CBI visited the area and decided to exhume the bodies on 15 January 2004. On 28 January 2004, a team of experts from All India Institute Medical Sciences (AIIMS) and CFSL, New Delhi, exhumed the bodies. On 29 January and 1 February 2004, a grave was located which revealed skeletal remains, clothes, bangles, and plastic salt bags. On 19 April 2004, the chargesheet was filed before the Chief Metropolitan Magistrate, Ahmedabad (Rural). The case was committed to the Court of the District and Sessions Judge, Panchmahals, Godhra on 18 May 2004. Subsequently the case was transferred to Mumbai at the behest of the Supreme Court. The special court also observed that 'the Hon'ble Supreme Court of India not only ordered the investigation in the present case to be carried out by the CBI but also directed the State Authorities to keep off from the petitioner (the prosecutrix) vide order dated 25 September 2003 in Criminal M.P. No. 8850/2003 in W.P. (Cri.) No. 118/2003' (ibid. at para 403).

29. *State of Gujarat* v. *Jaswantbhai Chaturbhai Nai and 19 Ors*, Sessions Case No. 634 of 2004 at para 285.

30. Ibid. at para 403.

31. Ibid. at para 410.

32. Ibid. at para 450.

33. Ibid. at para 451.

34. Who were these men? Bilki's aunt Sugrabi, who was once elected for a five-year term as a member of the *gram panchayat* from the village of Randhikpur, which had 100–150 Muslim households, testified in court that the accused were from the village and the family knew the men who had raped and killed Bilkis' family. She knew, since their childhood, Radheshyam Shah, Bipin Joshi, Kesharbhai Vohania, Pradip Modhiya, Bakabhai Vohania, and Mitesh Bhatt. Of these, Radheshyam Shah was the only lawyer in Randhikpur, known as Lala Vakil, Bipin Joshi was known as Lala Doctor, and Soni was a shopkeeper. She also knew Ramesh Chandana and his wife Pramilaben, who had served as a *sarpanch* of Randhikpur for over a decade.

35. *State of Gujarat v. Jaswantbhai Chaturbhai Nai and 19 Ors*, Sessions Case No. 634 of 2004 at para 453.

36. Ibid. at para (ix).

37. Ibid. at para 30.

38. Ibid. at para 436.

39. Ibid. at para 437.

40. The sentence and the acquittal are under appeal.

41. *State of Gujarat v. Jaswantbhai Chaturbhai Nai and 19 Ors*, Sessions Case No. 634 of 2004 at para 403.

42. Ibid. at para 451.

Appendix 1

The Criminal Law (Amendment) Act, 1983

THE CRIMINAL LAW (AMENDMENT) ACT, 1983 [Act No.43 of 1983] received the assent of the President on 25-12-1983. Act published in Gazette of India. 26-12-1983 Part II-S.1. Ext. p. 1 (No. 53). An Act further to amend the Indian Penal Code, the Code of Criminal Procedure, 1973 and the Indian Evidence Act, 1872. Be it enacted by Parliament in the Thirty fourth year of the Republic of India as follows:

1. Short title, insertion of new Section 228A

This Act may be called THE CRIMINAL LAW (AMENDMENT) ACT 1983.

2. Disclosure of identity of the victim of certain offences, etc. in the Indian Penal Code (hereinafter referred to as the Penal Code), after Section 228, the following section shall be inserted, namely:

228A. (1) Whoever prints or publishes the name or any matter which may make known the identity of any person against whom an offence under s. 376, s. 376A, s. 376C or s. 376D is alleged or found to have been committed (hereinafter in this section referred to as the victim) shall be punished with imprisonment of either description for a term which may extend to two years and shall also be liable to fine.

(2) Nothing in sub-s. (1) extends to any printing or publication of the name or any matter, which may make known the identity of the victim if such printing or publication is:

(a) by or under the order in writing of the officer in charge of the police station or the police office making the investigation into such offence acting in good faith for the purposes of such investigation: or

(b) by or with the authorization in writing of, the victim: or

(c) where the victim is dead or minor or of unsound mind, by or with the authorization in writing of, the next of kin of the victim;

Provided that no such authorization shall be given by the next of kin to anybody other than the chairman or the secretary, by whatever name called, of any recognized welfare institution or organization.

Explanation: For the purposes of this sub-s. 'recognised welfare institution or organisation' means a social welfare institution or organization recognized in this behalf by the Central or State Government.

(3) Whoever prints or publishes any matter in relation to any proceeding before a court with respect to an offence referred to in sub-s. (1) without the previous permission of such court shall be punished with imprisonment of either description for a term which may extend to two years and shall also be liable to fine.

Explanation: The printing or publication of the judgment of any High Court or the Supreme Court does not amount to an offence within the meaning of this section.

3. Substitution of new sections for sections 375 and 376. In the Penal Code, for the heading 'of rape' occurring immediately before s. 375 and for ss. 375 and 376, the following heading and sections shall be substituted, namely: Sexual offences

375. Rape: A man is said to commit 'rape' who, except in the case hereinafter excepted, has sexual intercourse with a woman under circumstances falling under any of the six following descriptions:

> Firstly: Against her will.
>   Secondly: Without her consent.
>   Thirdly: With her consent, when her consent has been obtained by putting her or any person in whom she is interested in fear of death or of hurt.

Fourthly: With her consent, when the man knows that he is not her husband, and that her consent is given because she believes that he is another man to whom she is or believes herself to be lawfully married.

Fifthly: With her consent, when, at the time of giving such consent, by reason of unsoundness of mind or intoxication or the administration by him personally or through another of any stupefying or unwholesome substance, she is unable to understand the nature and consequences of that to which she gives consent.

Sixthly: With or without her consent, when she is under sixteen years of age.

Explanation: Penetration is sufficient to constitute the sexual intercourse necessary to the offence of rape.

Exception: Sexual intercourse by a man with his own wife, the wife not being under fifteen years of age, is not rape.

376. Punishment for rape: (1) whoever, except in the cases provided for by sub-s. (2), commits rape shall be punished with imprisonment of either description for a term which shall not be less than seven years but which may be for life or for a term which may extend to ten years and shall also be liable to fine unless the woman raped is his own wife and is not under twelve years of age, in which case, he shall be punished with imprisonment of either description for a term which may extend to two years or with fine or with both: Provided that the court may, for adequate and special reasons to be mentioned in the judgment, impose a sentence of imprisonment for a term of less than seven years.

(2) Whoever,

(a) being a police officer commits rape

   i) within the limits of the police station to which he is appointed; or

   ii) in the premises of any station house whether or not situated in the police station to which he is appointed; or

   iii) on a woman in his custody or in the custody of a police officer subordinate to him; or

(b) being a public servant, takes advantage of his official position and commits rape on a woman in his custody as such public servant or in the custody of a public servant subordinate to him; or

(c) being on the management or on the staff of a jail, remand home or other place of custody established by or under any law for the time being in force or of a women's or children's institution takes advantage of his official position and commits rape on any inmate of such jail, remand home, place or institution; or

(d) being on the management or on the staff of a hospital, takes advantage of his official position and commits rape on a woman in that hospital; or

(e) commits rape on a woman knowing her to be pregnant; or

(f) commits rape on a woman when she is under twelve years of age; or

(g) commits gang rape shall be punished with rigorous imprisonment for a term which shall not be less than ten years but which may be for life and shall also be liable to fine;

Provided that the court may, for adequate and special reasons to be mentioned in the judgment, impose a sentence of imprisonment of either description for a term of less than ten years.

Explanation 1: Where a woman is raped by one or more in a group of persons acting in furtherance of their common intention, each of the persons shall be deemed to have committed gang rape within the meaning of this sub-section.

Explanation 2: 'Women's or children's institution means an institution whether called an orphanage or a home for neglected woman or children or a widows' home or by any other name, which is established and maintained to the reception and care of women or children.

Explanation 3: 'Hospital' means the precincts of the hospital and includes the precincts of any institution for the reception and treatment of persons during convalescence or of persons requiring medical attention or rehabilitation.

376A. Intercourse by a man with his wife during separation. Whoever has sexual intercourse with his own wife, who is living separately from him under a decree of separation or under any custom or usage without her consent shall be punished with imprisonment of either description for a term which may extend to two years and shall also be liable to fine.

376B. Intercourse by public servant with woman in his custody: Whoever, being a public servant, takes advantage of his official position and induces or seduces, any woman, who is in his custody as such public servant or in the custody of a public servant subordinate to him, to have sexual intercourse with him, such sexual intercourse not amounting to the offence of rape, shall be punished with imprisonment of either description for a term which may extend to five years and shall also be liable to fine.

376C. Intercourse by superintendent of Jail, remand home, etc. Whoever, being the superintendent or manager of a jail, remand home or other place or custody established by or under any law for the time being in force or in a women's or children's institution takes advantage of his official position and induces or seduces any female inmate of such jail, remand home, place or institution to have sexual intercourse with him, such sexual intercourse not amounting to the offence of rape, shall be punished with imprisonment of either description for a term which may extend to five years and shall also be liable to fine.

Explanation 1: 'Superintendent' in relation to jail, remand home or other place of custody or a women's or children's institution includes a person holding any other office in such jail, remand home, place or institution by virtue of which he can exercise any authority or control over its inmates.

Explanation 2: The expression 'Women's or children's institution shall have the same meaning as in Explanation to sub-s. (2) of s. 376.

376D. Intercourse by any member of the management or staff of a hospital with any woman in that hospital. Whoever, being on the management of a hospital or being on the staff of a hospital takes advantage of his position and has sexual intercourse with any woman in that hospital, such sexual intercourse not amounting to the offence of rape, shall be punished with imprisonment of either description for a term which may extend to five years and shall also be liable to fine.

Explanation: The expression 'hospital' shall have the same meaning as in Explanation 3 to sub-s. (2) of s. 376.

4. Amendment of Section 327: In the Code of Criminal Procedure, 1973 (hereinafter referred to as the Criminal Procedure Code), s. 327 shall be renumbered as sub-s. (1) of that section and after it, as so renumbered, the following sub-ss shall be inserted, namely:

(2) Notwithstanding anything contained in sub-s. (1), the inquiry into and trial of rape or an offence under s. 376, s. 376A, s. 376B, s. 376C or s. 376D of the Indian Penal Code shall be conducted in camera:

Provided that the presiding Judge may, if he thinks fit, or on an application made by either of the parties, allow any particular person to have access to, or be or remain in, the room or building used by the court.

(3) Where any proceedings are held under sub-s. (2) it shall be not be lawful for any person to print or publish any matter in relation to any proceedings, except with the previous permission of the court.

5. Amendment of the first schedule.

In the first schedule to the Criminal Procedure Code, under the heading 'I: Offences under the Indian Penal Code'.

(a) after the entries relating to s. 228, the following entries shall be inserted, namely:

6. Insertion of new Section 114A

After s. 114 of the Indian Evidence Act 1872, the following section shall be inserted namely, 114A Presumption as to absence of consent in certain prosecutions for rape: In a prosecution for rape under clause (a) or clause (b) or clause (c) or clause (d) or clause (e) or clause (g) of sub-s. (2) of s. 376 of the Indian Penal Code, where sexual intercourse by the accused is proved and the question is whether it was without the consent of the woman alleged to have been raped and the states in her evidence before the court that she did not consent, the court shall presume that she did not consent.

The Law on Character Evidence (IEA)

Section 155(4): The credit of a witness may be impeached in the following ways by the adverse party, or, with the consent of the court, by the party who calls him:

> (4) when a man is prosecuted for rape or an attempt to ravish, it may be shown that the prosecutrix was of a generally immoral character.

The Indian Evidence Act 2002

Act No. of Year: No. 4 of 2003
Enactment Date: [31st December 2002]
Act Objective: An Act further to amend the Indian Evidence Act, 1872. BE it enacted by Parliament in the Fifty-third Year of the Republic of India as follows:

3. Amendment of Section 155: In s. 155 of the principal Act, clause (4) shall be omitted.

Relevant Laws on Kidnapping and Abduction of Minors and Women (IPC)

Section 363: whoever kidnaps any person from India or from lawful guardianship, shall be punished with imprisonment of either description for a term, which may extend to seven years, and shall also be liable to fine.

Section 366: whoever kidnaps or abducts any woman with intent that she may be compelled, or knowing it to be likely that she will be compelled, to marry any person against her will, or in order that she may be forced or seduced to illicit intercourse, or knowing that it is likely that she will be forced or seduced to illicit sexual intercourse, shall be punished with imprisonment of either description for a term, which may extend to 10 years, and shall also be liable to fine: and whoever by means of criminal intimidation as defined in this code or of abuse of authority or any other method of compulsion, induces any woman to go from any place with intent that she may be, or knowing that it is likely that she will be, forced or seduced to illicit sexual intercourse with another person shall also be punishable as aforesaid.

THE SCHEDULED CASTES AND SCHEDULED TRIBES (PREVENTION OF ATROCITIES) ACT, 1989

No. 33 of 1989

[11th September 1989]

An Act to prevent the commission of offences of atrocities against the members of the Scheduled Castes and the Scheduled Tribes, to provide for Special Courts for the trial of such offences and for the relief and rehabilitation of the victims of such offences and for matters connected therewith or incidental thereto.

Be it enacted by Parliament in the Fortieth Year of the Republic of India as follows:

CHAPTER I

Preliminary

1. Short title, extent and commencement—

(1) This Act may be called the Scheduled Castes and the Scheduled Tribes (Prevention of Atrocities) Act, 1989.

(2) It extends to the whole of India except the State of Jammu and Kashmir.

(3) It shall come into force on such date as the Central Government may, by notification in the Official Gazette, appoint.

2. Definitions—

(1) In this Act, unless the context otherwise requires—

(a) 'atrocity' means an offence punishable under s. 3;

(b) 'Code' means the Code of Criminal Procedure, 1973 (2 of 1974);

(c) 'Scheduled Castes and Scheduled Tribes' shall have the meanings assigned to them respectively under clause (24) and clause (25) of Article 366 of the Constitution;

(d) 'Special Court' means a Court of Session specified as a Special Court in s. 14;

(e) 'Special Public Prosecutor' means a Public Prosecutor specified as a Special Public Prosecutor or an advocate referred to in s. 15;

(f) words and expressions used but not defined in this Act and defined in the Code or the Indian Penal Code (45 of 1860) shall have the meanings assigned to them respectively in the Code, or as the case may be, in the Indian Penal Code.

(2) Any reference in this Act to any enactment or any provision thereof shall, in relation to an area in which such enactment or

such provision is, not in force, be construed as a reference to the corresponding law, if any, in force in that area.

Chapter II

Offences of Atrocities

3. Punishments for offences of atrocities—

(1) Whoever, not being a member of a Scheduled Caste or a Scheduled Tribe,

    (i) forces a member of a Scheduled Caste or a Scheduled Tribe to drink or eat any inedible or obnoxious substance;

    (ii) acts with intent to cause injury, insult or annoyance to any member of a Scheduled Caste or a Scheduled Tribe by dumping excreta, waste matter, carcasses or any other obnoxious substance in his premises or neighbourhood;

    (iii) forcibly removes clothes from the person of a member of a Scheduled Caste or a Scheduled Tribe or parades him naked or with painted face or body or commits any similar act which is derogatory to human dignity;

    (iv) wrongfully occupies or cultivates any land owned by, or allotted to, or notified by any competent authority to be allotted to, a member of a Scheduled Caste or a Scheduled Tribe or gets the land allotted to him transferred;

    (v) wrongfully dispossesses a member of a Scheduled Caste or a Scheduled Tribe from his land or premises or interferes with the enjoyment of his rights over any land, premises or water;

    (vi) compels or entices a member of a Scheduled Caste or a Scheduled Tribe to do 'beggar' or other similar forms of forced or bonded labour other than any compulsory service for public purposes imposed by government;

    (vii) forces or intimidates a member of a Scheduled Caste or a Scheduled Tribe not to vote or to vote to a particular candidate or to vote in a manner other than that provided by law;

(viii)   institutes false, malicious or vexatious suit or criminal or other legal proceedings against a member of a Scheduled Caste or a Scheduled Tribe;

(ix)   gives any false or frivolous information to any public servant and thereby causes such public servant to use his lawful power to the injury or annoyance of a member of a Scheduled Caste or a Scheduled Tribe;

(x)   intentionally insults or intimidates with intent to humiliate a member of a Scheduled Caste or a Scheduled Tribe in any place within public view;

(xi)   assaults or uses force to any woman belonging to a Scheduled Caste or a Scheduled Tribe with intent to dishonour or outrage her modesty;

(xii)   being in a position to dominate the will of a woman belonging to a Scheduled Caste or a Scheduled Tribe and uses that position to exploit her sexually to which she would not have otherwise agreed;

(xiii)   corrupts or fouls the water of any spring, reservoir or any other source ordinarily used by members of the Scheduled Caste or the Scheduled Tribes so as to render it less fit for the purpose for which it is ordinarily used;

(xiv)   denies a member of a Scheduled Caste or a Scheduled Tribe any customary right of passage to a place of public resort or obstructs such member so as to prevent him from using or having access to a place of public resort to which other members of public or any section thereof have a right to use or access to;

(xv)   forces or causes a member of a Scheduled Caste or a Scheduled Tribe to leave his house, village or other place of residence, shall be punishable with imprisonment for a term which shall not be less than six months but which may extend to five years and with fine.

(2) Whoever, not being a member of a Scheduled Caste or a Scheduled Tribe—

(i)   gives or fabricates false evidence intending thereby to cause, or knowing it to be likely that he will thereby cause, any member of a Scheduled Caste or a Scheduled

Tribe to be convicted of an offence which is capital by the law for the time being in force shall be punished with imprisonment for life and with fine; and if an innocent member of a Scheduled Caste or a Scheduled Tribe be convicted and executed in consequence of such false or fabricated evidence, the person who gives or fabricates such false evidence, shall be punished with death;

(ii) gives or fabricates false evidence intending thereby to cause, or knowing it to be likely that he will thereby cause, any member of a Scheduled Caste or a Scheduled Tribe to be convicted of an offence which is not capital but punishable with imprisonment for a term of seven years or upwards, shall be punishable with imprisonment for a term which shall not be less than six months but which may extend to seven years or upwards and with fine;

(iii) commits mischief by fire or any explosive substance intending to cause or knowing it to be likely that he will thereby cause damage to any property belonging to a member of a Scheduled Caste or a Scheduled Tribe shall be punishable with imprisonment for a term which shall not be less than six months but which may extend to seven years and with fine;

(iv) commits mischief by fire or any explosive substance intending to cause or knowing it to be likely that he will thereby cause destruction of any building which is ordinarily used as a place of worship or as a place for human dwelling or as a place for custody of the property by a member of a Scheduled Caste or a Scheduled Tribe, shall be punishable with imprisonment for life and with fine;

(v) commits any offence under the Indian Penal Code (45 of 1860) punishable with imprisonment for a term of ten years or more against a person or property on the ground that such person is a member of a Scheduled Caste or a Scheduled Tribe or such property belongs to such member, shall be punishable with imprisonment for life and with fine;

(vi)   knowingly or having reason to believe that an offence has been committed under this Chapter, causes any evidence of the commission of that offence to disappear with the intention of screening the offender from legal punishment, or with that intention gives any information respecting the offence which he knows or believes to be false, shall be punishable with the punishment provided for that offence; or

(vii)   being a public servant, commits any offence under this section, shall be punishable with imprisonment for a term which shall not be less than one year but which may extend to the punishment provided for that offence.

4. Punishment for neglect of duties—

Whoever, being a public servant but not being a member of a Scheduled Caste or a Scheduled Tribe, wilfully neglects his duties required to be performed by him under this Act, shall be punishable with imprisonment for a term which shall not be less than six months but which may extend to one year.

5. Enhanced punishment for subsequent conviction—

Whoever, having already been convicted of an offence under this Chapter is convicted for the second offence or any offence subsequent to the second offence, shall be punishable with imprisonment for a term which shall not be less than one year but which may extend to the punishment provided for that offence.

6. Application of certain provisions of the Indian Penal Code—

Subject to the other provisions of this Act, the provisions of s. 34, Chapter III, Chapter IV, Chapter V, Chapter V-A, s. 149 and Chapter XXIII of the Indian Penal Code (45 of 1860), shall, so far as may be, apply for the purposes of this Act as they apply for the purposes of the Indian Penal Code.

7. Forfeiture of property of certain persons—

(1)   Where a person has been convicted of any offence punishable under this Chapter, the Special Court may, in addition to awarding any punishment, by order in writing, declare that

any property, movable or immovable or both, belonging to the person which has been used for the commission of that offence, shall stand forfeited to government.

(2) Where any person is accused of any offence under this Chapter, it shall be open to the Special Court trying him to pass an order that all or any of the properties, movable or immovable or both, belonging to him, shall, during the period of such trial, be attached, and where such trial ends in conviction, the property so attached shall be liable to forfeiture to the extent it is required for the purpose of realization of any fine imposed under this Chapter.

8. Presumption as to offences—

In a prosecution for an offence under this Chapter, if it is proved that –

(a) the accused rendered any financial assistance to a person accused of, or reasonably suspected of committing, an offence under this chapter, the Special Court shall presume, unless the contrary is proved, that such person had, abetted the offence;

(b) a group of persons committed an offence under this Chapter and if it is proved that the offence committed was a sequel to any existing dispute regarding land or any other matter, it shall be presumed that the offence was committed in furtherance of the common intention or in prosecution of the common object.

9. Conferment of powers—

(1) Notwithstanding anything contained in the Code or in any other provision of this Act, the State government may, if it considers it necessary or expedient so to do—

(a) for the prevention of and for coping with any offence under this Act, or

(b) for any case or class or group of cases under this Act, in any district or part thereof, confer, by notification in the Official Gazette, on any officer of the State government, the powers exercisable by a police officer under the Code in such district or part thereof or, as the case maybe, for such case or class or group of cases, and in particular, the powers of arrest, investigation and prosecution of persons before any Special Court.

(2) All officers of police and all other officers of government shall assist the officer referred to in sub-s. (1) in the execution of the provisions of this Act or any rule, scheme or order made thereunder.

(3) The provisions of the Code shall, so far as may be, apply to the exercise of the powers by an officer under sub-s. (1).

Chapter III

Externment

10. Removal of person likely to commit offence—

(1) Where the Special Court is satisfied, upon a complaint or a police report that a person is likely to commit an offence under Chapter II of this Act in any area included in 'Scheduled Areas' or 'Tribal areas' as referred to in Article 244 of the Constitution, it may, by order in writing, direct such person to remove himself beyond the limits of such area, by such route and within such time as may be specified in the order, and not to return to that area from which he was directed to remove himself for such period, not exceeding two years, as may be specified in the order.

(2) The Special Court shall, along with the order under sub-s. (1), communicate to the person directed under that sub-s. the grounds on which such order has been made.

(3) The Special Court may revoke or modify the order made under sub-s. (1), for the reasons to be recorded in writing, on the representation made by the person against whom such order has been made or by any other person on his behalf within thirty days from the date of the order.

11. Procedure on failure of person to remove himself from area and enter thereon after removal—

(1) If a person to whom a direction has been issued under s. 10 to remove himself from any area—

(a) fails to remove himself as directed; or
(b) having so removed himself enters such area within the period specified in the order, otherwise than with the permission in

writing of the Special Court under sub-s. (2), the Special Court may cause him to be arrested and removed in police custody to such place outside such area as the Special Court may specify.

(2) The Special Court may, by order in writing, permit any person in respect of whom an order under s. 10 has been made, to return to the area from which he was directed to remove himself for such temporary period and subject to such conditions as may be specified in such order and may require him to execute a bond with or without surety for the due observation of the conditions imposed.

(3) The Special Court may at any time revoke any such permission.

(4) Any person who, with such permission, returns to the area from which he was directed to remove himself shall observe the conditions imposed and at the expiry of the temporary period for which he was permitted to return or on the revocation of such permission before the expiry of such temporary period shall remove himself outside such area and shall not return thereto within the unexpired portion specified under s. 10 without a fresh permission.

(5) If a person fails to observe any of the conditions imposed or to remove himself accordingly or having so removed himself enters or returns to such area without fresh permission the Special Court may cause him to be arrested and removed in police custody to such place outside such area as the Special Court may specify.

12. Taking measurements and photographs, etc. of persons against whom order under Section 10 is made—

(1) Every person against whom an order has been made under s. 10 shall, if so required by the Special Court, allow his measurements and photographs to be taken by a police officer.

(2) If any person referred to in sub-s. (1) when required to allow his measurements or photographs to be taken, resists or refuses to allow the taking of such measurements or photographs, it shall be lawful to use all necessary means to secure the taking thereof.

(3) Resistance to or refusal to allow the taking of measurements or photographs under sub-s. (2) shall be deemed to be an offence under s. 186 of the Indian Penal Code (45 of 1860).

(4) Where an order under s. 10 is revoked, all measurements and photographs (including negatives) taken under sub-s. (2) shall be destroyed or made over to the person against whom such order is made.

13. Penalty for non-compliance of order under Section 10—

Any person contravening an order of the Special Court made under s. 10 shall be punishable with imprisonment for a term which may extend to one year and with fine.

CHAPTER IV

Special Courts

14. Special court—

For the purpose of providing for speedy trial, the State government shall, with the concurrence of the Chief Justice of the High Court, by notification in the Official Gazette, specify for each district a Court of Session to be a Special Court to try the offences under this Act.

15. Special Public Prosecutor—

For every Special Court, the State government shall, by notification in the Official Gazette, specify a Public Prosecutor or appoint an advocate who has been in practice as an advocate for not less than seven years, as a Special Public Prosecutor for the purpose of conducting cases in that court.

CHAPTER V

Miscellaneous

16. Power of state government to impose collective fine—

The provisions of section 10-A of the Protection of Civil Rights Act, 1955 (22 of 1955) shall, so far as may be, apply for the purposes of imposition and realization of collective fine and for all other matters connected therewith under this Act.

17. Preventive action to be taken by the law and order machinery—

(1) A District Magistrate or a Sub-divisional Magistrate or any other Executive Magistrate or any police officer not below the rank of a Deputy Superintendent of Police may, on receiving information and after such enquiry as he may think necessary, has reason to believe that a person or a group of persons not belonging to the Scheduled Castes or the Scheduled Tribes, residing in or frequenting any place within the local limits of his jurisdiction is likely to commit an offence or has threatened to commit any offence under this Act and is of the opinion that there is sufficient ground for proceeding, declare such an area to be an area prone to atrocities and take necessary action for keeping the peace and good behaviour and maintenance of public order and tranquillity and may take preventive action.

(2) The provisions of Chapters VIII, X and XI of the Code shall, so far as may be, apply for the purposes of sub-s. (1).

(3) The State government may, by notification in the Official Gazette, make one or more schemes specifying the manner in which the officers referred to in sub-s. (1) shall take appropriate action specified in such scheme or schemes to prevent atrocities and to restore the feeling of security amongst the members of the Scheduled Castes and the Scheduled Tribes.

18. Section 438 of the Code not to apply to persons committing an offence under the Act—

Nothing in s. 438 of the Code shall apply in relation to any case involving the arrest of any person on an accusation of having committed an offence under this Act.

19. Section 360 of the Code and the provisions of the Probation of Offenders Act not to apply to persons guilty of an offence under the Act—

The provisions of s. 360 of the Code and the provisions of the Probation of Offenders Act, 1958 (20 of 1958) shall not apply to any person above the age of eighteen years who is found guilty of having committed an offence under this Act.

20. Act to override other laws—

Save as otherwise provided in this Act, the provisions of this Act shall have effect notwithstanding anything inconsistent therewith contained in any other law for the time being in force or any custom or usage or any instrument having effect by virtue of any such law.

21. Duty of government to ensure effective implementation of the Act—

(1) Subject to such rules as the Central Government may make in this behalf, the State government shall take such measures as may be necessary for the effective implementation of this Act.

(2) In particular, and without prejudice to the generality of the foregoing provisions, such measures may include:—

  (i) the provision for adequate facilities, including legal aid, to the persons subjected to atrocities to enable them to avail themselves of justice;

  (ii) the provision for travelling and maintenance expenses to witnesses including the victims of atrocities, during investigation and trial of offences under this Act;

  (iii) the provision for the economic and social rehabilitation of the victims of the atrocities;

  (iv) the appointment of officers for initiating or exercising supervision over prosecutions for the contravention of the provisions of this Act;

  (v) the setting up of committees at such appropriate levels as the State government may think fit to assist that government in formulation or implementation of such measures;

  (vi) provision for a periodic survey of the working of the provisions of this Act with a view to suggesting measures for the better implementation of the provisions of this Act;

  (vii) the identification of the areas where the members of the Scheduled Castes and the Scheduled Tribes are likely to be subjected to atrocities and adoption of such measures so as to ensure safety for such members.

(3) The Central Government shall take such steps as may be necessary to co-ordinate the measures taken by the State governments under sub-s. (1).

(4) The Central Government shall, every year, place on the table of each House of Parliament a report on the measures taken by itself and by the State governments in pursuance of the provisions of this section.

22. Protection of action taken in good faith—

No suit, prosecution or other legal proceedings shall lie against the Central Government or against the State government or any officer or authority of government or any other person for anything which is in good faith done or intended to be done under this Act.

23. Power to make rules—

(1) The Central Government may, by notification in the Official Gazette, make rules for carrying out the purposes of this Act.

(2) Every rule made under this Act shall be laid, as soon as may be after it is made, before each House of Parliament, while it is in session for a total period of thirty days which may be comprised in one session or in two or more successive sessions, and if before the expiry of the session immediately following the session or the successive sessions aforesaid, both Houses agree in making any modification in the rule or both Houses agree that the rule should not be made, the rule shall thereafter have effect only in such modified form or be of no effect, as the case may be; so, however, that any such modification or annulment shall be without prejudice to the validity of anything previously done under that rule.

Appendix 2

It was not until 1971 that the National Crime Records Bureau's (NCRB) annual publication, *Crime in India*, provided official statistics on the number of cases of rape reported in the country. More than two decades later (in 1995), the NCRB started recording statistics concerning crimes specific to women as a separate chapter. The objective of reading official crime statistics to analyse the extent of violence against women has been furthered by the report published by the Centre for Women's Development Studies (CWDS), which provides an analysis of the statistics that concerned crime against women reported between 1995 and 1999. Although Gujarat, when compared to other states, falls in a 'lower-medium range', showing neither very high nor extremely low rate of rape, the states[1] (along with Daman and Diu and Pondicherry), has recorded 'low levels of crimes against women despite high overall crime rates' (CWDS Report 2002: 10). The rate and incidence of rape in Gujarat indicate an increase in the number of rape incidents that were reported to the police between 1996 and 1998 (see Table 1). Included here are figures that show the rates of kidnapping and abduction of girls and women (see Table 2). The CWDS report (2002) shows that during the disposal of criminal cases in courts during 1988 and 1999, only 15 per cent of the total crimes tried by courts comprised cases of crimes against women (see Table 3). During this period, rape had one of the lowest convictions rate amongst all crimes against women (see CWDS Report 2002). The statistical picture of judicial delay has not changed in Gujarat, in the last two decades, if anything it

Table 1　Number of rape cases between 1995 and 1999:
State-wise breakup

S. No.	STATES/UT	1995	1996	1997	1998	1999
1.	ANDHRA PRADESH	856	812	947	869	895
2.	ARUNACHAL PRADESH	25	37	43	32	39
3.	ASSAM	588	580	717	744	703
4.	BIHAR	1,312	1,453	1,457	1,421	1,447
5.	GOA	19	10	15	16	18
6.	GUJARAT	309	306	375	368	331
7.	HARYANA	311	336	373	364	372
8.	HIMACHAL PRADESH	116	132	129	128	109
9.	JAMMU & KASHMIR	109	157	166	178	170
10.	KARNATAKA	263	222	244	233	301
11.	KERALA	266	389	588	589	423
12.	MADHYA PRADESH	3,119	3,265	3,518	3,354	3,561
13.	MAHARASHTRA	1,362	1,444	1,246	1,154	1,320
14.	MANIPUR	12	14	9	13	12
15.	MEGHALAYA	17	33	37	42	27
16.	MIZORAM	41	49	52	84	71
17.	NAGALAND	16	9	17	13	11
18.	ORISSA	553	617	679	799	820
19.	PUNJAB	96	178	184	219	282
20.	RAJASTHAN	1,036	1,162	1,255	1,266	1,198
21.	SIKKIM	3	9	7	7	7
22.	TAMIL NADU	268	327	324	362	430
23.	TRIPURA	75	90	98	73	72
24.	UTTAR PRADESH	1,808	1,854	1,457	1,605	1,593
25.	UTTARANCHAL	787	855	824	757	819
26.	A & N ISLANDS	5	7	9	4	6
27.	CHANDIGARH	5	9	9	11	16
28.	D & N HAVELI	1	3	2	7	3
29.	DAMAN & DIU	2	1	1	0	4
30.	DELHI UT	372	484	544	438	402
31.	LAKSHADWEEP	0	0	0	0	0
32.	PONDICHERRY	2	2	4	1	6

Source: CWDS Report, 2002.

Table 2 Number of cases reported in Gujarat (1995–9)

Year	Rape	Abduction/Kidnapping (Girls/Women)
1995	309	**974**
1996	306	**864**
1997	375	**973**
1998	368	**1,182**
1999	331	**1,074**

Source: CWDS Report, 2002.

Table 3 Rape cases in all criminal courts in 1998–9

Rape Cases All India	1998	1999
No. of Cases that came on trial including pending cases	58,655	62,466
Pending cases	83%	82.46%
Trials completed	16.6%	17.23 %
Convictions	**26.46%**	**27.43%**

Source: CWDS Report, 2002.

has worsened. Per the latest Crime in India (2011) statistics, Gujarat has a pendency rate of 92.9 per cent cases, which places the courts in Gujarat amongst the first five states in the country unable to dispose the high rates of pending cases (see Tables 3, 4, and 5). Gujarat's percentage to pendency to an all India total is 11.5 per cent, the second highest contributor to the rate of judicial delay, after Maharashtra, which scores 17.7 per cent. The time taken for hearing a case ranges from six months to more than ten years. Gujarat has an appallingly poor record in completing criminal trials and each year the number of cases of rape that come up for hearing is on the increase.

Table 4 Disposal of rape cases by courts during 2011

Crime Head	Total No. of Cases for Trial Including Pending Cases from Previous Year	Cases Withdrawn By Govt.	Compounded or Withdrawn	No. of Cases			Pending Trial at the End of the Year
				In Which Trials were Completed			
				Convicted	Acquitted or Discharged	Total	
RAPE (Sec. 376 IPC)	95,065	3	166	4,072	11,351	15,423	79,476
CUSTODIAL RAPE	9	0	0	0	1	1	8
OTHER RAPE	95,056	3	166	4,072	11,350	15,422	79,468

Source: Table 4.9, Disposal of IPC Cases by Courts During 2011, NCRB, http://ncrb.gov.in/, accessed on 23 September 2012.

Table 5 Percentage of rape cases disposed by courts during 2011

| Crime Head | Cases Withdrawn by Govt. | Compounded or Withdrawn | Percentage of Cases to Total Cases for Trial | | | Pending Trial at the End of the Year | Conviction Rate |
| | | | In Which Trials were Completed | | | | |
			Convicted	Acquitted	Total		
RAPE (Sec. 376 IPC)	0.0	0.2	4.3	11.9	16.2	83.6	26.4
CUSTODIAL RAPE	0.0	0	0	11.1	0	88.9	0
OTHER RAPE	0.0	0.2	4.3	11.9	16.2	83.6	**26.4**

Source: Table 4.11, Percentage of IPC Cases Disposed by Courts During 2011, NCRB, http://ncrb.gov.in/, accessed on 23 September 2012.

Table 6   Gender of the persons arrested in rape cases, 2010.

Crime Head	Male	Female	Total	Percentage to Total	
				Male	Female
Rape Section 376	26,357	717	27,074	97.4	2.6
Custodial Rape	10	0	10	100.0	0
Other Rape	26,457	717	27,064	97.4	2.6

Source: Table 12.2 Persons Arrested Under IPC Crimes During 2010 (Crime and Head–Wise and Gender-Wise), Crime in India 2010, National Crimes Record Bureau, GOI.

NOTE

1. The total crime rate (per million persons) calculated as an average three year rate shows that Gujarat along with Rajasthan, Madhya Pradesh, and UT Chandigarh form a contiguous region marked by high crime rates (CWDS Report 2002: 8). The CWDS analysis of crime statistics shows that a high crime rate does not necessarily imply that the rate of crime against women would be high as well. Moreover, 'rape cases composed a high proportion (34 per cent) of cases with the lowest CAW (crimes against women) rates' (CWDS Report 2002:11).

Appendix 3

❧❧

One of the first cases to challenge the PoA Act on the grounds of constitutional validity was dismissed by a full bench in the Rajasthan High Court in 1993 (see Naval 2001). In *Jai Singh and Another* v. *Union of India and Others*,[1] the petitioners argued that punishment of 'a caste Hindu for the offences under Section 3 of the Act', which excluded 'Shudras or Scheduled Tribes' as perpetrators, amounted to 'hostile discrimination' between the caste Hindus and those who were not caste Hindus.[2] Dismissing the petition, the Rajasthan High Court insisted that historical discrimination makes it reasonable to classify 'the accused belonging to one caste or other' to 'represent one class; as long as 'they are treated alike or similarly'.[3] *Haresh Kumar Singh and Ors* v. *Union of India (UOI) and Ors*[4] dismissed twenty-two applications that challenged the PoA Act and attempted to quash the case. The high court explained the notion of reasonable classification as follows:

> Article 14 of the Constitution prohibits class legislation and not reasonable classification. It does not provide that uniform law should be made for all citizens. It only provides that amongst the equal, law should be equal. In other words, the like should be treated alike. ... The basis of classification may be historical, geographical or other relevant grounds depending upon the policy and object of the Act and evils sought to be remedied ... Two conditions must be fulfilled before a classification can be held valid; (i) the classification must be founded on intelligible differentia which distinguishes persons or things which are grouped together from others left out of the group;

(ii) that differentia has a rational relation to the objects sought to be achieved by the Act.[5]

The Patna High Court ruled that the PoA Act is founded on a reasonable classification and not on arbitrary or discriminatory discrimination against people who do not belong to these groups. Hence, the PoA Act does not violate Article 14 of the Constitution.

In *Dr Ram Krishna Balothia* v. *Union of India (UOI) and Ors* the petitioners, mostly upper-caste Hindus and Muslims, argued that 'the entire Act is based on caste discrimination and therefore infringes Article 15(1) of the Constitution and it is not saved under Article 15(4) of the Constitution'.[6] True, Article 15(1) says that 'the state shall not discriminate against any citizen on grounds only of religion, race, caste, sex, place of birth or any of them'.[7] Yet it is clear it also insists that 'nothing in this article or in clause 2 of Article 29 shall prevent the State from making any special provisions for the advancement of any socially and educationally backward classes of citizens or for the Scheduled Castes and Scheduled Tribes'.[8] The court had no difficulty then in holding that Article 15(4) 'embodies the doctrine of protective discrimination',[9] and further clarified that special provisions would include all efforts to make Dalits, tribals and backward classes 'live with dignity' and 'self-esteem'.[10] The Act 'is one of the legislative measures intended to do justice to members of Scheduled Castes and Scheduled Tribes, the most oppressed section of the society, by affirmative action'.[11] While the PoA Act was found to be constitutionally valid, s. 18 was found to violate Articles 14 and 21 (right to life), and was struck down. The court observed that the denial of anticipatory bail as provided under s. 438 CrPC precludes the possibility of courts considering whether the procedure was reasonable or not. This is especially important when 'false cases are foisted for purpose of disgracing or humiliating or harassing innocent persons'.[12] Since s. 18 of the act applied to all offences under its ambit and did not differentiate between minor or major atrocities, the Madhya Pradesh High Court believed that the PoA Act 'is capable of being misused considering the wide amplitude of the offences created thereunder. The wider the amplitude of the offence, the greater is the scope for misuse.'[13]

On review, the Supreme Court[14] disagreed on several counts:[15] First, the constitutional validity of s. 18 has to be 'viewed in the context of the social conditions which give rise to such offences and the apprehension that perpetrators of such atrocities are likely to threaten and intimidate their victims and prevent or obstruct them in the prosecution of these offenders, if the offenders are allowed to avail of anticipatory bail.'[16] Second, the 'Statement of Objects and Reasons' of the PoA Act makes it manifest that 'when members of Scheduled Castes and Scheduled Tribes assert their rights and demand statutory protection, vested interests try to cow them down and terrorize them'.[17] Third, the court held that 'in these circumstances, if anticipatory bail is not made available to persons who commit such offences, such a denial cannot be considered as unreasonable or violative of Article 14, as these offences form a distinct class by themselves and cannot be compared with other offences'.[18] Fourth, anticipatory bail 'cannot be granted as matter of right. It is essentially a statutory right conferred long after the coming of force of the Constitution. It cannot be considered as an essential ingredient of Article 21 of the Constitution. And its non-application to a certain special category of offences cannot be considered as violative of Article 21'.[19]

NOTES

1. AIR (1993) RAJ 177.
2. Ibid. at para 60.
3. Ibid. at para 61.
4. MANU/BH/0319/1996.
5. Ibid. at para 10.
6. MANU/MP/0032/1994 at para 3.
7. Ibid. cited at para 6.
8. Ibid. cited at para 6.
9. Ibid. at para 7.
10. Ibid.
11. Ibid. at para 10.
12. Ibid. at para 21.
13. Ibid. at para 23.
14. *State of MP and Another* v. *Ram Kishna Balothia and Another*, MANU/SC/0239/1995: (1995) SCC (3) 221.

15. Ibid.
16. Ibid at para 6.
17. Ibid at para 6.
18. Ibid at para 6.
19. Ibid at para 7.

Bibliography

❧❧

Arasu, Ponni and Priya Thangarajah, 'Queer Women and Habeas Corpus in India: The Love that Blinds the Law', *Indian Journal of Gender Studies*, 19(3), 2012, pp. 413–35.

Agamben, Giorgio, *Homo Sacer: Sovereign Power and Bare Life*, Stanford: Stanford University Press, 1998.

———, *Potentialities: Collected Essays in Philosophy*. Stanford: Stanford University Press, 1999.

Agnes, Flavia, 'The Anti–Rape Campaign: The Struggle and the Setback,' in *Struggle against Violence*, Chhaya Datar (ed.), Calcutta: Stree, 1983.

———, 'Protecting Women against Violence? Review of a Decade of Legislation, 1980–1989', *Economic and Political Weekly*, 27(7), 1992, pp. WS19–WS33.

———, 'Violence against Women: Review of Recent Enactments', in *In the Name of Justice: Women and Law in Society*, Swapna Mukhopadhyay (ed.), Delhi: Manohar, 1998.

———, 'Law, Ideology and Female Sexuality: Gender Neutrality in Rape Law', *Economic and Political Weekly*, 57(9), 2002, pp. 844–47.

———, 'To Whom Do Experts Testify? Ideological Challenges of Feminist Jurisprudence', *Economic and Political Weekly*, 40(18), 2005, pp. 1859–66.

Agrawal, Girish and Colin Gonsalves, *Dalits and the Law*, New Delhi: Human Rights Law Network, 2005.

Albin, R.S., 'Psychological Studies of Rape', *Signs: Journal of Women in Culture and Society*, 3(2), 1977, pp. 423–35.

Amos, Dean, 'On Rape, Age, Identity and Survivorship, Lectures on Medical Jurisprudence: Lecture Delivered at the University of London', *The London Medical Gazette Weekly Journal of Medicine and Collateral Sciences*, Saturday, 9 April 1831, pp. 33–9.

Anagol, Padma, *The Emergence of Feminism in India, 1850-1920*, London: Ashgate, 2006.

Aretxaga, Begoña, *Shattering Silence: Women, Nationalism and Political Subjectivity in Northern Ireland*, New Jersey: Princeton University Press, 1997.

Association for Advocacy and Legal Initiatives (AALI), *Choosing a Life … Crimes of Honor in India: The Right to, If, When and Whom to Marry*, Lucknow: AALI, 2004.

Auden, W.H. 'Law Like Love', *W.H. Auden: Selected by the Author*. England and Australia: Penguin Books with Faber and Faber, 1958.

Austin J. L., *How to do Things with Words: The William James Lectures delivered at Harvard University in 1955*, in J. O. Urmson and Marina Sbisà (eds), Oxford: Clarendon Press (2nd edition), 1975.

Balagopal, K., 'Post-Chundur and Other Chundurs', *Economic and Political Weekly*, (26)42, 1991, pp. 2399–405.

Basu, Srimati, 'Judges of Normality: Mediating Marriage in the Family Courts of Kolkata, India', *Signs*, 37(2), 2012, pp. 469–92.

Baxi, Pratiksha, 'Rape, Retribution, State: On Whose Bodies?', *Economic and Political Weekly*, 35(14), 2000, pp.1196–200.

————, '*Habeas Corpus* in the Realm of Love: Litigating Marriages of Choice in India', *Australian Feminist Law Journal*, (25), 2006, pp. 59–78.

————, 'Adjudicating the Riot: Communal Violence, Crowds and Public Tranquility', *Domains* (Special Issue), 3, 2007, pp. 70–105.

————, 'Justice is a Secret: Compromise in Rape Trials', *Contributions to Indian Sociology* (44), 3, 2010, pp. 207–233; and republished in Flavia Agnes and Shoba Venkatesh Ghosh (eds), *Negotiating Spaces: Legal Domains, Gender Concerns, and Community Constructs*. New Delhi: Oxford University Press, 2012, in association with Majlis Legal Centre.

————, *Habeas Corpus: Juridical Narratives of Sexual Governance*, Centre for the Study of Law and Governance, Working Paper Series CSLG/WP/09/02, New Delhi: Jawaharlal Nehru University, 2009.

Baxi, Upendra, Vasudha Dhagamwar, Raghunath Kelkar, and Lotika Sarkar, 'An Open Letter to the Chief Justice of India', *Supreme Court Cases*, (4), 1979, pp. 17–22.

————, 'Discipline, Repression and Legal Pluralism', in *Legal Pluralism Proceedings of the Canberra Law Workshop VII*, Peter Sack and Elizabeth Minchin (eds), Pink Panther: Australia, 1985.

————, *Towards a Sociology of Indian Law*. New Delhi: Satvahan Publications, 1986.

————, *Inhuman Wrongs and Human Rights: Unconventional Essays*, Delhi: Har Anand Publications, 1994.

————, 'The Second Gujarat Catastrophe', *Economic and Political Weekly*, 37(34), 2002, pp. 3519–31.

Baxi, Upendra, 'The Gujarat Catastrophe: Notes on Reading Politics as Democidal Rape Culture', in *The Violence of Normal Times: Essays on Women's Lived Realities*, Kalpana Kannabiran (ed.), Women Unlimited: New Delhi, 2005.

Baynes, C.R., *Hints on Medical Jurisprudence, Adapted and Intended for the use of Those Engaged in Judicial and Magisterial Duties in British India*, Madras: Pharoah & Co., 1854.

Bell, Diane, Pat Caplan, and Wazir Karim, *Gendered Fields Women, Men and Ethnography*, London: Routledge, 1993.

Berti, Daniela, 'Hostile Witnesses, Judicial Interactions and Out-of-court Narratives in a North Indian District Court', *Contributions to Indian Sociology*, 44(3), 2010, pp. 235–63.

—————, 'Courts of Law and Legal Practice', in *A Companion to the Anthropology of India*, Isabelle Clark-Deces (ed.), UK: Wiley–Blackwell, 2011.

Béteille, André, 'Race, Caste and Gender', *Man, New Series*, 25(3), 1990, pp. 489–504.

Bhatnagar, Rakesh, 'Woman Can Marry Her Rapist if She Wishes: Chief Justice of India', *Daily News and Analysis*, 8 March 2010, available at http://www.dnaindia.com/india/report_woman-can-marry-her-rapist-if-she-wishes-chief-justice-of-india_1356464.

Bhatt, Aparna, *Supreme Court on Rape Trials: A Manual of Best Practices of the Supreme Court*, New Delhi: Combat Law Publications, 2003.

Borneman, John, 'Until Death Do Us Part: Marriage/Death in Anthropological Discourse', *American Ethnologist*, 23(2), 1996, pp. 215–8.

Brownmiller, Susan, *Against Our Will: Men, Women and Rape*, New York: Simon and Schuster, 1975.

Burgess-Jackson, Keith, *Rape: A Philosophical Investigation*, Sydney: Darmouth Publishing Company Limited, 1996.

Butalia, Urvashi, *The Other Side of Silence: Voices from the Partition of India*, Delhi: Kali for Women, 1998.

Butler, Judith, *Excitable Speech: A Politics of the Performative*, New York and London: Routledge, 1997.

Card, Claudia, 'Rape as a Weapon of War', *Hypatia*, 11(4), 1996, pp. 5–18.

—————, 'The Atrocity Paradigm Revisited', *Hypatia*, 19(4), 2004, pp. 212–22.

Carlen, Pat, *Magistrates Justice*, London: Martin Robertson, 1976.

Cattaneo, Lauren Bennett and Lisa A. Goodman, 'Through the Lens of Therapeutic Jurisprudence: The Relationship between Empowerment in the Court System and Well-Being for Intimate Partner Violence Victims', *Journal of Interpersonal Violence*, (25), 2010, pp. 481–502.

(Centre for Women's Development Studies), 'Crimes against Women: Bondage and Beyond—Revelation of Data', report, New Delhi: Centre for Women's Development Studies, 2002.

Chakravarti, Uma, 'Conceptualising Brahmanical Patriarchy in Early India: Gender, Caste, Class and State', *Economic and Political Weekly*, 28(14), 1993, pp. 579–85.

Chakravarti, Uma, *Gendering Caste: Through a Feminist Lens*, Calcutta: Stree, 2003.

————, 'From Fathers to Husbands: Of Love, Death and Marriage in North India', in *'Honour': Crimes, Paradigms and Violence against Women*, Lynn Welchman and Sara Hossain (eds), London: Zed Books, 2005.

————, 'Rhetoric and Substance of Empowerment: Women, Development and the State', in *Contested Transformations, Changing Economies and Identities in Contemporary India*, Mary E. John, Praveen Kumar Jha, and Surinder S. Jodhka, (eds), New Delhi: Tulika, 2006.

Chaterji, Roma and Deepak Mehta, *Living with Violence: An Anthropology of Events and Everyday Life*, London: Routledge, 2007.

Chevers, Norman, *A Manual of Medical Jurisprudence for Bengal and the North Western Provinces*, Calcutta: F. Carbery, Bengal Military Orphan Press, 1856.

Chowdhry, Prem, 'Enforcing Cultural Codes: Gender and Violence in Northern India', in *A Question of Silence? The Sexual Economies of Modern India*, Mary E. John and Janaki Nair (eds), New Delhi: Kali for Women, 1998.

————, 'Private Lives, State Intervention: Cases of Runaway Marriage in Rural North India', *Modern Asian Studies*, (38), 2004, pp. 55–84.

Clark, Anna, *Women's Silence, Men's Violence: Sexual Assault in England 1770-1845*, London: Pandora, 1987.

Cohn, Bernard S., 'Anthropological Notes on Disputes and Law in India', in *American Anthropologist* 67(6), special issue: 'Ethnography of Law', Laura Nader (ed.), Arlington: American Anthropological Association, 1965.

Cover, Robert, 'Violence and the Word', in *Narrative, Violence, and the Law: The Essays of Robert Cover*, Martha Minow, Michael Ryan, and Austin Sarat (eds), Ann Arbor: University of Michigan Press, 1995.

Cuklanz, Lisa, *Rape on Trial: How the Mass Media Construct Legal Reform and Social Change*, Philadelphia: University of Pennsylvania Press, 1996.

Darian-Smith, Eve, 'Precedents of Injustice: Thinking about History in Law and Society Scholarship', *Studies in Law, Politics, and Society*, 41, special issue: 'Law and Society Reconsidered', 2007, pp. 61–81.

Das, Veena, 'Sociology of Law', in *ICSSR: A Survey of Research in Sociology and Social Anthropology*, vol. 2, Bombay: Popular Prakashan, 1974.

————, *Critical Events: An Anthropological Perspective on Contemporary India*, New Delhi: Oxford University Press, 1995.

Das, Veena, 'Sexual Violence, Discursive Formations and the State', *Economic and Political Weekly*, 31(35–7), 1996, pp. 2411–23.

————, 'Introduction: The Personal Sphere and Its Articulation', in *The Oxford India Companion to Sociology and Social Anthropology* (II), Veena Das (ed.), New Delhi: Oxford University Press, 2003.

Das, Veena, *Life and Words: Violence and the Descent into the Ordinary*, New Delhi: Oxford University Press, 2006.

Davies, Margaret, *Delimiting the Law: 'Postmodernism' and the Politics of Law*, London: Pluto Press, 1996.

Dayan, Joan, 'Held in the Body of the State: Prisons and the Law', in *History, Memory, and the Law*, Austin Sarat and Thomas R. Kearns (eds), Ann Arbor: The University of Michigan Press, 2002.

de Certeau, Michel, *Heterologies: Discourse on the Other*, Manchester: Manchester University Press, 1986.

Dhagamwar, Vasudha, 'The Lodipur Rape: After Mathura, What?', *Mainstream*, (3), 1980, pp. 1–6.

————, *Law, Power and Justice: The Protection of Personal Rights in the Indian Penal Code*, Delhi: Sage, 1992.

Douglas, Mary, *Purity and Danger*, Harmondsworth: Penguin, 1970.

Dua, Veena, 'A Woman's Encounter with Arya Samaj and Untouchables: A Slum in Jalandar', in *The Fieldworker and the Field: Problems and Challenges in Sociological Investigation*, M.N. Srinivas, A.M. Shah, and E.A. Ramaswamy (eds), New Delhi: Oxford University Press, 1979.

Dubinsky, Karen, *Improper Advances Rape and Heterosexual Conflict in Ontario, 1880-1929*, Chicago and London: University of Chicago Press, 1993.

Dumont, Louis, *Homo Hierarchicus*, London: Paladin, 1972.

Durkheim, Emile, *The Division of Labour*, New York: Macmillan, 1933.

Dwyer, Rachel, 'The Erotics of the Wet Sari in Hindi Films', *South Asia*, 23(1), 2000, pp. 143–59.

Epstein, A.L., 'The Case Method in the Field of Law', in *The Craft of Social Anthropology*, A.L. Epstein, (ed.), Delhi: Hindustan Publishing Corporation, 1978.

Feldman, Allen, *Formations of Violence: The Narrative of the Body and Political Terror in Northern Ireland*, Chicago: Chicago University Press, 1991.

Feldman, Hannah J.L., 'More than Confessional and the Subject of Rape', monograph, USA: Whitney Museum of Art, 1993.

Felman, Shoshana, 'Forms of Judicial Blindness: Traumatic Narratives and Legal Repetitions', in *Law in Everyday Life*, Austin Sarat and Thomas R. Kearns (eds), Ann Arbor: The University of Michigan Press, 2002.

Ferguson, Robert A., 'Untold Stories in Law', in *Law's Stories: Narrative and Rhetoric in Law*, Peter Brooks and Paul Gewirtz (eds), New Haven and London: Yale University Press, 1996.

Fernando, Franco, Jyotsna Macwan, and Suguna Ramanathan, *The Silken Swing: The Cultural Universe of Dalit Women*, Calcutta: Stree, 2000.

Foucault, Michel, *Discipline and Punish: The Birth of the Prison*, New York: Vintage Books, 1977.

————, *The History of Sexuality, Volume I, An Introduction*, trans. from French by Robert Hurley, Allan Lane: London, 1979.

———— (ed.), *I, Pierre Riviére, Having Slaughtered My Mother, My Sister and My Brother: A Case of Parricide in the 19th Century*, London: University of Nebraska Press, 1975.

Franklin, Sarah, 'Science as Culture, Cultures of Science', *Annual Review of Anthropology*, (24), 1995, pp. 163–84.

Galanter, Marc, 'The Modernization of Law', in *Modernization: The Dynamics of Growth*, M. Weiner (ed.), New York: Basic Books, 1966.

————, 'The Abolition of Disabilities: Untouchability and the Law', in *The Untouchables in Contemporary India*, J.M. Mahar (ed.), Tucson: University of Arizona Press, 1972.

————, *Competing Inequalities: Law and the Backward Classes in India*, California: University of California Press, 1984.

————, *Law and Society in Modern India*, New Delhi: Oxford University Press, 1989.

Gammon, Julie, 'A Denial of Innocence: Female Juvenile Victims of Rape and the English Legal System in the 18th Century', in *Childhood in Question: Children, Parents and the State*, Anthony Fletcher and Stephen Hussey (eds), Manchester: Manchester University Press, 1999.

Gandhi, Nandita and Nandita Shah, *The Issues at Stake: Theory and Practice in the Contemporary Women's Movement in India*, New Delhi: Kali for Women, 1992.

Gangoli, Geetanjali, *Indian Feminisms: Law, Patriarchies and Violence in India*, Hampshire, UK: Ashgate, 2007.

Garfinkel, Harold, *Studies in Ethnomethodology*, New York: Prentice Hall, 1967.

Gell, Alfred, *The Anthropology of Time: Cultural Constructions of Temporal Maps and Images*, Oxford: Berg, 1992.

Ghosh, Shrimoyee N., '"Not Worth the Paper It's Written on": Stamp Paper Documents and the Life of Law in India', conference paper presented at Anthropology Graduate Conference 'Tracing Documents', Baltimore: Johns Hopkins University, April 2012.

Gluckman, Max, *The Judicial Process Among the Barotse of Northern Rhodesia*, Manchester: Manchester University Press, 1955.

Government of India (GoI), Indian Penal Code (Act 45 of 1860).

———, Indian Evidence Act, 1872 (Act 2 of 1872).

———, The Special Marriage Act, 1954 (Act 43 of 1954).

———, The Protection of Civil Rights Act, 1955 (Act 22 of 1955).

———, The Untouchability (Offences) Act, 1955 (Act 22 of 1955).

———, Immoral Traffic (Prevention) Act, 1986 (Act 104 of 1956).

———, Prevention of Immoral Traffic in Women and Girls Act, 1956 (Act 104 of 1956).

———, Suppression of Immoral Trafficking Act, 1956 (Act 104 of 1956).

———, Criminal Procedure Code, 1973 (Act 2 of 1974).

———, The Criminal Law (Amendment) Act, 1983 (Act 43 of 1983), Gazette of India, Part II-S Ext. p. 1 (No. 53), 26 December 1983.

———, Terrorist and Disruptive Activities (Prevention) Act, 1985 (Act 31 of 1985).

———, The Scheduled Castes and Scheduled Tribes (Prevention of Atrocities) Act, 1989 (Act 33 of 1989).

———, Notification No. 777/VIII 9-4(2)—87, dated 31 July 1989, UP Gazette, Extra, Pt. A, Sec. (kha), 2 August 1989.

———, The Indian Evidence Act, 2002 (Act 4 of 2003).

———, The Criminal Law (Amendment) Act, 2005 (Act 2 of 2006).

———, Protection of Children from Sexual Offences Act, 2012 (Act 32 of 2012).

Gonsalves, Colin and G. Agarwal, *Dalits and the Law*, New Delhi: Human Rights Law Network, 2005.

Goodrich, Peter, *Languages of Law: From Logics of Memory to Nomadic Masks*, London: Weidenfeld and Nicolson, 1990.

———, *Law in the Courts of Love: Literature and Other Minor Jurisprudence*, London and New York: Routledge, 1996.

Government of Gujarat, 'Scheduled Caste and Scheduled Tribes (Prevention of Atrocities) Gujarat Rules, 1995', available at http://www.sje.gujarat.gov.in/showpage.aspx?contentid=1630&lang=English.

Griffin, Susan, 'Rape, the All American Crime', *Ramparts*, September 1971, pp. 26–35.

Grover, Vrinda, 'The Elusive Quest for Justice: Delhi 1984 to Gujarat 2002', in *Gujarat: The Making of a Tragedy*, Siddharth Vardharajan (ed.), New Delhi: Penguin, 2002.

Gujarat High Court, *Criminal Manual*, Ahmedabad: Gujarat High Court, 1977.

Gupta, Akhil and James Ferguson (eds), *Anthropological Locations: Boundaries and Grounds of a Field Science*, Berkeley: University of California Press, 1997.

Gupta, Alok, 'Section 377 and the Dignity of Indian Homosexuals', *Economic and Political Weekly*, 41(46), 2006, pp. 4815–23.

Guru, Gopal, 'Dalit Women Talk Differently', in *Gender and Caste*, Anupama Rao, (ed.), New Delhi: Kali for Women, 2003.

Haldar, Piyel, 'In and Out of Court: On Topographies of Law and the Architecture of Court Buildings—A Study of the Supreme Court of the State of Israel', *International Journal for the Semiotics of Law*, 7(20), 1994, pp. 185–200.

Hameed, Syeda, Ruth Manorama, Sheba George, Malini Ghose, Farah Naqvi, and Mari Thekaekara, *How Has the Gujarat Massacre Affected Minority Women? The Survivor's Speak: Fact-finding by a Women's Panel*, report, Ahmedabad: Citizen's Initiative, 16 April 2002.

Hansen, Thomas Blom, *Urban Violence in India: Identity Politics, 'Mumbai' and the Postcolonial City*, Delhi: Permanent Black, 2001.

Hartog, Hendrik, 'Abigail Bailey's Coverture: Law in a Married Woman's Consciousness', in *Law in Everyday Life*, Austin Sarat and Thomas R. Kearns (eds), Michigan: Michigan University Press, 1995.

Herman, Judith Lewis, *Trauma and Recovery*, New York: Basic Books, 1992.

Holden, Livia, *Hindu Divorce: A Legal Anthropology*, Aldershot: Ashgate, 2008.

Huff, Jennifer K., 'The Sexual Harassment of Researchers by Research Subjects: Lessons from the Field', in *Researching Sexual Violence Against Women: Methodological and Personal Perspectives*, Schwartz Martin (ed.), California: Sage, 1997.

Human Rights Watch (HRW), *Broken People: Caste Violence against India's Untouchables*, New York: Human Rights Watch, 1999.

————, *Dignity on Trial: India's Need for Sound Standards for Conducting and Interpreting Forensic Examinations of Rape Survivors*, New York: Human Rights Watch, 2010.

Hussain Nasser, *The Jurisprudence of Emergency: Colonialism and the Rule of Law*, Ann Arbor: The University of Michigan Press, 2003.

————, 'Beyond Norm and Exception: Guantanamo', *Critical Inquiry*, (33), 2007, pp. 734–53.

Hyde, Alan, *Bodies of Law*, Princeton: Princeton University Press, 1997.

International Initiative for Justice (IIJ), *Threatened Existence: A Feminist Analysis of the Genocide in Gujarat*, Bombay: New Age Printing Press, 2003.

James, A., and C. Jenks, 'Public Perceptions of Childhood Criminality', *British Journal of Sociology*, 47(2), 1996, pp. 315–31.

Jaoul, Nicolas, 'The "Righteous Anger" of the Powerless Investigating Dalit Outrage over Caste Violence', *South Asia Multidisciplinary Academic Journal* 2. special issue: 'Outraged Communities', 2008, available at http://samaj.revues.org/document1892.html.

Jaoul, Nicolas, *A Strong Law for the Weak: Dalit Encounters in a District Court of Uttar Pradesh*, unpublished draft paper, France, 2011.

Jeganathan, Pradeep, '"Violence" as an Analytical Problem: Sri Lankanist Anthropology after July, '83', *Nethra: Journal of the International Centre for Ethnic Studies*, 2(4), 1998, pp. 7–47.

Jervis, John, *Transgressing the Modern: Explorations in the Western Experience of Otherness*, United Kingdom: Blackwell, 1999.

Jha, Prita, 'Compromise in Criminal Justice Trials: Communal Violence in Gujarat 2002', unpublished draft paper, Ahmedabad: Nyayagraha, 2011.

John, Mary E., 'Dalit Women in Western Ethnography', in *Gender and Caste*, Anupama Rao (ed.), New Delhi: Kali for Women, 2003.

John, Mary E. and Janaki Nair (eds), *A Question of Silence? The Sexual Economies of Modern India*, New Delhi: Kali for Women, 1998.

Joint (Parliamentary) Committee (JPC), 'The Criminal Law (Amendment) Bill', report, New Delhi: Lok Sabha Secretariat, 1982.

Jong, Ferdinand de, 'The Social Life of Secrets', in *Situating Globality: African Agency in the Appropriation of Global Culture*, Wim Van Binsbergen and Rijk Van Dijk (eds), Leiden and Boston: Brill, 2004.

Kamble, N.D., *The Scheduled Castes*, Delhi: Ashish Publishing House, 1982.

Kannabiran, Kalpana, 'A Ravished Justice: Half a Century of Judicial Discourse on Rape', in *De-eroticising Assault: Essays on Modesty, Honour and Power*, Kalpana Kannabiran and Vasanth Kannabiran (eds), Calcutta: Stree, 2002.

————, 'Sexual Assault and the Law', in *Challenging the Rule(s) of Law: Colonialism, Criminology and Human Rights in India*, Kalpana Kannabiran and Ranbir Singh (eds), New Delhi: Sage, 2008.

Kannabiran, Vasanth and Kalpana Kannabiran, 'Caste and Gender: Understanding Dynamics of Power and Violence', in *Gender and Caste*, Anupama Rao (ed.), New Delhi: Kali for Women, 2003.

Kapur, Ratna, *Law and the New Erotic Justice: Politics of Postcolonialism*, Delhi: Routledge, 2005.

Karlekar, Malavika, 'Domestic Violence', in *The Oxford India Companion to Sociology and Social Anthropology (II)*, Veena Das (ed.), New Delhi: Oxford University Press, 2003.

Kelkar, R.V., *Lectures on Criminal Procedure*, Delhi: Eastern Book Company, 1980.

Kolsky, Elizabeth, '"The Body Evidencing the Crime": Gender, Law and Medicine in Colonial India', PhD dissertation, New York: Columbia University, 2002.

————, '"The Body Evidencing the Crime": Rape on Trial in Colonial India, 1860–1947', *Gender & History*, 22(1), 2010, pp. 109–30.

Koselleck, Reinhardt, *The Practice of Conceptual History: Timing History, Spacing Concepts*, Stanford: Stanford University Press, 2002.

Kripke, Saul A., *Naming and Necessity*, Harvard: Harvard University Press, 1980.

Krishnan, P.S., *Empowering Dalits for Empowering India: A Road-Map*, New Delhi: Manak Publications, 2009.

Kumari, Ved, 'State's Response to the Problem of Rape and Dowry', in *Women and the Law: Contemporary Problems*, Lotika Sarkar and B. Sivarammaya (eds), New Delhi: Vikas Publishing House, 1994.

Law Commission, 'Law Commission of India Forty Second Report, Indian Penal Code', New Delhi: Union Ministry of Law, 1971.

———, 'Law Commission of India Eighty Fourth Report on Rape and Allied Offences: Some Questions of Substantive Law, Procedure and Evidence', Delhi: Union Ministry of Law, 1981.

———, Law Commission of India: One Hundred and Seventy Second Report on Review of Rape Laws Delhi: Union Ministry of Law, GoI, 2000.

Lees, Sue, *Ruling Passions: Sexual Violence, Reputation and the Law*, Milton Keynes: Open University Press, 1997.

Llewellyn, Karl and E. Adamson Hoebel, *The Cheyenne Way*, Oklahoma: Oklahoma Press, 1941.

Lok Sabha, 13th Session (Seventh Lok Sabha), 'Debate on Criminal Law Amendment Bill' (18, 21 November and 1 December 1983), Lok Sabha Secretariat, New Delhi, 1983.

———, 12th Session (Tenth Lok Sabha), 'Debate on Scheduled Castes and the Scheduled Extent and Tribes (Prevention of Atrocities) Bill' (14 August 1989), Lok Sabha Secretariat, New Delhi, 1994.

———, 12th Session (Thirteenth Lok Sabha) 'Short Duration Discussions (RU: Regarding Atrocities on Dalits)' (29, 12 March 2003), available at http://indiankanoon.org/doc/452722.

Lyon, I.B., *Lyon's Medical Jurisprudence for India with Illustrative Cases*, 6th edition, edited and revised by L.A. Wadwell, Calcutta: Thacker, Spink and Co., 1888/1918.

———, *Lyon's Medical Jurisprudence for India with Illustrative Cases*, 7th edition, edited and revised by L.A. Waddell, Calcutta and Simla: Thacker, Spink and Co., 1888/1921.

———, *Lyon's Medical Jurisprudence for India with Illustrative Cases*, 10th edition, edited and revised by S.N. Gour, Calcutta: Thacker, Spink and Co., 1888/1953.

Mackinnon, Catherine, *Toward a Feminist Theory of the State*, Cambridge: Harvard University Press, 1989.

Mahapatra Dhananjay, 'In First Video Trial of Rape, Girl Stands Her Ground', *The Times of India*, 3 October 2007, available at http://articles.

timesofindia.indiatimes.com/2007-10-03/india/27977864_1_video-conferencing-minor-girl-video-conference-room.

Malik, Bela, 'Untouchability and Dalit Women's Oppression', in *Gender and Caste*, Anupama Rao (ed.), New Delhi: Kali for Women, 2003.

Mandal, Saptarshi, 'The Burden of Intelligibility: Disabled Women's Testimony in Rape Trials', *Indian Journal of Gender Studies*, 20:1, 2013, pp. 1–29.

Mangubhai, Jayshree P. and S.J. Aloysius Irudayam, 'Building a Subaltern Women's Perspective', in *Challenging the Rule(s) of Law: Colonialism, Criminology and Human Rights in India*, Kalpana Kannabiran and Ranbir Singh (eds), New Delhi: Sage, 2008.

Marcus, George E., 'The Uses of *Complicity* in the Changing Mise-en-Scene of Anthropological Fieldwork', *Representations*, (59) special issue: 'The Fate of "Culture": Geertz and Beyond', 1997, pp. 85–108.

Marcus, Sharon, 'Fighting Bodies, Fighting Words: A Theory and Politics of Rape Prevention', in *Feminists Theorise the Political*, Judith Butler and Joan Scott (eds), New York: Routledge, 1992.

Mardorossian, Carino M., 'Towards a New Feminist Theory of Rape', *Signs*, 27(4), 2002, pp. 743–75.

Mateosian, Gregory M., *Reproducing Rape: Domination Through Talk in the Courtroom*, Cambridge: Polity Press, 1993.

Mathur, Kanchan, 'Bhateri Rape Case: Backlash and Protest', *Economic and Political Weekly*, 27(41), 1992, pp. 2221–4.

Mattley, Christine, 'Field Research with Phone Sex Workers: Managing the Researcher's Emotions', in *Researching Sexual Violence against Women: Methodological and Personal Perspectives*, Martin Schwartz (ed.), California: Sage, 1997.

Mayaram, Shail, 'New Modes of Violence: The Backlash against Women in the Panchayat System', in *The Violence of Development: The Politics of Identity, Gender and Social Inequalities in India*, Karin Kapadia (ed.), New Delhi: Kali for Women, 2002.

Mehta, Deepak, 'Writing the Riot: Between the Historiography and Ethnography of Communal Violence in India', in *History and the Present*, Partha Chatterjee and Anjan Ghosh (eds), Delhi: Permanent Black, 2002.

Mehta, Deepak and Roma Chatterji, 'Boundaries, Names, Alterities: A Case Study of a "Communal Riot" in Dharavi, Bombay', in *Remaking a World Violence, Social Suffering, and Recovery*, Veena Das, Arthur Klienman, Margaret Lock, Mamphela Ramphele, and Pamela Reynolds (eds), Berkeley: University of California Press, 2001.

Mendelsohn, Oliver, and Mariko Vicziany, *The Untouchables: Subordination, Poverty and the State in Modern India*, New Delhi: Cambridge University Press, 1998.

Menon, Nivedita, 'Rights, Law and Feminist Politics: Rethinking Our Practice', in *In the Name of Justice: Women and Law in Society*, Swapna Mukhopadhyay (ed.), Delhi: Manohar Publications, 1998.

————, *Recovering Subversion: Feminist Politics Beyond the Law*, Urbana: University of Illinois Press, 2004.

Menon, Ritu, and Kamala Bhasin, *Borders and Boundaries: Women in India's Partition*, New Delhi: Kali for Women, 1998.

Merry, Sally E., *Getting Justice and Getting Even: Legal Consciousness among Working-class Americans*, Chicago: Chicago University Press, 1990.

————, 'Courts as Performances: Domestic Violence Hearings in a Hawai'i Family Court', in *Contested States: Law, Hegemony and Resistance*, Mindie Lazarus-Black and Susan F. Hirsch (eds), New York: Routledge, 1994.

————, 'Rights Talk and the Experience of Law: Implementing Women's Human Rights to Protection From Violence', *Human Rights Quarterly*, 25(2), 2003, pp. 343–81.

Modi, Jaising Prabhudas, Rai Bahadur, *A Textbook of Medical Jurisprudence and Toxicology*, 2nd edition, Calcutta: Butterworth, 1920/1922.

————, *A Textbook of Medical Jurisprudence and Toxicology*, 6th edition, Bombay: Butterworth, 1920/1940.

————, *Modi's Textbook of Medical Jurisprudence and Toxicology*, 17th edition, edited and revised by Natwar J. Modi, Bombay: Tripathi, 1920/1969.

————, *Modi's Textbook of Medical Jurisprudence and Toxicology*, 18th edition, edited and revised by Natwar J. Modi, Bombay: N.M. Tripathi, 1920/1972.

————, *Modi's Textbook of Medical Jurisprudence and Toxicology*, 22nd edition, edited and revised by B.V. Subrahmanyam, reprint, Delhi: Lexisnexis Butterworths, 1920/2002.

————, *Modi's Textbook of Medical Jurisprudence and Toxicology* [1920], 24th edition (Reprint), edited and revised by K. Kannan and K. Mathiharan, Delhi: Lexisnexis Butterworths, 2001.

Mody, Perveez, 'Love and the Law: Love-Marriage in Delhi', *Modern Asia Studies*, 36(1), 2002, pp. 223–56.

————, *The Intimate State: Love-Marriage and the Law in Delhi*, Delhi: Routledge, 2008.

Monir, M., *Principles and Digest of the Law of Evidence (I and II)*, Allahabad: University Book Agency, 1989.

Moog, Robert S., 'Conflict and Compromise: The Politics of Lok Adalats in Varanasi District', *Law and Society Review*, 25(3), reprint, 1991, pp. 545–69.

Moog, Robert S., 'The Significance of Lower Courts in the Judicial Process', in *The Oxford Companion to Sociology and Social Anthropology (II)*, Veena Das (ed.), New Delhi: Oxford University Press, 2003.

Moreno, Eva, 'Rape in the Field: Reflections from a Survivor', in *Taboo: Sex, Identity and Erotic Subjectivity in Anthropological Fieldwork*, Don Kulick and Margaret Wilson (eds), London and New York: Routledge, 1995.

Nader, Laura, *The Life of the Law: Anthropological Projects*, Berkeley: University of California Press, 2002.

———, 'The Anthropological Study of Law', special issue: 'Ethnography of Law', Laura Nader (ed.), *American Anthropologist*, 67(6), Arlington: American Anthropological Association, 1965.

Nader, Laura and H. Todd (eds), *The Disputing Process: Law in Ten Societies*, New York: Columbia University Press, 1978.

Nampoothiri, P.G.J. and Gagan Sethi, *Lest We Forget History: Tracing Communal Violence in Gujarat 2002*, Bangalore: Books for Change, 2012.

Narayana, P.S., *The Scheduled Castes and Scheduled Tribes (Prevention of Atrocities) Act, 1989 & Rules, 1995 with Protection of Civil Rights Act, 1955 & Rules, 1977*, Hyderabad: Gogia Law Agency, 2011.

Narrain, Arvind, '"That Despicable Specimen of Humanity": Policing of Homosexuality in India', in *Challenging the Rule(s) of Law: Colonialism, Criminology and Human Rights in India*, Kalpana Kannabiran and Ranbir Singh (eds), New Delhi: Sage, 2008.

Narrain, Arvind and Alok Gupta (eds), *Law like Love: Queer Perspectives on Law*, Delhi: Yoda Press, 2011.

National Crime Records Bureau (NCRB), 'Crimes in India 2001', New Delhi: National Crimes Record Bureau, 2003.

Naval, T.R., *Law of Prevention of Atrocities on the Scheduled Caste and Scheduled Tribe*, New Delhi: Concept Publishing Company, 2001.

Nordstrom, Carolyn, 'Rape: Politics and Theory in War and Peace', *Australian Feminist Studies*, 11(23), 1996, pp. 147–62.

'No Fresh Hearing in Rape Cases', *Hindustan Times*, 3 April 1980, pp. 1, 5.

O'Barr, William M., *Linguistic Evidence: Language, Power and Strategy in the Courtroom*, United Kingdom: Academic Press, 1982.

O'Neal, Robert J., 'Court Ordered Psychiatric Examination of a Rape Victim in a Criminal Rape Prosecution—Or How Many Times Must a Woman be Raped', *Santa Clara L. Rev.*, 18(1), 1978, pp. 119–55.

Panini, M.N. (ed.), *From the Female Eye: Accounts of Women Fieldworkers Studying their Own Communities*, Delhi: Hindustan Publishing Corporation, 1991.

Patel, Girish, *Law, Society and Girishbhai: Letters to the Editor*, Ahmedabad: Girishbhai Patel Sanman Samiti, 2009.

Parker, A., M. Russo, D. Sommer, and P. Yaeger, *Nationalism and Sexualities*, New York: Routledge, 1992.

People's Union for Democratic Rights (PUDR), 'Custodial Rape: A Report on the Aftermath', Delhi: People's Union for Democratic Rights, 1994.

————, 'In Custody: An Investigation into 5 Cases of Sexual Assault', A Fact Finding Report into 5 Cases of Custodial Rape in the Capital City. Delhi: People's Union for Democratic Rights, 2004.

Philips, Susan U., *Ideology in the Language of Judges: How Judges Practice Law, Politics and Courtroom Control*, Oxford: Oxford University Press, 1998.

Pillai, P.S., 'A Reply to "An Open Letter to the Chief Justice of India"', Supreme Court Cases 1: 22–24, 1980.

Pinney, Christopher, 'The Lexical Spaces of Eye-Spy', in *Films as Ethnography*, Peter Ian Crawford and David Turton (eds), Manchester: Manchester University Press, 1992.

————, *Camera Indica: The Social Life of Indian Photographs*, Chicago: University of Chicago Press, 1998.

Pitre, Amita, 'Sexual Assault Case and Forensic Evidence Kit: Strengthening the Case for the Use of the Kit', Conference Paper, New Delhi: Tenth International Women and Health Meeting, 21–5 September 2005.

Poizat, Michel, *The Angel's Cry: Beyond the Pleasure Principle in Opera*, Ithaca and London: Cornell University Press, 1992.

Pound, Roscoe, 'Law in Books and Law in Action', *American Law Rev.* 44, 1910, pp. 12–36.

————, 'Sociology of Law and Sociological Jurisprudence', *University of Toronto Law Journal*, 5(1), 1943, pp. 1–20.

PUCL, 'A Study of Kothi and Hijra Sex Workers in Bangalore, India', report, Bangalore: Peoples' Union for Civil Liberties, Karnataka, 2003.

Punalekar, Devyani, 'Atrocities on and Agonies of Gujarat Dalit Women', in *Dalit Women in India: Issues and Perspective*, P.G. Jogadand (ed.), New Delhi: Gyan Publishing House, 1995.

Puri, Jyoti, 'GenderQueer Perspectives', in *Law like Love: Queer Perspectives on Law*, Arvind Narrain and Alok Gupta (eds), Delhi: Yoda Press, 2011.

Rabinow, Paul, *Essays on the Anthropology of Reason*, Princeton: Princeton University Press, 1996.

Raes, Koen, 'On Love and Other Injustices: Love and Law as Improbable Communications', in *Love and Law in Europe*, Hanne Petersen (ed.), England: Ashgate. 1998, pp. 27–51.

Randeria, Shalini, 'Carrion and Corpses: Conflict in Categorizing Untouchability in Gujarat', *European Journal of Sociology*, 30(2), 1989, pp. 171–91.

Randeria, Shalini, 'Politics of Exchange and Representation among the Dalits of Gujarat/Western India', PhD dissertation, Berlin: Free University of Berlin, 1992.

Rao, Anupama (ed.), *Gender and Caste*, New Delhi: Kali for Women, 2003.

————, 'Understanding Sirasgaon: Notes Towards Conceptualising the Role of Law, Caste and Gender in a Case of "Atrocity"', in *Signposts: Gender Issues in Post-Independence India*, Rajeswari Sunder Rajan (ed.), Delhi: Kali for Women, 1999.

————, *The Caste Question: Dalits and the Politics of Modern India*, Los Angeles and Berkeley: University of California Press, 2009.

Ratanlal, Ranchhoddas and Keshavlal Thakore Dhirajlal, *The Law of Evidence (Act I of 1872)*, 21st edition, edited and revised by Y.V. Chandrachud and V.R. Manohar, Nagpur: Wadhwa and Company, 1916/1999.

————, *The Indian Penal Code (Act XLV of 1860)*, 28th edition, fourth reprint, edited and revised by Y.V. Chandrachud and V.R. Manohar, Nagpur: Wadhwa and Company, 1896/2001.

————, *The Code of Criminal Procedure (Act II of 1972)*, edited and revised by Y.V. Chandrachud and V.R. Manohar, Nagpur: Wadhwa and Company, 1930/2002.

————, *The Indian Penal Code (Act XLV of 1860)*, 32nd edition (reprint), edited and revised by Y.V. Chandrachud, V.R. Manohar, et al. Nagpur: LexisNexis and Butterworths, 1896/2011.

Reddy, Narayan K.S., *The Essentials of Forensic Medicine and Toxicology*, Hyderabad: Sri Lakshmi Art Printers, 1990.

Rege, Sharmila, 'Caste and Gender: The Violence against Women in India', in *Dalit Women in India: Issues and Perspective*, P.G. Jogadand, (ed.), New Delhi: Gyan Publishing House, 1995.

————, 'A Dalit Feminist Standpoint', in *Gender and Caste*, Anupama Rao, (ed.), New Delhi: Kali for Women, 2003.

Roy, Srila, 'Melancholic Politics and the Politics of Melancholia: The Indian Women's Movement', *Feminist Theory*, 10(3), 2009, pp. 341–57.

Rubin, Gayle, 'The Traffic in Women: Notes on the "Political Economy" of Sex', in *Toward an Anthropology of Women*, Rayna Reiter, (ed.), New York: Monthly Review Press, 1975.

Saarth Gujarati Jodani Kosh, Ahmedabad: Gujarat Vidyapeeth, 1987.

Sakhare, Seema, 'Law on Rape in Operation', in *Women and the Law: Contemporary Problems*, Lotika Sarkar and B. Sivarammaya, (eds), New Delhi: Vikas Publishing House, 1994.

Saksena, H.S., *Atrocities on Scheduled Castes: The Law and the Realities*, New Delhi: Serial Publication, 2010.

Sankaran, Kamala, 'Dalit Identity and the Law', in *Towards Dignity: Access, Assertion and Aspiration of Dalits in India*, Aseem Prakash, (ed.), forthcoming.

Sankaran, S.R., 'Social Exclusion and Criminal Law', in *Challenging the Rule(s) of Law: Colonialism, Criminology and Human Rights in India*, Kalpana Kannabiran and Ranbir Singh, (eds), New Delhi: Sage, 2008.

Sarat, Austin (ed.), *Law, Violence and the Possibility of Justice*, Princeton: Princeton University Press, 2001.

Sarat, Austin, and Thomas R. Kearns, 'Writing History and Registering Memory in Legal Decisions and Legal Practices: An Introduction', in *History, Memory, and the Law*, Austin Sarat and Thomas R. Kearns, (eds), Ann Arbor: The University of Michigan Press, 2002.

———, 'Introduction', in *Law in Everyday Life*, Austin Sarat and Thomas R. Kearns, (eds), Ann Arbor: The University of Michigan Press, 1995.

Sarkar, Lotika, 'A Human Rights versus a Patriarchal Interpretation', *Indian Journal of Gender Studies*, 1(1), 1994, pp. 69–92.

Sarkar, Tanika, *Hindu Wife, Hindu Nation Community, Religion and Cultural Nationalism*, New Delhi: Permanent Black, 2001.

———, 'Semiotics of Terror: Muslim Women and Children in Hindu Rashtra,' *Economic and Political Weekly*, 37(28), 2002, pp. 2872–6.

Satish Mrinal, Discretions, Discrimination and the Rule of Law: Reforming Rape Sentence in India. Unpublished PhD thesis, Yale Law School, Yale University, February, 2013.

Saxena, K.B., *Report on Prevention of Atrocities against Scheduled Castes, Policy and Performance: Suggested Interventions and Initiatives for NHRC*, New Delhi: National Human Rights Commission, 2004.

Scully, Diana and Joseph Marolla, '"Convicted Rapists" Vocabulary of Motive: Excuses and Justifications', *Social Problems*, 31(5), 1984, pp. 530–44.

Sen, Rukmini, 'Law Commission Reports on Rape', *Economic and Political Weekly*, XLV(44), October 30, 2010, pp. 81–87.

Sengoopta, Chandak, *Imprint of the Raj: How Fingerprinting was Born in Colonial India*, London: Macmillan, 2003.

Shankar, Shylashri, *Scaling Justice: India's Supreme Court, Anti-Terror Laws and Social Rights*, New Delhi: Oxford University Press, 2009.

Shivam, Vij, 'A Mighty Heart', *Tehelka*, 13 October 2007, available at http://www.tehelka.com/story_main34.asp?filename=hub131007A_MIGHTY.asp, accessed on 9 August 2012.

Siddique, Ahmed, *Criminology: Problems and Perspectives*. Lucknow: Eastern Book Company, 1993.

Singh, K.S. (ed.), *The Scheduled Castes, People of India: National Series (II)*, New Delhi: Oxford University Press, 1993.

Singh, K.S. (ed.), *People of India: Gujarat XXII (3)*, Mumbai: Popular Prakashan, 2002.

Singh, Ujjwal Kumar, 'The Silent Erosion: Anti-Terror Laws and Shifting Contours of Jurisprudence in India', *Diogenes* (53), 2006, pp. 116–33.

———, *The State, Democracy and Anti–Terror Laws*, New Delhi: Sage, 2007.

Singha, Radhika, *A Despotism of Law: Crime and Justice in Early Colonial India*, New Delhi: Oxford University Press, 2000a.

———, 'Settle, Mobilize, Verify: Identification Practices in Colonial India', *Studies in History*, 16(2), 2000b.

Sivakumar, Chitra, 'An Apprenticeship Marked with Frustration: College Students in Mysore', in *The Fieldworker and the Field: Problems and Challenges in Sociological Investigation*, M.N. Srinivas, A.M. Shah, and E.A. Ramaswamy (eds), New Delhi: Oxford University Press, 1979.

Sivakumaran, Sandesh, 'Male/Male Rape and the "Taint" of Homosexuality', *Human Rights Quarterly*, 27(4), 2005, pp. 1274–1306.

Smart, Carol, *Feminism and the Power of Law*, London: Routledge, 1989.

Smart, Carol and Neal, Bren, *Family Fragments?* Cambridge: Cambridge Polity Press, 1999.

Srinivas, M.N., *Village, Caste, Gender and Methods: Essays in Indian Anthropology*, New Delhi: Oxford University Press, 1996.

Stone, Julius, *Social Dimensions of Law and Justice*, Delhi: Universal Law Publishing Company, 1999.

Strathern, Marilyn, *After Nature: English Kinship in the Late Twentieth Century*, Cambridge: Cambridge University Press, 1992.

Strier, Franklin, *Reconstructing Justice: An Agenda for Trial Reform*, Chicago: Chicago University Press, 1996.

Takhtani, Aradhana, 'A Multi-Faceted Study of Society and Culture', *The Times of India*, 13 April 1997, p. 3.

Tarlo, Emma, *Clothing Matters: Dress and Identity of India*, Chicago: University of Chicago Press, 1996.

Taslitz, Andrew E., *Rape and the Culture of the Courtroom*, New York: New York University Press, 1999.

Taussig, Michael, *Defacement: Public Secrecy and the Labour of the Negative*, Stanford: Stanford University Press, 1999.

Taylor, Alfred Swaine, *Medical Jurisprudence*, edited with notes and additions by R. Eglesfeld Griffith, Philadelphia: Lea and Blanchard, 1845.

———, *Medical Jurisprudence*, 4th American edition, edited with additions by Edward Hartshorne, Philadelphia: Lea and Blanchard, 1845/1856.

———, *The Principles and Practice of Medical Jurisprudence*, London: John Churchill & Sons, New Burlington Street, 1865.

Taylor, Alfred Swaine, *A Manual of Medical Jurisprudence*, 6th American edition, revised and edited by Clement B. Penrose, Philadelphia: Lea and Blanchard, 1844/1866.

Tekchandani, Bharti, *Efficacy of the Enforcement System in Delivering Justice to Raped Scheduled Caste Women: A Report Prepared for Scheduled Caste Development Wing, Ministry of Welfare, Government of India*, New Delhi: Multiple Action Research Group, 1995.

Teltumbde, Anand, *Khairlanji: A Strange and Bitter Crop*, New Delhi: Navayana, 2008.

Thapan, Meenakshi (ed.), *Anthropological Journeys: Reflections on Fieldwork*, New Delhi: Orient Longman, 1998.

Thoinot, L., *Medico Legal Aspects of Moral Offenses*, trans. from the French and enlarged by Arthur W. Weysse, Philadelphia: F.A. Davis Company, 1898/1911.

Torrey, Morrison, 'When Will We Be Believed? Rape Myths and the Idea of a Fair Trial in Rape Prosecutions', *U.C. Davis Law Review*, (24), 1991, pp.1013–46.

Turner, Victor, *Schism and Continuity in an African Society*, Manchester: Manchester University Press, 1957.

Uberoi, Patricia (ed.), *Social Reform, Sexuality and the State*, Delhi: Sage, 1996.

Varghese, Rose, 'Sentencing in Rape Cases: Legislative Cases and Judicial Practice in the Context of Gender Justice and Atrocities against Women', PhD dissertation, Bangalore: National Law School of India University, 1992.

Vatuk, Sylvia, '"Where Will She Go? What Will She Do?" Paternalism towards Women in the Administration of Muslim Law in Contemporary India', in *Religion and Personal Law in Secular India: A Call to Judgment*, Gerald James Larson (ed.), Bloomington and Indianapolis: Indiana University Press, 2001.

Vigarello, Georges, *A History of Rape: Sexual Violence in France from the 16th to the 20th Century*, translated from the French by Jean Birell, Cambridge: Polity Press, 2001.

Vij, Shivam, 'A Mighty Heart', *Tehelka*, 13 October 2007, available at http://www.tehelka.com/story_main34.asp?filename=hub131007A_MIGHTY.asp.

Virdi, Jyotika, 'Reverence, Rape—and then Revenge: Popular Hindi Cinema's "Woman's Film"', *Screen*, 40(1), 1999, pp. 17–37.

Vishwanath, K., 'Shame and Control: Feminism, Sexuality and the Body, paper presented at the seminar on *Femininity, The Female Body and Sexuality in Contemporary Society*, New Delhi: Nehru Memorial Museum and Library, 1994.

Walby, Sylvia, 'Towards a Theory of Patriarchy', in *The Polity Reader in Gender Studies*, Polity Press (ed.), Cambridge: Polity Press, 1994.

Welchman, Lynn, and Sara Hossain (eds), *"Honour": Crimes, Paradigms and Violence against Women*', London: Zed Books, 2005.

White, Lucie, 'Why Do You Treat Us So Badly? On Loss, Remembrance and Responsibility', *Cumberland Law Review*, (26), 1995, pp. 809–16.

Winkler, Cathy, and Penelope J. Hanke, 'Rape Attack: Ethnography of the Ethnographer', in *Fieldwork under Fire: Contemporary Studies of Violence and Survival*, Carolyn Nordstrom and Antonius C.G.M. Robben (eds), California: University of California Press, 1995.

Index

❧❧

Nader, Laura, xxviii, 322
Nair, Janaki, 38–39, 201
Nampoothiri, P.G.J., 353
Naqvi, Farah, 362n14
Narayana, P.S., 289
Narrain, Arvind, 6, 103
National Commission for Women
(NCW), 26–27
National Crime Records Bureau
(NCRB), 384, 387–388
Naval, T.R., 287–288, 299,
334n10, 390
Naz Foundation case, 6
Neal, Bren, 129
non-cognizable offences, 5, 166n9
non-state law, 276n4
non-state *panchayats*, 226n43
Nordstrom, Carolyn, xxiv, xlvin2

O'Barr, William M., xxvi
offences
cognizable, 166n9
non-cognizable, 5, 166n9
sexual, 3, 24, 29, 102–103, 175,
180, 366
unnatural sexual, 5–6, 24,
114n66
O'Neal, Robert J., 107n11
Open Letter (Mathura Open
Letter), xxiv, 16–18, 54n41,
54n42, 55n46, 342
out-of-court settlement, xlii, 174.
See also compromise

panch, 204–206, 229n79, 230n80,
231n91
panchayats, xlixn7, 35, 177–179,
181–182, 226n43, 226n75,
229n79, 321–322, 364n34
panchnamma, 193, 203–207,
230n80, 322, 357

of clothes, 206, 344
panch witnesses, 204–206,
231n91
Panini, M.N., xlixn4
pardon, 187, 189
Parker, A., 332
past sexual history clause, 8, 18–19,
62, 79, 82, 103, 128, 180, 346
pathology, 3, 6, 24, 72–73, 103
patriarchy
Brahmanical, 37, 58n111
caste-based, 37, 222, 266,
306–308. *See also* atrocity
imperial, 64
patriarchal power, 3, 8, 138,
222, 293, 313
patriarchal virtue, 293
penetration, interpretation of, 5–6,
23–24
absence of hymen/hymeneal
injuries, 72, 80–82
British medical experts, early
views, 70–72
common-law definition, 25
'complete intromission' and
'non-intromission,' 70–72
medical expert's testimony,
89–93
in Modi's textbooks, 92
partial penile penetration,
xxxvi, xxxix, 4, 5, 61, 63, 72,
91–93, 147, 173, 346
under sub-ss. 376 (rape) and
377 IPC (unnatural sexual
offence), 24, 27
People's Union for Democratic
Rights (PUDR), 7
perjury, xlii, 108n13, 144, 240,
345
phallocentric social order, 9, 83, 93,
103, 122, 166n3, 308, 332

About the Author

❧

Pratiksha Baxi is Associate Professor at the Centre for the Study of Law and Governance, Jawaharlal Nehru University, New Delhi. She holds a doctoral degree from the Department of Sociology, Delhi School of Economics, University of Delhi.

Baxi has an abiding interest in researching the social life of law, violence, and gender. She has published widely on rape, sexual harassment, 'honour crimes', mass violence, medical jurisprudence, politics of judicial reform, access to justice, and feminism.

Baxi initiated and continues to lead the *Law and Social Sciences Research Network* (*LASSnet*),anchored at the Centre for the Study of Law and Governance, Jawaharlal Nehru University. This interdisciplinary network has brought together more than five hundred scholars, researchers, and lawyers from different parts of the world.

Baxi was also the founder member of the *Gender Study Group* (1992–1997) and *Forum against Sexual Harassment* (1998–2002), University of Delhi, which among other issues, worked on preventing and redressing sexual harassment in the academia.